THE
Teen Health
Book

W. W. Norton & Company

New York ■ London

THE

Teen Health
Book

A Parents' Guide
to Adolescent Health
and Well-Being

Ralph I. López, M.D.

For information about permission to reproduce selections from this book, write to
Permissions, W. W. Norton & Company, Inc., 500 Fifth Avenue, New York, NY 10110

All product names used herein are trademarks of their respective owners.

The text of this book is composed in Adobe Garamond with the display set in Eng Gothic
Composition by Sue Carlson
Illustrations by Ralph I. López
Manufacturing by the Haddon Craftsmen, Inc.
Book design by Judith Stagnitto Abbate/Abbate Design
Production manager: Amanda Morrison

Library of Congress Cataloging-in-Publication Data

López, Ralph I.
    The teen health book : a parents' guide to adolescent health and well-being /
Ralph I. López.
        p.   cm.
    Includes bibliographical references and index.
    ISBN 0-393-02046-0
    1. Teenagers—Health and hygiene. 2. Teenagers—Psychlogy. 3. Adolescence. I. Title.
RJ140 .L67 2002
613'.0433—dc21
                                                                    2001044819

W. W. Norton & Company, Inc., 500 Fifth Avenue, New York, N.Y. 10110
www.wwnorton.com

W. W. Norton & Company Ltd., Castle House, 75/76 Wells Street, London W1T 3QT

1 2 3 4 5 6 7 8 9 0

To my wife, Paula, and to our daughter, Abigail.
They both taught me what parenting is about.

Contents

Acknowledgments   *13*
Introduction   *15*

Part One ▌ **The Onset of Puberty and the Changes It Brings**   **21**

Chapter 1 ▪ *Does Your Teen Need a New Doctor?*   *23*
            Changing Thoughts on Teen Health Care   *23*
            Toward a More Teen-Friendly Environment   *24*
            An Increasing Need for Privacy   *24*
            The Importance of Confidentiality   *25*
            Considering a New Doctor   *26*
            Finding the Right Patient-Doctor Match   *26*
            Shifting Responsibility   *27*

Chapter 2 ▪ *Puberty: Your Developing Child,*
               Your Developing Teen   *30*
            So What Exactly Is Puberty?   *31*
            Talking (Out Loud) about Puberty   *31*
            Puberty Is More Than Body Changes   *32*
            Growth before Puberty   *34*
            How Male/Female Growth Is the Same   *34*
            Glandular Changes   *36*
            Skin Changes   *36*
            Male Growth Pattern   *36*

Measuring Genital Development: The Tanner System   *38*
Male Facial Hair   *42*
Testosterone Makes Itself Known   *43*
Same-Gender Talks Work Best at This Age   *43*
Female Growth Pattern   *44*
Pubertal Growth in Girls   *44*
Menstruation   *48*
So When Will It Start?   *49*
Talking about Menstruation   *52*
Moving On   *54*

Chapter 3 ■ *The Emotional Life of the Adolescent*   *55*
The Nature of Adolescence   *56*
But Who Are They?   *56*
Internal Pressures   *58*
External Pressures   *62*
Normal and Coping?   *65*
Coping or Depressed?   *66*
Suicide   *67*

Part Two ▌ Health and Lifestyle Issues   **71**

Chapter 4 ■ *The Sleep-Deprived Teen*   *73*
Sleep Physiology   *73*
Teen Sleep Requirements   *74*
Why Teens Don't Sleep   *75*
Helping Your Teen Fit In More Sleep   *77*
Sleep Disorders   *78*

Chapter 5 ■ *Teens, Nutrition, and Eating Disorders*   *83*
Eating Well and Judging Nutritional Value   *84*
What Calories Mean to Your Teen   *86*
How Food Sources Vary   *88*
The Need for Fat   *90*
Teens and Cholesterol   *93*
What Vitamins and Minerals Do   *96*
Guiding toward Better Eating   *100*
Weight Issues   *102*
Eating Disorders   *106*
Teens and Special Diets   *114*

Chapter 6 ■ *The Teen Obsession: Skin* 118
    Acne 119
    Allergic Skin Reactions and Dermatitis 126
    Fungal Skin Infections 132
    Viral Skin Infections 134
    Moles and Spots 137
    The Importance of Sunscreens 137
    Tattoos and Piercings 138

Chapter 7 ■ *Teens and Sports: Sports-Related Injuries* 143
    The Importance of the Physical Exam 144
    The Importance of Nutrition 146
    Body Types and Their Effect on Sports Participation 149
    Suiting Up Properly 150
    The Rise (and Fall?) of the Early Developer 154
    The Female Athlete 154
    General Health Problems 155
    Injuries and Treatment 158
    Remembering What Is Important 172

Part Three ■ **Teen Sexual Practices and Issues** **175**

Chapter 8 ■ *Sexuality and the Adolescent* 177
    Sex and the Teen 178
    But What Are They *Doing?* 179
    "What Is Normal?" 181
    Talking to Your Teen 184
    Teaching or Reaffirming Values 187
    The Homosexual Teen 189
    "Coming Out" 192

Chapter 9 ■ *Birth Control* 195
    Abstinence, the Rhythm Method, and Withdrawal 196
    Intrauterine Devices 197
    Barrier Methods 197
    Hormonal Methods 204
    Newly Released Birth Control Methods 212
    Pregnancy 213
    Helping Your Teen (Both Sons and Daughters)
      "Do the Right Thing" 218

Chapter 10 ■ *Sexually Transmitted Diseases*   *220*
How Prevalent are STDs?   *221*
Viral Infections   *222*
Bacterial Infections   *228*
Syphilis   *232*
Fungal Infections   *233*
Parasites   *234*
Teen Awareness   *236*

Part Four ▌ **Teen Substance Abuse**   **239**

Chapter 11 ■ *What Parents Need to Know about Substance Abuse*   *241*
Learning about Alcohol and Drug Abuse   *243*
Recognizing a Drug User   *244*
Finding the Right Time   *244*
The Information Pipeline   *247*
The Discovery: Your Teen Is Drinking or
   Using Drugs   *248*
Getting Additional Advice or Help   *250*
Putting a Teen into a Rehabilitation Program   *252*
Is This an Emergency?   *252*
Improving Your Knowledge   *252*

Chapter 12 ■ *Teens and Alcohol*   *254*
Alcohol as Part of the Teen Scene   *254*
What Parents Should Know about Alcohol   *257*
Measuring Alcohol Consumption   *257*
Responsible Drinking   *260*
So You Think Your Teen's Been Drinking   *262*
If Your Teen Comes Home Drunk   *265*
If the Shoe Fits   *267*
Helping Your Teen   *268*
The Party Scene   *269*
The Underage College Years   *269*

Chapter 13 ■ *Teens and Smoking*   *273*
Marketing to Teens   *274*
Why Teens Start   *274*
The Effects of Nicotine   *275*
Other Means of Taking in Nicotine   *276*
The Gateway Theory   *277*

Quitting   *278*
Forming New Habits   *284*

Chapter 14 ■ *Marijuana*   *285*
A Few Definitions   *286*
Understanding the Chemistry of Pot   *287*
How Pot Is Used   *289*
The Mind-Altering Aspects of Pot   *290*
Drug Testing   *293*
"How Can I Know What My Teen Is Doing?"   *295*
Long-Term Use of THC   *298*
Pot Is Illegal, but That's a Small Deterrent   *298*
Therapeutic Use of Marijuana   *299*

Chapter 15 ■ *Hallucinogens and Stimulants*   *300*
About Hallucinogens   *301*
Hallucinogens   *302*
Stimulants   *308*

Chapter 16 ■ *Other Frequently Used Drugs*   *315*
Inhalants   *315*
Amyl Nitrate, or "Poppers"   *317*
Ketamine, or "Vitamin K"   *317*
GHB   *318*
"Roofies"   *318*
Klonopin   *319*
Opiates   *319*
Barbiturates and Quaaludes   *322*

Part Five ▌ **The Adolescent, Head to Toe: Common Ailments**   **325**

Introduction   *327*
Whole Body Issues   *330*
Immunizations   *330*
Fatigue   *338*
The Head   *347*
Headaches   *347*
The Eyes   *352*
The Nose   *355*
The Ears   *358*
The Mouth   *362*
The Throat   *365*

The Neck Area   *368*
  Neck Pain   *368*
  The Glands   *369*
The Spine and Back   *377*
  The Spine   *377*
  The Back   *381*
The Shoulders, Chest, and Heart   *384*
  The Shoulders   *384*
  The Chest   *386*
  The Heart   *400*
The Abdomen and Digestive System   *409*
  The Esophageal Area   *409*
  The Stomach   *411*
  The Abdomen   *415*
  The Liver   *420*
  The Umbilicus, or Belly Button   *427*
The Urinary Tract   *428*
  The Bladder   *428*
  The Kidneys   *431*
The Female Reproductive System   *436*
  Timing of the First Pelvic Exam   *436*
  The Pelvic Exam   *437*
  The Rate of Female Development   *440*
  Menstruation   *442*
  Disorders of the Reproductive System   *457*
The Male Reproductive System   *464*
  The Prostatic Gland   *464*
  The Penis   *465*
  The Scrotum   *467*
  The Testicles   *468*
The Hips, Legs, and Feet   *474*
  Hip Problems in Adolescents   *474*
  The Legs   *475*
  The Knees   *476*
  The Lower Leg   *479*
  The Feet   *479*
  The Toes   *480*

Web Sites for Parents and Teens   *483*
Index   *487*

Acknowledgments

This book started years before a single word was ever written. I owe a great deal to my first mentor, Father Timothy Healy, S.J., who took a frightened eighteen-year-old freshman in English class and said, "Ralph, you should write some more." To my eventual colleague and friend, whom I miss terribly, I thank you for teaching me the power of the written word. Next I want to thank a wise, kindly, and knowledgeable mentor, Dr. Robert Masland, who molded my perspective on adolescent medicine during my fellowship at Boston Childrens' Hospital. Fresh from gathering a massive amount of medical information from two great medical institutions, I was still naive about patient care. It was Dr. Masland who taught me how to understand and how to listen to the teenager.

But the book began to take shape with printed words when I met my agents, Sarah Jane Freymann and Judith Riven. They approached me with the same idea for a book that I had been considering for a long time. The fit was immediate. They took me by the hand and guided me through the maze of the publishing world; without them, I would still be wondering how to get my words into print. They are also responsible for Kate Kelly, my editor. Anyone who has ever written a book and thinks that they do not need an editor is ingenous. They just have to find their Kate. I had feared that an editor would distort my voice and my tempo. Within one day of reading my words, Kate had managed to be faithful to their sound and the result has been a seamless collaboration. We have become friends.

I want to thank Amy Cherry at W. W. Norton for putting in countless hours checking the manuscript and offering advice. Thank you also to Dr.

David Fields, Dr. John Franklin, Dr. Michelle Green, and Elyse Sosin, M.A., R.D., for taking the time to make sure I was accurate.

I want to thank my daughter, Abigail, for teaching me the joy of being a father through her childhood, her adolescence, and now as a grown woman. You know you have done something right when you can say that you not only love your daughter but you like her. Lastly, I want to thank my wife, Paula, for being there all these years. She put up with so many apartment moves during my training that packing soon became easy. She also did not whimper a word of concern when I told her I was leaving academic medicine to start a private practice. If the Vatican ever considers someone Jewish for sainthood, I propose my wife stand in the front of the line.

Introduction

No one entertaining the idea of having a baby imagines the pleasures of having a teenager. There may be images of baby's first smile, first step, first word, and even of special talks with a grown child, but never, never, in the history of mankind, were these words uttered: "Honey, I can't wait to have teenagers!"

Most parents enter parenthood and do well with their on-the-job training. They find ways to calm the crying baby and comfort the toddler, and their school-aged children go off to the classroom and seem to thrive. For the first ten to eleven years after childbirth it all seems so easy. Then, with a mere bud of a breast or a little extra testosterone, the young child is transformed into a brooding, moody, secretive, and often unpredictable being.

What's happening? Parents become perplexed and find that kissing a skinned elbow or hugging the player on a losing soccer team no longer suffices. There's no telling what will next erupt from the teen who now lives in your house.

My role as a doctor of adolescent medicine has been to smooth the transition to the teen years for both teen and parent and to help families navigate through the next ten or twelve years of life. The purpose of this book is to share with readers what I have been doing in my practice for over thirty years.

My practice deals with high school and college students. Questions about when physical examinations are needed, what shots are appropriate for school or for travel, what is the expectation of growth for this or that teen abound daily. The harder questions about sex, drugs, and depression are also the routine of my day.

I finished my pediatric training in 1969, just in time to witness the pangs of the 1960s revolution from the safe distance of the medical establishment. I watched the early experiments with "sex, drugs, and rock and roll" and thought, just as everyone else, that we had seen some mysterious and sinister virus infect our young people's behavior. Yet, a part of me understood that a piece of this behavior was normal, and I wanted to learn more about this strange creature called "the adolescent." With that in mind, I spent a fellowship learning about this developmental period and began a career in 1971 in caring for adolescents.

Many of my patients start seeing me at eleven years old and stay through and after college. Sometimes, it is hard to find the endpoint when I can move them on to an internist. They enter with camp forms, with college forms, with working paper requests, and with a range of maladies that include a textbook of concerns. Some come simply because they are tired of Smurfs on the wall or the picture of Big Bird that adorned their pediatrician's office. They feel like Gulliver in the land of the Lilliputians . . . too big to sit in the now too-small chairs. Some come because they feel that their "baby doctor" just isn't someone who will listen to their concerns about sex or puberty.

Others are sent because they need to discuss a unique concern for adolescents. Teens with eating disorders have become more common and even younger patients are now "dieting." "Is it normal for her to lose weight?" asks the worried parent. To deal with this complicated illness requires a great deal of experience with teens and with their parents. Another parent may have concerns about her son or daughter's sexual activities and she may feel it's time for a new approach. Many parents and teens view the change in doctors as an opportunity to approach a particularly difficult problem. The adolescent who comes with the camp or school form in hand slowly works his way to problems with school, with peers and drugs, or with a concern about that abdominal pain that he is ignoring. Some struggle to finally say that they are concerned about issues of gender identity.

Over the years, I have also had an opportunity to meet kids in their classrooms where they greet me with a pile of 4 x 6 cards on which they anonymously write questions. I answer them as forthrightly as I can. It usually takes about fifteen minutes before they are raising their hands and asking direct questions. If you show you will listen, they seem ready to talk. On other occasions I lecture to parent groups. Notes are furiously taken (most of the time by mom) and I watch, delighted, as a point is driven home and the parents turn to each other in acknowledgment. It is often the case that a lively discussion arises at the end of the talk and parents regale one another with tales of their problems. We have a group therapy session for fifty or more!

In this book, I've tried to share with you all that I've learned about adolescents—medically and otherwise.

What I Hope You'll Take Away from This Book

As teenagers go from middle school to college, their bodies change and their attitudes adjust to their bodies. Parents need guidance in knowing the usual concerns about the health care of the teenager, including the changes that puberty brings.

The decision of whether to accompany the teen to the office or to let him go alone may seem trivial to some, but it is a monumental decision in the eyes of teens. How and when do issues of confidentiality enter into the care of the adolescent? Can the parent call without the teen knowing? Suddenly the medical care of the teenager appears so difficult. It was so easy, so clear when she went to the pediatrician.

The majority of this book is devoted to the day-to-day medical concerns of parents of teenagers. A day does not go by in my office that I am not asked if a patient should be seen, or if something is a reasonable expectation with teenagers: "Is it normal for a teenager to sleep so much?" or "Will he grow any more?" Questions arise about acne, menstrual problems, headaches, stomachaches, chest pains, or a shoulder that clicks when moved.

For parents with athletic teens, a whole series of questions arise: What exams are required? How can we prevent injuries? What does the sports physical encompass? If a teen suffers a concussion, how soon can he play again? If she has a sprain, how do we treat it? Is it okay for growing adolescents to take supplements to bulk up? All of these questions arise daily in an adolescent medicine practice.

But in many ways these are the easy questions. When we enter the world of drugs we enter a domain that is much more difficult to deal with. It is painful for parents to witness a son or daughter coming home drunk after a party. That pain is compounded by the reality that "grounding" them is hardly the answer. Do we prohibit the use of alcohol altogether or is a certain amount okay? When, if ever, is the occasional joint not a problem? Should we do drug screens on our kids randomly? at their next physical? Parents ask, *"Gee, doctor, can't you simply do a urine test? He'll never know and if it comes back negative, we won't tell him we did it."*

Today's teens face a new group of drugs that didn't exist when their parents were young. Kids talk about "Vitamin K" or about who's doing "E," and parents need to know what they mean. Even the most sophisticated parent may not be current on the drug scene confronting our kids. With the rise of the Internet, adolescents have access to detailed pharmacological information. I am no longer surprised at the sophistication with which some teens will discuss the merits of a drug and minimize the risks because of the way it is metabolized. We can no longer say "It's bad for you." Today we need to know why and how it is bad before we convince teenagers who may have done their own research.

Another difficult area is sexuality. Our teens are being asked to grow up and enter a world of sexual participation often before they are ready. The seventh grader no longer is viewed as part of the pre-adolescent age group but rather as someone whom we need to reach with sexual information. Parents cannot pretend that their kid is immune to the risk of sexually transmitted diseases, they cannot think that the need for birth control can be delayed until well into the future. Information about prevalent sexually transmitted diseases is now presented in many middle school health classes. It falls on parents to keep informed so that they can discuss intelligently how they feel about sexual topics.

The one area of adolescent development we confront daily is that of the emotions. Bookstore shelves are filled with information about the dysfunctional emotional toils of the adolescent. Indeed, it is easier to find a book on anorexia nervosa or delinquent behavior than it is to find a book that covers the growth and development of the normal teenager experiencing normal stresses.

Distinguishing the normal mood swings of the teenager from the pathology of depression is quite difficult in this age group. A chapter is devoted to understanding the normal emotional life of adolescents and will help parents answer the question, "Is this normal for a teenager?"

By reading this book and paying attention to your teen, you'll soon find your level of expertise on the adolescent years has grown exponentially, making you a wiser and more compassionate parent.

In order to make it easier to find information about the medical ills of teenagers, the last part of the book covers the teen from head to toe. By putting the medical problems in this sequence, you can easily find a specific area—i.e., if you are concerned about neck pains, or chest pains, or stomachaches. Most parents and teens call and complain about a specific body part that is hurting, and Part Five, "The Adolescent, Head to Toe," makes it easier to group the possibilities.

One important note of caution is in order. Parents have to decide what their limits are, and they have to work as a team whether they are married or divorced. No physician, no guidance counselor, can tell you the "right way" to raise your child. Indeed, it is easier to spot what *not* to do in a situation than to direct parents in a step-by-step process.

I have been lucky in my career; I found a niche in medicine that makes me happy. I get to watch kids grow through the pangs of adolescence and witness the mostly successful outcome in their twenties. By providing facts and information—and raising some questions—I hope to help you appreciate what the underlying issues are for teenagers. By better understanding your teen and his or her medical care, you are better prepared to continue your role as a helpful, supportive, sympathetic adult who is still vitally important in your teen's life.

Part One

The Onset of Puberty and the Changes It Brings

Chapter 1

Does Your Teen
Need a New Doctor?

A few years ago, Gary, a high school junior, came into my office and sat in one of the chairs opposite my desk. He had been the patient of one of the most respected pediatricians in the area. I asked him if this was a routine visit or if something special was concerning him. He thought for a minute and answered, "No." Then he added, "Dr. Jones has been my doctor for years. He's real good." I sensed a pride in praising his childhood doctor. "Then why did you switch?" I asked. He smiled and stood up—all 6'3" of him: "Okay?"

Changing Thoughts on Teen Health Care

Today's adolescent benefits from the fact that there have been major changes in attitude toward the medical care of teenagers. The medical profession as a whole now recognizes that teens have a unique set of issues. While a few of us have chosen to specialize in adolescent health, many pediatric practices have opted to stay up-to-date on teen issues so that they, too, can provide the care the teenagers in their practices need.

In all aspects of their lives, teenagers need to feel that they are no longer "children." Despite the fact that they are not legally adults until age eighteen, they resent attempts to make them feel like youngsters. It is important for them to have a visible sign that the transition period is recognized. Is it a surprise that the Smurfs on the pediatrician's walls and the silly jokes as the ears are examined no longer amuse? The toys in the waiting room, the child-size chairs, the fellow patients who are babies all pose a threat to the teenager's sense of maturity. The logic is simple: If I don't see magazines for me, if I don't have an environment directed at my needs, I don't belong here. Let me out!

Toward a More Teen-Friendly Environment

If the teen is to be comfortable in the doctor's office, it has to be a teen-friendly one. The attitude of the office staff in recognizing the teen's transition into young adulthood can set a new stage in which teens are encouraged to assume some responsibility for their own medical care.

If you're evaluating whether or not to change doctors, the waiting room is the first place to begin to make a decision as to whether a particular practice will suit your teen's needs. A separate area for teens is ideal, though usually not possible in offices where space is at a premium. Teen reading materials, which can be as simple as having copies of *People* or *Rolling Stone* around, are a good offset to *Sesame Street* magazine and informational pamphlets from La Leche League.

The demeanor of the nurse or receptionist is also important. Calling out a nickname, or addressing the parent instead of the teen (as in "Would you like to bring Johnny in now?") is no longer appropriate. More adult-styled exam rooms will make the adolescent more comfortable. The Muppets posters, the infant scale, the open door all indicate "child" to the teen.

An Increasing Need for Privacy

Starting at about age thirteen or fourteen, your teen should begin to have private time with the doctor. This can be a gradual process. You might leave him for the actual physical exam, and let him call you back in later. But teens shouldn't feel like they were dropped off: The eighteen-year-old who is really sick may want you in the room. However, they should see that parents are supportive of the fact that they have a private life, which will begin to include the state of their health.

If you have an appointment with a new doctor, some physicians prefer to meet with the teenager alone before bringing in the parents. My own style is to meet with both parents and teen to take a medical history and to set guidelines for the professional relationship. This way both parent and teenager are present to hear about how I run the practice (after-hour calls, appointment length, etc.). Later on, a parent may come in at the beginning or the end of the appointment (or both, depending on the nature of the visit), but the teenager should see the doctor and be examined by the doctor without a parent there. Particularly if you are opting to remain with your "old" pediatrician, this new manner of handling the visits forces both your teen and the doctor into a new relationship. Both doctor and teen patient need to start forging a relationship that is just between the two of them.

Adolescent medicine specialists and pediatric offices addressing the needs of teenagers will offer teen girls a paper robe to wear after disrobing for a physical exam. Preventing her from feeling vulnerable and exposed is a first step toward treating her with the same respect an adult patient would receive. Some girls will want their mother present during the examination, while others prefer a female nurse to be in the room. In most cases, the physician's manner and tone will put the patient at ease.

The Importance of Confidentiality

A common complaint from the teens who switch to my practice is the sense that their "baby doctor" is somehow allied with their parents. They feel the doctor is more their parents' doctor than their own. Unfortunately, this is sometimes true. When their patients are babies and children, pediatricians tell parents about every cold, every sore, and every sprain. Parents may well expect that information disclosure to continue into their child's teens. Questions about smoking, alcohol, pot, and sex are on all parents' minds. They want to know if their son or daughter is involved in risky behaviors or is thinking about it. The latter is often true; the former is not. If parents can't elicit this information from their teens, they may turn to their teen's doctor. Most parents understand that they are crossing a boundary line by asking a doctor to break patient confidentiality, but their parental needs often overtake their judgment.

The pediatrician who unwittingly divulges that the cough is a "smoker's cough" has just about lost a patient. The parent who gets the pediatrician to do a "urine test for drugs, *just to be sure*" will probably have to find a new physician if the teen finds out. And what if such a test is positive? Does the parent who couldn't confront her son with her suspicions, now tell him that she knows about the teen's drug use for sure? I can imagine the response: "Dr. Jones did what!? Forget it, I'm not going back. Ever!"

One patient told me recently that he hated his old doctor because the doctor had told his mother something the boy had told him in confidence. I did not know all the details of the incident, but the message being sent by my new patient was clear. I assured him of confidentiality but cautioned that, if I felt the need to discuss something with his parents, I would discuss it with him first. He paused, looked at me, and nodded that this was an acceptable agreement. I looked at his mother and she concurred.

Considering a New Doctor

Referral from friends is the most common way of finding a new doctor, but if you're looking for doctors who specialize in treating adolescents, try contacting the Society for Adolescent Medicine (1916 NW Copper Oaks Circle, Blue Springs, Missouri 64015; 816-224-8010; www.adolescenthealth.org). The organization can send you a list of any members who practice in your area.

If there are no adolescent medicine specialists in your area, then start looking for a pediatrician who enjoys working with teenagers. Your best bet will be to search among those who are old enough to have raised teens themselves. I know that I became a better pediatrician when my daughter was born. The doctor who has lived through these stages with children has generally gained wisdom and compassion that can be found in other doctors but may be more difficult to come by.

Finding the Right Patient-Doctor Match

Let's face it, some doctors do not particularly want to see teenagers as patients. They may have chosen pediatrics because they really like young children, and the idea of serving the adolescent population is simply not to their taste. However, there is also an economic reality to taking care of teenagers.

An office visit with a teenager is longer than that of a first-grader with an earache or a baby the doctor saw just last month. The busy office of a typical pediatrician is capable of seeing as many as three to six patients in one hour. Babies can be given an overall physical and an immunization in as little as fifteen minutes. The nurse can weigh the child, the nurse can give the vaccines, and the nurse may even be the one to go over diet with the mother.

If a doctor seeing teenagers relies too heavily on staff members for the drawing of blood, taking of height and weight, and blood pressure, the teen may feel slighted. But more important, the doctor is missing the opportunity to build a relationship with the teen, which may open the door to important communication about sensitive issues. Typically I allow twenty to thirty minutes for a regular visit and, in almost all cases, time is spent covering some question that has nothing to do with the appointment. A first visit, in which I meet parents in addition to the teen, is a scheduled hour!

Another issue to consider is whether or not the current pediatrician, or the one you are considering using, is willing to stay up to date on the issues that will affect your teen. Menstrual irregularities, acne, pace of growth, and learning disabilities are just a few of the topics in which a pediatrician or adolescent medicine doctor must be well-versed.

Patients who lose weight or show other symptoms of an eating disorder are frequently referred to someone with enough experience and time to handle the issues that involve both the patient and the family. Doctors seeing adolescents must also be willing to counsel on birth control (a full discussion will follow in the chapter on birth control). They may encounter a pregnant teenager who has no one to counsel her. The physician may have to fill this role.

Shifting Responsibility

As of age eighteen, your teen is considered old enough to take charge of his medical care. From that age on, the doctor will have to ask your teen's permission to share any medical information with you. That's why it's so very important that you teach your teen to take charge of his own medical care.

At some point, kids will feel that they can make their own appointments. I prefer that the parent know they are doing it but, logistically, it is usually easier for the teen to determine what appointment time can be fit in around soccer practice and piano lessons. Parents should, however, stress to their children that making an appointment is making a commitment; many physicians charge for their time if patients do not show up or if they show up late. (If a teen wants an appointment without the parent's knowledge, the doctor has to be willing to potentially absorb the cost of an office visit. If the visit has to do with sexual topics or relates to drugs, then the teen can make the appointment with full rights, as this is protected confidentially. If he has strep throat, he can't!)

One way of educating teenagers about their medical care is to give them access to their lab results. In most cases, I will ask the teen if she wants to call for her lab results, or if she prefers her parents to call. Many don't realize that they can do this and welcome the idea. On the other hand, some aren't quite ready for this adult responsibility. That's fine. But the gesture on my part goes a long way in making them feel that they have a right to this information.

> **Billy is a somewhat heavyset** *fifteen-year-old who has constantly fought the "battle of the bulge." Diets, admonitions, and entreaties have gone unheeded. When I saw him, I suggested that part of the exam include blood work to check cholesterol levels and triglycerides (fats) in the blood. I asked him if he wanted to call me for results. He hesitated but then said he would call in a few days. As it turned out, his cholesterol and fats were quite high and he admitted to me that these represented not the empty stomach that I had wanted before the tests but a fairly large breakfast of eggs, pancakes with syrup, and bacon. When he heard the blood values he was shocked. "What should I do?" he asked. The obvious answer of losing weight and changing his diet were simple enough; the question was would he do it. On his own, he suggested that he be given a month to lower the numbers; if this didn't work, he would meet with a nutritionist. I told him that, because of his age, I needed to inform his parents but that I would ask them not to pressure him about his diet. At his follow up a month later, his weight had dropped by six pounds. His cholesterol and triglyceride levels were much better and he continues to lose weight weekly. He takes enormous pride in knowing that he is doing this by himself. I am convinced that, had I called his parents first, this great outcome would have been missed.*

Occasionally, test results cannot be shared with a teen either because it is devastating news or because parents absolutely forbid it. Parents do have such a legal right. For example, I have had several teens with rare disorders whom I felt needed chromosome analysis. It is difficult enough to share my concern with parents, let alone the teen. In each case I consulted with the parent and simply drew an extra tube of blood at the annual visit. If the results showed a problem, the parents and I together discussed it with the teen. Legally a physician must share this information with the parent if the child is a minor. If the patient is over eighteen not only does she need to know the results, she needs to give consent to do the initial test.

The exception to informing parents about blood test results is for those in which the information is privileged. Tests done for sexually transmitted disease or pregnancy legally cannot be shared with anyone other than the patient.

(This is mandated on a state-by-state basis.) However, I usually strongly suggest that the teen talk with her parents, and I offer to be present during the discussion. In some cases teens may actually request that treatment or test bills be sent to them. HIV testing is a good example. A teen may choose not to tell his parents about the test and will pay the laboratory directly. In New York even a physician needs special permission from the patient just to let another doctor know that the test was done!

The Ideal Medical Visit for the Teenager

In the best-case scenario, the following criteria will be met for a successful adolescent office visit.

1. The environment should be one that reflects the age of the teenager.
2. The office staff and especially the physician should view the teen as the primary patient. The teen should be addressed by name and spoken to directly; comments and questions should not be directed to the parent.
3. Examination rooms should have adult-size examining tables. Scales, ear speculum, and overall equipment should be consistent with the age of the patient.
4. The patient should have a chance to discuss issues alone with the physician, and a parent should not be present for the physical examination unless the teen requests. Parents may accompany the patient into the consultation room, and policies about seeing the patient alone, billing, broken appointment policies, and above all, confidentiality need to be directly presented to both parent and teen.
5. Parents should have a chance to express their concerns, but the teen should be guaranteed an equal opportunity to voice concerns. If the issue is complex, the doctor should be willing to make another appointment for further discussion.
6. Teenagers should be given privacy to get undressed and dressed without the physician in the room. Gowns are optional for boys but are almost always mandatory for girls.
7. Any procedure that is new or painful should be explained, including the drawing of blood.
8. Parents should be included in the treatment plan for illness.
9. A well-run office will have a reminder plan and will send out notices for follow-up examinations or the need for additional immunizations.

Chapter 2

Puberty: Your Developing Child, Your Developing Teen

P uberty. What a term. It sounds like a disease, as in "He has a bad case of puberty!" Or imagine the plaintive cry of parents pleading, "Is she through puberty yet?"

In Neil Simon's *Brighton Beach Memoirs*, the older brother is discussing some of the facts of life with Eugene (his younger and very sexually curious brother). Eugene is aghast to learn that his most secret needs and fantasies are shared by others who are going through this "pooberty" stuff. Eugene is an "innocent victim of puberty," who can't quite figure out why his dreams of being Willie Mays are being replaced by thoughts about the cute neighbor girl.

Today, Eugene would be better prepared. His school would have had courses in sex education and the mysteries of genital "plumbing" would have been studied. Teachers would have voiced words that he never thought could be uttered in public, and he, along with his classmates, would likely have had to suppress laughter borne out of discomfort. As an added bonus, he could easily borrow a friend's candid full-color magazines or log on to the Internet to add to his information base.

Clearly, the Eugene of the twenty-first century would not be so naive. Anxious and confused? Yes. Naive? No.

Despite access to factual information from a variety of sources ranging from sex education class and the Internet to magazines and that "know-it-all" friend, your teen still needs your guidance in navigating a clear pathway through puberty. As parents, many of us have vowed to differ from our own parents by having open conversations about previously forbidden subjects. The changes occurring in your child's body offer a topic about which your teen is extremely curious, and this is one of your early opportunities to lay the groundwork for open discussions.

But first, you need to know what you're talking about.

So What Exactly Is Puberty?

The terms "puberty" and "adolescence" are often used interchangeably when talking about teenagers. This is an error of usage. The former refers to the physical changes that take place in the teenager; the latter refers to the attitudes and feelings of the teen as a result of these changes. Ideally, the two phenomena take place at the same time.

It doesn't require a great deal of skill to acquire the physical changes. Anyone who has been lucky enough to come from a healthy background with appropriate nutrition manages to get the right amount of puberty at the right time, though the wide variation in what is the "right" time for each individual often leads to teen—and even parental—angst. One need only visit a middle school to see that there is no norm for the onset of puberty—girls at age thirteen can be flat-chested or ready for the cover of *Seventeen*; boys may fall into the Mutt or Jeff category, with a lanky long-legged basketball player loping along next to his much shorter friend.

Adolescence is a different matter. The maturation of the body forces an inner struggle. Teens must deal with new and difficult concepts about themselves, their peers, and their families. They face pressure to conform, they have decisions to make, and they are filled with emotions to sort out. It is a confusing time.

How teens cope with the issues that arise from the physical changes brought on by puberty will have a direct effect on how easily they make the transition into the adult world. That's why your position as "tour guide" and role model is so important right now. Being able to talk about the changes your child is going through is part of your job in the coming years. The tone you set at this time can make a difference in how your child feels about puberty.

Talking (Out Loud) about Puberty

If you, as a parent, should be so lucky as to be asked direct questions about the sexual developmental process, you have a wonderful opportunity to mold healthy attitudes and dispel fears. However, most parents have had scant opportunity to practice the delicate art of talking about body changes and sex, so these conversations often become awkward. It's one thing to identify what an "erection" is; it's another thing altogether to tell a son what to do about it if it happens in math class.

Being the parent of a young teenager requires you to prepare for these questions and to answer them. Probably the most important aspect of dealing with puberty and teenagers is the ability to convey that you are comfortable with the topic; that you can say what I refer to as the "silent" words—the words that many people have such a hard time saying that they unconsciously pronounce them more softly than the rest of the words in the sentence: "When your breasts are developing . . . " or "Did you hurt your penis?" Unfortunately, by doing this you make clear to your teenager that the subject of sexuality, or at least of breasts or penis, is difficult for you, and perhaps it will be best not to burden you with so sensitive a subject. In time, the teenager will learn not to bother you at all. He'll think to himself: "Why make Mom or Dad uncomfortable? I'll figure it out for myself."

If your teen is to turn to you for guidance, you need to make it clear that you are just as prepared to discuss bodily functions and sex—using the correct terms—as you are to talk about last night's baseball game or the family vacation you're planning. (Part Three will provide you with the factual information you'll need for these discussions.)

Be honest with yourself. If sexual topics make you blush and stammer, then your first exercise is to learn to say the "silent" words in the same tone of voice you would say any other word.

Puberty Is More Than Body Changes

No one wills puberty. You don't sit down and think that it would be a good idea to make your breasts grow a certain amount, or have your testicles begin to get larger.

The enormity of the bodily upheaval of puberty is now a part of distant history for most parents. We seldom, if ever, look at our bodies and remember that at one time the curves were not there, that we did not have to shave, and that bras, jock straps, tampons, and the need for birth control were not always part of our consciousness. We take these for granted the way we take for granted the fact that we have eyebrows.

Silent Word List

The "silent words" are presented in alphabetical order. You must judge your own level of difficulty:

Breast
Clitoris*
Intercourse
Masturbation
Menstruation
Penis
Pubic Hair
Scrotum
Testicle
Vagina

Take this list and say the words out loud. Some of you may feel comfortable with these words, but many people are quite tongue-tied, particularly at the thought of uttering them in conversation with their teen. Go into training before you get into the real confrontation. (Firefighters don't wait for the actual fire to see how to carry someone out of the burning building; they practice repeatedly.)

Once you can say the words, practice saying them with your spouse, and see how he or she handles them, too. Those of you who have preadolescents should start practicing now. Those who have teenagers, take a crash course quickly.

But imagine how you would feel if, somehow, your eyebrows started to go through slow but noticeable changes. What if they became bushier, changed color, or changed shape . . . and you could do nothing to control the changes that were occurring? You would, at a minimum, stare daily at the mirror to see the impact of the new eyebrows on your face and on your personality. Would you try on new hats? Would you change your facial expression? Would you worry about what people would think about your suddenly different eyebrows?

This is the way that the teenager feels as his or her body starts to change. The changes are puberty; the feelings are adolescence.

---

*This one is particular difficult to say, partly because people hear it pronounced in a variety of ways. According to *Dorland's Medical Dictionary*, the preferred way of saying it is "klit'-o-ris" with the emphasis on the first syllable.

Growth before Puberty

At birth most babies are about nineteen to twenty inches long. They then undergo an astronomical growth spurt of about ten inches during their first year. At no other time will the human being grow as much, and at no other time will the calories required to sustain that amount of growth be as great. In the second year, the child will grow about five inches. Growth then begins to slow down to a manageable two to two-and-a-half inches per year. That is, until the beginning of puberty.

When doctors measure human growth, there are critical proportions that tell how well a child is growing. One of the most meaningful measurements is the assessment of the crown to pubis: pubis to heel ratio. Rather than simply measuring the whole length, the child is divided into the proportion between the distance from the top of the head to the top of the pubic bone (that's the hard bone just at the end of the belly where the pubic hair begins), and from there to the heel.

At infancy, a baby is nearly twice as long at the top of his body than at the bottom. Think about the way children fall and where they strike their heads. Toddlers, just taking their first steps fall and land on their foreheads, while two-year-olds hit their noses, and three-year-olds catch the chin. A child's center of balance dictates how he lands. As the child grows, the ratio eventually becomes more and more even so that by age ten there is a crown to pubis: pubis to heel ratio of 1. This explains the beautiful symmetry seen in ten-year-olds on the athletic fields. They are balanced and graceful. But not for long. Here comes puberty.

This body symmetry as well as the side-by-side growth of boys and girls suddenly changes at about the eleventh birthday. In a strange twist of fate, boys—many of whom are destined to eventually outgrow most girls—grow at a lesser rate than girls do. As a result, the sixth- or seventh-grade boys sit on the sidelines watching their female counterparts blossom, getting taller, curvier, and more mature-looking and sounding. What a way to begin your sexually promising years—by growing *less*. Is it any wonder that boys are forever trying to find some way to show that they have arrived at a new plateau?

How Male/Female Growth Is the Same

The major growth of the skull takes place during the first six years. At the beginning of an adolescent's growth spurt, the skull grows more; however, on a

Glasses? For Me?

The need for glasses and teenagers' willingness to wear them are two different issues, but the last thing you want to do is to buy very expensive glasses or contacts for your teenager. Not only does the eye change shape as teens grow—necessitating frequent prescription changes—but there is a mathematical probability nearing 100 percent that they will either be lost or broken shortly. Look for fashionable but less expensive frames. If you buy frames your teen hates, he'll never wear the glasses.

relative basis it is not very significant. Most of the growth is accounted for by a thickening of the bone itself.

Of more importance is the fact that there is a reshaping of the jaw. The upper jaw, or *maxilla*, does not grow at the same rate as the lower jaw, or *mandible*. Hence, for a while, there is an asymmetry of the upper and lower jaws, and again it will take a few years before the normal occlusion (the meeting of the upper and lower teeth) takes place. Commonly, teens will note a small "clicking" sound at the edge of the jaw where the maxilla and mandible joint meet in front of the ear. In fact, this growth process can create a temporary joint problem—TMJ, temporomandibular joint syndrome—that is similar to a sore shoulder from pitching incorrectly. Teens may complain of headaches, or even earaches. It often goes away as the teen matures, but if not, it can be corrected by an orthodontist.

Along with the shift in the shape of the jaw, there is a reshaping of the eyes. The eyeball itself should assume a fairly round shape, with a slightly elongated front to back diameter. As puberty progresses, there is an increase in this anterior to posterior distance, and the net result is a change in the ability to focus on an object. Many teenagers will suddenly find themselves in need of glasses at this point, because their eyes elongate too much.

An often-overlooked aspect of facial growth is the fact that the skin must shift while the face is growing. If there is contemplation of any plastic surgery to the face, the rate of facial growth has a lot to do with the decision of *when* to perform the surgery. Since a girl's ultimate growth is reached two to three years after the onset of her first menstrual period, it is easier to time such a surgical procedure. In boys, growth may continue throughout their teenage years until age twenty or twenty-one. If elective surgery is to take place it should be done at a time when the face itself has finished changing.

Glandular Changes

Everyone remembers the wonderful odor of baby powder on the skin of the infant. Forget that olfactory memory and welcome the new scent of puberty. Both genders undergo dramatic shifts of body odor as their sweat glands enlarge. There are a series of small glands, called the eccrine glands, located throughout the body that allow us to control our body temperature by sweating. With the onset of sexual changes, and under the influence of sexual hormones, the apocrine glands also begin to proliferate. These glands are located in the "sexual" areas—the axilla (the armpit has to be considered "sexual" because it grows hair at puberty) and the groin. When it comes to sweating, these greatly outpace the eccrine glands. Since young teenagers are not well-known for their fondness of showering, they may need to be gently reminded. Girls are not excluded from this problem, but in my experience, boys are more careless about hygiene. Nevertheless, I sometimes have to tactfully remind a girl that daily showers are a good idea.

Parents who tire of arguing about the need for good hygiene may find that humor helps: "John, you smell bad. Please lower your arm before the dog dies." Later on, interest in the opposite sex will make nagging unnecessary. Soon enough, access to the bathroom by other family members will become almost impossible.

Skin Changes

Acne is *the* scourge of the teenager and is a major pubertal change—so major, and so long-lasting, that it will be covered in its own chapter (see Chapter 6).

Male Growth Pattern

While most male body growth is on hold during the early years of puberty, there is a further indignity for boys: Hands and feet go through growth spurts of their own before the rest of the body does. Most parents are very much aware of this change as they are forever lamenting: "I just bought you a new pair of sneakers in June. Do you really need a new pair already? It's only August." And there he stands, with his toes already at the end of shoes that still have several months of wear left.

The first sign of hand growth generally comes in the form of awkwardness.

At dinner a formerly coordinated young teen knocks over his glass with hands that now seem to have overlong fingers. Compared to the rest of his body, the proportions are all wrong; it is as if he were wearing baseball gloves and fins. Try picking up a small piece of jewelry while wearing a catcher's mitt; this is the clumsiness felt by the young teenager experiencing his growth spurt.

So it is that the young adolescent loses his previous grace and trades it in for this new ill-fitting costume that comes with puberty. In another year or so the length of the arms and legs will begin to catch up to the larger hands and feet so that his symmetry returns. You would think this would make everyone happy, but it turns out that the growth of arms and legs happens independently of his trunk. Now the male teen looks like he has been stretched by his appendages like Gumby. The trunk has not changed sufficiently during all of this growth to maintain a proportional body. All you need to do is watch the way pants and jackets fit the young thirteen- or fourteen-year-old male to appreciate the disproportionate way that the body grows. If you could buy clothes that allowed him to "grow into them," the tailor would have to make the sleeves two inches longer and the pants would have an extra two inches trailing over the shoes.

If you've never asked to look at your child's record of growth on the pediatrician's growth chart (kept as part of your child's medical records), do so now. It tells a lot about the pattern of growth. You'll see how your son's growth fits in relation to what is "normal" for his age. Some boys will be very tall, while others will be perfectly normal but shorter. "Normal" for your child is a consistency of growth along one of the chart lines.

Unfortunately, our society tends to view short stature—particularly for males—as undesirable; sometimes it is, and a work-up is warranted for someone who is not growing within this wide range of "normal." However, Chihuahuas make Chihuahuas, and Great Danes make Great Danes, unless of course, they intermarry and then you can't predict which parent your child will take after. In other words, some mix of your own height and that of your spouse is very likely to predict the height of your offspring.

Doctors also plot weight on the same chart, and this, too, is normal if it follows its own symmetry and parallels the pattern for height for your child. (Weight for boys is a little more difficult to plot because they gain weight erratically, depending on their growth spurts.)

To sustain growth for the male, the refrigerator door should have strong hinges during the adolescent years. This, too, is normal. (Weight issues for adolescents are covered in Chapter 5. They are as important to the adolescent male as to the female, so if you're concerned that your son is overweight or underweight, I urge you to read that chapter.)

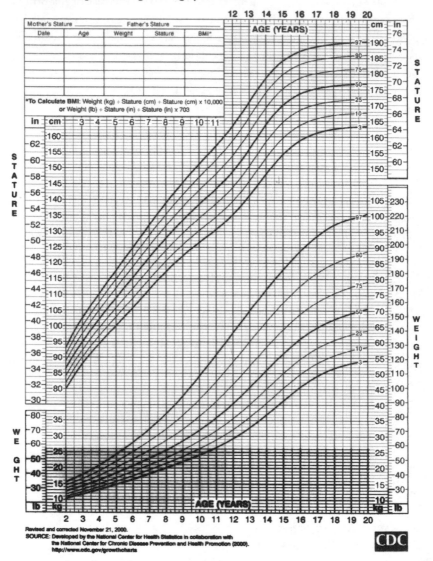

2 to 20 years: Boys
Stature-for-age and Weight-for-age percentiles

Revised and corrected November 21, 2000.
SOURCE: Developed by the National Center for Health Statistics in collaboration with the National Center for Chronic Disease Prevention and Health Promotion (2000). http://www.cdc.gov/growthcharts

Measuring Genital Development: The Tanner System

Rather than always discussing the development of the genital stages by testicular size, a Sexual Staging System has been developed to enable us to discuss the youngster's point in puberty. This was developed in England by Dr. J. M. Tanner of the Institute of Child Health during the 1950s. He described five stages of pubescent development in terms of genital, pubic hair, or breast tissue development. This allows us to speak of the relative stages of puberty: "Now that he has reached Stage 3, you can anticipate . . ."

The easiest way to remember the different stages is to remember that the first stage will identify the child without any pubertal changes; the fifth stage is the fully mature adult body. With this understanding, we can focus more fully on the stages in between. First, we'll address what happens to the adolescent male; later in the chapter, you'll learn what to expect with girls.

Tanner Stages of Male Sexual Changes

■ First Stage

In this stage, the boy has no pubic hair and the testicles are about 2.0 centimeters (2.54 centimeters equals an inch). This is the standard little-boy look that you photographed while he was taking his baby bath and will later cause him a great deal of embarrassment when you show them off.

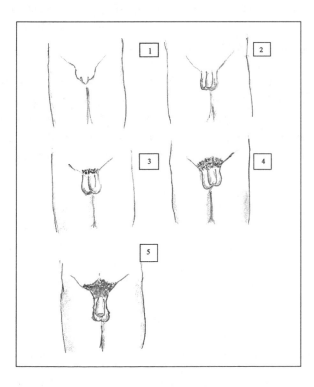

■ Second Stage

Now there is a very slight increase in the size of the testicles—from 2.0 to 2.4 cm. We may not even notice that the stage has arrived. The scrotum now appears a bit thinner in texture and it takes on a slightly red appearance. The scrotum hangs a bit more than last year. That's basically all he has to show for the new stage in his development.

The penis grows lengthwise, but for now little is gained in girth. Some slight, straight pubic hairs at the base of the genitals will begin to grow in. At this point in development, the youngster will invariably giggle as the physician tries to examine his genitalia, checking for a hernia or any testicular masses. A variant of the discomfort is the little dance that takes place as the physician gently examines the scrotum. The teen still giggles uncontrollably, and while raising a leg off the floor, does a little jig, saying "Are you done?!" As the teen matures, this examination becomes routine and is simply accepted.

■ Third Stage

In the third stage, all sorts of changes begin to happen. There will be a rapid growth spurt—three to four inches will be gained in height over one year, and a brief glance will reveal a lot of changes in the genital area, or as it is sometimes called, "down there." Remember, "down there" is near South America. Avoid this phrase, for it signals your own unwillingness to deal with the reality of the sexual changes. (Keep practicing your "silent words" list.)

Pubic hairs become curly and coarse (the color is variable and hopefully matches the natural hair of the head). Sometimes in a dark-haired individual some thin straight hairs are mistaken for pubic hairs and an alarm goes off that "he is developing too rapidly!" The differentiation of the quality of the hair is critical.

Pubic hair eventually reaches out to the thighs, and in most males, has a point of growth that reaches up into the abdomen. Eventually the hair will have the appearance of a normal triangle with the point going up. (In girls the triangular point goes down.)

The scrotum now continues to enlarge as the testes grow inside; the scrotal skin appears coarse, and "ruggae" or folds are evident. Occasionally, small plugs of oil follicles dot the scrotum's surface and give it a "pebbly" appearance. The teen may be concerned that these plugs represent an infection, or may mistake them for a sexually transmitted disease. Most of the time, there is no infection although these oily plugs can get infected when irritated. (For more information, see Chapter 10, "Sexually Transmitted Diseases.")

The penis elongates further, and almost all boys will have slight breast development at this stage. The low level of circulating female hormones, unbalanced by sufficient amounts of male hormones, cause the incredibly sensitive

Genital Growth in Boys

Prior to the 1950s it was difficult to categorize the degree, or level, of genital development in the adolescent. One would have had to measure the testicles by directly grasping the teste and comparing it to a ruler. Since then a device called the "orchidometer" was invented. Essentially a series of increasingly larger egg-shaped (or testicular-shaped, if you will) plastic balls, it allows you to quantify the size of the testicle by volume. They are sequentially numbered so that charting growth is easy to do. I must admit that no matter how carefully I explain the procedure of measuring the testicle to the boy (or parent) the degree of apprehension is incredible on both their parts. The boy who needs this type of measurement performed (and it should *not* be done routinely!) obviously has some degree of initial concern, so measuring just makes it worse. However, in a situation in which the boy is not developing well, this is a critical test and must be done at each visit if there is concern.

breast tissue to respond. The net result is true breast tissue in the male. This is hard to explain to boys, but they are generally reassured when you tell them that it happens to most men, including their father, at their age. This breast tissue is called adolescent gynecomastia, and we will discuss it further in the medical care section. This part of male puberty is one of the best kept secrets of all men.

■ Fourth Stage

Here the most evident change will be the quantity of pubic hair that has sprouted. The hair is now thicker, curlier and coarser, and has spread to the greater area of the mons veneris, the bone you can feel under the hair ("mons" is Latin for mountain; "veneris" is for Venus; "mons veneris" is the "love mountain"). The pubic hair in the fourth stage does not fully reach out to the thighs.

With the testes growing even more, the scrotum continues to get darker and larger. All the while the penis maintains its growth not only in length, but also in thickness. The fourth stage is filled with all types of functional surprises; "wet dreams" (involuntary ejaculation during sleep) and spontaneous erections are the norm. There is nothing sexual about math class, and yet in the middle of the discussion on Pythagorean theory a boy may feel an uncomfortable swelling. Hormones gone crazy! And embarrassment rampant. The young teenager can't fully control the equipment yet. His testosterone factory is working overtime and it will take a while before he learns to control this new phenomenon.

Sensitivity Always

While eventually your son may take over the changing of the bed linen, initially, mom is likely responsible for cleaning the sheets. Questions about what happened to stain the sheet should not be asked. It is also not cute to joke about it, to make light of it, or to question with feigned ignorance. "Gee John did something bad happen last night? Are you all right?" The stare, the scowl, and the stomping of feet in flight will give you the answer.

If a discussion about erections (at night or in school) does come up, the best way a father can handle it is by reassuring his son: "I understand, John. For a while, you will have them at odd times, like when you wake up, but soon your hormones will be under your control. I promise." Unfortunately, some competitive fathers can't resist smirking with remarks like "Don't worry. I had worse ones." The point of parenting is to help, not to compete.

This heightened testosterone level is also the same hormone that accounts for the difference in aggressive behavior in the male. Whether you are a sixteen-year-old city boy or one from the rural countryside, aggressive behavior is predicated on testosterone. This is also true with antelopes, mice, and apes.

■ Fifth Stage

Abundant adult pubic hair now covers the entire mons veneris, but the penis may continue to grow until the twenty-first birthday, a fact often greeted with applause by the teenage boy. The genitalia is now adult.

Male Facial Hair

A sure sign that the teenage male is looking forward to maturity is the innocent question of when to shave, often asked when the hair is nothing more than "peach fuzz."

In most cases the mustache is the first to be noted. The sideburns grow longer and by the mid-teens most boys have to face the daily ritual of shaving. Full beards seldom grow in the early years; there isn't a high enough hormone level to produce a full beard. I cannot think of a single high school student in my practice with a full beard.

I am not an advocate of shaving before it is necessary. It irritates the sensitive still-soft skin of the teen, to say nothing of the damage done by aggressive work with a razor.

However, it is also a mistake to dampen your son's enthusiasm. Before you tell him "not yet," balance the possibility of damage to his face against the possible damage to his ego.

Testosterone Makes Itself Known

Being the parent of a son requires an appreciation of the remarkable hormone, testosterone, which is increasingly believed to be the chemical that causes a type of thinking and aggression that is uniquely male. It is no accident that teen males greet each other by punching and pushing. This primitive but effective way of establishing "maleness" is as old as time.

Of course, testosterone plays a part in other aspects of masculinity. Erotic dreams are common in this age group and the stimulation, although in dreams, is sufficient to produce an ejaculation. The teen male generally has his first ejaculation at roughly the age of fourteen, a fact never mentioned in class by a single male in the history of mankind. (This in contrast to the ever-discussed "first period" by girls in sixth or seventh grade.) The morning erection is the result of unregulated production of testosterone. The only consolation available to the boy is that, in time, this all disappears as the testosterone release self regulates.

Although testosterone accounts for physical aggression, one cannot blame testosterone for all of the male teenager's pranks. Aggressive behavior where someone gets hurt may be predicated on testosterone, but it does not exonerate the teen's actions. This is a good time to discuss feelings, behavior, and self-control with your son.

Same-Gender Talks Work Best at This Age

While gender equality and neutrality are admirable changes that are affecting our society, there are certain discussions that are best handled by adults of the same gender as their teen. To the teenage boy, another man, and only a man, understands the embarrassment of an erection misplaced—the quick flip onto his stomach to hide an erection when Mom comes to wake him up in the morning. For the same reason, menstrual management is best left to Mom, an aunt, or a stepmother. What could men possibly know about the agony of getting your period on the first day of school?

Early adolescence is not the time to say, "Your mother (or father) can discuss that with you just as well as I can." Teenagers want to hear it from an adult (parent, stepfather, stepmother, uncle, aunt) who has gone through a similar experience. Later on there will be plenty of opportunity for realizing that a sensitive human being is all that's really required for almost any type of intimate conversation.

What parents of both genders must do is identify with either their son or daughter. Never dismiss your teen's concern with a quick and simple diagnosis that trivializes it.

Female Growth Pattern

While girls experience some of the disproportionate growth experienced by boys, the degree of disproportion is less evident. We don't associate girls with the image of the Frankenstein-like arms and legs sticking out of their clothes. Their spurt of growth is much less than that of boys, and it is more easily defined because the onset of the menstrual flow signals the beginning of the end of the growth spurt. In other words, once menses start, the growth spurt begins to wane.

Pubertal Growth in Girls

Girls have a distinct timetable for pubertal changes, and there is a Tanner System that marks their changes as well. Like the boys, stage one is a child's body with no development; stage five is the fully matured adult body.

First a word about pubic hair and breasts.

Pubic Hair

The girl may show an adult pattern of pubic hair distribution in as little as two years from first development. It is also possible to show pubic hair before the development of breast tissue. About a third of girls do so, and it should not be a cause for alarm. However, if the pubic hair appears when a child would still be classified as a "little girl," then a medical workup is in order. Generally, we accept ten years as a reasonable age at which to see pubic hair. Lately there is some evidence that even girls as young as eight can develop pubic hair and be normal.

Breasts

In almost all cases, the first changes of puberty that are noticed are changes in the breasts. This development alone forces girls to deal with the sexual impact of puberty. (It's hard not to contend with sexual issues when you look down and see this new growth.) Frequently one of the breasts develops faster than the other. In fact, it may well be that at the conclusion of the entire process, there will be asymmetry of the breasts. In most cases the degree of difference is not sufficient to cause concern.

Occasionally, because of increased body fat it may be difficult to adequately, and correctly, judge the stage of breast development.

Tanner Stages of Female Sexual Changes

■ Stage One

In this stage we see a little girl with no development at all, whose chest is indistinguishable from a little boy.

■ Stage Two

At this time there is a small amount of pubic hair, usually straight, present on the labia majora (the outer fatty folds of the genitals) and perhaps some on the mons veneris. Just as for boys, darker-haired girls may show a slight amount of fine hair, which is not considered true pubic hair.

The first sign of breast development is a slight budding of the breast tissue, the areola (colored part) slightly widens and the papilia, or nipple, is more erect. Most girls are between nine and thirteen years old at this stage. Many girls will develop breast tissue prior to developing pubic hair.

■ Stage Three

At this stage we see the beginning of curly pubic hair over more of the mons veneris. Menstruation will start for many girls at this time, and the breasts will enlarge further, and will begin to show contour. One could draw a smooth curve that would include the breast and the elevation of the nipple and areola.

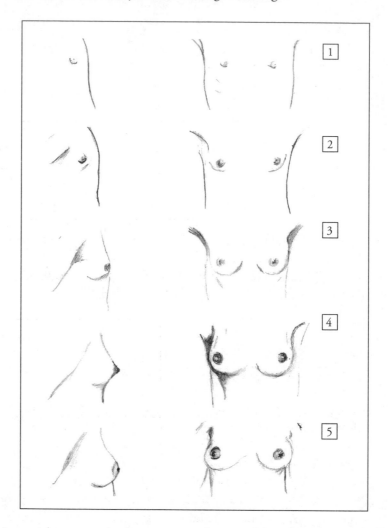

Most girls are ready for menstruation at this point since, if all goes smoothly, there will be a concomitant development of the genital area. Usually girls are in the seventh to ninth grades at this stage, which would put them as young as twelve or as old as fourteen, but the range is quite variable. Some may not have their first cycle until stage four of breast development. About 4 percent of girls will menstruate normally and without much in the way of breast development. Since that is the exception, we watch those girls carefully for any signs of endocrine abnormality.

■ Stage Four

Thicker, curlier and coarser hair covering almost the entire mons appears by stage four. This increase is distinguished from the fifth stage by the fact that

"When Does She Need a Bra?"

oday bras are less a rite of passage because they have become fashion accessories. Young girls start wearing sports-style bras to dance and gymnastics classes long before they need them, and even true "underwear" bras are part of the look of young girls today.

Most girls want a bra even before it is remotely necessary, and the less that is made of the issue the better. Without necessarily voicing her concern, your daughter may be worried that her nipples "show" under her shirt, which is as good a reason for getting a bra as true tissue development.

Rather than making the purchase of a bra a "landmark event," simply take your daughter shopping. Start at a department store, not one of the stores specializing in sexy lingerie. With the younger set, the message is key: You're buying her "underwear" not "sex appeal." As with the discussion about wet dreams, everyone will likely be more comfortable if shopping for a bra is done when on an outing with mom or with the significant female in a girl's life.

the hair does not reach out to the thighs. This is exactly the same as the male's stage four.

The breast now undergoes a distinct change and the areola and nipple form a secondary mound. The breast now has a contour to the breast tissue and a "bud" made of the areola. Some normal, mature women stay at stage four breast development. Some girls even skip this stage and progress directly to stage five. By stage four, one would expect that 90 percent of girls would have had their first menstrual cycle.

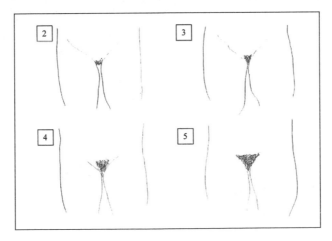

When the Developmental Stages Don't Match Up

O ccasionally there are times when a girl will only have breast development or only pubic hair. Consult with your daughter's doctor if you have any concern. This often requires testing to determine if there is an abnormality in the production of hormones, or if it is due to an increased responsiveness in the end organ (breasts or pubic hair) to normal circulating pre-pubertal hormones. The discussion of precocious pubertal development is complex, but suffice it to say that if the breasts develop remarkably early (younger than age eight), a consultation is in order to ascertain if there is an overproduction of estrogen, and if so, from where. The presence of early pubic hair and no breast development should prompt a similar search. The physician has to weigh the child's age in relation to this isolated development to gauge whether it is prudent to intervene with laboratory tests, sonograms, X rays, and CAT scans.

■ Stage Five

The mature female has abundant adult-type hair over the entire mons, reaching to the beginning of the thighs. Note that the pubic hair, or "female escutcheon" (from the Latin for "shield") has a triangular shape with the point of the triangle down, and the flat side up. This has some importance in the assessment of an overproduction of male hormones: if the normal flat top has hair creeping up to the umbilicus (belly button), it need not signify a problem, but when coupled with acne or menstrual abnormalities, it is probably wise to have your daughter's physician investigate. The argument is simple: since the male escutcheon has a point up, then a point up would be consistent with male hormones. (Also see "The Female Reproductive System" section of Part Five, "The Adolescent: Head to Toe.")

The breast grows to its adult size with the areola and nipple no longer forming a secondary mound. In most cases, there is an interval of about one and a half to four years from the beginning of the development to the completion.

Menstruation

After their first menstrual period, girls often go to school the next day and proudly announce the event to their friends. This single event marks a clear difference between the "little girl" and the "young woman."

In the United States, the mean age of menarche (first menstruation) occurs at 12.5 years of age. Generally, an American teen starts menstruating between the ages of eight and sixteen. These are standard guidelines and allow the physician to judge whether menstruation has started too early (precocious puberty; see discussion on p. 441 in Part Five) or too late (primary amenorrhea: no period by the age of eighteen; none by the age of sixteen is called delayed menarche; see discussion in Part Five).

Prior to the first menstrual flow the normal girl will gain a huge amount of weight—forty pounds over the previous four years! If you continue to look at the rate curve, you see that girls will continue to gain weight but at a less dramatic rate. Most girls are upset to hear this is normal; even mothers gasp at the information.

Moreover, the increased weight will not be distributed evenly. Most girls will have a greater distribution below their waist. Indeed, most girls are built like pears by the time of their first menstruation. At this time, girls have to deal with their appearance whether they want to or not. As their bodies change, the last thing they want to hear is Daddy saying something, presumably well-intended, like "Sweetheart, you seem to be gaining a little on the bottom. Maybe you better watch the extra ice cream." Or Mom saying something like: "Margaret, haven't you had enough cookies? You have to watch your figure now."

Eating disorders will be discussed later in the book, but it is important to note that the eleven- or twelve-year-old who has not reached her menarche is at risk if she starts to diet at this point. Girls need the right amount of calories and protein in order to menstruate; but of more importance is the fact that they need the right amount of nutrition in order to achieve normal growth. Although eating disorders are now evident in all social groups, they are more likely to be found in the upper and middle classes. How ironic that, until recently, malnutrition was only seen in the poor in underdeveloped countries, but that in the United States at present we are most likely to see growth problems from malnutrition in affluent social groups.

So When Will It Start?

Prior to the onset of the first period there are some clues that allow one to predict that menarche is due. The girl has usually reached genital and breast stage three. The girl may also have a slight clear vaginal discharge; it has no odor, nor is there any discomfort associated with the discharge. It is normal, but the

Girls Weight Gain

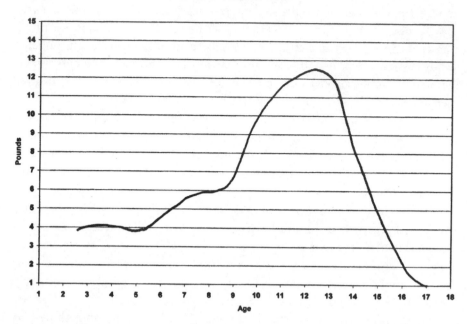

Weight Gain before Menses:

■ 4 years before menses, there will be a weight gain of about 8 pounds.
■ 3 years before menses, there will be a weight gain of another 10 pounds.
■ 2 years before menses, there will be a weight gain of another 12 pounds.
■ 1 year before menses, there will be a weight gain of another 13 pounds.

Age will vary but not the years before menses

young girl doesn't always know that and often needs reassurance that all is well. Throughout life many women will notice that prior to the onset of the menstrual flow there will be some "physiologic leukorrhea" (this is known as "normal discharge"). Along with the discharge, another clue that will help prepare the girl for the prospect of her first period is the developing of axillary (armpit) hair. Generally speaking, the presence of axillary hair and a physiologic leukorrhea heralds the onset of menarche within six months.

The initial menstruation that takes place is not a "genuine period" since there is usually no previous ovulation. What causes menstruation in the first place is the fact that the female has not gotten pregnant in the previous month; with the lack of appropriate levels of progesterone, the endometrium (lining of the uterus) will slough and bleeding will begin. In most cases, the young

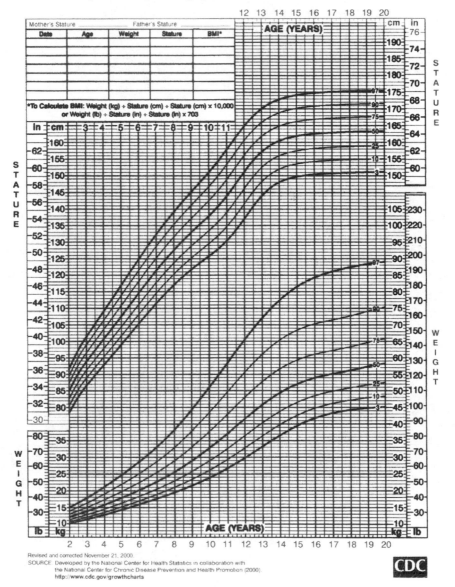

2 to 20 years: Girls
Stature-for-age and Weight-for-age percentiles

Revised and corrected November 21, 2000.
SOURCE: Developed by the National Center for Health Statistics in collaboration with
the National Center for Chronic Disease Prevention and Health Promotion (2000).
http://www.cdc.gov/growthcharts

teenager will have to wait a year or more before monthly ovulation occurs. When this happens, it will bring more regularity to the menstrual cycle. In the early years what is being shed is the build-up of some endometrial lining that is affected by estrogen; since there is no ovulation there is no secondary boost

Change in the Age of Menarche

Throughout the world there has been a steady fall in the age of menarche. In the United States, we began keeping statistics only after the early 1900s, when the mean age was approximately seventeen years of age. Better nutrition, plain and simple, is the critical factor that affects the onset of menstruation. One study compared Japanese girls before World War II and after. The girls from the pre-war study had onset of menses ages that were later than for those girls who had better nutrition after the American occupation. When the pre-war Japanese girls were compared to Japanese-American girls from California, the California girls had earlier onset of menses. In time, as Japanese society developed a better economy and better nutrition, there was no difference between Japanese girls and those of Japanese heritage in the United States.

with the progesterone hormone. Without progesterone the endometrial lining is at risk for irregular bleeding (shedding) since progesterone holds the lining in place. As a result, the young teen will have irregular cycles and unless there is so much bleeding that anemia is a potential problem, irregularity is part of the "normal" menstrual history for most girls. Nonetheless, if periods remain irregular for more than a year, you should discuss this with your physician.

Talking about Menstruation

Perhaps in the Dark Ages (about thirty years ago for some), menstruation was on the "silent word" list. But school-aged boys and girls of today know that girls "bleed" every month, and they know it is a natural phenomenon. Yet there is still need for a mother-daughter discussion. First, it is important to discuss the mechanics of dealing with the blood by providing answers to questions such as these: "Does it come out all at once?" "Will I have warning?" "What if I am wearing a white dress?" "Can people tell?" "What if I am at camp or at school?" And the ever constant: "Does it hurt?"

Each parent has to judge how ready their daughter will be for the first menses. Be sure to tell your daughter that the first menses should not be painful. The reason for pain is that ovulation releases progesterone and some chemicals that cause uterine contractions. These chemicals generally do not come with first periods since there is no ovulation.

As to potential embarrassment, reassurance is again in order. What young girls fear is their lack of control over the situation. Explain that their period will not begin with a volcanic gush, and tell them that they will, indeed, have enough time to excuse themselves to go to the women's room before anything embarrassing occurs.

To be up-to-date with a menstrual discussion, it is important not to revert to some of the unfortunate terms and information that were used only a few years ago. Terms such as "your friend," "the scourge," and "the curse" must go the way of the bustle. The information should be delivered factually and calmly, because part of what you're trying to convey is an attitude. Lines like "You have to endure this" or "When I was a girl I used to stay home the first day of my period" are out of place. Today's girls need to be given a can-do spirit, and they should know that even when menstruating, they are going to be able to do everything they want—from swimming at the beach to running a meeting in a corporate board room.

Additional sensitivity is required if your daughter is maturing at a different rate than her friends. The girl who is the only one in the class who's had her period has no one to talk with and will be quite self-conscious until someone else in her class begins developing; the older girl who has not menstruated feels odd and worries about what might be wrong with her.

You also will soon need to address the use of sanitary napkins versus tampons. In some cultures, it is taboo to insert anything in the vagina before marriage. For most families, however, the tampon is a perfectly safe and reasonable alternative, even for young adolescents. Using tampons provides freedom and gives a teenager a greater feeling of control, which provides enormous relief about the entire menstrual process.

To find a type that is right for your teen, shop for any brand, but look for one labeled "junior" or "teen." You may need to experiment with buying several different brands before your daughter is satisfied. While it may be a little difficult at first for a young teen to get the hang of inserting the tampon, it will fit in easily if the girl is relaxed and catches on to aiming it at the right angle. Send her to the bathroom with a full box of tampons, and let her read the directions (there are clear ones in every box that explain the angle as upward and back), and tell her to experiment. The motivated teen will learn to use tampons pretty quickly.

Today's tampons are perfectly safe and, contrary to the advice that was given during the Toxic Shock Syndrome crisis, they can be worn through the night. TSS occurred in some women who used a tampon that had an artificial fiber in it. The fibers were making microscopic cuts that allowed bacteria to enter the blood stream. The removal of these tampons from the market has generally eliminated the danger of Toxic Shock Syndrome.

Moving On

So here we are. We have discussed the bodily changes that are taking place in the two sexes. I hope that reading about them helps you understand the dramatic and exciting changes your teen is experiencing. What's more, you are now prepared to openly discuss these topics with your teenager.

Chapter 3

The Emotional Life
of the Adolescent

If puberty is defined by all of the body changes that are taking place, then adolescence is the direct result of all of these changes. The tranquillity of the child's thinking is disrupted by the pubescent changes, and suddenly the parent is confronted with a sullen, moody, secretive, volatile, narcissistic, sexual, and "difficult" person in the household. What happened, and equally important, is this normal? The latter is a question that is put to me daily.

It is still a mystery to me why parents cannot vividly recall their own teenage years. Is the process so awkward and painful that we have a built-in memory block that forces amnesia for those years? Perhaps it is important for our own parenting ability to be able to distance ourselves from the insecurity that surrounded those years. Few adults can look back and say truthfully that their teenage years were blissful. Memories of wanting to belong, or feeling self-conscious about our body, and the embarrassments of our young journey into the sexual arena are best forgotten or embellished.

If parents reading this book could summon their own memories (the actual ones, not the ones they may have fabricated over the years), they would be better able to understand their teenagers. Go to your own parents' house and pull out family photos, preferably those when you were your own teenager's age, and start the slide show of your own years. It will help as we discuss the tools that teenagers use to survive. When you were a teen, you used the very same tools.

The Nature of Adolescence

Adolescence is about a psychosocial and psychosexual time. Teens undergo bodily changes and want to see how their new image affects others. In time, the need to understand their place in the sexual arena invites the opposite sex in some sort of sexual game. A boy will no longer show interest by punching a girl, but may go out of his way to walk beside her. The girl will no longer call boys "yucky" but may slowly begin to realize that the "gross kid" in the fifth grade is actually "sort of cute."

The class that was once homogenous in body is now showing a large variation in development, and this affects their social development as well. The earlier developers—the girls who are now wearing bras, and the boys who are beginning to develop muscles—are viewed as "sexual" even if they haven't a clue what that might entail. Some become leaders of a peer group often only because of a special physical trait. Ask the teenager about the "good looking" kids in the class and they often have no problem in total recall. Indeed, they will be able to tell you that there is a ranking order to all of this that is somehow understood. Even teachers fall into the trap of looking upon the more physically developed as "mature," and parents may expect more of these early developers. But adolescents are all the same underneath—personalities trying to find themselves and decide who they are going to be.

But Who Are They?

To better understand teenagers, parents might first consider the three questions adolescents must answer as they pass from childhood to adult status. When they are answered, the teen has become an adult.

The Three Critical Questions:
1. Who am I?
2. Who am I sexually?
3. How do I become independent?

Who Am I?

This is a question that is first answered concretely by the child, and the answer lies in age, in gender, in culture, and where the teen lives. She can be an eleven-year-old named Julie who lives in New York and whose family hails from a particular culture. That is identity enough until she begins to undergo puberty.

Slowly this question takes on a more abstract meaning. It goes to the heart of who they are. Teenagers begin to wonder: "What are my values? What do I believe in? Are the values given to me by my parents the same ones that I want to embrace?" Teenagers' sense of themselves no longer is an easy answer. As they progress through adolescence, they begin to have more and more complex insights.

In the midst of all this, teens have the added burden of not being able to be a single being. They feel great pressure to appear in three personas. There is the teenager that you get to see at home. Then there is the public teenager for the adult world; I get to see a bit of that in my office. Lastly, there is the teenager who is out there with his friends. Make no mistake about it. They may all be quite different and you only get to see one side of their world. Watch the awkwardness when you greet one of his friends. Does your teen behave as he normally does with the peer group or, with you by the door, does he revert to the son role? Movie theater dates with your child are no longer possible because her peers may spot her with her mother. It is best to leave the two worlds separate when appropriate.

Who Am I Sexually?

While some teens will be struggling with the issue of gender preference (see Chapter 8 for a further discussion), this question concerns how teens present themselves as a male or as a female. Each culture, each social group, and each generation has a scale that is acceptable. How teens dress, how they talk, and their choice of peer groups all define "masculine" and "feminine" behavior.

Eventually, as they come to terms with their sense of self, their sexual identity will begin to fall into place. At some point Julie, now eighteen, will understand herself more fully and have a better idea of how she wants other females to view her.

How Do I Become Independent?

The last task of adolescence begins slowly as the twelve-year-old argues that it is acceptable to go to the movies alone, to be left unsupervised, or to be allowed the privilege of selecting clothes that define self and sexuality. It means that he wants to be able to manage some decisions and be allowed to correct his mistakes by himself. The teen mantra becomes "I'm old enough now to do that."

Parents can help with such simple things as setting a fixed allowance. The teen learns to manage money and learns the lesson of spending foolishly and being penniless on the weekend. Parents who leave their pockets open to the teenager are only perpetuating dependence.

Commitments to appointments are part of this process. When teens make an appointment or a pledge, they need to honor it. If parents make excuses to the authorities and get them out of trouble, they teach a lesson that they are powerful and the teenager needs them. The idea of parenting is to turn the reins of responsibility over to the next generation.

In my own practice, I see teenagers who fail to show up for SAT tutors, who fail to keep appointments with physicians, and who change their minds easily about a musical instrument. If this goes on without consequence, the lesson is obvious. They can forgo responsibility and their parents will bail them out. They must learn that their actions have consequences and that future authorities will not always listen to mommy and daddy.

Some people never really grow up—they never really understand about taking responsibility for themselves—and it is usually because they spent their adolescence being rescued by others. The kindest favor you can do your teen is to help her gain independence one step at a time. By her late teens, she'll be ready to shoulder many adult-size responsibilities.

Internal Pressures

In addition to trying to figure out the three critical questions, teens have both internal and external pressures that make their lives even more difficult. Before judging a teenager's bad mood too harshly, consider the other issues with which he is coping.

Teen Insecurities

Teenagers have a fragile defense system. Theirs is a world of apprehension, misinformation, and doubt. They harbor secret anxieties about what they perceive they *should* know. How are they to understand that their confusion is the same as the other kids when no one ever is willing to say, "I don't know, either!" Bravado and cover-up are common.

When they find a sympathetic and, hopefully knowledgeable, adult, they worship the relationship as only a pupil can with a mentor. If you are not there, they will find someone else to answer their mysteries.

Feelings of Isolation

Teenagers feel isolated. They feel intensely that no one really understands them. Puberty, alone, is enough to cause inner agitation. The teen is discovering a body that has new angles and new feelings, and the sense of wonder that this all brings makes him feel unique. Yes, they know that others have gone through puberty, but they fear that their puberty, and their adolescence is different: "How can it be that my mother or father ever had these feelings?"

If they are lucky, an older sibling of the same sex will be there to share the big secret that she is not alone in these weird feelings. Parents who toss aside a casual "It's normal, don't worry about it" have forgotten their own adolescence.

Don't volunteer a dialogue about puberty and feelings since your timing may be inappropriate. Wait for the moment when you get a question that opens up the discussion and just do a little at a time. That's all they want, for now. They need to integrate your thoughts and advice and see if it works. If the advice is wise and to the point, the teen will come back for more.

Teens Want to Be Different

As part of the separation process, teens work hard to be different, often creating open rebellion against authority figures—including you. It's their way of assuring that decisions are all theirs.

Rebellion doesn't mean that they want to do bad things. Rather, it's about seeing what they can do. As parents, you must set limits, and you and your spouse must agree. This is an art: If the limits you set are too rigid, you are asking for problems, since teens will want to go to that limit and just a bit more. Likewise, if the limit is too vague they will take advantage. For example, if you say "Come home before dark" when you want her to be home by 8, you are in trouble because the teenager will view "dark" as as "whenever I notice it's dark," which may be 9:30! Look at how clear the message is when you say "Come home by 8."

Teenagers whose parents are divorced have a particularly difficult time with limits. Unless the two parents can come together and agree, the teen is left with two sets of values and two sets of rules. In the end, neither parent takes charge of the situation and the teenager is left in the middle wondering which is the right set of rules. As painful as it may be for the divorced adults, they need to find a common ground for the rules of parenting. I know that it is easier said than done, but if you want to help guide your teen through adolescence, it's a task that must fall on united parental shoulders.

Parents Must Be Parents

Though they may be tempted to include you in their world now and then, teens really can't. They now must rely more on peers and less on the support and advice of parents—though they still very much need you as an authority figure.

Since each generation thinks that theirs has invented youth, it is reasonable for teens to feel a certain amount of skepticism about whether parents truly understand them, and as a result, peers become a source of solace. A best friend is precious. You, as a parent, cannot be your teenager's best friend. It will be a flawed relationship—you cannot set boundaries while still being viewed as a friend. Parents are told some things and friends are privy to others. Parents have obligations and responsibilities that are distinct from friendship, and if those are tempered by friendship the parent does not come across as authoritative. Adolescents need a same-age "best friend" because this helps them become independent. A child tells a parent everything (at least one hopes so), but as he grows, he must turn to others, or he will never become truly independent. To clarify, I do not mean that you cannot be "friendly" with your teen nor spend time doing fun things. It is the specific relationship of "best friend" that is the issue.

If you want a friendly relationship with your teen, when your teen asks a question, don't lecture. Communication must be a dialogue with you talking occasionally and listening more. You'll be amazed at what you'll learn.

Friends Rule

As teens discover what is important to them, they will associate with different groups at different times. They are not being fickle but rather they are experimenting with their identity. Parents may be mystified as to why the group of kids who were once their child's universe are no longer even mentioned.

What if the group is "bad"? As a parent, you may well think a new group of kids is "bad," but it is a word that is so open to interpretation that I suggest you not use it. It pre-judges the group and immediately puts your own teen on the defensive. Instead try to understand the attraction of the group. You may begin to appreciate what attracts your teen. If, as you say, the group is bad, then why is it so appealing to your teen?

When you ask your teen why he hangs out with a certain group, don't expect him to be able to answer on the spot; allow time to slowly draw out the reasons. Since you are not privy to the social hierarchy in school or the politics of your teen's peer group, don't presume who are his friends. Never invite a teenager to your house without checking with your own to see if that is acceptable. And remember: Your perception of a teen's character may be based on the behavior that is accorded the adult world, which may belie a darker reality. Behind the scenes, your son or daughter may see a side that is far from that proper and well-mannered phony. The neatly dressed teen who is polite to you may well be the local bully or even the local drug dealer. Listen to your teen's judgment and respect his decision not to associate with your choices.

If you remain certain that the group is "bad," first consult your spouse. You may learn more information about the group in question. Secondly, be painfully honest with yourself and with your spouse as to the reasons why you see the group, or a particular teen this way. Clothes, hair style, economic status, and, regretfully, culture and race, may all play a part in your perception. None of these may enter into your teenager's frame of reference and, hence, your arguments will fall on rather deaf ears.

Be sure of your facts before you discuss any of this with your teen. Rumors, insinuation, and "feelings" do not constitute sufficient evidence to argue the point that the group will have a bad effect. If, however, you have evidence that shows the group in a bad light, sit down with your teen and calmly present your argument.

Rational Thinking Is Not the Norm

Teenagers tend to view problems as black or white and cannot fully comprehend the gray zones of arguments. Gray becomes an area that they learn after their teens. Listen to their solutions, and you are hearing the words of righteousness. They have an uncanny ability to simplify an argument so that it sounds right, even if you instinctively feel that something is wrong. Teenagers have an innate sense of legal argument. But beware of their logic. It is often flawed but hard to unravel because of all the extraneous stuff they throw in: "Mom, why can't I tattoo myself? Don't I own my body?" Does she, you ask yourself? If I say yes, I am doomed by this argument. If I say no, I'm not sure I can back it up with solid reasons. When caught in that bind, ask for time to think about it. You do not owe, as part of your parental contract, *immediate* and correct answers to your teenager. "Good point! Let me think about it for a while." Make sure you do and eventually respond.

Teenagers Have Heavy Thinking to Do

Teenagers will spend time thinking about thinking. They go into the sanctum of their room and stare at the ceiling. They are working hard as they deal with issues of life, death, and the meaning of it all. These are legitimate concerns and, since answers are not easy, they will go back to their ceiling for some more thinking. This occurs normally as the teenager's body forces him to deal with the cycle of life and death. They are, after all, capable of procreation. Let them think, and don't intrude. But if you get an opportunity to enter that sanctum, and you are posed a question like, "Hey, Dad, did you ever wonder why we are here? I mean on earth? It's sorta weird . . . ," you are doing something right. Grab the moment to have a philosophical discussion.

On the darker side, some of the "heavy thoughts" teens have concern suicide. This is an alarming thought, but as the thinking becomes more abstract, the notion of nonexistence and death may arise. It is important to take this seriously without panic. See page 67 for more information about teenage suicide.

External Pressures

Appreciating the teenager's inner struggles changes our perspective of the swagger that they often project. Underneath there is a constant struggle to understand what is happening as physical changes bring about an upheaval of feelings. These are common to both sexes, to all generations, and to all cultures. Every one of us had to deal with our struggle for identity and expression at some time in our lives. But if all of us struggle in the same way why do some teenagers have a harder time? To answer that we have to understand that internal pressures are not the only ones confronting the teenager.

Adoption

The adopted teen *can* deal with adolescence normally, but there has to be an appreciation that questions of identity are especially significant. Most teens can look at their parents and, at a minimum, judge whether they will be tall or short. The adopted teen has no such luxury. The way the issue of adoption has been handled makes this pressure greater or lesser.

Culture

Ideally the teenager's home culture is the same as the greater outside culture. The tools for identity, for sexual expression, and for how to deal with issues of independence are standardized. But, if the family culture is different from the larger one—i.e., the family has emigrated—conflicts about behavior are inevitable. The teenager, with justification, will respond to the parent's disapproval with, "You put me here. What do you expect? I have to survive out there!"

Death

The death of a parent throws off the normal balance of parenting. Even if the death took place during childhood years, the teenager will again feel the loss during puberty as questions arise that would have been answered by the absent parent. Feeling that the remaining parent may be having a hard time coping, the teenager may also feel a need to compensate and "take care" of that parent, or "not bother" the parent with problems.

Disease

Since children and teens need to feel protected by the parents, it is assumed that the parents are healthy enough to do so. The parent who is ill poses a dilemma for the adolescent struggling for independence and rebellion. As with death, a disease in the family poses a question of who becomes the caretaker. We should also not forget the toll that an ill sibling takes on the family and, ultimately on the teenager who has to watch the dynamics of attention shift to the ill child. For example, in anorexia nervosa (see Chapter 5) there is so much emphasis on the starving teen that the others are often neglected.

Divorce

Perhaps there is no more common external stress on this generation of teens than divorced parents. Divorce is not normal; but it is prevalent. With 50 percent of marriages succumbing to divorce, it is some consolation to know that many of your teen's classmates have to deal with the same issues. But your home has a particular tempo and rhythm, with rules and regulations about behavior. If the marriage had not dissolved, the teen would have only one set of rules to deal with. With divorce, there are often two sets, even in the most amicable separations. The extra burden of stepparents and stepsiblings, or half siblings, is not to be underestimated. An entire book can be written about the role of stepparents in the life of a teenager. Suffice it to say, that rarely can a stepparent do much right in the eyes of the adolescent.

Puberty Abnormalities and Physical Disabilities

Since adolescence is predicated by bodily changes, it logically follows that any abnormality in those physical changes will throw off how the teenager feels. Too early, too late, too much, or too little are all problems. No change at all can be devastating, as is seen with some illnesses. Also, physically disabled teens may have to cope all over again with how their disability is perceived. The loss does not have to be visible. Several of my patients are hearing impaired, and the idea of publicly proclaiming their difficulty by wearing hearing aids has caused a great deal of stress for them.

Religion

As adults we can embrace a spirituality, a religion, that we hope to pass on to our children. However, it does not always follow that the teen will embrace, at that point in life, the same religious tenets. Indeed, the parent may be aghast to hear blasphemous statements about their beliefs. The good news is that this rebellious time may only be a passing phase of experimentation. If the parents can discuss religion openly and have valid reasons for their beliefs, and (this is critical) if they practice what they preach, many teens will come back to the fold.

Normal and Coping?

Looking at these stresses, internal and external, one realizes how difficult and confusing it is to be a teenager. As adults, this confusion seems to us a distant memory. If one were to say that an adult were idealistic, volatile, abstract, rebellious, and thought about suicide, we would consider this behavior abnormal and possibly dangerous. Yet, these are the very normal behaviors of teenagers—no wonder parents worry. What parents need is a sense of what is okay and what is not. How do you identify the teen in trouble if the normal one looks so difficult?

The individual who is functioning well generally does so by existing in three spheres of life. (A potential fourth sphere can be added later in our discussion.) We all have jobs, we all live in a family setting, and we all have friends with whom we choose to spend time. The schematic illustrates this point.

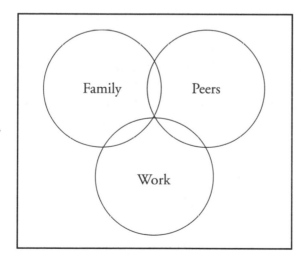

Family. We all are, in some way or another, a member of a family. Father, mother, son, daughter, brother, sister all define roles that we play within the family. If we are doing well in that sphere, we derive emotional support as a member.

Work. Each of us has a job to do. Mine is going to the office and practicing medicine. Yours may be in an office or managing a household, or both. Your teenager's job is school. If you do well in your job, there is a sense of accomplishment. This sphere gives us a sense of responsibility and fulfillment.

Peers. Our friends are people that we select because they suit our needs and we enjoy their company. When we interact with friends another part of who we are is fulfilled.

The Whole Teen

The notion of the spheres is that the contented individual is doing well in all three. Since each provides a different aspect of nurturance we derive a feeling of satisfaction from belonging to a good family, doing well in our work, and having a group of friends that treat us well.

If one of the spheres is failing, for whatever reason, the other two have to fill the gap. For example, if home is a problem, then one's work and friends have to make you feel good about yourself. You may work longer hours and spend more time with your friends than usual as you avoid home. Alternatively, if you are struggling with the work environment, your home and your friends have to be there for you. Lastly, if your friends turn against you, you cry at home and bury yourself in the workplace.

When two spheres fail, it is impossible to expect the remaining one to do all of the nurturing. One cannot just work, or just be a parent, or just party with friends and feel satisfied. If there are problems with all three spheres, you are usually depressed.

One of my patients, feeling overwhelmed by his school, told me that I was missing a fourth sphere. He insisted that spirituality was missing; I have no problem adding it for some, but not for all.

Coping or Depressed?

Now look at your teenager. Judge how he is doing in the family, as a student, and with his choice of friends. If you can say that all spheres are working well, your teen is probably okay. Don't ask for a totally smooth ride, but accept the bumps along the way as part of the price of adolescence. If he is not doing well in school, and his friends pose a problem, where can he go? Despite your love and all your good intentions, you cannot provide everything for your teen. If the home life is disrupted (i.e., divorce, death, or disease in the family), and he is not doing well in school, he will seek out his friends and want nothing more than to be with them.

Once all three spheres are not working you have a depressed teen who needs help. However, don't expect to find the traditional behaviors that we associate with adult depression. Mood swings, avoidance, poor choice of clothes, lack of interest or sullen behavior may not be part of depression for a teenager, but part of the developmental phase. Generally, the depressed adult does poorly at work; not necessarily the teenager. Indeed, the straight-A student may have only school and nothing more going for her. She has isolated herself from friends and she dreads going home to the shouts and screams of an impending divorce. Soon even the A's will not be enough to provide her with something to look forward to.

If your teen is failing in two or three of these spheres, you need to get some professional advice on how to handle the situation. Start with your teenager's doctor and ask for an evaluation. Some pediatricians will automatically refer you to mental health professionals since they feel that despression is best handled by them. What counts is experience and a willingness to work with the teenager and knowing when the issues require that the family be brought in. If the family is disrupted and mother and father are yelling, it makes no sense to expect that the teenager in individual therapy will be able to make the changes needed. Too often it is easier to blame the behavior of the angry and hurt teenager on nothing more than his age, and to fail to see family factors that have to be addressed for the anger to abate.

Sometimes medications will be required to deal with a depression or anxiety in the adolescent. Nonmedical therapists are not licensed to prescribe, so be prepared to see a *psychopharmacologist* if the therapist is not a psychiatrist (an M.D.).

Suicide

The depressed teenager is always at risk for suicide. Statistics show that for every one completed adult suicide there will be roughly seven failed attempts. With teenagers the attempt-to-completed ratio can be as high as 50 (or even 100). With this in mind we have to be vigilant that the adolescent's attempt doesn't inadvertently succeed.

Psychiatrists will talk about suicide ideation or suicide gestures. The former is meant to convey that there are *thoughts* of hurting oneself but nothing has been done; the latter implies that the individual actually acted out the thought. In both cases professional intervention is needed to sort out the issues.

Suicide ideation means that the individual thinks about dying and how it would be done. The true suicide's thoughts rarely include a future since he considers it irrelevant. A teenager may be thinking of death, yet have no notion of how it would come about; in the next sentence he may tell you that he still wants to go to college but is scared. Why worry about college if you are going to take actions to die? The trained professional will gauge the level of intention and guide the family appropriately.

The classic *suicide gesture* in the adolescent years will take place in the home, while parents are there or are soon expected, often following an argument with a friend or family member. The teen may be a sixteen-year-old girl who has had some problems or just experienced a loss (her boyfriend broke up with her, a friend or even a pet died). She will take pills from the medicine cabinet while leaving a note, or calling a friend to tell her what happened. Realize that the call and the pills give professionals a clue that, although serious and dangerous, this is a cry for help and that she wants to be saved. By taking pills at home, there is a good chance of rescue since parents can take her to the hospital and usually help her. Likewise, shallow cuts on the wrist are signals that there is a problem and she seeks relief. Yet the cuts give time for rescue.

Studies on suicide attempts talk about intention and lethality. What was the intention of the suicide and how was it done? It is far more lethal to do something where the probability of rescue is low. Any time that a teenager attempts and fails suicide with hanging, with a gun, or by jumping out a window, one must be especially concerned. Most of the kids who survive such an attempt actually wanted to die and were not trying to get attention. Realize that the lethality is high in each of these as compared to pills and cuts. All attempts are serious, but some are more lethal and worrisome than others. Another rule of thumb is that statistically boys are more likely to succeed in killing themselves while girls are more likely to attempt suicide and be rescued.

Teenagers involve themselves in risk-taking behavior. It is often characteristic of adolescents that they will try things that are dangerous as a way of testing themselves. They will drink, they will court the danger of a sexually transmitted disease by having unprotected sex, or they will drive at high speeds. Sometimes it takes a composite look at the life of the teenager to realize that their behavior is a form of suicide gesture. It is hard to prove that to kids, but it is important that parents understand the subtle ways that kids can hurt themselves. There is often a fine line between teen bravado and teen depression.

Since parents are often concerned that the stresses of adolescence may lead to suicide, there is consolation in knowing that no one casually commits suicide. No one suddenly decides to die. We have a built-in need to live, and it rarely is tested for most people. Your teen does not want to die and thinking about it or even gesturing it does not mean that this is what she wants. However, the death of a teenager may occur because of a brinkmanship that played too close to being lethal. The pills that were taken in the hopes of being pumped later, or the speed chase for thrill simply were more than could be handled.

Since all teens will ponder death, parents need some guidelines to decide whether they need professional help. The following is a list of common precursors to suicide.

1. Discussions of death, either verbally or through art or poetry
2. Discovering that the teenager has accumulated pills or a rope and discusses death
3. Previous suicide attempt
4. Self-destructive acts: automobile accidents that were nearly fatal; drunk driving
5. Self-mutilation: cutting herself has become common
6. Recent loss of someone close
7. Giving away things that were considered important
8. Dramatic shift of performance in school

I don't want to close this chapter giving readers a sense that many teenagers will commit suicide. Be reassured that the suicide attempt is the exception by far. Most kids will go through their adolescent years and think about death, but few will be so distraught that they will make an attempt. Nevertheless, we must be aware of the possibility, even though it is remote.

Along with the changes of puberty teenagers have a lot of internal and external pressures to cope with before they can establish adult status. With knowledge and understanding, you can help them through these changes. We now move on to the day-to-day issues of health that parents of teenagers must deal with as their teen moves from childhood to adolescence.

Part Two

Health and Lifestyle Issues

Chapter 4

The Sleep-Deprived Teen

I f you were to spend a day or so in my office, you would find that the questions regarding teens and sleep cover two ends of the spectrum. A parent will call in the morning to say: "He seems to be sleeping too much! Could this be a sign of mono? Could this be a sign of drugs?" That afternoon another parent will arrive for an office visit with the opposite report, but the same conclusion: "She doesn't get enough sleep, and she is exhausted all the time. Could this be a sign of mono? Could this be a sign of drugs?"

So what exactly is going on during puberty, and what sleeping patterns constitute "normal?" Before we deal with the teenager we need to understand sleep itself.

Sleep Physiology

Normal sleep consists of four distinct stages, which range from light sleep (Stage 1) to deep sleep (Stage 4). Moreover, there is a distinction made between two types of sleep: REM (*R*apid *E*ye *M*ovement) and NREM (*n*on-*R*apid *E*ye *M*ovement). Throughout a normal sleep cycle we go from one stage to the other in a fairly rhythmic fashion. During deep sleep, blood pressure actually drops, and heart pace and breathing slow. If we do it right, we should awake rested and refreshed for another day. If we interfere with the process, we can look forward to more than a bad hair day.

There are major differences between REM and NREM cycles. We know

from studies what occurs in each phase. During REM, the brain is quite stimulated, with a lot of electrical activity taking place (measured by an electroencephalograph, or EEG). There is evidence that if we do not get enough REM
sleep we do not function well the next day and our ability to learn and remember will suffer. During NREM sleep the brain is quiet, but some vital body
processes take place: growth hormone (GH), prolactin (involved in lactation),
and hormones from the testicles and ovaries are released. Teens and adults have
different REM and NREM sleep patterns, with teens requiring more NREM
than the adult (about 75 percent of sleep).

The concept that we need "a good night's rest" to stay physically healthy,
as well as mentally alert, is actually valid. During a night in which a sleeper does
not go through the natural sleep stages, researchers have found that the
immune system is temporarily alerted. Our lymphocytes, the white cells
responsible for producing antibodies to thwart infections, take a direct hit in
sheer numbers and even in their ability to produce the natural chemicals of
protection, all by having poor sleep! We need both a certain amount of these
cells and we need them fully functional in order to stay healthy. Sleep interferes
with both. It is not too far-fetched a conclusion that one *needs* enough sleep.
Our own parents were right after all.

Teen Sleep Requirements

I am often asked, "What is one of the most common problems you see in your
practice?" The unequivocal answer is that kids are "tired all the time." Suggesting that teens alter their patterns of sleep and go to bed early is met with laughter by both parents and teens. The idea of giving up study time or party time
is simply ludicrous, yet it's an important issue that deserves your attention.

Most adults require about eight hours of sleep, but that figure does not per-
tain to the teenager who is growing rapidly. The need for frequent sleep is as
normal for the teen as the need to look in the mirror for a quick check to see
if she still looks okay. This is especially true for the teen undergoing a growth
spurt. During rapid growth periods, the teen will grow more than the two to
two-and-a-half inches per year that was the norm prior to puberty. Boys grow
at a rate of nearly four inches per year, which is about the same growth rate as
a two-year-old. We let the toddler take naps because we understand that the
growing child needs to rest. So, too, do teenagers, but they rarely nap and may
not even get enough sleep at night. No one has clear numbers on what is
"enough" sleep for adolescents, but let's assume that the bare minimum needed

is the adult-required eight hours. Since teens are also growing, one could easily extend the *need* to more than that.

If there is a difference in sleep requirements by gender, I am unaware of any studies that prove it. However, by observation it would appear that boys sleep more. Is that because they are undergoing more growth than girls? Certainly the caloric requirement for the male during a rapid growth spurt far exceeds that of girls, and boys' growth can be as much as twice what a girl will experience. Moreover, when most girls are finishing their pubertal changes, boys are still going strong with body and brain changes.

Why Teens Don't Sleep

Part of the problem that confronts the teenager when it comes to sleep deprivation is the interference of two abnormal activities. One is school and the other is weekends.

School should not start as early as it does. It is that simple. If we could have teens sleep during the morning hours and start classes around 10 A.M. or even 11 A.M., we would solve part of the teen sleep problem immediately. Any teacher will tell you that the amount of sleep deprivation in schools is astounding. As the enthusiastic teacher discusses the history of mankind or the latest discovery in science, yawns and head bobbing are interspersed with the occasional openly heard snore. The teenager's need for sleep simply prevents them from being a fully functional individual at an early hour.

Our society thrives on our children doing well and doing a lot. We expect them to not only do their school work, but to go to tutors, ballet and piano lessons, after-school football, baseball, soccer, tennis, volleyball, swimming, lacrosse, track and field, and gymnastics practice, and to join yearbook, the debate team, and chess club. Then we must account for phone time, a part-time job, and, oh yes, dinner. By the time the teen starts homework it is clear that sleep before midnight is a luxury afforded to few. Most high schools start classes close to 8:00 A.M. If a "good night's sleep" is a full eight hours, then the latest we should see teens go to sleep is 11 P.M., so that they can be up by 7:00 to 7:30 A.M. to begin their day. I know of few teens who can manage good grades and a full schedule of activities and consistently hit the pillow by that hour. Most are lucky if they are snuggled in bed by midnight. I cringe at the thought of the farm kids who also have chores in the morning before school.

The second abnormality in the teen schedule is weekends. It turns out that the brain, for all of its incredible powers, cannot tell Saturday from Wednesday. From Sunday through Thursday, teens are well aware that they have school the next day. They, as best as possible, plan for the next day by setting their bedtime for a particular hour. Let's call that Sleep Time 1. Then, logically assuming that Friday is quite different because of no school on Saturday, they decide that they will relax and have fun (translation: "party") on Friday night. This makes a lot of sense to all. Except that they set a new sleep pattern: Sleep Time 2. They logically conclude that they can sleep the extra time on Saturday and do. In fact, many have been known to sleep through Saturday— all of it. Saturday night a dilemma approaches; some need to wake up early to do school work or attend church on Sunday, while others compromise by making Sunday into a somewhat more relaxed day and still working but not as hard. Regardless, there is a new time to go to bed, Sleep Time 3.

Sleep researchers learned a long time ago that we function best if our inner biological clock is not teased into too much change. Like insects, we need sunlight and dark cycles for our bodies to function, and we need constant rhythms (our circadian rhythms). If we try to shift from one sleep pattern to another, we throw off this rhythm. The international traveler or the shift worker who goes from an 8 A.M.-to-4 P.M. schedule to a 4 P.M.-to-midnight shift can testify to the difficulty in changing one's body rhythms to suit a new schedule. The same occurs with the teenager who stays up very late Friday and Saturday, sleeps late the next day to compensate, and then tries to re-adjust to a new wakeup time Monday morning. Unfortunately, teens, too, must yield to the need for constancy in bedtimes. The price of ignoring this schedule and assuming that they can go from Sleep Time 1 to 2 or 3 and back again is exhaustion. In fact, what they are actually doing is lengthening and shortening their internal 24-hour clock and paying a price for it.

Another issue that sometimes affects weekend sleep is alcohol. Despite being underage, many teens include alcohol in their efforts to have a good time. Unfortunately, alcohol interferes with the ability to sleep because it interferes with the normal REM and NREM patterns of the brain. If we are required to go through all the stages in order to feel rested, then it is easy to appreciate how alcohol does not provide a good night's sleep. With as little as a couple of drinks, a sleeper stays in the first two stages and does not proceed to the restful deep-sleep stage. Try telling that to teenagers who are out partying and argue that they can handle a couple of drinks. They may not appear to be impaired, but their sleep will be. Once again, the teenager loses.

Helping Your Teen Fit In More Sleep

So what can you do to help your teen get more sleep?

If we expect our teens to function in all their scheduled activities, they need more than 24 hours. So we allow teens to stay up late, reward them with an extended curfew on the weekends, hope they catch up on sleep on the same weekend, and wonder why they are yawning constantly during the school week. Some alternatives are to have them go to sleep by eleven, settle for lower grades, start classes later, skip all the extra activities at school, and not pressure them by asking them to allow time for SAT tutors. I can hear you laughing. In summary, the teenager needs more sleep and seldom gets it. The solution is outrageously simple and nearly impossible to impose.

If our teens were to learn some time management and a few ground rules for sleep, they might improve their chances of getting a good night's rest.

1. One has to be realistic in deciding how much can be squeezed into a day. If the teenager *has* to be on a sports team, or any club after school, then it is imperative that homework begin as soon after dinner as possible. If our goal is to finish homework as close to 11 P.M. as possible, then dinner should end by 7 or 8 P.M. so that several hours of work can be accomplished. This generally means that television viewing is out for the night. Of course, it would be ideal to ask the teenager to limit afterschool activities, but in a world where we are asking our teens to thrive and to compete, the message becomes mixed. On the one hand we want them to take advantage of every opportunity available to them, and yet we want them to rest when they come home. As a parent, you need to monitor your teen's activity level, and at some point you may have to intercede and suggest that the schedule is just "too much."

2. If your child is not quite a teen, there is still time to instill good homework and sleep habits. Homework is best done at a desk in the bedroom. The child who does homework in a common room can't help but be distracted by family members and the television. Also teach your teen that the bed has one major purpose and that is to sleep.

3. From middle school on, teens feel that a night without talking to their friends on the phone or on the Internet is the equivalent of Siberian banishment. Too many parents permit this. Teens are given their own phones and their own Internet connections so that they won't disturb

the rest of the family. Unfortunately, in most cases the amount of time spent "communicating" with their friends is often in the range of an hour or more per night. This is simply too much, and you, as a parent, need to set rules about how much and when calls can be made and the Internet accessed. Internet access is so easy for kids that they log on and time just melts. If the computer is in the teen's bedroom, Internet time becomes hard to monitor, but you must. Or let the teen have a computer, but remove Internet access. Don't be afraid to take a stand; the Internet is a privilege similar to driving. If you drive responsibly, you get the use of the car. It is no different with the Internet. Be similarly conscious of telephone time. No one wants to ruin a teen's life by denying social access, but lengthy nightly phone calls are not necessary.

4. Similarly, a television and VCR in a teen's bedroom can interfere with time management. Reduce access or remove the electronics from their rooms. Yes, that means they may have to watch television with you and/or siblings on occasion. There may be squabbling over what show to watch, but it will be better than fighting daily over homework and the time they get to bed.

5. Even teens need a routine for going to sleep. Playing exciting games on Nintendo or on the computer or watching television programs that are disturbing will make the sleep transition difficult. I, personally, do not sleep well after watching a movie about a chainsaw killer chasing young girls in the woods and chopping off appendages. Do you?

Sleep Disorders

In addition to the "normal" sleep deprivation of most teens, more serious sleep disorders affect some teens.

Insomnia

If a person has interrupted sleep, can't get to sleep, or if the sleep cycle itself is shortened, this is considered insomnia, and this uncomfortable condition does not spare the teenager. Often this is a temporary situation brought about by medication (remember that caffeine is a drug and that many sodas have caffeine) or by a stressful environment. For teenagers stress comes from dealing with their sense of identity, their sexual expression, and what they want to be when they grow up! Given what they have to deal with, an occasional night of insomnia doesn't seem too unlikely.

In my practice, chronic insomnia, where a person's sleep is affected for prolonged periods, is not a frequent problem. Often patients who recently started antidepressants will complain of sleep disturbances. Usually, this is a short-lived problem, and patients adjust to the medication. Similarly, patients who start stimulant medications for Attention Deficit Disorder have to be careful that they do not take too large a dose or a dose too late in the day, as most of the medications for ADD can alter the sleep cycle.

I'm not a big proponent of using medications to help kids sleep. It strikes me as a bad message of "better living through chemistry." I avoid the benzodiazapines (Valium family) unless absolutely necessary and then use them for a few days only. A short-acting hypnotic (sold by prescription as Ambien) can be useful, since there is little chance of rebound depression the next day. But my choice is to try less dramatic options.

An age-old remedy is drinking a glass of warm milk. Personally, I could never understand warm milk as tasty but it does work for some since it contains a naturally occurring sedative, tryptophan. If your teen doesn't complain about congestion and is not allergic to milk, it's worth a try. Or you might try Benadryl, which is sold over the counter for allergies and has the side effect of sedation. Benadryl should not be used for more than a night or two—breaking the cycle is your goal in using a mild chemical sedative.

The ideal way of curing insomnia is to be consistent about bedtime and bedtime routines. No one will get over insomnia if he tries to sleep at different hours. If your teen has insomnia, consult with your physician, as there is no possible way that your teen is efficient in school. Today many major hospitals have sleep disorder centers to study an individual's sleep pathology.

One natural remedy you may have heard of is melotonin. This naturally occurring hormone seems to work for some, but there isn't enough research available to allow physicians to comfortably recommend how, when, and how much to use. It strikes me as a bit premature to use this as a sleep medication. Certainly, in the growing child and teenager, we have to take the fast-occurring body changes into account as we consider any medication.

Like everyone else, teenagers will sleep better if they have ten to fifteen minutes to relax before falling asleep. If you see a light on under your teen's door, and you know she's thumbing through *Vogue* at 11 P.M., that's actually good use of her time—let her unwind on her own.

Seasonal Affective Disorder

At times, people simply do not get enough sun. They seem to be fine and then, slowly and inexplicably, begin to recede into depression as daylight hours lessen. With less sun, the person appears to "wilt" and a gradual depression sets in. When doctors used to recommend a vacation in the sun, it was felt that the change of pace was the remedy. It may, in fact, have more to do with the sun itself than anything else. Sun and its effect on our brain serotonin is just being appreciated. It appears that, for some, sunlight is as necessary for stabilizing moods as it is for some flowers to grow!

Teenagers may compound the problem by not going out during the daytime on weekends as they try to "catch up" on their sleep. A sixteen-year-old patient came in and casually mentioned that she was just not feeling well and felt tired. She had transferred to a new school and was noted to be exceptionally bright and creative. After a normal examination and normal laboratory results it was felt that she was adjusting to her new school, and some psychotherapy was undertaken in an effort to keep tabs on the situation. Slowly, she got better and the need for discussion disappeared. Summer went well and as school started in the fall, she seemed on track for a good year. Somewhere around November she called and said she felt awful. As we talked, she seemed depressed and complained of the same symptoms of the previous year. I noted that the first visit was also in November and suggested that, with the end of Daylight Saving Time, she could be suffering from SAD (Seasonal Affective Disorder).

The solution for SAD is either to stimulate one's serotonin level in the brain by increasing exposure to light or by trying medication that increases the serotonin level directly. There are lights specially made (the wave spectrum of the light is critical) for SAD and the person literally works, or sleeps, with these lights on. The idea is to mimic an extended day—a cheap way of going to the Bahamas. Alternatively, the selective serotonin reuptake inhibitors (SSRI) often work quite well in overcoming the feelings of the person suffering from SAD.

Further questioning of my patient revealed that her father had similar symptoms and was being treated with Prozac. A few weeks after starting one of the SSRIs, she began to feel much better and remains on a low dose. Her therapist suggested that we might lower the dose for the summer or stop it altogether.

Sleepwalking or Somnambulism

Although this phenomenon occurs primarily in the prepubertal child, an occasional teenager will present with signs of sleepwalking. The typical patient has no recollection of the event and during the event it is quite difficult to awaken him. He is in a deep Stage 3 or 4 sleep. Statistically, it is more common in boys, and most of the time it disappears by the age of twelve. Fortunately, it is rare and it is unusual for a patient to get hurt. But there are situations where a referral has to be made to a sleep center.

One of my patients found herself outside her house in New York City. Clad in her pajamas only, she had gotten up, walked down three flights of stairs, opened the front door and stood, confused and cold, on a city street wondering how she got there. The first part of the solution was to have a special lock requiring an inside key; a wise move since the safety of the person is any family's first priority. (However, because this presents a fire hazard, it is important to only lock the door in this way until the sleepwalking problem is under control.) The second was an assessment of the patterns of sleep. In this case, although we eventually had a successful outcome, there were illicit drugs in the picture. Her sleep patterns were being disrupted by street drugs.

If your teen has a single episode of sleepwalking, note it and tell your doctor. If the problem recurs a second or third time, your physician may decide to either medicate prior to sleep or refer you to a sleep disorder center.

Other Sleep-Related Issues

There are other problems associated with sleep, such as enuresis (bed-wetting), night terrors, and sleep apnea. The first two are likely to have disappeared by the teen years, but some young teens will still have problems with bed-wetting. Treatment for the teen bed-wetter may include the use of a nasal spray hormone to minimize urine production and behavior modification in terms of fluid intake and urination prior to bedtime. If the enuresis persists into the middle teens, one should search for evidence of anxiety or other physical problems.

An occasional patient will present with issues of sleep apnea, in which breathing stops briefly during the night. These patients need an ear, nose, and throat evaluation for evidence of obstruction of the breathing passages. Often, a referral needs to be made to a sleep center so that the teen's sleep patterns can be monitored fully. Although the only sure way of diagnosing sleep apnea is through the center, teens with this problem often have certain characteristics, such as huge tonsils or adenoids or a broken or crooked nose that obstructs breathing. Pronounced snoring is another symptom.

Another candidate is the extremely obese child who has difficulty lifting his chest. While sleeping his breathing can be so labored that he can stop breathing. Although this is incredibly frightening to read, there are compensatory systems in the body that force the patient to take a breath. Sleep apnea can be treated but first it has to be diagnosed. (For information regarding fatigue illnesses that can make a teenager extraordinarily tired, please refer to "Fatigue" in Part Five, "The Adolescent, Head to Toe.")

The admonition from your own parents about the need to sleep more during the growing years essentially was correct. But we live in a culture that regularly tries to cram more than twenty-four hours into a day and where success demands that you are up on the latest news, technology, and social skills. We teach these values to our children by our style and by our words. We want them to do well in school, perform extracurricular tasks, participate in family activities, and, when all this is wrapped up, to "Get a good night's sleep." Impossible. As parents you need to take a hard look at your own expectations and what messages you are giving about time management. Some parents would rather bear with sleepy teens than have them give up football, wresting, ballet, or SAT classes. Decide your priorities before you complain about a tired teen.

Chapter 5

Teens, Nutrition, and Eating Disorders

T eenagers experience a rapid growth spurt during adolescence, and, as a result, they require a change in caloric requirements. Unfortunately, this overwhelming need for sound nutrition occurs just at the time they are spending more time away from the family than ever before. After-school dates, meeting friends for meals on weekends, and going away during the summer are all a part of normal teen life. Within the family itself the demands on the teenager's time is such that many are allowed to eat alone in their rooms, often take-out food instead of a home-cooked meal. Throw into this mix worry about eating disorders and diseases such as diabetes, and it's no wonder that a frequent concern voiced by parents is: "Is my teen eating properly?"

When it comes to food, there are four major issues that face teenagers and their parents today:

1. **Teen bodies need good nutrition.**   Refer to Chapter 2 on puberty to be reminded of how much growth takes place during these years. Teens often turn to fast food, which is rarely nutritious.
2. **Teens (and adults) of today are more sedentary than previous generations.**   The use of cars for even short trips, watching TV, or sitting in front of the computer have contributed to the current obesity epidemic.
3. **Society honors an unhealthy view of proper body type, and teens are greatly affected by this.**   Even a teen whose weight is normal by medical chart standards may be viewed by peers, or by the family, as being "a bit overweight." This distortion of appropriate body size leads to unhealthy eating.

4. Some teens may require—or wish to follow—a special diet. Parents need to discuss restricted diets with their teens and figure out how they fit the teen's health and lifestyle.

With these forces in play in the adolescent world, how does a parent monitor proper nutrition for the teenager? Before beginning to discuss issues such as "fast food," or total calories, or how to deal with special situations such as the vegetarian teen, we need to discuss some nutritional basics.

Eating Well and Judging Nutritional Value

The best way to teach healthy eating, of course, is by modeling it. The teen whose mother diets excessively or who watches Dad sitting down in front of the television to consume a bucket of fast-food fried chicken is learning poor eating habits. Almost every family today has a hectic lifestyle, but it is still important to make a point of scheduling a few family meals each week. Plan a meal that draws from the four basic food groups. An ideal way to feed a family is to put out platters of foods containing a protein, vegetables, starches, and a salad, and let family members serve themselves. As a parent, you're offering a nutritionally sound base, but you've given each individual choice and control over portion size—a good way to teach healthy eating. Meals together also offer an ideal time to "stay connected" with your teen, so there are many reasons why it's worth trying to schedule a family dinner several times a week.

If you think your teen might be willing to learn a little about healthy eating, pick up a book on nutrition or contact the U.S. Department of Agriculture, which produces *Dietary Guidelines for Americans.* The FDA has a web site that offers a great deal of information about foods, supplements, and most nutritionally related questions. (The explanation of the food pyramid is located at www.cfsan.fda/gov-dms/fdpyrmid.html.) Other good web sites include www.nal.usda.gov/fnic, the site of the government's food nutrition information center, and www.nutrition.gov for questions regarding proper nutrition. The motivated teen can be given web site addresses; one particularly geared for young people is www.library.thinkquest.org/1091/rda.html. The interested teen will benefit more if you talk about the reasoning behind certain meal planning. This will give him a basic understanding of what constitutes a healthy meal.

I suggest tacking the Food Guide Pyramid to the refrigerator to use as a guide. In time, it will become second nature to prepare meals based on this guide. To eat according to the pyramid, families should consume more vegetables, fruits, and pasta in their diet, which will help eliminate the high-fat content of most diets.

Food Pyramid

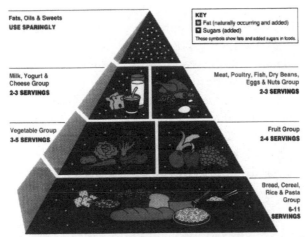

Credit: U.S. Department of Agriculture and the U.S. Department of Health and Human Services (USDA and DHHS).

The pyramid lists specific serving sizes, and it is difficult to give one serving without understanding what is being eaten. As examples, the pyramid would suggest the following:

Serving Sizes	
Whole grains, breads, rice, pasta	1 slice bread 1 ounce ready-to-eat cereal ½ cup cooked cereal, rice, or pasta ½ bagel or English muffin 1 small tortilla
Fruits	1 medium piece fresh fruit ½ cup chopped fresh or canned fruit ¾ cup fruit juice
Vegetables	½ cup raw, leafy vegetables ½ cup cooked or chopped raw vegetables ¾ cup vegetable juice
Fish, skinless poultry, lean meat, nuts, eggs	2–3 ounces poultry, fish, lean meat 1 to 1½ cups cooked dry beans 2 tablespoons peanut butter = 1 ounce of meat 1 egg = 1 ounce of meat
Low-fat or nonfat milk, yogurt, cheese	1 cup of milk or yogurt 1½ ounces of cheese

Nutritional daily requirements, or recommended daily allowances (RDA), established by the government in 1989 and expected to be revised this year, is another tool provided by the government to give us guidelines for our average need for calories, vitamins, and minerals (see below for a summary of the caloric needs for all strata of the population).

One other point regarding serving sizes requires reading the label. It is one thing to see a listing for calories and serving size; it is another to appreciate how many servings are in the package. A perfect example is the ice cream carton. It may be deceiving to find that the rich chocolate ice cream contains 270 calories per serving. It's another to understand that there are eight servings in the carton totalling 2,160 calories!

In addition, it is helpful to keep these measurements in mind:

Nutritional Measurements

1. One tablespoon = 3 teaspoons
2. One ounce (oz.) = 2 tablespoons
3. One cup = 16 tablespoons = 8 oz. = "a glass"
4. One "serving" = ~3 ounces (see below for specific group)

A shift in eating habits can mean a rather drastic change in teen cuisine. Teens frequent fast-food restaurants because they are easy, cheap, and convenient. Parent and teen together should look at some of the books that have been written recently giving caloric and fat content of food from fast-food chains.

If you as a family become more acquainted with what you are eating, it will help your teen gain a better perspective on eating.

What Calories Mean to Your Teen

To the teen dieter, calorie-counting can be all-consuming, yet calories (often written as *kcal*) are important to teens of all sizes because this is the "energy" unit that powers our bodies. Teens need only a few more calories (5 percent to 6 percent of daily requirements) than adults to compensate for their growth. The caloric requirement just to breathe and perform all of the body's metabolic functions *without doing any activity* is called the Resting Energy Expenditure (REE). (The Basal Metabolic Rate, BMR, is very similar to the REE.) Just as a parked car with an idling motor uses gas, so, too, does a body at rest consume calories. If we drive the car, we need more gas; if we are active we need more calories. In order to calculate the total daily energy requirements, you add the activity level to the REE. Once an individual attains nearly adult size, the major variable becomes the calories spent on increased activity. The following table lists the mean values for teens and assumes a "normal" activity level. It does not include sports.

Average Height–Weight and Caloric Tables

Males:

Age	Weight (lbs.)	Height (in.)	REE kcal/day	Total with average activity
11–14	99	62	1440	2500
15–18	145	69	1760	3000
19–24	160	70	1780	2900

Females:

Age	Weight (lbs.)	Height (in.)	REE kcal/day	Total with average activity
11–14	101	62	1310	2200
15–18	120	64	1370	2200
19–24	128	65	1350	2200

As you know, different kinds of activity will affect caloric needs. The caloric requirements of a person playing a musical instrument are much less than someone who is doing manual labor. A male teen on a quiet day may require only about 2500 kcal, but on a day when he is playing basketball the needs may jump to 4000 kcal. A girl's needs will range from 2000 to 3000 kcal by comparison even when she is playing soccer or basketball. Girls will often say that they can survive quite well on 1200 calories per day. As you can see from the above table, unless they don't move at all, they can't. Also note that since girls reach maximum adult height sooner than boys do, their caloric needs even out, and their caloric "average activity" stabilizes at about fourteen (or two years after they start menstruating). Boys are still growing throughout high school and adjustments are made for this change.

The following table illustrates how an activity can burn calories and how the energy expended and the weight lost can be put back with foods that contain the same calories. As you can see, the hard work of one hour is gone with one slice of chocolate cake!

Energy Activity and Comparable Foods		
Activity	Calories	Foods
Walking at 3 mph for 105 minutes	400	Hamburger, ¼ pound
Walking at 3 mph for 60 minutes	250	Chocolate cake, 1 slice
Running at 8 mph for 19 minutes	250	One buttered roll
Aerobic dancing for 38 minutes	250	Chili with beans, ¾ cup
Walking at 3 mph for 26 minutes	100	Plain doughnut
Running at 8 mph for 8 minutes	100	Marshmallows, 4
Aerobic dancing for 15 minutes	100	Pretzels, 1 ounce

How Food Sources Vary

A food product containing 100 kcal will deliver 100 units of energy for a person to metabolize, or if taken in excess, to store in the body as fat. Protein and carbohydrates have the same caloric value of 4 kcal/gm (kilocalories per gram). A 100-gram meal of protein or carbohydrates will give the individual 400 kcal regardless of the source. On the other hand, fat contains 9 kcal/gm so that the same 100 grams of fat would yield 900 kcal of energy. From a caloric or energy point of view, then, the body is perfectly content with either 100 grams of carbohydrate or protein, or with 45 grams of fat; all three will provide the same energy and calories for the body to burn or store. However, our body *needs* the protein since it cannot manufacture protein without consuming it. It can, however, take protein and carbohydrates and convert them into fat, but fat and carbohydrates can never become protein. Hence, proper nutrition requires that you eat about 0.4 grams of protein a day per pound of body weight; a normal adult will need about 60 to 70 grams of protein a day depending on size. (One ounce of meat has 7 grams of protein, so a 2–3 ounce serving would give us 14–21 grams. With three servings, the teen could have 42–63 grams from this group alone. With the addition of three servings from the milk group, another 24 grams of protein is added for a daily total that is sufficient.) Without an adequate intake of protein, we lose muscle mass and become malnourished, even if the total caloric intake is appropriate.

Table of Foods and Calories	
Carbohydrate	4 kcal per gram
Protein	4 kcal per gram
Fat	9 kcal per gram

For a teen who is fighting a weight battle, eating high-calorie foods can quickly do away with the value of an activity. A "Quarter-pounder" is standard teen fare. Then add French fries and a malted shake for a satisfying meal. It took an hour and forty-five minutes to walk to the fast-food store but only 10 minutes to get back the calories plus excess that will yield fat.

A typical teen meal may consist of one of the following:

1. The hamburger meal:
   Hamburgers may vary from 400 to 600 kcal depending on toppings. In some fast-foods chains that have 80 percent lean burgers, the calories drop to 230 without toppings. "Veggie burgers" run 100 to 200 kcal.
   French fries ("large serving"): 450 kcal
   Shake ("small" chocolate): 360 kcal.
   Total: roughly 1300 kcal
   (*Note*: a "Double Whopper with cheese contains 1010 kcal; add 310 kcal extra for a serving of onion rings)
2. Pizza:
   In determining a pizza's calories one has to calculate size and toppings. A Domino's Deep Dish Pizza is 477 kcal for two slices without toppings. Pizza Hut hand-tossed style is 560 kcal for two slices, while its "Pizzeria Stuffed Crust" is 860 kcal for two slices.
   Soda: If the soda is a "diet" soda then the kcal are zero to one. If it is a "regular" soda then the calories are 150 kcal for a 12 oz. (small) soda. Since a teaspoon of sugar contains about 16 kcal, a small soda is the equivalent of 9 teaspoons of sugar.
   Total: about 750 kcal
3. Chicken pot pie meal:
   Kentucky Fried Chicken's "Chunky Chicken Pot Pie" has 770 kcal.
   One ear of corn on the cob: 150 kcal
   Macaroni and cheese (1 order): 180 kcal

   Cornbread (1 piece): 228 kcal
   Soda: 150 kcal
   Total: 1478 kcal
 4. Reuben sandwich:
   A Reuben sandwich (containing Russian dressing, meat, cheese, and cooked cabbage) has about 530 kcal.
   Soda: 150 kcal
   Total: roughly 680 kcal
 5. Mexican food:
   The Mexican meal is often heavy in fat because of the deep-fried meat and cheese toppings. A typical meal ordered by a teen might be:
   Mexican rice: 190 kcal
   Refried beans with cheese sold as "pintos and cheese": 190 kcal
   Chicken quesadillas (1): 410 kcal
   Nachos (1 serving of 3.5 oz): 320 kcal
   Soda: 150 kcal
   Total: 1260 kcal
 6. Chips as an entire meal:
   It is not unusual for a teen to view a bag of chips as an entire meal. One bag of corn chips contains about seven to eight servings at 148 kcal per serving = 1036 to 1184 kcal, one bag of cheese puffs has 1256 kcal, and one bag of potato chips contains 1217 kcal.

From a nutritional point of view, fast-food stores give teens protein and energy, but teens need to understand what they are eating. For the ease of having that quick lunch, they will pay a price in fat, in salt, and in calories.*

The Need for Fat

Despite the argument that "you can never be too thin" as a mantra of models and some advertisers, too thin is actually bad for one's health. We need fat for body insulation, for caloric storage, for hormone production, and for vitamin absorption. Women with a low percentage of body fat will stop producing estrogen, will not ovulate, and will be at risk for osteoporosis. Men will lower

---

*Sources: *The Most Complete Food Counter* by Annette B. Natow, Ph.D., R.D., and Jo-Ann Heslin, M.A., R. D. (Pocket Books, New York, 1999), and *The T-Factor 2000 Fat Gram Counter* by Jamie Pope, M.S., R.D., and Martin Katahn, Ph.D. (W.W. Norton & Company, New York, 1989, 2000).

their testosterone levels, and their sex drive will be compromised. The issue on fat is one of moderation. How much is enough? How much is too much? Here's how to tell:

Lean Body Mass is the weight of the body without stored fat; it allows for "essential fat" that the body requires. The 200-pound teen with lots of muscle mass has a very different body from the 200-pound teen with excess fat. The box below lists the norms and the dangerous percentages of body fat. In general, females have a higher percent of their weight as body fat.

At 5'8" and 215 pounds, *sixteen-year-old Jan was overweight by any standard, and the jokes about his "chubby" body were no longer humorous. To lose weight, he embarked on a rigid diet and exercise program. The fat literally melted off his body. He lost 65 pounds and everyone admired his achievement. But he had lost weight so rapidly that he could not stop. When I saw him for a consultation, he was frightened that he was going to "have to eat" and become fat again. His percentage of body fat was so low that I felt it important to measure his male hormone, and indeed, at sixteen, it was less than that of an eleven-year-old male. He admitted that his sexual drive had been "different" lately but he was so consumed with dieting that it had not mattered. He met all the criteria for anorexia nervosa; the only unusual part was that he was a male.*

With therapy he slowly began to relax the rigidity of his eating and, soon, as the percentage of his body fat increased, his testosterone increased. No hormonal treatment was given; he just ate correctly and his testosterone climbed back into a normal range as he gained weight.

One way of defining our weight as normal is to proportion it to our height; this is known as the Body Mass Index, or BMI. This allows actual calculations as opposed to "thinking" that one is overweight. It is defined as weight in kilograms divided by the square of height in meters. Although that sounds complex, the actual calculations for the BMI are simple. You need two numbers, height and weight, and a calculator. One can either use the pound and inch sys-

Percentages of Body Fat

	Normal Body Fat	Minimum Allowed	Dangerous
Males	13% to 17%	7% to 10%	less than 7%
Females	20% to 27%	14% to 17%	less than 12%

tem or you can covert the numbers into the metric system. I also found many Internet sites that allow you to enter the numbers in the American system and it will give you a quick readout. Search "BMI" on the Internet. The general calculations are listed below.

Metric system:

1. Weight in pounds divided by 2.2 = weight in kilograms
2. Height in inches multiplied by .0254 = height in meters
3. Square that number (#2): height in meters × height in meters
4. Divide #1 by #3 (kilograms divided by meters squared) = BMI

As an example: a 71-inch, 150-pound person has a BMI of 21

1. 150 pounds divided by 2.2 = 68.18 kilograms
2. 71 inches multiplied by 0.0254 meters = 1.80 meters
3. 1.80 meters × 1.80 meters = 3.24 square meters
4. 68.18 kilograms divided by 3.24 meters = 21.0

The American system is simpler and uses the following formula:
$$BMI = (pounds/height)/height × 703$$

1. 150 pounds divided by 71 inches in height = 2.113
2. Divide #1 by 71 inches in height (again) = 0.02976
3. Multiply #2 by 703 = 20.918

By using the BMI we can make statements about obesity that eliminate style and fashion as norms. The system provides a standard for the teen who says, "That's too much for me. I know my body." A rule of thumb to follow is that your BMI should be between 22 and 23 in order for it to be average and

BMI Ranges

22–23	Average or normal
25–29	Overweight
30–35	Obese
35–40	Morbidly obese

normal (see BMI curves for age and gender). If a teen is in the 25–29 range, this would be considered overweight. The "obese" person is in the 30 to 35 BMI range. Once the number approaches the 40s, we speak of *morbid obesity.* Morbid obesity can also be defined as "double your ideal body weight" or "100 pounds above your ideal weight." These individuals, whether teenagers or not, are complicated and often need an endocrine workup. Often they have a strong family history of obesity, and they will have tried diets, exercise, and even weight loss medications.

When considering whether or not a teen is "getting heavy," it is important to know that girls may put on weight just before they get their first period. Parents should be aware of this and not make a point of asking the girl to lose weight. Check with your physician to see if your daughter is following a normal rate of weight gain during the sixth through eighth grades. Boys, on the other hand, do not have a large gain of weight without a comparable increase in height to compensate. See Chapter 2 to be reminded of information about puberty and growth curves.

Later in the chapter, we will discuss how to manage weight issues.

Teens and Cholesterol

While teens definitely need a certain amount of body fat, it is important to remember that, just like adults, when it comes to consuming fat, they need to be mindful of the type of fat they are eating. Most saturated fats come from animal fats (beef, veal, pork, poultry, and whole milk) and small amounts from fish. This grouping constitutes about half of the fat in the American diet. Fats from vegetable products make up the unsaturated fats and are the "good" fats, the ones with which we should be cooking.

For years, no one cared about teenagers and cholesterol, since arteriosclerosis takes years to develop. Today most parents are aware that teens need to be screened for cholesterol since poor eating habits in childhood can lead to high cholesterol, and the groundwork for heart disease can be laid early. It is important, however, that the teenagers not feel that they are at immediate risk since it will generate anxiety.

There are two types of cholesterol: the high-density lipoproteins (HDL) and low-density lipoproteins (LDL). The former is the "good" cholesterol that does not stick to the blood vessels to form plaque. The more your cholesterol is made of HDL the better it is for your body. The LDL cholesterol (the clogging kind) is "bad," and the person with a high LDL is at risk for heart disease.

Triglycerides are also checked at the same time as cholesterol. These are free

Cholesterol levels		
Good cholesterol	HDL	*Total* cholesterol should be between 120–190 for teens
Bad cholesterol	LDL	LDL should be below 125 for teens

fatty acids that are circulating throughout the bloodstream. When blood is "spun" in a doctor's office, you can see the fat floating in the cloudy serum if it is too high. (Think of adding pure cream to your blood and you get the idea of the cloudy nature of triglycerides.) Over time a patient with elevated triglycerides is at risk for heart disease and diabetes mellitus type II or "non-insulin dependent diabetes." Drinking a great deal of juice or alcohol, or eating in fast-food restaurants can cause a patient's triglyceride level to rise. Usually the patient's diet alone will alter the triglyceride blood level, but there are some people who are genetically predisposed to having high levels.

Getting an accurate reading when measuring the cholesterol or triglyceride level in teens is important but not always easy to do. If the patient has recently eaten hamburgers, French fries, eggs, bacon, and buttered bread, expect the triglycerides to be elevated and that there be some alteration of the cholesterol, since cholesterol measurement is dependent on the triglycerides. In particular, the calculation of the LDL fraction of cholesterol (the "bad" one) is highly dependent on total triglycerides. If cholesterol must be measured and the patient has eaten, you will get a close enough but not fully accurate measurement of the cholesterol. My preference is to do it on an empty stomach. For accuracy, blood cholesterol triglyceride tests should be taken after a twelve-hour fast. These are important measurements and should be done properly. I have seen kids who were told that their blood fats were too high become obsessed with the idea that they will die young, or parents who have become so controlling of their teen's diet that the issue of autonomy surfaces.

Ian came in for a *first visit and had a routine blood screen at 10 A.M. Since the blood is always spun before sending it to the lab, it was quickly apparent we had a problem, since the cloudy serum implied a high fat level. I called him, and he admitted that he had eaten before he came to the office. He then rattled off the breakfast he had eaten about an hour before coming in: "Three eggs, two pancakes, several pieces of bacon, two slices of buttered bread, orange juice, and coffee." I suggested that we draw blood again, and since there was a family history of cardiovascular disease, it was done within a week.*

On an empty stomach his cholesterol and triglycerides were normal. Had the blood tests not been repeated Ian might have been told that he had a "cholesterol problem," which would have alarmed both his parents and himself. What he had instead was a big, fat-filled breakfast. However, the cholesterol values did confirm that when he ate badly, he put himself at risk for the future.

The teenager with high cholesterol is not at immediate risk. Health precautions taken now are actually to protect the forty-five-year-old your teenager may become. I have a responsibility to tell the parent that a teen's cholesterol or triglycerides are elevated. Since teens tend to make things very black and white, it is important not to panic them. All you are looking for is an adjustment of diet. Here's how I generally put it:

"Virginia, I got your lab values back. They're basically normal except for a slight elevation of cholesterol. By the way, did you eat something for breakfast that might have changed the numbers? No? Well, okay, the value is a bit high, and I would like you to watch your diet for a few months. Just choose chicken or fish over red meat, and if you can, cut back a bit on the chocolate. Don't go overboard, and we'll repeat this in a few months. Okay?"

Most kids are comfortable with this approach. Some parents want me to scare them into eating well, but that only backfires.

There are some medical conditions, other than familial tendency, that can elevate the cholesterol. Low thyroid levels, renal disease, and liver disease can elevate the cholesterol. Ironically, in starvation patients (as seen in anorexia nervosa), the cholesterol can be elevated. Since this can be problematic when talking to a patient with anorexia, I usually say even more mildly, "Your cholesterol is a bit elevated. This is seen in starvation, and it goes away as soon as the body gets more calories. We will watch it as you get better."

Because learning to eat properly is important throughout life, the best thing you can do is begin demonstrating for your teen how to watch fat intake. The government recommends Americans reduce fat intake to less than a total of 30 percent of the daily diet of 2000 calories (about 600 calories). Of that only 10 percent should be saturated. Like most parents, you likely have little knowledge or control over what your teen eats early in the day, so try to plan to serve a meal low in saturated fat for dinner as often as you can.

Besides cholesterol issues, one of the more common parental concerns about teenage eating styles has to do with vitamins and minerals. Parents often ask me which vitamin/mineral supplements are necessary for their teen. They have an implicit understanding that telling teens to take vitamins is one more struggle in parenting and they need to know that it will be worth it. What, then, are vitamins and minerals, and do teens need supplements?

What Vitamins and Minerals Do

A vitamin is an enzyme that helps the body with chemical reactions. Minerals are nutrients (calcium, iron, magnesium, zinc, manganese, copper) that the body also needs for these reactions to take place. Neither, contrary to what parents may think, stimulate appetite nor contain calories; however, both are critical for normal growth.

Teen requirements for vitamins and minerals are much the same as what is required for adults, and while I am frequently asked, "Should my teen take vitamins, doctor?" the answer can be a guarded "No." Taking a general supplement that contains all the vitamins and minerals is not usually harmful but, as a rule, it is not really necessary. Even with teens' poor eating habits, it is actually hard to become vitamin deficient in the modern world unless the person has an eating disorder or a malabsorption syndrome. In our society, the RDAs can be met with a reasonable diet, partly because these requirements can be averaged over the week; a teen needn't eat "perfectly" every day, since most foods are fortified. Sometimes parents themselves are big believers in vitamins and take several vitamin supplements. Teens don't need this; vitamins can be toxic and the notion of giving a teen or a child mega-doses of anything because of their availability and low cost is unwise.

There are two types of vitamins: fat-soluble and water-soluble ones. Those that are fat-soluble require fat in the digestive system to digest properly, so a person who is deficient in fat or following an extremely low-fat diet may become unable to absorb those vitamins. The water-soluble ones will be excreted in the urine if taken in excess.

Each vitamin and mineral has a particular function in the body, and when it comes to teens the following are the ones that are most important.

Fat-Soluble Vitamins

1. **Vitamin A** is needed for skin healing, vision, and immune system function. Sources are primarily the "yellow vegetables," such as carrots

and pumpkin. Fish liver (especially cod), salmon, milk, and eggs also contain vitamin A. Deficiency is rare but is seen in cases of malabsorption. Cases of excess vitamin A used to occur when high doses of vitamin A were recommended for acne; this is rarely a problem today. Government RDA is 800 mcg for teen girls and 1000 mcg for teen boys. If one eats too much of the "yellow vegetables," the carotene in them will cause the skin to yellow. This "carotenemia" is distinguished from jaundice (a liver condition) in that the eyes are not yellowed with too much carotene. If skin yellowing occurs, it is a sign that too much carotene is being consumed.

2. **Vitamin D,** of which milk is the main source, works in conjunction with calcium to fortify bones. With patients where milk, or dairy in general, is a problem, supplements may be recommended. Unless malabsorption interferes or lack of sun (which helps synthesize D) is a factor, most diets contain sufficient D. The requirement for both sexes is about 5 mcg. A cup of milk has about 25 percent of the RDA.

3. **Vitamin E** is recognized with growing importance as an antioxidant and in preventing certain diseases. There is suggestive evidence that it can protect against cancer and heart disease. One form of E is contained in vegetable oils (soybean, corn, cottonseed, and safflower); another is found in wheat germ, nuts, and green leafy vegetables. For years this vitamin has been known to be critical for neurological development, for muscle function, and for red cell membrane formation; currently, its role in preventing arteriosclerosis is being further evaluated. The "antioxidant" effect of vitamin E is felt to prevent the bad effects of LDL (the "bad" cholesterol) that must be oxidized before it exerts its negative properties. Requirements range between 8–10 mg.

Water-Soluble Vitamins

1. **Vitamin C,** also called ascorbic acid, is critical for survival. It facilitates the absorption of iron, and vitamin C did away with the disease of scurvy. It is primarily found in peppers, most greens, tomatoes, strawberries, and all citric fruits. Our diet is also fortified with C from "C-enriched" foods. Perhaps the most frequent reason teenagers take (or more frequently, are given by a parent) Vitamin C supplements is to help fight the common cold, though there is no conclusive medical proof that it works. Vitamin C passes into the urine when taken in excess, but medically, it is impossible to recommend high doses for

teens and be assured of scientifically proven safety. The body requires 60–90 mg per day (the amount in 2/3 cup of orange juice), yet health food stores commonly stock C capsules of 1000 mg for a daily dose.

An additional warning: Orange juice is the main source of C for many teens, and boys often consume large amounts at one sitting. Orange juice is acidic and can cause gastric irritation with possible heartburn (see p. 409). Simply changing this habit (juice all in one gulp) can often improve heartburn.

2. **B vitamins,** which used to be referred to as B_1, B_2, or B_6, are now primarily referred to by specific names. Thiamin (B_1), riboflavin (B_2), niacin (B_3), and pyridoxine (B_6) deficiency will be seen only in the most malnourished patient. A warning is in order. Doses of B_6 in excess of 200 mg per day over prolonged use, which had been advocated for premenstrual symptoms, have resulted in cases of nerve damage (reversible with discontinuation of the pyridoxine). Normal requirements for B_6 are less than 2.0 mg/day, and diets rich in chicken, fish, kidney, liver, pork, and eggs each provide 0.4 mg for every 100 gram serving. Rice, soybeans, oats, peanuts, and walnuts are also good sources, while dairy products provide very little B_6. Frozen foods and processed foods lose a great deal of vitamin B_6—as much as 70 percent of the original B_6 content.

3. **Vitamin B_{12}** (cobalamin) has maintained its old "12" number in usage and is needed for hemoglobin formation. Since we cannot make B_{12} within the body, we must consume it. It is primarily available in meat but strict vegetarians can get B_{12} by eating Grape-Nuts cereal, which supplies the adult RDA with only ½ cup. Another source of B_{12} for a vegetarian is a yeast called Red Star T-6635 (1–2 teaspoons) per day. One of the common illnesses in which we see a B_{12} deficiency is in the eating disordered patient whose diet is low in B_{12}. An unusual form of anemia, called pernicious anemia, results from a deficit of B_{12}. Although some adults may get B_{12} shots routinely from their physicians, in the absence of pernicious anemia there is no rationale to administer it to a teenager. Some physicians will advocate "extra" B_{12} but there is no rationale for this treatment.

4. **Folic acid** is required for hemoglobin (red cell) synthesis. It is widely available in dried beans, liver, yeast, leafy vegetables, and legumes. As with other vitamins, processing and storage of foods can lose the folate activity of the food. The current RDA is 200 mcg per day, though this is being reevaluated, and newer dietary guidelines have raised it to 400 mcg.

Minerals

Calcium, iron, and zinc are the most important minerals for teenagers.

1. **Calcium** is vital for bone density, and foods rich in calcium include dairy products, sardines with bones, and green leafy vegetables. With calcium, supplements are usually necessary. We require approximately 1300 mg of calcium per day, yet most people, including teens, do not consume this amount. The food pyramid suggests three servings of the dairy group, which will provide about 900 mg. The rest can be made up with supplements or with the addition of another serving from this group. Since calcium is present in so many foods, most mixed diets will provide adequate amounts. Check with your child's doctor to see if she recommends a calcium supplement. So many supplements are now available that it is hard to keep up. Even Tums, a stomach antacid, has 200 mg of calcium! With calcium, it is best to follow these guidelines:
   • Avoid the bone meal calcium sources as some may contain lead.
   • Anyone taking calcium should drink plenty of water as large amounts of calcium (greater than 2500 mg/day) may lead to calcium stone formation in those who are prone to developing stones. Take 500–600 mg at a time.
   • Iron interferes with the absorption of calcium, so if iron pills are necessary, they should be taken at a different time than calcium-rich foods or supplements.
   • Zinc levels may be compromised by calcium, so a teen should increase daily "fortified" cereal or supplement the diet with zinc after speaking to the doctor.
2. **Iron** is crucial for hemoglobin formation. Iron comes from two sources: *Heme* iron is readily absorbed and comes primarily from liver, red meat, clams, shrimp, and sardines. Other fish and poultry contain very little heme iron. *Non-heme* iron is more difficult to absorb and is found in enriched oatmeal and pasta, cereals, soybeans, red kidney beans, lentils, and figs, with lesser amounts in raisins, bananas, peanut butter, and brown sugar. Some foods such as ascorbic acid (vitamin C) help absorb the non-heme iron, while teas, bran, and antacids inhibit absorption. Iron depletion or iron deficiency anemia occurs in cases of massive blood loss, gradual (and undiscovered) bleeding, such as from an intestinal tract lesion or sometimes from extremely heavy menstrual

periods mounting up. If the intake of iron does not keep up with these losses, there will be a gradual iron deficiency that can be measured by a blood test. (An eating disordered patient or a vegetarian who has not paid attention to consuming the proper minerals may also register an iron deficiency.) Iron supplements are not necessary for most teenagers. Vegetarians can get adequate iron without eating meat, but they need to pay attention to what they eat. The RDA for iron is about 15 mg/day for most women, while for males the level drops to about 10 mg. When reading supplemental labels look for the term "elemental" iron. Some supplements will advertise iron in the 100-milligram range but provide only 15–50 mg of elemental iron for absorption.

3. **Zinc** has recently been recognized as an important mineral for promoting growth, appetite, and skin healing. It is one of the elements that is now a standard supplement for any patient who has lost a great deal of weight for any reason. Although the RDA is 12–15 mg/day, in situations of stress, such as with anorexia nervosa, your doctor may prescribe a higher dosage. The current RDA for girls is 12 mg and for boys about 15 mg day.

An additional note on supplements: A recent phenomenon with teenage boys is purchasing supplements at the health store (or weight-lifting shop) to improve sports performance. These often purport to have all the necessary RDAs plus supplements to burn fat, lose weight, and increase muscle mass. Many of these contain ephedra, which is a stimulant closely related to amphetamine. It is not recognized as a safe supplement and taking anything containing it should be discouraged. (For more about supplements to build muscle mass, see Chapter 7, "Teens and Sports: Sports-Related Injufires.")

Guiding toward Better Eating

If you expect change in your teen's eating patterns, set aside time and explain the calories that are consumed in each meal. There are many books on the market that will list calories and some also include individual food chains. (The Internet is another source of information, but check with your physician to be sure the information is accurate.)

If you are informed and provide healthy family meals as often as possible, your next task is informing your teen of what you know about food. Cooking

Dietary Reference Intakes (DRIs), Including Recommended Daily Allowances (RDAs) and Adequate Intakes (AIs)

	Vitamin A (mcg)	Vitamin C (mg)	Vitamin D* (mcg)	Vitamin E (mg)	Thiamin (B1) (mg)	Riboflavin (B2) (mg)	Niacin (B3) (mg)	Vitamin B6 (mg)	Folate (Folic Acid) (mcg)	Vitamin B12 (mcg)	Calcium (mg)	Iron (mg)	Zinc (mg)
Males													
9-13 yrs	600	45	5	11	0.9	0.9	12	1	300	1.8	1300	12	15
14-18 yrs	900	75	5	15	1.2	1.3	16	1.3	400	2.4	1300	12	15
19-30 yrs	900	90	5	15	1.2	1.3	16	1.3	400	2.4	1000	10	15
Females													
9-13 yrs	600	45	5	11	0.9	0.9	12	1	300	1.8	1300	15	12
14-18 yrs	700	65	5	15	1	1	14	1.2	400	2.4	1300	15	12
19-30 yrs	700	75	5	15	1.1	1.1	14	1.3	400	2.4	1000	15	12

Reprinted with permission from *Recommended Dietary Allowances: 10th Edition* and *Dietary Reference Intakes*. Copyright 1989, 2001 by the National Academy of Sciences. Courtesy of the National Academy Press, Washington, D.C.

*These numbers represent the Adequate Intake (AI), which is believed to cover the needs of all individuals in the group.

is no longer limited to one gender, and the more time you can spend with your teens in the kitchen, the better prepared they will be to create a lifestyle featuring healthy eating.

The College-Bound Teen

The "freshman 15" does not refer to a baseball team and its reserves but rather to the fifteen pounds generally gained by young college students away from home. Meals and alcohol are now their responsibility, and fast food, the cafeteria, and erratic hours all contribute pound by pound. Spend some additional time with your teenager talking about making healthy selections when away from home.

Weight Issues

The teenager today is confronted with unrealistic body images. Both genders have standards, set by magazines, television, and even parents, that are difficult if not impossible to meet. The muscled male of the magazines is not commonly possible and the thin runway model may be paying a huge price in dieting to look as skinny as she does. Many normal weight teenagers have a low regard for their own looks because they do not fulfill this unattainable media image. Some are just built with larger or stockier frames; it becomes akin to saying that anyone who does not have blond hair (naturally) is unattractive.

In my practice, young teens are brought in because they are "too heavy." A parent will ask me to look into a "glandular" problem, or "to put him on a diet" so that he can lose weight quickly and join the competitive adolescent market.

"He is so unhappy, doctor. We have tried everything, and he refuses to stop eating junk food. Don't you have a diet he can follow? I'm sure he will do it if you tell him."

This issue is very difficult for me because, realistically, I know that there is little chance that the youngster will change as quickly as his parents would like. It takes an enormous amount of willpower to avoid the fattening foods of our world and to take the time to exercise. The youngster is fighting a lifestyle and, often, genetics. (No one in medicine today would deny that there is an obesity gene.) No matter how much I tell parents that the weight is not all their child's fault, it is hard for them to accept. We view overweight as a failure of sound thinking or a form of self-destruction. Often kids don't know where to begin; they just know that they want to lose weight, but the anxiety only causes them to seek comfort by eating something. Parents make the mistake of saying something like: "He's so handsome. If only he could lose weight . . ."

Here's what is helpful to know about weight issues and teens.

When a Teen Is Overweight

The overweight or obese teen often doesn't know where to begin. She is told that she needs to eat less and exercise more, but both seem impossible. She claims hunger, and she claims fatigue with exercise. To make matters worse, her parents are constantly telling her that she needs to do "something" about her weight, which makes her anxious, and she eats even more. I can assure any parent who has a teen who is overweight that it is not a state she desires.

Begin with your physician and establish a goal weight and a time frame to reach it. Realize that a sudden and dramatic loss is unacceptable during the growth phase of puberty. Parents often ask for "pills" so that their kids can lose weight. This desperate plea has to be denied. There are several types of pills available, but there are risks. One group consists of amphetamine-like stimulants that decrease appetite and increase metabolism; it's like using speed to stop hunger. These pills are associated with high blood pressure, increased heart rate, as well as lung disease. The second pill is a thyroid hormone that increases metabolism and should only be used in cases of low thyroid. The third medication is a new one called sibutramine, marketed as Meridia. It interferes with the brain's perception of hunger, and its side effects have to be closely monitored. The FDA does not permit this medication for anyone under sixteen years of age, and it is only approved for a two- or three-month span. There are also pills such as orlistat (Xenical) that interfere with food absorption but can cause diarrhea and interfere with fat-soluble vitamin absorption. For a growing teen any of these products adds the extra risk of an unknown impact on growth.

During the summer, heavy kids may be sent to "overweight" camps. All will lose weight; that is almost a guarantee. Diet is closely monitored, and activity level is increased. The problem is that once home, teens have to maintain the same regimen. No cookies and cake, no hamburgers and fries; in brief, if teens go back to the old style of eating, they simply gain the weight back. In a way it only makes it worse since the kids feel a sense of failure.

Weight Loss Made "Easy"

The key to losing weight is simple. Our bodies are consumers of fuel and we either burn up the calories or they go into "storage" on hips, waist, thighs, etc. To lose weight, you must have a caloric input that is less than your caloric output: the body must burn more than is taken in. This can happen in one of two ways. By eating less than needed and letting the body burn off the stored calories, or by burning more than is eaten.

Done properly, dieting can work. Extreme diets, often touted even in the mainstream press, may leave a body without sufficient protein or proper nutrients. Anyone who is dieting must take care not to overdo it, and care must be taken in the message we give to the teenager to prevent an overreaction. A doctor or nutritionist must supervise a teen's diet plan.

Plan on something reasonable, like losing a pound a week, or even half a pound weekly. This requires a change of only 250–500 calories per day. One can either reduce the caloric intake by that amount or one can exercise the equivalent; ideally, a combination of the two is best. For every 500-calorie deficit per day there is approximately a pound loss per week; a 750-calorie deficit daily will lose 1.5 pounds per week.

1. As a parent, you can help by buying appropriate foods and avoiding having a teen's favorite fattening foods in the house. (Do you really need potato chips in the house, ever?)
2. Your body digests a meal in 30 to 45 minutes, and it takes about that long for the brain to appreciate that you are full. By eating slowly, your brain will naturally release dopamine, which will help you feel satisfied. Encourage your teen to sit down to eat and to eat slowly. Snacks should be limited and should be vegetables and fruits. (Never eat while standing, especially in front of the refrigerator.)
3. Remind your teen of the benefits of drinking water. Kids forget that soft drinks may contain a lot of calories. As a reminder, a can of soda with 150 kcal is the same as having 9 teaspoons of sugar! Water is filling and good for you.
4. Remind teens that alcohol is fattening (a very good reason for obeying the drinking law). Because it's nutritionally empty, alcohol falls in the category of "candy"—something unnecessary to consume.
5. Trim the fat off steaks, or serve lean chicken and fish.
6. Don't be fooled into buying "low fat" foods. Just because they are low in fat doesn't mean that they are low in calories.
7. Introduce your teen to salads!

8. Realize that some teens eat out of boredom or depression. Having a snack while sitting in front of the television will add weight, from inactivity and caloric increase.

One weight-loss method I find effective with young teenagers is to counsel "weight maintenance." When you plot the curves for the youngster's height and weight at a particular age, it will become apparent that by holding a weight for a year or so, the teenager can grow into the weight! (Just draw a horizontal line over the two years and plot the height and weight again. The same weight that today seemed too much on the twelve-year-old will do nicely on a frame that is six or seven inches taller and older by two years.) "Holding" weight is easier than losing, but not as easy as it sounds—a referral to a nutritionist is a good idea so a teen can learn about foods and quantities.

As an adjunct to a proper diet, exercise is necessary. This is the only safe way to burn up more calories than are consumed. Not only does the energy expenditure increase, but the exercise itself alters the desire for fatty foods and helps suppress hunger. If teens aren't getting regular exercise through a school program, the issue becomes a little more complicated. While walking, biking, and jogging are certainly excellent forms of exercise, they are weather-dependent and there is little variety to the activity. Health clubs are an alternative but a problematic one. Not only are they expensive, but many require that members be at least sixteen—and in some locations, eighteen years old. It may take some creativity to come up with ways to keep the exercise quotient high. However, parents can help their teens exercise and get some exercise themselves if they walk to more places instead of taking the car. Perhaps you can find an indoor community pool to join that isn't too expensive, or teens might find a yoga or karate class fun to join with a friend.

Ultimately a teen needs to have a genuine resolve to lose weight, since eating and exercise habits must be changed. An understanding doctor or a nutritionist can also be very helpful. But in the end, the desire has to come from the teenager to be successful.

The Genuinely Underweight

These are people who genuinely have an accelerated metabolism, or who do so much exercise that they burn up all the calories they consume. The rest of us may consider them thoroughly annoying when they complain that they can never gain weight. (Can you imagine such a thing? Some of us spell CHEESE-CAKE and gain weight!) These teens come into my office feeling too skinny and ask for "some shake or something" to gain weight. I look at them and try to understand as I recall that piece of cake I had to pass up at lunch.

The teenager who is too thin should have an evaluation to rule out pathology. The first step is to see the growth pattern and decide if this is the "natural" body type for the teenager. Pathologic causes of underweight can be conditions such as hyperthyroidism (because of increased metabolism) or malabsorption, which prevents digestion of food. These must be diagnosed and treated by a physician. If there is no pathology, then one looks at the gene pool and at the fact that the teenager is growing so quickly that all the calories are being consumed for rapid growth.

It is often the tall lanky basketball player who comes in and asks to be helped in filling out his six-foot frame. A simple calculation for the amount of calories needed to simply survive (REE), to grow, and to account for the extra exercise of his sport often yields astounding numbers. At 6'1" and still growing, one such youngster practiced about four hours a day and required somewhere between 5000 and 6000 calories per day. His father accompanied him for the visit, and when I finished all the math and told him the final tally, he looked at me and simply said, "Call his mother. She won't believe me."

This youngster needed some supplemental drinks to make the total calories, and we monitored his growth and weight just as we do the teen who is overweight. When the season ended, he went back to a more normal intake of 3500 calories!

When selecting supplemental drinks, buy the ones recommended by your teen's physician, ones that provide a balance of carbohydrates, amino acids, and fat. They are safe and have been used by many patients who cannot, for one reason or another, tolerate solid foods.

If it is felt that the reason for being thin is not genetic nor a growth spurt, and one cannot find a medical cause, then the search for an eating disorder begins. If a girl is not getting her period, either the first one or subsequent ones, weight has also to be considered as a possible factor.

Eating Disorders

While this section primarily focuses on anorexia nervosa and bulimia, one fairly new syndrome has been described as "fear of obesity," in which teens are so concerned about gaining weight or eating "bad foods" (for example, cholesterol in meat or mercury in fish) that they deliberately abstain from these foods and consequently restrict their calories too much. This is not considered anorexia nervosa because the dynamics of control are different (see anorexia nervosa below).

However, they are depriving themselves of calories, and both parents and teen need to be educated about proper eating. Often explaining to the parent that they may have oversold the message of proper nutrition is all that is required.

Although one could refer to the overweight teen as having an "eating disorder," the term is usually reserved for people who are losing weight excessively or who purge. There are basically three types of eating disorders:

1. the teen with anorexia nervosa who starves (restrictive eating disorder)
2. the bulimic teen who binges and then vomits
3. the bulimorexia teen who does both

Today eating disorders cross all economic boundaries, races, and cultures. It is not only a girls' disease. Any teen who decides to lose weight or who is involved in sports that have high risk for eating disorders should be monitored closely (see Chapter 7 about sports). In our society we have to be particularly alert to the girl who announces that she plans to "lose a few pounds." Even if it is felt appropriate to diet, she should be monitored by a parent or by a physician. Loss of menses is a red flag. Consult your teenager's doctor to see what weight is appropriate for your daughter's height. This will provide you both with a gauge. The beginning of an eating disorder will often start with an innocuous diet to lose just "a little weight" before the prom or some other occasion.

Eating disorders are psychological illnesses, and there are many things families can do to prevent setting the stage for problems with eating:

1. Stop complaining about being fat. Constant comments by parents about their own weight only adds the idea that being "fat" is terrible. This is especially true if the parent is in fact a normal weight.
2. Allow the teen to make choices at dinner. Serve the meal on a platter and allow each member to select their portions.
3. Don't criticize others for their weight. If you talk about strangers, the lesson is that others will talk about you and your weight as well.
4. If your teen is involved in a sport that is at risk for weight problems (dance, skating, etc.) be sure you realize the risk, and monitor weight and nutrition, even if the coach says to lose a few pounds.
5. Avoid the "You could lose a few pounds, dear" line.
6. Allow the teen a chance of expression through their clothes. This gives them control over their physical appearance that is taken away if you select their clothes or criticize their choices. Through food teens can quickly prove to you that they can control their physical appearance; this can jumpstart a serious problem you want to avoid.

I have never treated a patient with an eating disorder and had it "go away" or be cured on its own in a few weeks. The teenager with an eating disorder will require a great deal of attention. This is a complex and symbolic disorder where a person uses food and control issues to solve underlying problems. If the diagnosis is made early, the diet and unhealthy thought patterns may be less ingrained. You'll want a team of experts to help: A physician will be necessary to monitor the physical health. A nutritionist is usually included to help with food choices and with caloric planning, and a mental health expert, either a psychiatrist, a psychologist, or a social worker trained in eating disorders, will be needed to help the patient and the parents understand this illness. Tell a patient who is eating 850 calories per day that she needs to consume 2500 calories to turn the illness around, and you elicit panic and disbelief. Plan on many months of therapy and setbacks before the patient shows signs of recovery.

Although boys can have anorexia nervosa or bulimia, the likely candidate is the female high school student. Girls who seem to show symptoms of it for the first time in college were likely hiding the disease during high school or were "dieting" and doing so with everyone's approval.

Anorexia Nervosa

It is estimated that 1 percent of teenage girls will develop anorexia nervosa, and that most girls will binge eat or attempt to lose weight during adolescence. Girls who participate in gymnastics, track, dance, or ice skating are particularly at risk. Being thin is a premium in all of these sports. (Boys who wrestle may binge or purge to "make weight.") Certainly these sports can have healthy and well-nourished teens, but the reality of the demands to be thin and have a "good line" is a high priority in these sports. The girls wear outfits that accentuate their bodies, and the competitive nature of these sports encourages the athlete to get an edge where possible. It doesn't take too long to decide that losing weight will help. The image of the petite gymnast who wins medals is now etched in our minds; these girls need to be monitored closely. If menses is disrupted, see your physician, as this may be the first clue that there is a problem.

The term anorexia nervosa is a partial misnomer. The anorexia (lack of hunger) is real in that they are not eating, but not because they lose their appetite, and there is nothing "nervous" about the patient, rather they suffer from an underlying depression. These patients are so scared to gain weight that they deliberately suppress hunger and, in time, they actually do lose their appetite. For a while, they want to eat but feel guilty if they do. In time, it takes little to suppress appetite and after a few days of dieting it gets easier and easier. In most cases, the girl is perfectly normal in weight but she still feels a need to "lose a few pounds." Ask and you will be told that there is a particular part of their body that they feel is "too large." The usual places are the stomach, thighs, hips, or breasts. The peak incidences for this disorder occur at fourteen and again at age eighteen. Note that these two ages correspond with "new beginnings"—entering high school and college.

The diagnosis of anorexia nervosa rests on the history of poor food intake and a refusal to gain weight. The girl with anorexia sees "normal" (or even feel that they still have to lose a few more pounds) where others see emaciated. Ribs sticking out, hair falling out, lack of menses, dry sallow skin, and cold extremities all appear acceptable to them. The notion of gaining any weight, let alone putting on normal body fat, is a disgusting and frightening thought. They formulate rules and regulations, and any violation of these rules brings about guilt.

A good way of appreciating their plight is to examine traditional religions that impose a value on foods. Some religions and cultures prohibit certain foods or foods at certain times of the year. These are sacred rules, and violation brings about a sense of dishonor and guilt. One recognizes that one has transgressed a religious code of behavior. It is no different with the girl who has self-imposed rules of eating. She may say that only 20 peas can be eaten or that no oil or butter can *touch* the food. If the food is tainted by a violation of the rules, then she will feel guilt and shame. Logic alone will not turn the tide, no more than telling someone to eat pork if their religion prohibits it. She has set up the rules of her diet, and only she will be able to change them.

The damage from anorexia nervosa is many-layered: the most common

Diagnosis of Anorexia Nervosa

1. Refusal to maintain normal body weight
2. Intense fear of gaining weight or becoming fat despite being underweight
3. No other medical explanation for weight loss
4. Distorted perception of body shape
5. Amenorrhea (lack of menstrual periods)
6. Constipation: not a standard criteria but diarrhea raises the risk of other illnesses or may be a symptom of abuse of laxatives

findings are immediately visible. The thin hair that hangs with little or no curl attests to poor nutrition. The skin is dry and coarse with an increase in fine small hairs on the body as estrogen falls. Because they have lost fat, they lose insulation and they complain of being cold. In warm weather they have to wear gloves or sweaters. They tend to be sullen and are preoccupied with food. They will worry about their distended stomachs filled with stool, as constipation is common. Lastly, they lose their menstrual cycle. Teens tolerate each of these as long as they are losing weight; all will be reversed with the proper acquisition of weight. A sense of power accompanies the weight loss; to gain weight is to lose this power. It is a bad trade-off in their minds.

The girl who loses weight before her first menstrual cycle may compromise her growth; all girls who have lost weight just as their periods started should have an assessment of their "bone age" to determine how much more growth is left. This is a simple X ray of the wrist that tells us how mature the bones are and therefore how much growth is left. This is important in determining the amount of calories needed to turn around the anorexia. Concerns about having children later can be put to rest as the weight gain will trigger the brain and the ovaries to respond to the body fat and normal cycles will resume. Child bearing, if it were possible before, will be possible when weight is regained. It's as if they were going through puberty once again.

A major concern with this disease is the loss of bone density because of loss of estrogen. The loss of bone is reversible if estrogen and nutrition is replaced soon after the weight loss. If the disease has progressed to the point of osteoporosis (porous bones that are thinned out), it will take longer to heal, and the girl with anorexia nervosa actually is at risk for the same fractures as her grandmother.

Lastly, parents worry about their teen dying. Most parents have heard of celebrities who succumbed to this disorder. Fortunately, this outcome is rare, although possible. I have had patients as low as 60 pounds who refused to gain weight. The only solution was to intravenously feed them, and eventually nasogastric tubes could be placed to sustain life. It took months but the patients eventually left the hospital and were able to participate in psychotherapy.

As parents, here are clues to watch for:

1. The teen becomes obsessed with food magazines, diets, and nutrition. She will know the calories in foods and even the amount of fat.
2. She may begin to isolate herself from her friends and focus more and more on her diet.
3. She may actually prepare elaborate meals for the family and not eat them.

4. She will begin to give up sweets and fat with claims that she "isn't hungry." She may argue that she "ate a big meal at school" and needs to skip dinner.

5. She may become a vegetarian.

6. She may begin to exercise to the point of exhaustion.

7. She will complain that she is "fat" while being normal in weight.

8. Her hair becomes thin and brittle.

9. Her period will become irregular and may even stop.

10. If you find laxatives or diuretics, contact your physician!

Treatment is aimed at both the nutritional aspect and at the underlying psychological problem. The choice of outpatient treatment or hospitalization depends on several factors. Certainly if the weight is below 25 percent of ideal weight, or if the patient has life-threatening symptoms, hospitalization is inevitable. If the weight is too low, it is felt that one cannot do psychotherapy as the ability to think properly is compromised. Some therapists will admit the patient to the hospital simply to increase caloric input. Whether the patient eats voluntarily or by naso-gastric tube, the aim is to have the patient gain weight.

At first few teens will cooperate, as they feel that their resolve is being challenged. Soon, as trust enters into the equation, the teen will begin to understand that the staff is only interested in her welfare. Often parents are not allowed to visit during the first phase of hospital care as their presence may only aggravate the situation. Patients will talk about the need for "control," and they are using the disorder to set limits for themselves and for their family. Parents who innocently say something like, "Oh, just eat a little, dear. It's so easy and you can leave here!" only add fuel to the fire.

Today most patients are not hospitalized as the disorder is recognized sooner. The same team of specialists needs to work together to address three major points:

1. weight gain and resuming menses;

2. understanding the psychodynamics that brought about the problems in the first place and substituting new systems to deal with problems— one cannot starve to fix everything that is wrong;

3. family therapy to appreciate what the teen is going through and to change whatever the family's contribution to the disorder has been.

The outpatient treatment requires weekly visits to each member of the team. Often the teen with anorexia nervosa will try to maneuver the members so that she gets an ally and then can pit one against the other. A good team will read the clues immediately and tell her that the team shares all information. An example is the girl who gets weighed in my office or by the nutritionist and then declares that she doesn't want anyone else to know it. It's okay for the family not to know, but the team must. She may secretly exercise and ask parents not to tell. Don't participate in this deception. It's equivalent to giving whisky to the alcoholic. Exercise for them is the safeguard against gaining weight, and they will do it secretly.

> **Catherine was admitted to the** *hospital because at sixteen and 5'2" her weight was down to 85 pounds. She refused to eat and saw nothing wrong with her body. She had lost her menses and was pleased that she didn't have to deal with this "messy problem." While at the hospital she gained steadily and was progressing on schedule, when she suddenly stopped gaining further weight. We searched for clues that she was throwing up, that she could be hiding food, or that she was using laxatives. All came up negative. Frankly, I was puzzled and wondered if I had missed some diagnosis. Then came the clue. One of the nurses casually stated that Catherine was so delightful and she was so helpful on the ward. She would trail the nurses "all day" and help with the younger children. I asked if she literally meant "all day" and every nurse agreed that Catherine was everywhere. I measured the distance from Catherine's room to the nurses' station and to the last patient's bed. By calculating how many trips Catherine was making per day, it came out that she was walking miles while in the hospital. Under the guise of being helpful, she was exercising daily. When I confronted her, she smiled and acknowledged the ruse. In a way, it established our bond as she realized that I had taken the trouble to work it all out. She finally left the hospital short of her target weight but we felt—and were proven correct—that she could reach it as an outpatient. She is now functioning well in college and sees a therapist weekly to maintain her stability.*

Although this disorder is most common in the female teen, boys can also develop an eating disorder. They are harder to identify because they don't have something to "lose" like a menses. Yet, their male hormone level will also fall as they lose weight; and, hence, their sex drive. Clearly this is seldom mentioned and the problem goes unnoticed. The clues for males will differ slightly but they, too, will isolate themselves, be preoccupied with thoughts of foods and calories, and exercise strenuously. They become "gym rats" or run miles daily; all under the pretense that they are "getting into shape." Watch for falling weight and a continued desire to get thinner, along with a misconception about their appearance. Their treatment requires the same team approach.

Bulimia

This disorder will present differently than anorexia nervosa. The patient with anorexia nervosa feels out of control and uses food restriction to establish control. The bulimic patient feels out of control and will eat voraciously and then purge. The preferred choice of purging is vomiting; initially some use syrup of ipecac and, later, train themselves to do it on demand. Secretive at first, they will leave the table while others are still eating to eliminate the food as quickly as possible. Only when they sense "empty" is achieved do they feel good. Alternatively, they may use laxatives to cleanse themselves. I have had patients tell me that they will use as many as 50 laxative pills at a time to be sure that they got rid of all that was inside. Some will use diuretics either in pill form or as special diuretic herbal tea. Lastly, they will exercise.

Each of the purges has complications. Aside from altering nutrition, since they do not absorb the food they ate, vomiting can lead to tears in the esophagus and dental caries as the repeated acid of the stomach damages the covering of the teeth. Abrasions at the edges of the lips are common, and the chipmunk appearance of swollen parotid (salivary) glands attests to the dry mouth and the vomiting. Close observation will reveal cuts on the knuckles as the fingers are used to induce the vomit and teeth marks are left on the knuckles. The laxative abuser will develop malabsorption problems and potentially will have rectal bleeding from the repeated abuse. Both laxative and diuretic abusers will alter their electrolytes (body chemistry) and problems with sodium and potassium deficiency are seen. Stress fractures from excessive exercise and poor bone density are possible.

Frankly the patient who has bulimia may be a difficult one to diagnose. They can have normal weight or even be slightly overweight and their blood studies can be normal. Sometimes the only way is to catch them in the act.

Phyllis was not growing *appropriately, and when she was fourteen, I diagnosed hypothyroidism as the cause. She was started on thyroid medications and the results were dramatic in terms of her growth spurt. Because of the medications and the need to monitor her growth, she was in my office several times a year and blood work was done to check her thyroid. One week prior to graduation, her mother called to report that she had heard*

Phyllis throwing up right after a meal, and she confronted her with the suspicion that this was deliberate. She brought her into my office where Phyllis admitted that she had been hiding her bulimia for the past two years. Despite all the visits and all the blood work, she had managed to elude suspicion and detection. It was only in the last two weeks that her mother realized that she was leaving the table more quickly than usual and going directly to the bathroom. This was what alerted her to call me.

Many bulimics use the purge as a way of maintaining weight. They can "have their cake and eat it, too" and then throw up without gaining any weight. Often the bulimic teen had too many problems maintaining a diet and realized that purging was an easier solution. Because of their secrecy and their hiding of laxatives or diuretics, they may present to the doctor with unusual symptoms or unusual blood values. Diarrhea of unexplained origin is always suspect; throwing up blood after a forceful vomit is also rare in teens but something to consider in the bulimic patient. Low potassium is seldom seen without some evidence of deliberate and sudden fluid loss either through diuretics or laxatives. The body does a remarkable job in conserving potassium through kidney regulation, and it requires significant losses for the kidney to be unable to compensate.

Many therapists feel that the patient with bulimia needs medication to help with the impulsivity of their eating. Antidepressants and medications for obsessive behavior may be adjuncts to the therapeutic process. As opposed to the anorexia nervosa patient, who needs family therapy as part of the recovery process, the patient with bulimia tends to need more individual work. Unfortunately, many bulimic patients continue their behavior past the college years.

The *bulimorexia* patient has features of both. This patient will have intermittent bouts of starvation and then resort to binge-and-purge tactics. Clearly the therapy for this patient is complex as the shifting behaviors make it hard for both the medical and the mental aspect of management.

Teens and Special Diets

The Vegetarian Teen

When your teenager makes the decision to become a vegetarian, you should make sure that the teen's motives are genuine and not a ruse to eat less. Some teens will use being a vegetarian as an excuse to diet and avoid certain foods; they may actually be hiding an eating disorder. (Check the earlier section in this chapter if you have concerns.) Other teens feel a moral obligation to abstain from eating animal products but do not know how to compensate for the nutrients and calories contained in meat. Others get "grossed out" at the idea of eating an animal. There is more to being a vegetarian than just avoiding meat and meat products.

If your teenager seems genuinely interested in taking on this new lifestyle, your next step is to be certain it is done properly. If the parent is well schooled in proper nutrition, then well-planned and balanced vegetarian meals can be introduced. But this is not a time in your teen's life to guess about nutrition. I would prefer for you to check your sources and information. The vegetarian teenager should meet with a nutritionist soon after taking on this lifestyle. It is perfectly acceptable to be a vegetarian, indeed even a vegan, who will not eat eggs or drink milk. Vegetarian teens need more information about food values and a good understanding of how to get the nutrition needed for proper growth.

Hypoglycemia and the Teen

If a teen feels faint and weak after skipping a meal, this may be a sign of low blood sugar. However, hypoglycemia tends to be overdiagnosed. Any teen who feels dizzy and has other signs of hypoglycemia needs a fasting glucose test, a two-hour post-meal sugar test, a thyroid checkup, and a thorough assessment of his eating patterns and diet. A physician can diagnose hypoglycemia and set up a diet to keep your teen healthy and well.

Since the desire is to maintain a normal glucose level, the goal is to eat in such a way as to avoid shifts of insulin being released. This hormone, released by the pancreas, reacts to the presence of sugar in the blood. The more sugar, the more the insulin is released. To avoid a "yo-yo" effect, the person is advised to eat more protein and complex starches so that the insulin is not released too quickly, which forces the blood sugar into the hypoglycemic range. Secondly, more than the three meals a day with smaller servings can lower the glucose and insulin shifts. The use of the "glycemic" index should be introduced to help the patient recognize which foods trigger more insulin release.

The Glycemic Index (GI) gives carbohydrates a value based on how they will influence blood sugar. By measuring blood sugar two to three hours after eating a particular food, one can see how that particular food will influence the amount of sugar in the bloodstream. Since fat and protein do not raise sugar quickly, the index is limited to carbohydrates only. The higher the index, the more glucose is elevated in the bloodstream. We want a low index in order to

Glycemic Index

Glucose	100	Whole-grain bread	50
Baked potato	95	Fresh fruit juice	40
Honey	90	Red kidney beans	40
Cooked carrots	85	Milk products	30
Sugar (sucrose)	75	Chickpeas, stoneground	
White bread, corn, biscuits	70	whole-wheat pasta, lentils	30
Boiled potatoes	70	Fruit preserve (no sugar)	25
Bananas	60	Green vegetables, lemons,	
Peas	50	tomatoes, mushrooms	<15

prevent high and low sugar swings that make us feel sluggish and hungry. For a book with recipes that incorporate the Glycemic Index, see *The Glucose Revolution: The Authoritative Guide to the Glycemic Index* by Jennie Brand-Miller and Thomas M.S. Wolver, M.D. (Marlowe & Co., 1999). The chart above represents some of the carbohydrates in the Index.

The Food Allergic Teen

Allergic patients may feel tired, have vague symptoms, and possibly diarrhea when they consume offending foods, but a definitive diagnosis must be made by an allergist. If there is a strong suspicion of food allergy, notify your physician as some allergies can be fatal. For example, a peanut allergy may trigger a reaction so severe that the next time a peanut is consumed the individual will have trouble breathing. These individuals must wear "Alert" bracelets or necklaces to identify the potential problem in case of an emergency. Your physician will help you obtain these.

The use of the word "allergy" when applied to milk implies a genuine inability to handle the protein in cow's milk. These patients have an "allergic" reaction to milk. Also remember that the protein in cow's milk is bovine protein, and some allergic people will produce a lot of phlegm in response to this protein.

The more frequently used term "milk intolerance" or "lactose intolerance" is more common than appreciated. This can be an inherited disorder and, in the classic sense, the teen has inherited less lactase (an enzyme) to digest the milk's sugar, lactose. It is estimated that 15 percent of American whites have lower than normal lactase levels. Other groups will range from 50 percent in Mexican Americans to 90 percent in Asian Americans. As a result of not having enough lactase, the milk is not properly digested and the lactose sugar remaining will ferment. The patient will complain of gas, a sense of fullness, and cramps with possible diarrhea. Yet, anyone can develop the same symptoms if there is a large amount of lactose consumed. Even the most tolerant teen will become gassy, show abdominal pain, and some diarrhea after the fourth pizza slice and milkshake.

Milk is overrated as a necessary product—there are other ways to get the calcium a teen needs. If your teen doesn't like milk, chances are that he has discovered empirically that milk upsets his digestive system.

The Migraine Sufferer

Migraine headaches can be triggered by some foods. Anyone with migraine headaches should keep a food log every time a headache occurs. In time, the patient may find a common theme to the headaches. See "Migraine" in Part Five, "The Adolescent, Head to Toe."

Ours is a society in which we have low activity levels and yet our consumption of fast foods is high. When I ask parents about family dinners, they often joke about the home meals they have several nights per week as each member of the family chooses a different chain from which to bring home dinner. We are in the midst of an obesity epidemic as our kids sit in front of television sets and computer monitors.

Go back through this chapter and think about how you can revise your family's eating habits. We need to start teaching our teens about proper nutrition so that, when they leave for college, they can continue the lessons learned at family meals and reap the benefits of good nutrition.

Chapter 6

The Teen Obsession: Skin

A lucky few people have clear, beautiful skin throughout life, but most will have skin problems in their teens and will want to see a doctor at some point. Even the teenager who complains about having to see a doctor for a camp physical will be willing to see a dermatologist. The teenager with a pimple considers it a full-blown medical emergency, and something has to be done about it "yesterday." Teens know that we've come a long way from scrubbing with pHisoHex.

To understand skin problems, you first need to know something about skin. The skin is actually an organ that is divided into three layers. The *epidermis* is the top layer that peels daily. The *dermal* layer contains blood vessels and nerves and is susceptible to scarring if it is damaged. The lowest layer is the *subcutaneous,* which contains fat cells and more blood vessels. When a physician diagnoses a skin condition, he takes into account which layer is involved. During adolescence the skin is altered by hormonal changes as well as by sweat and bacteria. Teens also tend to spend more time outdoors, and therefore, they are susceptible to sun damage. All this translates into frequent skin lesions during the teen years.

This chapter deals with all types of skin problems, ranging from allergic skin reactions to eczema and warts, but if you are like most families, you'll find that acne and the issues of tattoos and piercings will be the skin topics of most interest. As responsible parents, be sure to give them one other piece of skin-oriented advice: Wear sunscreen. Sun damage sustained in youth lays the groundwork for adult skin cancer. Make sure your teen knows how important it is to protect against the sun.

Acne

There is no disease more associated with puberty than acne. Parents and teenagers view acne as inevitable, an unwanted part of "growing up." No one should take this condition lightly, for the physical scars and emotional trauma to the teen are immense. There really is such a thing as "a pimple emergency!" I have seen teens dread a prom because a pimple sits prominently on her forehead, or worse, her nose. Parental comments about ignoring it will only make the teenager feel that you have no understanding of her plight. The right answer is to tell the teenager that you will get her to the doctor to deal with the problem. There are excellent treatments that can make one aspect of their lives easier and more manageable. Even those parents whose economic level prevents access to private care can help their teens. All hospitals have dermatology clinics whose competent resident staff are more than willing to help. Seek them out.

What causes acne? To dismiss one old myth, it has nothing to do with the foods we eat. The days of banning chocolates and other sweets because of acne are gone. Acne is a disease of the hair-oil follicle (pilosebaceous unit) located in the dermal layer. (Since the hair follicle is critical to acne, pimples occur on the face, the chest, and the back where there are hair follicles; not on the hairless palms or on the soles of the feet.) The oil is called *sebum,* and this oil, along with flaked skin and bacteria, can irritate the hair follicle so that an inflamma-

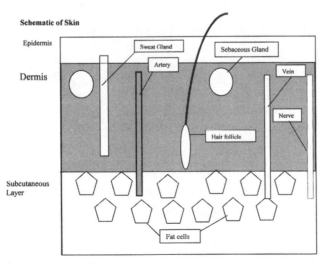

Note the arteries, veins, and nerves predominate in the Dermal layer. Fat cells are in the Subcutaneous Layer primarily.

tion results. Eventually there is so much oil in the follicle that it cannot come out of the narrow opening. The blackhead (open comedo) results from an excess of oil in the follicle with an opening at the top. The classic whitehead (closed comedo) occurs when the oil is unable to drain through a very small opening and is infected. The whiteness represents the pus that is trapped, and it can scar if ruptured.

The worst-case scenario is the lesion that has so much oil it starts to rupture sideways under the skin and the patient develops a *pustule* or *cyst*. Since the blackhead has an opening, it is amenable to being pushed out of the top without scars, but the deeper and more extensive the lesion, the more scarring can occur. Teens who squeeze their lesions with their nails will cause a scar at the site, as the nails will force the inflammation down into the dermal layer.

Young children do not get acne because their hair follicles are small and they do not have sex hormones affecting oil production. The critical hormone in all of this is testosterone (an *androgen)* and, therefore, boys tend to get worse acne. It is this fact that makes physicians look for excessive androgen production in girls whose acne persists. (See pp. 460 and 461 for a further discussion of hirsutism.)

While puberty, with its newly produced testosterone, is the prime time for acne, occasionally patients who are taking birth control pills with androgen properties, steroids, some seizure medications, and topical medications that clog the hair-follicle are subject to acne. In athletes who wear protective helmets and hairbands, the irritation will worsen the acne, and it is harder to treat. Girls may note an increase in their acne just before their periods as their hormone levels change.

Stress and acne have long been linked. One argument is that teens with acne are stressed because of it, another is that acne is caused by stress. One possible explanation is an increase in adrenal steroids associated with stress, but that hardly helps the teen who has acne. Whatever the reason, he needs treatment of his skin and not a lecture on dealing with stress.

Treatment

One can divide treatment of acne into two main categories: topical treatment and oral medication. A separate category involves cosmetic surgery for the lesions, and this will be covered below. Washing the area is important but not sufficient for acne treatment. Indeed, face washing and body washing should simply be part of good hygiene, but sometimes it takes acne to get some teens washing! Check with your doctor regarding proper washing for your teen's skin type.

Whatever treatment is used, your teen needs information as to what to expect. If the medicine is not working fast enough, or if there is a side effect that they can't tolerate, teens will frequently toss aside over-the-counter and prescription medications that, if given time, will do some good. Few cases of acne respond in a day or two, and none are "cured" during adolescence. The only way that acne treatment will succeed is if your teenager is fully informed and has reasonable expectations. Most doctors will tell patients that it will be a few weeks before they see the results, and—this is the hard part—it may get worse before it improves!

■ Topical Care

Most physicians begin treatment gradually, using topical care only. The patient who has very dry skin will do best with topical creams, while the oily-skinned patient will be able to tolerate gels, lotions, or solutions that have a drying effect on the skin.

Benzoyl peroxide. The gold standard for first-line care is any product containing benzoyl peroxide. It is available without prescription and, therefore, kids may not think it strong enough. Benzoyl peroxide, which comes in concentrations of 2.5%, 5%, and 10%, has antibacterial properties and also increases peeling, which helps in unclogging pores. It also comes as an alcohol- or water-based product, so your physician will recommend the one that is best for your teen. Some of the preparations come in the forms of a benzoyl peroxide wash or soap, and some are tinted to help hide lesions. Light-skinned patients tend to do best with a lower concentration to guard against too much peeling. The doctor may later see fit to increase the strength of it. (A very small percent of patients are allergic to the product.) In mild cases this may be the only acne treatment necessary, and if done regularly some teens see great improvements.

Salicylic acid. Another peeling agent is salicylic acid, and this, too, can be found in several over-the-counter products in concentrations from 0.5% to 2%. One popular form is the salicylic-acid–soaked pad, which the patient uses twice a day. Salicylic acid is the main ingredient in aspirin, so if your teen has aspirin sensitivity, this may not be the right product for her.

Other peeling agents. Other products may contain sulfur or even an abrasive agent to help peel the skin. Since sulfur has a bad odor, kids tend to avoid products containing it, but they can be effective. All of these are first-line medications meant to control early or mild acne. If more aggressive acne develops, the physician needs to prescribe more powerful products.

Retin-A and derivatives. Many years ago it was found that vitamin A could increase peeling, and patients were routinely given very high doses of oral vitamin A for acne care. Eventually it became apparent that there were side effects and potential toxicity in giving pure vitamin A in high doses. A newer solution is to coat the skin of the acne sufferer with the vitamin. With the advent of Retin-A (tretinoin), currently a prescription drug, patients could safely apply this derivative of vitamin A to their skin without the toxicity. The results were dramatic when the proper cream, gel, or solution of tretinoin was used. The solution fell into disfavor because of its extreme drying effect. Even the cream and gel caused some irritation. Patients had to tolerate extremely dry skin and irritation and a gradual adjustment to the medication, but many felt that it was worth it. Today there are newer versions of the retinoic acid derivatives (Differin, Tazorac) and some now come with added moisturizers to lessen irritation.

Whether a teen is using tretinoin or the newer derivatives, care must be taken because skin will dry considerably and a mild redness will be visible. Teens should be warned of this or they may stop taking the medication. Sometimes changing the dosage, the frequency, or the type (cream versus gel) will help the situation. Using this medication during the summer requires vigilant use of sunscreens, since the summer sun will accelerate the burning (photosensitivity) process.

Azelaic acid. A relatively new product, azelaic acid, is found in Azelex, a cream that claims to rival the effects of the retinoic acids. This product was first developed to decrease pigmentation for patients with dark spots; therefore, dark-skinned patients should use this cautiously. Since it is a prescription item, your physician will advise you.

Topical antibiotics. Antibiotics are often used topically in conjunction with a peeling agent. Most patients will leave the office with two prescriptions, one for a peeling pledget (as described above) and one for topical antibiotics. Your doctor will advise you on when to use each of them. The patient who has whiteheads is the ideal candidate for topical antibiotics. Almost all of the antibiotics are in the tetracycline or erythromycin family. (If your teen is allergic to these medications, it is important to tell the doctor.) The most common ones come in creams, gels, and in small pads packed in foil that are soaked with the antibiotic. These resemble the alcohol pads found in doctors' offices and,

The Importance of Following Directions

The biggest barrier to effective topical care is the teenager's reluctance to be consistent and patient about achieving results. There is no doubt that since most acne treatments require twice-daily applications, it is annoying and a constant reminder of the need for the acne care. Once they see results, most teens will continue to use the medicines, but the first few weeks are the worst. They need support and reminders for a while, but ultimately they need to be responsible for their own treatment.

although more expensive, are ideal for travel and are less "messy" than the other methods.

Combination prescription. One last prescription medication contains both benzoyl peroxide (5%) and a topical antibiotic (erythromycin). The advantage of this medication cream is that it is convenient, since the peeling agent and the antibiotic are applied together. Often it is used in mild to moderate cases, and since it is convenient it is popular with the teens. But it has a major drawback: After it has been mixed by the pharmacist, the preparation needs to be refrigerated. This poses some drawbacks during trips, particularly if your teen spends time camping.

■ Oral Medications

Systemic treatment for acne is the next step if topical care has failed. (One should not proceed to the use of oral medications if the failure is due to not using the medication. Although relatively safe, medications do have side effects. Treatment should not be undertaken simply because a teen is too undisciplined to use the topical medicines.) Some cases of acne are so severe that the physician will deem it necessary to bypass the topical route, or to augment it with oral medications from the very start of care.

Antibiotics. Oral medications are exactly the same antibiotics as the topical ones except more powerful. They are generally used once or twice a day. Erythromycin, clindamycin, tetracycline, and minocycline are the most common ones. Many physicians have stopped using tetracycline because it needs to be taken on an empty stomach. Since teens rarely pay careful attention to food intake, failure of tetracycline was frequent.

Minocycline is a tetracycline derivative and has replaced it in most cases because of its easier absorption. Taken in the generic form, its expense is reasonable, but it may have the side effect of upsetting the stomach. Newer versions are coated but so far these do not come generically and are quite expensive. One has to weigh cost in dealing with acne. Ampicillin, the standard for many children with ear infections, has also been used successfully. Some acne is so resistant to the standard antibiotics that the physician will have to resort to the newer, more expensive, cephalosporins to combat the skin infections. No matter which are used, they must be used for weeks, if not for months before one can see the full effects.

Females who are taking antibiotics for a long a time have to realize that they face an extra risk. As the antibiotic kills the skin bacteria it also alters the vaginal flora, and there is a high likelihood that they will develop a vaginal fungal infection. (See p. 458 in Part Five for further details.) Also, oral antibiotics must be avoided if there is any chance of pregnancy.

Accutane. The newest, and perhaps the most controversial prescription for acne is the use of an oral pill, retinoic acid in the form of isotretinoin, or Accutane. The use of this product is supposed to be limited to the patient whose acne is scarring and who has not responded to conventional topical or oral care. This treatment is not to be undertaken lightly and casually. I had one patient who went to a dermatologist for *one* lesion and, because she was a well-known actress, she was going to be put on Accutane! I yelled, and she wasn't.

When Accutane first was prescribed, patients were given three months of treatment with some requiring a second course; today most dermatologists feel that a five-to-six-month course is needed. Because a side effect of Accutane is to temporarily elevate cholesterol and triglyceride levels (see Chapter 5), monthly blood tests for both and for liver functions are standard. However, the major concern is the potential for birth defects if the patient becomes pregnant. A pregnancy test is usually mandatory before initiating treatment (even in the most protesting of virgins, many physicians will insist for legal reasons). Some will even insist that the patient be on the birth control pill for the time that they are on Accutane. So great is the concern about birth defects that each pill is packaged individually and has a pregnancy warning drawn on each foil. (It actually is a drawing, a pregnant woman with an X through her.)

A recent concern, borne out of anecdotal evidence and a well-publicized story of a young man who while on Accutane committed suicide, is the risk of depression while on this medication. No studies have shown that teens taking Accutane are more likely to be any more suicidal than the rest of their peer group. The argument that Accutane causes depression is impossible to prove or disprove because teens get depressed and teens get acne. But parents need to discuss their teen's mental health with the dermatologist if the acne problem is severe enough to warrant the use of Accutane. A teen with severe acne may well suffer from serious anxiety or depression because of it.

I have seen incredible success stories with this medication. Teens who refused to socialize, whose faces were scarred, and whose lives were miserable because of the constant daily care of their skin, had great results. Rarely will there be a need for more than a six-month prescription, and with proper use, the side effects of peeling, of dry lips, dry eyes and nasal passages can be tolerated. Teens should be reminded that sun, whether at the beach or on the ski slopes, is dangerous to unprotected skin when using Accutane. One of my patients wanted to go on Accutane so badly that he insisted on starting during his spring break. He was thrilled that the results were soon evident by May. Despite my cautions about the sun, he spent the summer at the beach and his sunburn was by far the worst I have ever seen!

Birth control pills. Teenagers on the low-androgenic birth control pill will generally see an improvement in acne. If a teen is under treatment for a disorder that necessitates going on the Pill, or if she decides it's appropriate to be on the Pill for birth control, she should reevaluate her skin care routine. She may be able to reduce the use of oral or topical treatments. This should be discussed

Acne Medication Chart	
Topical medications	Benzoyl peroxide: wash, soaps, cleaners, creams, gels
	Salicylic acids
	Retinoids
	Azelaic acid
	Sulfur
	Abrasives and drying agents
	Topical antibiotics
Oral medications	Antibiotics
	Isotretinoin (Accutane)
Surgical	Injections of steroids
	Abrasion

with a doctor. (Although the skin of a girl on the Pill *may* show some improvement, I don't use the Pill specifically for acne care.)

■ Surgery

Anytime that a needle or scalpel is involved, it is considered surgery. There are two reasons for surgical intervention: elimination or reduction of lesions or cosmetic repair of scars. Individual cysts can be injected with a diluted corticosteroid solution to help shrink the lesion. Repeated injections are sometimes needed. They can also be opened with a small scalpel.

Blackheads (open comedones) are also amenable to minor "surgery" by the dermatologist. If these are removed correctly, with proper care and instrumentation, and under sterile conditions, one can avert the progression of these to the scarring pustular lesions. (A little bit of alcohol and squeezing in front of the mirror does not constitute proper sterile technique.) Monthly, or even weekly visits to the dermatologist may be necessary to eliminate all blackheads.

A recent cosmetic trend has been to inject collagen into pitted areas. The depressed scarred areas are lifted by the collagen injections and the results can be quite attractive. However, any patient considering a collagen injection should first be tested for allergies to collagen. Laser is not currently a standard treatment. Dermabrasion is still used by some physicians but it is less popular today.

Allergic Skin Reactions and Dermatitis

Skin allergies are manifested as generalized throughout the body in the form of "hives" (urticaria), or more localized as a "contact" dermatitis. While teens' immune systems are no different than when they were children, their new lifestyle and variety of new things they encounter mean their skin reactions need to be considered separately. Think of your teen's exposure to chemicals in chemistry or biology class. She may find herself breaking out in a rash during a science experiment.

Hives

Urticarial reactions are commonly called *hives*, and they can occur all over the body. Sometimes it is easy to find the cause if the patient is on a medication such as an antibiotic. Other times it is impossible. Sometimes the attack may be brought on by cold weather. It will likely take a physician to decide the cause.

In most people attacks of hives are triggered by foods or by additives. I ask all my patients to write down everything they ate just before getting the rash. Strawberries that were eaten many times before without problem now trigger hives, but this determination can only be made if your teen has kept complete and unedited lists. If they are unaware of a food allergy and then exercise, this can make the reaction worse, as exercise seems to send the chemicals that cause the hives throughout the body much faster. One of my patients had so severe an allergic reaction (hives and faintness) that she bypassed me and went directly to the hospital. Later, we determined that she had eaten Chinese take-out before all the episodes, and we concluded that she was probably allergic to MSG. She also commented that she didn't feel bad immediately after the meal. In fact, she had gone to the gym! It was this combination of exercise following the allergic episode that triggered the severe problem.

Unfortunately, teens may take unprescribed medications or illicit drugs and not tell anyone. If a teen has an allergic rash, the trust between physician and teen is tested as the teen may not want his parents to know what he did. Or, he may not realize the relationship between the drug and the rash.

Generally we treat hives with antihistamines and perhaps with steroids regardless of the cause. Once the rash disappears and once the teen is no longer taking antihistamines, he should be tested by an allergist to determine what the cause might be.

Irritants Causing Allergic Reactions

Cosmetics. Cosmetics, including deodorants and perfumes, can cause allergic reactions. Adolescence is when colognes and perfumes, lipstick, mascara, hair dyes, and body lotions are used for the first time. Teens who are allergic to a product will show a rash wherever and whenever the cosmetics are used. Think of the obvious. If there is a rash under the armpit, an underarm deodorant is likely at fault. If there is a rash along the neckline, did she apply perfume there?

One patient had a rash under her breasts and along the sides where she had a stay in her bra to increase its support. She couldn't understand the rash until we put the bra on and showed all the contact points. Was it the laundry soap, the material, or the stays? To be sure, she would need to eliminate each. (In this case, it was eventually determined it was the detergent, and the family simply changed to another.) Anything that comes in contact with the skin is a potential cause for a rash.

Girls may want to buy "hypoallergenic" cosmetics and fragrance-free products if they are getting rashes, but that is not a guarantee. Basically, any product can cause an allergy and hypoallergenic products only make it less likely but not impossible to get a rash.

Jewelry. Jewelry in all price ranges can cause skin reactions; the usual culprit is nickel or copper content. The teen will have an itchy red eruption around the area where the jewelry is worn, and in extreme cases it may blister. Treatment consists of not wearing the jewelry and applying a topical steroid to halt the inflammation. Any metal, from earrings to a belt buckle to jewelry used in body piercing, can cause an allergic reaction. Hypoallergenic jewelry is recommended for pierced ears and any other type of body piercing.

Latex. Several of my patients have noted that they are allergic to latex, and that this has posed a problem with the use of condoms. (See Chapter 9 for a solution.) One also has to remember that latex is found in products other than condoms; for example, the tourniquet used in my office for taking blood is latex. Those who are allergic to it are often surprised at how many products contain it; they may encounter an allergen at a children's birthday party (the balloons) or when asked to help with the dishes (the rubber gloves).

Poison ivy. Teenagers who go to camps as counselors or as "seniors campers," increase the likelihood that they will get poison ivy each summer. Teens should be told that upon contact with the plant oil, they should immediately wash the area in an attempt to eliminate as much of it as possible. (Poison ivy can be spread by scratching, so be certain your teen knows not to touch it.) Calamine lotion is meant to make the lesions feel better; it is not a cure. Topical steroids of varying intensity are often prescribed for mild to moderate lesions. In severe cases, it may be necessary to start the teen on a course of oral steroids; a convenient dose package in decreasing doses is available by prescription. Anytime that one starts oral steroids, it is imperative that the dose be tapered and not stopped suddenly.

Eczema. When a child with eczema reaches adolescence, the eczema generally changes its appearance for reasons that are not understood. During the teen years, eczema tends to localize to specific areas and has a hard dry texture and appearance. The areas most often affected are the creases in front of the elbow and behind the knees. Teens will usually have a family history of eczema, and the lesions will come and go without explanation. Often they will have an associated allergic condition such as asthma or hay fever, but the eczema itself is not an "allergic" rash. Stress has not been proven to be a cause of eczema, though there is some suggestion that lesions *may* get worse under stress.

Nummular eczema. This type of eczema presents as coin-like lesions that may occur for the first time during puberty. When the lesion is scratched repeatedly, which some do habitually, the area becomes thick. Sometimes the eczema will be on the fingertips, and the patient will have peeling of his fingers.

Keratosis pilaris. Another variation of eczema is keratosis pilaris, in which the infection spreads beyond the hair follicle. The tendency for this type of eczema is inherited. Here the eruption is noticeable as small, white pus-filled areas. Thighs and upper arms are particularly prone to this and it be aggravated by scratching. The treatment involves using a mild lubricant. Sometimes topical steroids are prescribed; some physicians will use Retin-A.

Folliculitis

Folliculitis occurs quite frequently in adolescents and is a cosmetic issue. Folliculitis is an inflammation of the hair follicles, and it is due to either an infection or to physical or chemical irritation. Boys' faces and girls' legs are the common sites for the infection, and shaving is a primary cause. One will see redness and swelling of many small spots as each hair follicle is inflamed. If the infection stays in the epidermis and is treated properly, it will heal without scars. However, left unchecked it can go into the dermis with resulting scars. At that point pus oozes from the follicle. The most common infection is caused by staphylococcus that has become resistant to many common antibiotics. Although topical antibiotics may be used, the physician may have to prescribe newer oral antibiotics to deal with a large infection.

Teens usually cause this problem through aggressive shaving or waxing of the skin. Shaving is supposed to cut the hair at the base of the shaft as it leaves the skin. Hair is not supposed to be grabbed and plucked or the hair follicle may be left irritated. Teens who don't change razor blades often will use a single blade for weeks, allowing the blade to become pitted and "snag" hairs. Whether shaving the face or the legs, it is imperative to remember to change blades often.

Waxing, as inhumane as it sounds, requires placing hot wax on an area, smoothing a piece of cloth over it, then letting the wax and cloth cool and harden before yanking it off. Since waxing opens the pores, it is easy for an infection to set in. Once the sole province of women and their legs, waxing is now used on the "bikini" area, the upper lip, and even by boys on the chest and back. I hesitate to think of the pain, but I can attest to the folliculitis that occurs.

When folliculitis occurs in the beard area, the doctor needs to ascertain whether it is an infection due to bacteria or fungus, or whether it is caused by the hair turning in on itself (pseudofolliculitis barbae). This latter condition is common in individuals who have short, tight, curly hair, such as African-American males. The problem arises when the shaved hair curls into the skin causing an irritation. It is a reactive inflammation to the hair itself. Often the treatment requires the person to switch to an electric razor or to grow a beard. In some schools this is not an acceptable policy, so a medical solution may have to be offered. Barring this, the only other solution is to have the teen shave in a different fashion so that he does not cut the skin. The best way of shaving is to thoroughly hydrate the face, use a shaving gel, and shave the area, going with the grain, using a double-edge razor. The market has responded to the plight of African-American male's shaving by introducing specially made electric razors.

Impetigo

Impetigo and cellulitis are seen in teenagers if they ignore wounds. Parents usually attend to the slight cut sustained by a child, but teens rarely come to Mom and Dad now to share with them their latest cut, and sometimes there is no treatment. Impetigo is a bacterial infection that shows isolated pus-filled areas that are scattered; cellulitis, which involves confluent areas, is a spreading bacterial infection in the skin and the tissues beneath the skin that may show as bruising. Both can lead to significant complications and need to be aggressively treated. Oral antibiotics are the usual course unless the impetigo involves only a few lesions. If the impetigo is mild some physicians will treat with a topical antibiotic. There is an argument, however, that all impetigo should be treated with systemic antibiotics. Consult with your physician to decide.

Pityriasis Rosea

Pityriasis rosea is usually seen during the winter months, and although it is not proven, the suggestion is that it is due to a virus. In most cases there is a single lesion about one to three inches wide and located anywhere on the body but most commonly on the trunk. As it stands alone, it is hard to be sure what it is and often a mistaken diagnosis of ringworm is made. Within a few days the generalized rash gives the clue. A slightly red rash for Caucasians and a hyper-pigmented one for darker-complected patients will appear in lines that mimic a Christmas tree. Patients will complain of little except a mild itch and anxiety about the diagnosis. No treatment is necessary, though the patient needs a lot of reassurance, since the rash will last for about a month.

A correct diagnosis of pityriasis rosea is important because some fungal infections and secondary syphilis are just two of the diseases that may present similarly. The latter is, fortunately, rare in teens so one is usually left with a question of a fungal infection or pityriasis rosea.

Psoriasis

Psoriasis usually occurs initially during adolescence. This scaly, patchy disorder causes a great deal of anxiety and humiliation for most teens because it is quite visible. There is strong evidence that it may follow a streptococcal infection in patients who have a familial predisposition. The most common location is on the elbows and the knees. The anus, the belly button, the scalp, and the genitals are also potential sites. However, the teenager may never admit to these areas being involved. Since the sun's ultraviolet rays tend to heal the lesions, most patients do better in the summer months and worsen in the winter. Many have to take courses of topical steroids to get the disorder under control. Special light therapy is also used in an attempt to mimic the healing effects of the sun. A unique type of psoriasis is also associated with joint pains and swelling and psoriatic arthritis needs to be thought of in any patient with swollen joints.

Seborrheic Dermatitis (Dandruff)

Seborrheic dermatitis is a chronic disorder and has to be treated as such. We now understand that there is a fungal infection involved. Where the infant had "cradle cap," the adolescent has "dandruff." The white, yellowish scales will accumulate and shed, on their own or by scratching the area. The more the teen doesn't wash his scalp, the more dandruff will develop. The eyelashes and eyebrows are not spared, and by scratching these the same flaking will occur. Treatment now consists of lotions and shampoos, which contain the same medication used to treat the fungus of athlete's foot.

Fungal Skin Infections

Parents first encounter fungus when a baby gets diaper rash or thrush. After that, there is generally a long rest in dealing with these organisms until the pubertal years when we meet them again.

When doctors speak of fungal skin infections, we generally use the word "tinea" as part of the term. Hence, we have tinea pedis on the foot, tinea cruris in the groin, and tinea barbae on the face and beard. These are all seen in the teenager as well as two other common sites: the back and chest (tinea versicolor) and the body (tinea corporis). Scrapings of the area may be needed to confirm the diagnosis, but usually the clinical picture is fairly straightforward. It is a fungus and the treatment is antifungal medication.

Athlete's Foot

Athlete's foot is a misnomer. There is no need to be an athlete to get this fungal infection. The warm moist interiors of sneakers make the fungus quite at home as it invades the skin area between athletic and nonathletic toes alike. Being an athlete, however, makes for more sweat and, therefore, more of a possibility of getting infected. The floors in the locker room are often coated with the fungus and walking barefoot allows the fungus to spread. Some are lucky and will never get the fungus; a certain immune deficiency is present in those who pick it up.

Once infected it is hard to totally eradicate the fungus, and it may come back intermittently. Treatment involves allowing the foot to "breathe" and dry. Wider shoes, open-toed sandals, and topical applications of a fungal medication are standard. In severe cases the doctor may have to prescribe oral antifungal medication for the teen to take for several months.

"Jock Itch"

Tinea cruris is commonly referred to as "jock itch" but, again, you can be a couch potato and get it. Because humidity of the area is necessary to promote fungal growth, it is more common during the summer when teens hang out in wet bathing suits. Sweating adds to the humidity so that all athletic activities in the summer create a potential problem.

The fungus is often no different than the one on the foot and is often brought to the groin unintentionally. The individual with athlete's foot dries the foot with a towel and then dries his groin area. He has infected himself by using a wet towel to transfer the fungus. I tell all my patients who are prone to this infection that they either wipe downward or use two towels.

Most teens with this infection are uncomfortable because it is such a private place. They don't usually tell their parents until the infection and the itch are unbearable. By the time I see them, there is a half moon crescent of fungus infection surrounding the genitalia. By lifting the scrotum, one can see the irritation and speculate as to the discomfort. Girls are not absolved of the disorder, and they can get the fungus under their breasts. The irritation of a large breast rubbing against the chest is thoroughly uncomfortable. When the folds of skin are involved we refer to it as intertrigo, but it is still a tinea infection. Girls are also treated with topical antifungal creams or, in severe cases, with oral antifungal medications.

Nail Infections

Infections of the nails (onychomycosis) are difficult to treat and often require months of topical and oral antifungal antibiotics. These are often treated by dermatologists and diagnosis frequently requires scraping and culture of the infected area. Fungal infections of the nail are a risk of artificial fingernails.

"Ringworm"

When you tell a teenager that she has tinea corporis she nods and says okay. When you tell her that it is the same as "ringworm," she gasps. The only part of the name that is true is "ring," since the lesions are coin shaped. There is no "worm" to this, and it is the same fungus that can infect other areas of the body. One clue as to the diagnosis is the fact that tinea lesions have sharp, irregular edges with a flaky component. Transmission of ringworm is through contact (nonsexual). Ringworm is a fungus and therefore contagious and is treated with antifungal creams either topically or orally, depending on the amount of lesions.

Tinea Versicolor

Tinea versicolor is a fungus that normally is on the skin but with heat and sweating it becomes problematic. Teens who are very active in summer sports are particularly prone to it. With this fungus, the person will have pigmented oval-shaped circles (they can be white or brown) approximately a half-inch long, usually on the shoulders, back, and chest. If a teen has been in the sun these spots really stand out against the tanned skin, since each lesion serves as a sunscreen and therefore the affected area is less pigmented and clearly visible. Commonly, the doctor will prescribe a lotion containing selenium sulfide or an antifungal cream to be applied daily for several weeks. If stopped too soon, the lesions will recur. Even after treatment the different colored area will remain until more sun exposure evens out the skin color.

Viral Skin Infections

Apart from sexually transmitted diseases (see Chapter 10), there are several viral lesions of the skin that affect teenagers. They are common in this age group and basically fall into three categories: warts, herpes simplex, and herpes zoster. Sometimes the distribution and site of the lesions make the diagnosis easy, but there are times when the only way of confirming is with a biopsy and a referral to a dermatologist.

Warts

Warts are due to viral invasion of the epidermal layer and are benign. As with most viral infections, they eventually go away but it may take months or years. Most teens will want these unattractive bumps eliminated, but the fact that it can hurt to remove them usually delays treatment. All they need to hear is "cut it off" or "burn it off," and the wart becomes more attractive. But they'll be more interested in getting rid of it once they find out they can spread warts to themselves or others through scratching.

■ Common Warts

Looking at warts under magnification is like looking at craggy rocks. They come in all forms and shapes, and they tend to be harder than the surrounding tissue. The simplest wart is the verruca vulgaris or the "common wart." Since the point of treatment is to cut the wart down to the base, the doctor can literally remove it with a scalpel. The wart can also be removed using electrical cautery, which "burns" off the wart, or by using liquid nitrogen to "freeze" it off. All three can leave scars. Milder abrasive agents such as salicylic acid (an aspirin derivative) can also be used by the doctor, but these take longer. Over-the-counter versions of these are sold either in a liquid or in small pads. The patient has to apply the medication himself and keep doing so until the wart is removed. This is clearly cheaper but requires patience on the part of the teen and parents.

Some warts are flat, and they are dealt with in a different way. Because of the visibility of the flat wart on the face and extremities one has to be aware of the potential for scarring. Moreover, these do not respond easily to the previous treatment. Instead, a slower approach with Retin-A–type creams may be used. You should not try over-the-counter wart removers on these; they are best left to the dermatologist.

■ Plantar Warts

Many times adolescents will come in for a physical and parenthetically mention they have "something on their foot." Plantar warts are found specifically on the pressure points of the foot and differ from common warts in that they grow inward. They may be painful and calloused and, depending on whether or not the teenager has picked at them, are either solitary lesions or clumps of many.

Looked at carefully, there is a well-organized surface pattern to the wart, as opposed to a callus formation or corn. The problem is not what to do but when to do it. If the wart is removed, it will affect walking for a while and can interfere with their academic, sports, or social life. All of the treatments available for the common wart apply to the plantar wart.

Warts in the genital area are discussed in Chapter 10, "Sexually Transmitted Diseases."

Herpes Simplex Virus

"Cold sores" and "fever blisters" are in fact an infection of herpes simplex virus (HSV) Type I; it is more completely discussed in Chapter 10. Once a person is infected with this virus, it lies dormant in the body, waiting for an opportune moment to express itself. Sun, trauma to the area, menstruation, and perhaps stress and fatigue are all triggers that produce lesions of the herpes simplex virus. HSV-1 can affect any part of the body, but the lip is the most frequent site.

This is a contagious lesion and can be spread by contact. (It is reassuring to know that the virus of the lip is less virulent and less likely to express itself than the one in the genitalia.) From the first signs (sometimes a tingling sensation) it takes several days before the painful, small, burning blisters break out. As with any viral infection, the patient may have a low-grade fever and local swelling of the lymph glands. The initial sores may last for a few weeks before they begin to dry up and disappear. But while the blisters heal, the virus continues to reside in the nerve root of the area, waiting to flare up again. The subsequent lesions are usually less severe, but they keep coming back.

Since the lesions are located in the epidermis, scarring is unlikely. Because of the burning, some patients will keep touching the area and incur a bacterial infection on the site. Once that happens, impetigo may occur, and this may lead to a scar. The lesson: leave it alone. With the advent of antiviral drugs, it is now possible to treat mouth lesions aggressively. At the first sign of recurrence, taking either Acyclovir or one of its derivatives, Valtrex or Famvir, will help. You might want to have an extra prescription on hand. This way you or your teen needn't worry about reaching the doctor if a recurrence happens on a weekend. Patients soon learn to recognize the tingling feeling in the area that precedes the first small blister.

Lesions on the skin can be difficult to diagnose. A biopsy or a trained eye is needed to properly identify the cause. If there is a history of oral labial herpes or "fever blisters," then it is a bit easier to deduce that the skin lesions may be HSV.

In some patients the lesions will recur so frequently that a six-month course of antiviral medications is prescribed. Before undertaking so definitive and expensive a course, it is important that a dermatologist confirms the diagnosis. When in doubt the only way of confirming that the lesions are HSV is with an analysis or culture of the fluid in the blister.

"Shingles" (Herpes Zoster or Varicella)

Herpes zoster or "shingles" is the late manifestation of the same virus that causes chickenpox. This can occur among teenagers. There is an intense burning sensation along the nerve route, and the small blisters that appear neatly clustered along the path of the nerve confirm the diagnosis. As an example, if the right side of the chest is involved, the lesions will stop just at the breastplate since the other side is served by a different nerve. It is this sharply demarcated line that aids in the diagnosis of "shingles." Patients tend to be quite ill with fever and headache and are uncomfortable to the point where pain medication is prescribed. If your teen is complaining of pain from shingles and doesn't want to go to school, believe him. As with HSV, antiviral medication is started but in higher doses and for a longer period of time. All the precautions one uses with chickenpox should be followed.

Moles and Spots

All moles and freckles represent lesions that have extra pigment. The one exception is the "halo" nevus, in which pigment is lost. Most moles or freckles are benign. Some patients have extensive spots all over their backs and bodies. Not only is it hard for them to see or remember what they first looked like, it may be hard for most doctors to catalog them and be sure of their size and position and color. In such cases, it is worthwhile seeing a dermatologist, who will photograph the spots and follow them at regular intervals for comparison.

Dermatologists classify moles, or *nevi*, by appearance and by where they are located in the skin layers. We don't need to go into detail except to say that a good rule of thumb is that any skin area that is changing or growing needs to be evaluated. When in doubt, the physician should remove the mole and send it for a biopsy.

While I was a resident, one of my interns noted a spot on his back that looked quite innocent. He also complained of a plantar wart. He decided that he would have one or the other removed but not both because he thought it was too much cutting. As is the case with many doctors, he managed to convince one of the surgeons who passed by the emergency room to look at both and remove one. It was decided he needed to walk so the plantar wart stayed and the back lesion was removed, rather casually with the idea that this was a cosmetic decision. A week later the pathologist called with alarming news. The "innocent lesion" turned out to be a malignant melanoma, a complex cancer of the skin. The young intern's life was saved because of the plantar wart. This particular intern had been in Africa with the Peace Corps and was fair-skinned. The amount of sun he had been exposed to was considerable, but this never occurred to anyone until after the diagnosis.

The Importance of Sunscreens

When they are small, we take responsibility for putting sunscreens on our children. Now, in adolescence, they need to take on this responsibility for themselves.

We have finally come to the realization that the dark sexy tan may look great, but it causes damage to the skin. Teenagers are particularly at risk because many spend a great deal of time in the sun. Many also look on sunscreens as something to be avoided at all costs. They are wrong! Sunscreens are effective and necessary.

Some of the ultraviolet rays of the sun will damage the skin. Make sure your sunscreen has some protection against UVA-II. The products on the market contain chemicals that absorb the UV light waves or block their path to the skin by coating it with a layer of zinc oxide. In order to have some uniformity, a standard sun protection factor (SPF) has been created. The higher the SPF the longer it takes to produce a sunburn, and, therefore, the more protection the compound affords. What is not clear from the labels are the variables—the amount of humidity, heat, and wind—that can affect the product's performance.

If you can, get your teen to put sunscreen on before leaving the house. Also tell him to reapply after excessive sweating or swimming. A major unanswered question is whether sunscreens protect against skin cancer. There is no definitive study but at present the current feeling is that they do offer some protection if used appropriately.

As for the ever-present baseball cap on some male teens' heads—nothing better in the world. See if your daughter won't throw one on, too.

The tanning salon is another sun-related issue to address with your teen. Despite all the warnings about the dangers of the sun, people still go to a salon and *pay* to get a damaging suntan. The idea is to avoid "tan lines" and to "look gorgeous." As stupid as this sounds, remember that teenagers don't believe that bad things will happen to them. Why else would they take up smoking? Is it so much of a difference to smoke in the face of overwhelming evidence of cancer from smoking than to deliberately tan? Simply put, forbid your teen from going to these salons and make it clear that this is a strong position on your part. Treat this as seriously as you would any other "risk-taking behavior" on the part of the teen.

Tattoos and Piercings

Tattoos and piercings have become part of the teenager's quest for individuality. I have patients who have tattooed every conceivable part of their body. One has a tattoo of a mongoose and a python that represents the struggle of life and death that covers her entire back. Frankly it is an exceptional work of art, although I prefer art on walls.

Kids from all walks of life are getting small hearts, flowers, and intricate Asian and mythical symbols etched onto their bodies. Many choose to place it in a private location in some misconceived belief that parents will not notice it. One clever teenage girl claimed that the design on the small of her back was "temporary," and she kept getting it redone so that it would look good. She managed to fool her mother for a few months with this deception.

As for the "why" of tattoos and piercings, every teen will argue that these measures are personal expressions. They view it as a way of saying something unique about who they are. One patient, who is interested in film, had a strip of film tattooed on his back with the intention of filling in the frames with important people in his life as he aged. Another had an eagle drawn on her arm when she was discharged from the hospital; she told me it represented her sense of freedom. Others just think it is "cool" to have a rose above the breast or an anchor near the pubic area. It is hard to convince the teen that they are changing and the tattoo that represents them today may not be an expression of who they will eventually become.

What exactly is a tattoo? By introducing small particles of ink into the dermal layer you slowly produce a picture that is the ultimate in George Seurat's style of *pointillism,* in which the artist used thousands of dots to form a picture. But since our bodies are designed to reject foreign particles, why doesn't the dermal layer reject these foreign ink pieces? Ordinarily, the immune system's macrophages go around gulping foreign debris. The problem with the tattoo ink is that the pieces are too big for the macrophage; it can't eat them. So the tattoo artist makes thousands of small punctures (with sophisticated probes) and drops ink into the skin. The macrophage is powerless.

Every teenager with a tattoo has told me that they got it from a "professional" who used a "sterile technique." A recent trend among tattoo artists is to use disposable needles that they deliberately show in the sterile package to the client. This helps, but there are still reports about Hepatitis C (see p. 423) associated with tattoos. Some physicians routinely check for the Hepatitis C virus in newly tattooed patients. In addition, the concern about a needle contaminated with HIV continues to exist.

Tattoos are illegal in some states, but the determined teen will still find a way of doing it. The receiver of the homemade tattoo often will be the one that gets infected with bacteria (see "Impetigo," p. 130).

Before teens get a tattoo they have to remember that this is a lifelong commitment. Teens need to be reminded that BEATRICE will always be on their arm. Or that attractive swan that encircles your navel may not look great as you get older and the wings begin to fall and stretch. Regretfully, teenagers are not always going to think of the future. Tattoos are cool, and they have lots of friends who are doing it, so what's the problem?

Tattoo Removal

If you awake on Sunday morning to see your teen with a new adornment that is permanent, your response may be to call the doctor. Tattoos are much harder to get off than to put on, and removal is infinitely more expensive. This now becomes a medical procedure that could qualify as surgery. In previous generations, all we had was salabrasion, in which salt was rubbed on the tattoo until it scarred and lightened it. That was the "state of the art" when I was in the Navy in 1971, and a young corpsman would come in after shore leave begging to remove NANCY from his arm. Today the laser beam has changed the process. With a special laser, not just your run-of-the-mill laser, but a "Q-switched YAG laser," the dermatologist can direct the beam onto the dermal layer and slowly burst the ink particles into something more digestible for the body to remove as foreign matter. Each treatment lasts for 30 to 45 minutes and can cost hundreds of dollars. The size of the tattoo and the patient's tolerance for the slight burning sensation will determine the number of treatments. Count on several.

If your tattoo artist was prone to using blue or black inks, then you have a good chance that with enough treatments your tattoo may be removed without scars. Orange and purple also seem to remove well. However, if your adolescent has a colorful green or yellow tattoo, the laser will not do as well in removing these inks.

If you aren't going to be happy if your teen comes home with a tattoo, make this clear to your teen now. I know this is hardly something that parents imagine their teens doing. But preventive care with teens requires that you think of every possibility, even the remote ones. If you don't talk to your teen ahead of time, any discussion may be too late.

Piercings

The reason why a teen would endure the pain of a pierced nipple or tongue escapes most parents. And to pay money for it only adds to the confusion. When I ask patients—even those from "very good families"—to say "ah," I frequently find barbells sticking out of their tongues. One patient had his eyebrow pierced, and it got infected. It became so swollen that no matter how much he twisted the ends, he was unable to get it out, and I finally had to cut it. (For my office I have acquired cutting pliers specifically for removing these bars after they cause an infection or before a parent loses sanity. Sometimes I feel like a wire-cutting electrician!)

Teens argue that piercing is sexy and an expression of individuality. Tongue piercing is supposed to intensify sexual pleasure and the genital pierces are meant to evoke erotic images and also add to sexual pleasure. The belly button has almost become *passé* as a fashion statement, and many parents see it as a lesser evil. Girls currently wear low-waisted pants and skirts so that the belly button and its piercing deliberately show.

There is no medical reason not to get piercings other than the fact that they can get infected. Once these pierced parts get infected, pus will develop and scar tissue will form. One rarely worries about scars on the tongue after a removed barbell; however, the same casual concern should not prevail on the face, the breasts, or the genitals. I have seen scars in all these places and any sense of the erotic is quickly gone. A common place for infection is the top portion of the ear, where there is cartilage and little blood supply. I have had to remove many earrings from here because the infection will not heal as long as the foreign body (the earring) is present. I have seen piercings made of pieces of wood, glass, and small barbells. I even have a boy who had his genitalia pierced. He had a "Prince Albert," a ring through the urethral opening. When he eventually removes this ring, he will have two streams of urine—one through his natural urethra and one through the hole left by the ring. He has no intention of removing the ring since he sees it as beautiful. I have tried in vain to persuade him that he is wrong. I keep trying.

In some patients, even the most simplistic procedure on the earlobe may cause a large scar as the tissue grows over. Some patients develop keloids (large overgrown scars that are obvious and difficult to treat) every time they have any type of wound. If your teen has a keloid from a long-ago injury, be sure to warn her that a piercing may eventually become a keloid. If it is on the face, a keloid can be disfiguring.

Sometimes teens use piercing and tattoos as a way of making a statement about their feelings. The role of the adult here is to try to understand their messages so we can appreciate what is going on in their lives and try to prevent them from having to continue these types of measures in expressing themselves. I have had several kids heavily into the drug scene using the tattoos and body piercing as identification with a group. When they got clean and sober, they removed the hardware. I do not mean that each kid with a tattoo or a piercing is into drugs. But all it does is raise suspicion and should be used to promote conversation.

Again, a bit of planning is in order. If you and your spouse make it clear that piercing is not acceptable, then you stand a better chance of preventing it. Tell kids that piercing hurts, that it leaves permanent holes, and that you do not consider it something that, as parents, you can allow. Tell them in no uncertain terms that you disapprove *before* they get it done. You might also discuss an appropriate age before which your teenagers cannot get pierced. Perhaps by then they will have thought better of it.

Chapter 7

Teens and Sports:
Sports-Related Injuries

S ports are an integral part of teenagers' lives, and the advantages of physical activity far outweigh the downside of potential injury. However, compared to adults, adolescents engaged in sports are at a disadvantage. At twelve, an adolescent's eye-hand coordination is still developing. Even for older adolescents, muscle development is not complete; the limbs are growing faster than the trunk of the body, making coordination difficult; and the judgment process is not yet mature because teens' brains are not yet fully developed—sometimes the bravado of succeeding in sports and impressing everyone overtakes the good judgment to sit out a game because of an injury. In addition, throughout puberty the bones are fragile since they still have cartilage at the growth plates.

As long as we maintain an attitude that competition is fun, that kids should enjoy participating in sports, and that parents are there for support, the sense of confidence and pride that can be instilled is priceless. Healthy bodies do, indeed, bring about sound minds. However, if sports are all about winning and parents forget who is actually wearing the sports equipment, then we have created a situation that is guaranteed to cause trouble. The recent trend of parents becoming overly involved in kids' sports has received national attention with news reports about irate parents verbally and physically assaulting coaches. The pressure to win at all costs extracts a huge toll on teenagers and their families.

Some nonathletic parents may feel out of place if their teen plays a sport that they don't understand. As a parent all you need to do is show up for the games and give support. Who knows? You may even get to understand and appreciate the subtleties of the game. Sports should be a healthy outlet and parents need to be there to show approval and interest. The adolescent engaged in sports is channeling a tremendous amount of physical energy into a leap, a throw, a swim, or a great landing. That natural energy exists in all teens and it needs an outlet; sports are a healthy avenue for that.

Even if your greatest physical exertion during adolescence involved moving the black queen in a chess tournament, you can still make a great contribution to your child's good health by encouraging physical activity and being supportive. The soccer mom's or dad's role doesn't end at the Pee Wee league. Even if all you do is drive home several sweaty, muddy sixteen-year-olds who just finished a game, this continued support is valuable. Asking your teen to explain the game and its rules shows your interest, and few teens will fail to glow at the chance to educate an interested parent.

You may want to extend your interest and encouragement to include participating in an activity together. Whether it's taking up jogging for the first time so that the two of you can do it together, signing her up for the tennis lessons she wants to take, or attending soccer games and exhibiting good sportsmanship as you cheer on the team, your interest and encouragement can make the difference in whether or not your teen lives life as a couch potato or understands the importance of exercising regularly.

In addition to building strong muscles and burning calories, participating in exercise releases the same "feel good" neurotransmitters (serotonin and dopamine) in the brain that we release with any pleasurable activity. At a time when parents are so worried about drugs, it is far preferable for teens to feel the "runner's high" of dopamine than to seek that high from illicit drugs. One doesn't have to be on an organized team for that feeling; one simply has to move the body from point A to point B. Help your teen learn to enjoy doing just that.

The Importance of the Physical Exam

We've all read of the teen athlete who died on the basketball court or football field because no one knew he had a heart condition. Most schools mandate that teenagers visit a physician for clearance before allowing participation in a sport. In fact your teen's annual examination asks if the student is allowed full activity or not. However, for a student who is on a varsity sport, or for one who is participating in an activity with specialized risk (deep sea diving, for example), it is important that a more thorough examination be performed. Both the annual examination form and the sports clearance form are legal documents and should be treated as such. Answer the questions fully. Asking the doctor to "just fill it out" so the teen can play undermines the purpose of this rule: to protect your child.

One of the critical parts of the examination is assessing cardiovascular function. Benign heart murmurs are often detected in teenagers, and these need to be noted but they are not necessarily reasons for disqualification. Blood pressure in the anxious teen may be elevated and should be repeated at the end of the visit. Hopefully the teen will have calmed down by then and will have normal pressure. Some physicians insist that an electrocardiogram be done on every teen who is going to play sports. Although not a mandate, it is not a bad idea and is up to the discretion of your physician.

If your teen has had antecedent cardiac surgery, or if there is a heart murmur noted that was not previously identified, the teen should be seen by a cardiologist prior to clearance. Mild abnormalities of heart rate or a few extra heartbeats do not always pose a problem. However, if the athlete has a history of a rapid heartbeat while resting or feels many skipped beats, then a cardiologist is needed. Some rare but lethal conditions may present with fainting episodes, and these patients, too, need extra attention during the sports evaluation.

Reasons for disqualification for a sport are rare, but they do occur. Teens with heart disease, with liver abnormalities, with asthma, or with a missing paired organ (an eye for example) may not participate in some sports. There are guidelines in all states that serve the physician in making a judgment about the teenager. At the annual physical, a state health form containing disqualification reasons for contact and noncontact sports allows the physician an opportunity to review these guidelines. In New York, for example, growth retardation disqualifies a teen from participating in a contact sport, but not a noncontact sport. Likewise, the absence of an eye is reason to prevent a contact sport. Check with your physician and the local school authorities to verify your teen's ability to participate. In general, the risk of injury increases with a contact sport even though the athlete may not physically come into contact with another player. For example, gymnastics is classified as a contact sport because of the tumbling and falling that is integral to the sport. The following is a list of the types of sports based on the amount of contact or collisions.

Types of Sports		
Contact Sports or Impact	**Limited Contact**	**No Contact**
Basketball	Baseball	Aerobic dancing
Boxing	Bicycling	Archery
Football	Diving	Badminton
Hockey: field and ice	Field events	Fencing
Martial arts: karate	Gymnastics	Field sports: e.g., shot put
Lacrosse	Horseback riding	Golf
Rodeo	Skating: ice and Rollerblade	Riflery
Rugby	Skiing	Running
Soccer	Softball	Swimming
Wrestling	Squash	Table tennis
	Volleyball	Tennis
		Track
		Weight lifting

The Importance of Nutrition

All athletes place extra demands on their bodies. Teenagers, whose height and weight are constantly changing, need to match their diet to their other changing physical needs. (For an overview of nutrition and teenagers, see Chapter 5.)

Most athletes store energy for sports by eating more. Athletes have to eat enough before an event so that energy is readily available for the demands of the sport. Energy is produced when glucose is released into the bloodstream. Digestion transforms all food into glucose, but different foods break down at different rates. As an example, pure table sugar breaks down rapidly and gives an immediate rise in energy, but the release falls equally quickly as insulin is stimulated in response. Rice and pasta break down more slowly and provide a longer steadier release of glucose. A "glycemic index" identifies which foods convert rapidly into glucose (high glycemic index) and which convert slowly (low index). An athlete needs to have a steady release of glucose during an event in order to maintain adequate energy levels and hence needs foods with a low index *before* the event and foods with a high index after the activity. (Also refer to Chapter 5, "Teens, Nutrition, and Eating Disorders.")

This is the basis for "carbo loading"—eating a lot of carbohydrates prior to a sporting event. A meal high in complex starches (50 percent of total calories) with about 15 percent of protein is recommended. The use of pasta or rice or lentils makes the equation easy to attain. Teens should allow two to three hours for digestion before a competition. Fat in this meal should be minimal, as fat will only delay gastric emptying and cause problems during the event; lastly, it should be low in salt to prevent fluid retention. People who attempt rigorous sports without properly adhering to good nutrition are expecting their bodies to perform without proper fuel. The result may well be a collapse on the field.

Water is critical in all sports, but the timing is also important. A teen should drink 16 ounces of water two hours before exercise and another 10 to 15 ounces of water fifteen minutes before a running sport. Add 6 to 12 ounces for every twenty minutes of participation. The football or soccer player will need to drink every 45 minutes, especially on a hot day. Some of the newer flavored sports drinks are acceptable but be sure to avoid those that contain caffeine, as this promotes increased heart rate, diarrhea, and forces one to urinate more often.

Supplements in Sports

One of the few supplements that may be useful are vitamins and minerals, particularly for the female athlete who may need additional iron. If a female athlete is on a diet that is iron-poor and she is menstruating normally, it will take very little time for her to develop an iron-deficiency anemia. Periodic checks of hemoglobin are in order to assure that she is not too low in her iron stores. For other information on vitamins see Chapter 5, "Teens, Nutrition, and Eating Disorders."

Other supplements are inappropriate. Yet with the level of competition increasing in high school, some coaches and parents are sending a message to teenagers that winning is all-important. This trend is hurting our teens and sports, and it encourages the use of supplements that are unhealthy.

One example of inappropriate and dangerous supplement use is the use of steroids. Male hormones or anabolic steroids increase muscle mass but the price paid is dramatic. Fluid retention, elevated glucose loads, suppression of normal testicular function, breast enlargement in males, and personality changes (aggressiveness) are all side effects. In females who take testosterone, breasts diminish and excess muscle mass develops. Some of the products, especially oral steroids, can cause liver problems. The teenager, impetuous and impatient to get a bigger, stronger body, may foolishly take oral androgens and place himself at greater risk. Yet even though most people realize the danger of these steroids, there is still a prevailing notion that *some* anabolic steroids are acceptable. Professional athletes take "nutritional" supplements that contain milder androgens. My office was deluged with requests from teens to take an over-the-counter natural male hormone, androstenedione, when two famous baseball stars revealed they were taking them. Androstenedione is secreted by the adrenal gland and has male hormonal properties. Since "more" is better in the minds of teenagers, it would stand to reason that they would be attracted to this quick method of building up their muscles. Why wait for your own testosterone to work when you can buy some at the store? The fact that androstenedione is "natural" has also contributed to its popularity. It is banned in the Olympics, and it should be banned everywhere. The adolescent needs to go through puberty with the proper amount of hormones dictated by nature. The addition of androstenedione will only accelerate and ultimately shorten puberty in the male; in the female it will cause virilization. Moreover, anytime there is an outside source of testosterone, the natural production will fall and testicular shrinkage in the male may ensue.

The second "natural" product that has recently been in the news is creatine or creatine kinase. This is a combination of three amino acids that is believed to increase muscle mass if taken before an event. It is normally found in the meats we eat and can actually be good for you. However, the problem is that powdered creatine is given in doses that far exceed what we would consume daily. No one knows what the long-term effects are on growing muscles. Since we don't know, we can't accept it as safe for teenagers. Regretfully, the teen mindset works in the opposite way. Since you don't know that it is bad for you, it may actually be okay to use it. Sales of this product have skyrocketed since prominent athletes have admitted taking it. Along with "andro" and creatine, we now have DHEA-S. This, despite its promises, should be avoided. (See "The Female Reproductive System" section of Part Five, "The Adolescent, Head to Toe," for the effects of DHEA-S on females.) The side effects are the same as androstenedione.

"Fat-burning" products also abound in health stores. These are touted as a quick fix for the problem of increased weight. Most contain ephedra, which is a first cousin to epinephrine or adrenaline. It is a stimulant that increases blood pressure, heart rate, and can cause insomnia. Some of the fat burners contain a "natural" thyroid extract, and this, too, can cause thyroid dysfunction if taken without monitoring. Use of diuretics and caffeine to lose weight can cause potentially dangerous low blood pressure during an event.

Finally, some athletes don't understand that illegal drugs can impair performance. Despite all of the warnings about the dangers of marijuana, many teens still believe that they can perform as well if not better while on pot. Until they quit and realize the difference, it is hard to convince them otherwise. (See Part Four, "Teen Substance Abuse.")

Body Types and Their Effect on Sports Participation

Some sports, such as gymnastics or track require, a lean body, and the teenager who chooses such a sport has to be monitored for growth and for the development of eating problems. Female gymnasts, for example, have been pushed toward a prepubescent body type that can more easily perform certain moves. The wrestler whose coach wants him to wrestle at a lower weight level also faces the need to lose weight. Weight loss for a sport should be undertaken carefully and only with supervision. Parents and coaches need to be realistic about what is possible and healthy, as eating disorders are a frequent outcome of an emphasis on maintaining a specific weight.

The other side of the equation is the sport that demands a heavier body. The coach, the teenager, or even the parents may feel that more mass is needed to compete. This weight increase has to be monitored to ensure that the result is an increase in the amount of muscle mass and not in the percentage of body fat.

A 200-pound teen who gains weight quickly may become obese, and does not have the same body type as the 200-pound muscled athlete who works out. Teens going through early puberty *cannot* attain large muscle mass simply

---

Sports That May Require Weight Loss

Dancing
Track; cross country
Gymnastics
Ice skating; figure skating
Wrestling
Swimming
Tennis
Cheerleading
Basketball: for some positions

because they don't have enough testosterone. Without testosterone they cannot get large muscle mass, only fat.

> **Douglas was growing rapidly** *and it was soon apparent that he would be close to six feet tall and weigh over 250 pounds by his second year of high school. This made him an ideal candidate for the position of tackle on the varsity football team. Shy and reserved, he welcomed the attention that he was getting. As a "down lineman" he was hard to budge at that weight, and the coach was pleased with his body. However, at sixteen, Douglas had lots of fat and little in the way of muscle. Despite objections on my part, he gained more weight, and by his senior year he had reached close to 300 pounds! He was told that he was being "recruited" for college ball, but he never reached beyond six feet and his skills would never take him to the professional ranks. In college, he "tore his knee" and he gained even more weight. He spent the next four years trying to lose all the fat he had gained for football while in high school.*

If your teen is into sports that require weight gain to participate, check with your physician since unmonitored gains may increase blood pressure, strain the heart, and in some, put excessive stress on the hips. Ultimately, weight is a lot harder to lose than it is to put on.

Suiting Up Properly

Whether it's selecting the right ski length or racquet size, or fitting a mouth guard, take the equipment preparation for a sport as seriously as you did the choice of the proper car seat when your teen was an infant. The principles are the same—good quality equipment that fits properly will increase the likelihood that your teen will be protected. Remember that your teen's continued

---

Sports That May Require Weight Gain

Wrestling: to go up in weight class
Weight lifting
Football: for some positions
Basketball: for some positions

growth may require new equipment more frequently, particularly with skates and skis.

Shoes should also be checked regularly because of the astounding growth rate during these years. Even if shoes fit, they must be checked for wear. The purpose of shoes is to provide support and cushioning for the pounding involved in running, jumping, and landing. New shoes will provide support for the foot, but in time, the comfortable shoe that you can slip on without untying provides little more than warmth! If the bottom of the shoe is worn, or the edges of the heels uneven, it is time to invest in a new pair. This is true for any athlete, but in the teenager it is critical that the shoes be constantly evaluated.

Warm-ups for Sports

Teenagers who go out and play without a warm-up put their bodies at risk for muscle and ligament injury. Not only are teen bodies not symmetrical (see Chapter 2 on how the body grows in spurts), but they have less muscle mass than adults. Hence, their muscles need even more stretching in order to withstand the strain of a sporting event. It is crucial that teens learn to warm up and stretch before participating in a sport.

There are standard exercises that all athletes should do and they are outlined by the American Academy of Pediatrics (www.aap.org) and by the American Academy of Orthopedic Surgeons (www.sportsmed.org). Their web sites are ideal sources for pamphlets and information. Tell your teen about them.

General Exercises: 3–5 Minutes before Most Sports
1. Jumping jacks
2. Stationary cycling
3. Running in place
4. Stretch muscles slowly and hold stretch for 5 seconds; repeat 3–5 times. See below for some sample exercises.

Stretching Exercises for Legs and Abdominal Muscles
Seated Exercises
1. **Seat straddle lotus.** Place the soles of the feet together and drop the knees to the floor. Push down on the knees with the elbows and lean forward while trying to bring the chin to the feet.
2. **Seat side straddle.** Spread the legs apart in a "V" and try to place both hands on one ankle, while bringing the chin to the knee.

(Many teens have "tight hamstrings" and cannot touch their toes; this is a great exercise for stretching the hamstrings.)

3. **Seat stretch.** Hold legs together and bring your hands to your ankles while touching the head to the knees.

Prone Exercises

1. **Lying quad stretch.** This exercise helps strengthen the front thigh muscles (the quadriceps). Lie on your back with one leg straight on the ground and the other leg turned in at the hip with the knee rotated to touch the other knee and the leg at a 90 degree angle. Press the knee to the floor and hold for 5 seconds.
2. **Knees to chest.** Lie on back with knees bent. Grasp the top of the knees and pull them up to the armpit area.

Standing Exercises

1. **Forward lunge.** The person looks like a fencer lunging with the back leg straight out while the front leg is bent at a right angle. Lunge forward on the bent leg and feel the stretch on that side's groin. Change positions after five seconds.
2. **Side lunge.** Stand with legs apart, back straight, and bend the left knee and stretch to that side. Hold for 5 seconds. Repeat on the other side.
3. **Crossover.** Cross your legs but keep the feet close together. With the legs kept straight, touch your toes.
4. **Standing quad stretch.** While standing, pull one foot to the buttocks and hold.

Done properly these will only take a few minutes and are worth the effort. To loosen the leg muscles, athletes in training should do these at home. Check with your trainer or physician to make sure that you are not overdoing it or that there are no contraindications to the exercises.

Weight Lifting

Sometimes teens lift weights just to build up their bodies; more often, weight training is undertaken in preparation for a team sport. My office receives many calls from parents who have concerns about their teens' weight lifting. They fear that they will hurt themselves, and they want some reassurance that the program undertaken is safe. There is nothing wrong with teenagers training with weights as long as certain rules are followed and there is a clear understanding of what is expected from the training.

The first myth to dispel is that weight lifting will stunt growth. It is important to remember that people in the weight lifting world may be secretly taking anabolic steroids, which affect growth. Teens who take these in an effort to build up muscle may accelerate muscle development but pay the price of shortening the pubertal growth period. As long as adolescents keep away from these drugs, have reasonable expectations, and use proper techniques, it is safe for them to "lift."

Understanding the terms is also helpful: *Weight lifting* is self-explanatory but vague. *Weight training* on the other hand, is meant to increase muscle mass. *Strength training* is meant to increase strength. Weight training is a cause of concern for the teen. If a teen wants to weight train, there must be sufficient testosterone to allow the muscle to bulk. If there isn't, he could lift all day and all he will do is lose weight and tire out and possibly damage his muscles, but he will not increase his muscle mass. Yet increasing his muscle mass may be the very reason he is lifting. In "power lifting," the idea is to do a few repetitions of very heavy weights. Such a lifter would lift 50 pounds or 100 pounds a couple of times and stop. But because the teen's bones are not fused and his muscles are normally underdeveloped, this can be potentially dangerous.

Strength training, on the other hand, is designed to increase strength; the lifter does many reps of a smaller weight. The overall weight lifted may be the same (3 reps of 100 pounds and 12 reps of 25 pounds both come out to 300 pounds lifted), but the strength training will make the muscles stronger and place less strain on the body. Teens are less likely to hurt their ligaments and muscles with the lower weight. In fact, it makes more sense to train this way for any sport since the injury factor is reduced both during the training and, because of the resulting stronger muscles, during the sport. A good guideline to follow is to do 15 repetitions of a particular weight. If one cannot do a set of 15, then the weight is too high for that exercise and the teen should use a lower weight.

Free weights are cheaper and more portable but they pose a problem. With free weights one can lift improperly and use the wrong muscles. For example, to do a two-hand curl with free weights one could swing the pelvis during the lift and use the back and abdominal muscles improperly. A coach or teammate should guide the lifter to prevent injury. Stationary machines make correct lifting easier because the way the weight is situated on the machine forces the body into the proper position. Another problem with free weights is that one needs to be properly spotted at higher weights. Barbells can become dangerous as the lifter tires, or tries too heavy a weight. Someone must be there to help catch the barbell if it falls.

Though machines are safer, this is problematic as many gyms do not permit teens to join as members. Fortunately, more and more schools are providing good facilities and good trainers who can outline the proper exercises and lifting techniques for teens. Also be sure to check with your physician as to the advisability of lifting for either weight training or strength training.

The Rise (and Fall?) of the Early Developer

Since physical competitions are organized by age, those who have an earlier pubertal development often excel in sports that require body mass and strength. They may also become more coordinated earlier than their classmates. The advantage for these early developers sometimes wanes as their classmates begin to catch up. The strong thirteen-year-old who could run through tacklers and throw faster and farther watches helplessly as the other kids begin to catch up and get taller and stronger; the star of the eighth-grade team becomes just good in tenth grade.

If you are the parent of this type of athlete, it is important to remain aware of what may be happening. It is incredibly hard for a young mind struggling for acceptance in a peer world to find himself faltering. We can best console by understanding and not making casual suggestions like, "You can always try another sport." His passion for the sport does not die overnight. It is important for parents to continue to show support for the now merely "good" athlete.

The Female Athlete

Girls now commonly participate in high-level, intense, and aggressive competitive sports. Girls now play contact basketball and field sports at a level that was unheard of twenty years ago. But new opportunities have created new injuries for the female athlete. Their bodies are certainly suited for competition, and there should be no concerns about menstruation interfering with activities. Because of earlier development girls will reach an adult physical status sooner than boys; by the tenth grade they may have fully developed bodies. Yet, their bodies require a higher percentage of fat in order to properly mature (many find this unacceptable), and the different joint angles (elbows, shoulders, and hips) pose challenges for training. The high school girl athlete has to be concerned not only about injuries but also has to be vigilant about proper nutrition. Girls are more at risk because they cannot afford to lose body fat, and they do lose some when training.

General Health Problems

Asthma and Asthma-like Reactions

Some athletes may find themselves wheezing and having difficulty breathing after brief exertion. If your teen experiences this problem, consult your doctor. Medications are available in the forms of inhalers and pills that allow participation for most asthmatic teens. Before using these on a teen who is in regulated competition, however, check with your physician and coach about medications. Olympic-level sports, for example, have banned certain medications, and medals have been taken away. Even with prescription medicines (for example, some asthma medicines have adrenaline-like properties) medals have been removed from athletes who had excercise-induced asthma and competed while taking commonly prescribed medication.

Breathing difficulties can also affect otherwise healthy athletes in the form of bronchial spasm. These spasms occur when training and competition move outdoors in the spring, when the cold air reaches the bronchi (the tubes in the lungs) and induces a spasm, making it difficult to expel the air from the lungs. (This same reaction can occur in the asthmatic, but the cause is an allergic reaction.) If you have a teen with this problem, consult your physician, as it is easily managed by using inhalers that prevent the bronchospasm before the event.

Heat-Related Illnesses

Runners, cyclists, and soccer, football, baseball, basketball, and tennis players are at risk for heat-related illnesses during hot weather. Anyone who participates in any type of sport needs to be taught the importance of proper hydration before and during a game.

During hot weather, athletes need to avoid the midday sun and dress appropriately (clothing that permits ventilation). They should also be mindful of the early signs of heat-related illnesses. Mild forms of heat injury are signaled by muscle cramps. With increased sweating and exposure to heat without drinking enough liquids, the possibility of heat exhaustion can occur. The lack of fluid volume makes the heart incapable of supplying blood to the brain and muscles. The athlete feels dizzy, nauseated, and may faint. With the excessive sweating that typically occurs at the beginning of the season, athletes lose salt, so fluid replacement, whether orally or intravenously, cannot consist of pure water. Plain water will only dilute the existing salt level (sodium) and can potentially make the situation worse. Sports drinks that do not contain caffeine provide water, glucose, and adequately balanced salts, and are good to drink while exercising. With additional conditioning during the season, the kidneys make the necessary corrections and less salt is excreted, so water will then offer adequate hydration.

Heatstroke is an extreme case of heat injury, where the heart does not have enough vascular fluid to pump, and requires admission to an emergency room. While waiting for trained personnel to arrive, a person should be moved to a shaded spot and the legs elevated to increase blood flow to the brain. Excess clothing should also be removed.

Fainting

Fainting may be part of a brain injury, but commonly it occurs because insufficient blood is reaching the brain. When we stand, our blood pressure drops, but normally there is a quick compensatory adjustment in our pressure to assure that the brain gets enough blood. Some people's blood pressure drops too quickly when they stand and they may even feel faint just getting up from a chair. These people must be sure that they have proper nutrition and fluids with salt if they participate in sports so that their blood pressure is adequate.

Others have an exaggerated response to a natural phenomenon. When we strain we can cause less blood to reach our brains as we bear down on a closed windpipe. This causes the heart to slow down and a "vasovagal" response occurs. This is so called because the blood vessels open up in response to a nerve (vagus) telling the heart to slow down. As we do that we feel dizzy and faint since less blood goes to our brain. This happens often with weight lifters and with the Victorian ladies who stopped breathing when they saw something frightful.

Another activity that can cause a feeling of lightheadedness is hyperventilating, or breathing so fast that there is low carbon dioxide tension in the body. During an attack, simply putting a paper bag over the athlete's mouth and having her rebreathe her own carbon dioxide will make her feel better. This is commonly seen in athletes who train for the first time in high altitude and are not conditioned to the low oxygen tension. For example, a New Yorker going to Denver might have difficulty in the high-altitude climate until he became accustomed to it. Skiers or athletes who travel to compete should talk to their physician. There are medications that can be used for altitude sickness.

Anxiety can also cause hyperventilation. Some people, feeling a sense of panic, breathe so fast that they become lightheaded because of a loss of carbon dioxide. The paper bag trick can also work here.

Sprains and Strains

When you stretch or tear a ligament—a rubber-bandlike attachment between two bones—you have a sprain. When you stretch or tear a muscle or a tendon, which attaches the muscle to the bone, you have a strain. They can be hard to distinguish and at times only an MRI can differentiate the two.

Most sprains are due to direct injury to the ligaments so that the ligament is stretched out of place or even ruptured. The blow does not need to directly hit the ligament—hitting the bone supported by the ligament can also cause injury. For example, landing on an outstretched hand or landing on the side of a foot may dislodge the ligaments at the wrist or ankles.

Strains can occur without direct trauma and can result from any movement done improperly over a short time, or even one done properly over a prolonged time (these are called repetitive stress injuries). Commonly, strains occur because of poor preparation, poor conditioning, or poor equipment, such as a tennis racquet that is too heavy for the user or ill-fitting shoes that cause leg strains.

Regardless of whether it is a strain or a sprain, the injury should receive the same type of emergency care until a proper evaluation can take place. Use the RICE method: *R*est the area, *I*ce it, *C*ompress it, and *E*levate it. Call your doctor to discuss whether you need an appointment. If the injury is so severe that the individual cannot move the joint at all or bear weight, then there is no question that a physician or a trainer should evaluate it. A mild injury may require little more than rest and slow rehabilitation involving prescribed exercises. A severe sprain or strain may require a cast or even surgery.

Sprains (ligaments) generally cause swelling and significant pain when the affected area is moved. A teen may say there was a loud "pop" or "snap" sound prior to the injury. Severity of sprains run from a stretched ligament to a partial tear to complete tears; the pain ranges from painful to unbearable. The patient with a full tear will not be able to bear weight and should be seen that day to immobilize the joint until a full assessment is done. In experienced hands, a full tear can be diagnosed on the playing field or in the office. Most orthopedists will order a scan of the joint for further assessment and treatment. A partial tear will leave the joint unstable but it can be examined in the office and assessed the next day as long as the pain is not unbearable and the joint is not swollen. Scans (often MRIs) are done by radiologists and will reveal the degree of tear. In some cases the orthopedist will want to perform an arthroscopic examination to be sure. A small incision is made, and an arthroscope (a narrow flexible tube) with a camera at one end is passed into the joint to assess the tear. If the tear is complete, the ligament will have separated from the bone and even the most stoic adolescent will writhe in pain. Surgery is inevitably required to suture the ligament back into place.

Strains will cause pain and weakness of the affected muscles with possible swelling. If the muscle is torn or if the tendon detaches from either end, the involved muscle is painful to move or even touch. Commonly, back strains are seen in sports that involve a lot of jumping, as in basketball. The player goes up for a rebound and lands the wrong way and twists her back. Another common injury is a hamstring pull, in which the muscle that connects the back of the thigh to the lower part of the leg is overstretched while running or leaping. As a result, the back of the leg cannot be extended without pain. Hamstring injuries are treated with rest, gradual stretching, and a physical therapy program that your doctor will coordinate.

Sadly, severe strains or sprains may incapacitate the athlete for months. Because of a misconception that it is "only" a sprain or strain, the athlete may resume activity before fully recovering. Too rapid a return to the sport will only aggravate the situation.

Injuries and Treatment

Head Injury

■ Concussion

This is one of the most frightening of all sports injuries and the one that may keep many parents from allowing their teens to participate in sports. Despite the estimated 300,000 concussions yearly in sports, most are mild and have to be put into perspective with the value of the sport. Rarely will a single concussion cause permanent damage. Problems occur when a teen returns to the sport too quickly and receives a second blow before being fully recovered.

In a classic concussion, the individual has a moment in which he is not conscious and has no recollection of the event. Recovery should be complete without any neurological deficit, though there may be amnesia for the actual injury. Since some athletes will continue to perform on the field (a so-called "ding" injury), it may well be that the unconscious moment is fleeting or actually absent. The mild concussion may be missed unless someone notes that the athlete cannot remember what happened. What matters most, then, is the element of memory loss.

Soon after a concussion the athlete will complain of a headache and feeling tired. There may be confusion, an altered state of awareness, and nausea or even vomiting. If a teen is throwing up or has severe nausea, contact your doctor or go to the emergency room. These may be symptoms of a concussion but they may also indicate internal bleeding. Today few physicians rely on routine head X rays to evaluate concussions as these are limited to the assessment of bony pathology. Rather MRI and CAT scans are used to assess brain damage.

Some standard questions are used to assess a concussion. If a teen who receives a blow to the head is asked where he lives and what his birthday is and stumbles for the answers, of if he cannot count backward from 100 by 7, he likely has suffered a concussion. Finally, see if he can walk a straight line. Your physician or trainer will do more elaborate testing.

There are various classifications for concussion but the American Academy of Neurology has listed three grades of concussions in increasing degree of seriousness. Grade 1 consists of transient confusion for more than 15 minutes and no loss of consciousness. Grade 2 consists of confusion for less than 15 minutes and no loss of consciousness. Grade 3 consists of loss of consciousness even for seconds.

For a period of forty-eight hours (some advise seventy-two hours) the teen with a concussion should be watched for any change in mental status. A post-concussion syndrome of headaches and exhaustion is expected. Vomiting and severe headaches or double vision warrant a further call to your physician. During this period, no sports or strenuous activities should be permitted. A teen should be allowed to return to sports only after a normal cognitive examination shows that all neurological functions are normal. The headaches that accompany the post-concussion syndrome will *not* go away immediately and may linger for months. Over time, the severity and the frequency of these headaches will wane.

Many school districts have restrictions on the number of concussions a teen can sustain and still participate in sports. Check with your high school to see what the ruling is in your district. A major concern is when and whether an injured teen can return to the athletic field. A second injury may cause "second impact syndrome," where the brain is still recovering from the first concussion and a new trauma causes further damage. Studies on professional athletes have demonstrated that less impact is necessary to create subsequent concussions. In fact, the blow may be so mild as to be missed. This is why it is so important not to permit a teen to become active too soon after a head injury. To complicate the issue, the younger the teen the longer the necessary recovery period.

Current thinking allows a teen with a "ding" injury (confusion clears rapidly; see above) to remain in the game. If there is doubt as to loss of consciousness, the athlete needs to be removed and assessed for mental status. You need an okay from a physician, not an "I'm fine" assertion from your teen. A thorough evaluation by your physician for memory, attention, cognitive thinking, and coordination are necessary before a teen should be put back into a game, and generally, teens are benched for one week following such an injury. Regardless of an upcoming "big game," it is important that a teen take at least a one-week rest. If after one week the teen is still unsteady or unclear in thinking, then a referral for further testing and image scanning of the brain may be in order. A Grade 3 (severe) warrants a month or more of rest before returning to the sport.

If more than one concussion has occurred, an individual is at risk for additional injury for several months afterward. Most physicians would terminate a season for any athlete who has sustained two concussions.

I have had teens with concussion in almost all sports. One teen, however, illustrated particularly well the fragility of the head in sports:

> **At fourteen, Jim was** *very athletic, had excellent eye-hand coordination, and could play most sports well. One September he and his parents accompanied his older brother to college. As the parents were helping his brother with the dorm move, Jim went for a ride on his brother's bike. While straddling the bike waiting for a traffic light to change, a car came along and brushed the side of the bike, knocking the bike, with Jim astride it, to the side. Jim struck the right temple of his head, immediately losing consciousness. Witnesses saw him convulse and throw up. He was rushed to the hospital where an MRI showed a subdural hematoma and several small bleeds in his right temporal lobe. Though it took months before he felt "all right," fortunately his recovery was complete.*

I use this instructive story in urging my patients to wear helmets when they are biking, in-line skating, or skateboarding. You don't have to be playing football or crashing into a tree on a ski slope to be at risk for a concussion. If a teen plays football, hockey, lacrosse, rides, or ski-jumps, head protection should be worn, but remember that soccer players, rugby players, gymnasts, and basketball players are also at risk. Helmets made after March 1999 must meet U.S. Consumer Product Safety Commission standards and carry a CPSC sticker.

■ Contusions of the Brain

A contusion is like a bruise to the brain, as if the brain were punched. The injury does not have to appear where the head was hit, as the acceleration-deceleration forces may bring about the "punch mark" at the other side of the brain. A contusion has all the features of a concussion, but it will be accompanied by immediate vomiting, which warrants more aggressive action. You need to take your teen immediately to the emergency room where they are better prepared to treat a potential "bleed." Head scans are usually indicated, and a physician will check for a contusion as well as internal bleeding, which may require aggressive care.

Eye Injuries

Contact lens have helped improve participation for many athletes. They allow clear vision, and athletes who couldn't participate because they wear glasses can now compete. However, the eye is still vulnerable to impact injury in sports in which an object is thrown. Blows to the eye with fingers, elbows, and knees also occur in contact sports. Eye guards are ideal protection. Some professional athletes use protective eye guards at all times, and this has made teenagers more accepting of this gear. Although not a mandate for many team sports, the use of protective glasses or a shield worn over contact lenses is encouraged for anyone in sports, particularly if they play baseball, racquetball, or contact sports like lacrosse. (Hockey is now played with a protective shield attached to the helmet.)

Laccrations around the eye are quite commonly seen in contact sports. If your teen sustains a cut around the eye, get a plastic surgeon to suture these lacerations or the scar may always be visible. The physician who greets the teen with a hockey injury in the emergency room can call the plastic surgical resident on duty to sew any facial lacerations.

An eye that sustains a blow and looks very bloody may be diagnosed as a hyphema, blood in the chamber of the eye. These injuries generally require hospitalization and may require surgery to evacuate the blood from the inside of the eye.

Ear Injuries

Ears are subject to sports injury blows, and though serious harm to a teen's ear is seen infrequently, there are several types of injury that can occur. The classic "cauliflower" ear is caused by repeated injuries and blood accumulation under the skin. Teens who choose to box or wrestle must wear protective helmets that cover the ears and prevent this type of injury. A direct blow to the ear (often with an open palm) may rupture an eardrum or dislocate the small bones inside the ear. A doctor should assess any damage. A third type of ear injury from a blow can cause an individual to hear high-pitched ringing in the ear that is quite annoying. This is called tinnitus and, in most cases, goes away after a period of time.

Nose Injury

Perhaps the most common facial injury is the broken nose. Since the nasal bones of the young teen are still being formed it takes a substantially harder force to fracture them than it would for an adult's bones. For that reason, they are not broken that easily, and at times it is hard to tell whether or not the nose is actually broken.

If the nose is bleeding and seems broken, concentrate on trying to stop the bleeding by placing cotton in the nose and waiting for the blood to stop. When you get to the doctor, X rays are usually ordered, but unless the teen is having difficulty breathing there is usually no immediate emergency. Sometimes the diagnosis is made a few days later, once the swelling subsides. Most nasal fractures can be treated after a final diagnosis. General anesthesia is usually necessary as few teens can withstand the anxiety of using only a local anesthetic to fix the nose. The procedure itself depends on the severity of the break. In general the point is to make the bones as straight and as attached as possible. This may require pushing and pulling of the bones under general anesthesia. If the break is an old one, the surgeon will have to break the nose and reset it properly.

A small laceration on the nose can be easily closed with butterfly bandages that bring the two edges together. Again, if the lesion requires sutures, think of getting a plastic surgeon for the job.

Injury to the Mouth

Mouth guards are helpful in minimizing dental injuries. Players of contact sports often wear these, but occasionally the trauma is so great that the guard fails and teeth are broken. If a tooth is knocked out, clean it with warm water (salt water is preferable but few have it lying around), and go to the dentist as soon as possible. Most teeth that are reimplanted within the first thirty minutes have a good prognosis. If the tooth is not implanted soon, it will not be capable of resetting. A cosmetic false tooth will be the solution.

Cervical Injury (Neck Injury)

The spine is always at risk in sports. With teenagers there is the added risk of undetected congenital spine abnormalities to complicate the picture and increase the risk. Most organized sports for high school and college athletes have immediate facilities to deal with spine injuries. The hallmark of proper care in the immediate aftermath of an accident is to be sure that the neck is not moved and that professional help is called for immediately. You should *never* try to move the injured player yourself, as movement of the neck may aggravate the injury.

Chest Pain

Chest pain is common in teenagers and can come from sustaining a blow or overstretching a muscle when playing sports to getting heartburn from eating too much (see p. 409). It is reassuring to note that the cause of chest pain is rarely cardiac pathology. Although possible, it is unusual for any intrinsic heart disorder to cause the pain.

Certainly anyone with severe chest pain may have pathology of the heart or of the pulmonary structure, and labored breathing may warrant a chest X ray. In most cases there will be no pathology internally and the X ray is normal. Often the pain is aggravated by motion of the chest and localized to the major muscles and/or to the point where the ribs meet the breastbone. If the muscle alone is involved, it is usually due to a strain. If the joints of the breastbone are tender, it is from a condition called Tietze's disease or costochondritis (see "The Chest" in Part Five). Treatment in both cases consists of analgesics (mild) and rest. Crew athletes and those who do a lot of push-ups are prone to this pain.

Parents sometimes call saying they are worried their teen has broken a rib. If the teen can cough or sneeze hard, it is unlikely that the rib is fractured. The sudden expansion of the chest in both of these actions causes an immense amount of pain if there is a fracture. Fractured and bruised ribs are treated with rest.

Breast injuries are rare, and blunt trauma to breast tissue will heal with rest.

Abdominal Pain

Abdominal pain sometimes accompanies a blow that knocks the wind out of a teen. There will be an agonizing few minutes during which the athlete will writhe in discomfort, but a few minutes later the pain usually subsides, and she can get up and continue playing.

One major concern in sports is the teen with a swollen spleen, which often is one of the side effects of infectious mononucleosis (see "Fatigue"in Part Five). If a direct blow occurs to the area near a swollen spleen, the spleen can rupture. For this reasons, teens who have had mono are generally restricted from playing any type of sport for as long as the spleen is swollen. Anyone who has mono should not go back to sports activity until cleared by a physician. Most teens with mono are in no position to want to play, so it's less an issue than you might expect.

Back Injuries

As part of the pre-sports physical, the back should be assessed for abnormal curves. (See "Scoliosis," p. 377, for details.)

When a teenager complains of back pain after a sport there is usually some trauma or spasm of a back muscle. Rest and analgesics are often sufficient. However, there should also be an evaluation by a doctor to see if a disc has been herniated. In this case, the teen will complain of severe pain down the back. Initially, heat is applied to the area and rest is recommended. Most patients will respond to a course of physical therapy and seldom require surgery.

In patients who complain of back pain, a urine specimen should be evaluated to rule out a kidney problem. The kidneys are located in the back and below the shoulder blades. By gently tapping over this area a physician can tell if the kidney is inflamed (the tapping elicits pain). The presence of microscopic amounts of blood in the urine of most players should not be surprising, as most contact sports will eventuate in trauma to the back in one way or another. A microscopic amount is to be expected after football, hockey, or basketball, etc.

If there is visible blood in the urine, a sonogram is in order to decide if there is a "fracture" of the kidney. In this case, the kidney is quite literally "broken" or lacerated. Your doctor would then refer your teen to a kidney expert to assess the damage with proper X rays.

Shoulder Pain

The shoulder is held in place by muscles and tendons. The shape of the joint is shallow in order to allow for the rotation of the shoulder. If the joint were a strong ball-socket type (as in the hip), it would not have such a wide range of motion. As a result, the shoulder's integrity is directly related to the strength of the muscle groups holding it in place. Since the growth plates of the arm (humerus) are not fully fused until growth is complete, no young teen has a strong enough shoulder to withstand certain forces.

Throwing, serving in tennis, and tackling all require immense muscle strength. Too often young teenagers try to accomplish more than is reasonable at their age, resulting in muscle strains. Teens who are involved with sports that rely heavily on moving the shoulder (lifting, volleyball, basketball) often injure the deltoid, which forms the mass of the shoulder. Teens who are involved with hard throwing (baseball, tennis, football quarterbacks) are at risk for rotator cuff tears. In contact sports, one sees injuries that range from slight separations to complete separations, in which the shoulder is literally popped out of place (displaced). One major concern with shoulder separations is a high recurrence rate unless there is proper rehabilitation and rest.

In most shoulder injuries, a change in the movement of the shoulder mechanics or stopping the movement altogether is needed. Young teens should not be allowed to throw curve and slider balls, as the force required to make the ball move erratically is greater than the muscle capacity for this age group. Similarly, improper tackling techniques can cause shoulder injuries.

If an injury results in shoulder muscles being stretched one way and the neck the other, the bundle of nerves that runs down the neck to the shoulder can be temporarily damaged. The athlete feels an immediate sense of an electric shock running down the arm (think of the sense you feel when you hit your "funny bone" in the elbow). If the injury is severe enough, the arm becomes numb as the nerve conduction is temporarily disrupted. These "burners" or "stingers" are seen in contact sports. Typically, normal sensation returns, but you should contact your physician since the same symptoms can arise from a pinched nerve.

The shoulder also meets the collarbone at the acromion-clavicular (AC) joint, and sometimes a shoulder injury results in a fractured clavicle. Falling on the shoulder is a common cause for the fracture. Fortunately, this injury requires a simple splinting (a "Figure 8" splint applied to both shoulders, which forces them back) and withdrawing from sports temporarily.

Athletes who participate in "throwing" sports are also prone to elbow injuries. "Tennis elbow" (tendonitis) is caused by improper use of the elbow. A change of racquet to one that fits properly and a change in swinging technique should alleviate the painful elbow. The same kind of injury is seen in baseball, when a player throws too hard, or as above, with too much curve to the throw. Falling on the elbow when the arm is fully extended can also cause great pain, and may result in a muscle strain or a fully dislocated elbow.

If there is pain running down the inside part of the arm to the fourth and fifth (the pinky) fingers, it is an ulna nerve injury. It may be transient, coming from a blow to the nerve directly at the elbow (the "funny bone" isn't funny and it's not a bone), or it could signal an entrapment of the nerve due to a fractured elbow.

Hand Injuries

The most common injuries to the hand involve "jamming" the fingers and fractures. In the former, the finger is hit by something (usually a ball) while the finger is fully extended, and it is "jammed" into the joint, causing pain and swelling. Blood may enter the capsule space of the joint making the finger intensely tender. X rays may be needed to exclude a fracture and if none is present, then all that is required is splinting the finger. While waiting for a proper splint, the affected finger can be "buddy taped" to the next one so that the normal one serves as a temporary splint. If the finger is fractured or dislocated, a splint is also usually the remedy. An orthopedist or sports medicine physician often splints fractures of the metacarpal bones (long bones of the hand) or of the thumb.

Sometimes while on the field, a finger becomes dislocated and the trainer will "pull it" back into the joint. As painful as this sounds, it actually relieves some of the pain. Many physicians will X ray the finger to assure that there is no concomitant fracture. This is particularly true in the younger teen who is still growing and has wide-open growth plates.

Wrist Injuries

Wrist injuries are seen in the same situations as elbow injuries. The small bones of the wrist can be damaged both from throwing and from falling but the latter is more commonly a cause of a fracture or a sprain. There are a series of small bones in the wrist and they, although small, can be fractured. X rays do not always show the fracture and continued pain warrants a reassessment of a possible fracture. Commonly the wrist is injured in skateboarding, in-line skating, and snowboarding, as the outstretched hand breaks a fall and, as a result, the bone. Treatment of a wrist fracture often requires a cast and, depending on the bone involved, it may take months to heal. Wearing wrist guards can help prevent fractures.

Hips

The hip is an incredibly strong ball-joint socket. It is not easily broken or knocked out of place, yet in all contact sports it can happen.

Genital Injury

For obvious reasons, the most common injury will be trauma to the testicles. The use of protective cups in sports has gained support from many teens and we are seeing fewer of these injuries. Some teens argue that they do not wear cups because they are uncomfortable. Let them know it will be much more uncomfortable if they injure their testicles. As they themselves would so eloquently put it, "Deal with it!" In most cases of trauma, the injury can be treated with rest and a support strap to diminish the pain of the dependent testicle. A doctor should be seen if the pain persists or if there is swelling. The male athlete with a single testicle is often warned, if not prohibited by some states, from contact sports.

"Jock itch" is common simply because of the increased sweating and friction in the groin. This is actually a fungal infection (see Chapter 6, "The Teen Obsession: Skin").

Knee Frontal View

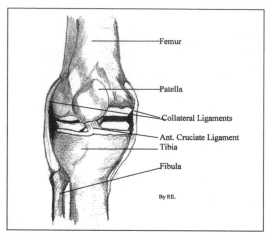

Knees

When our prehistoric ancestors decided to stand up, they never expected that their descendents would rely on the knee to support them. Yet athletes jump repeatedly while dribbling a ball, withstand the impact of another player tackling them at the knee, and even manage to go downhill on snow with two small sleds attached to their feet. Simply stated, our knees were not meant for the abuse of most sports. Moreover, since teenagers are not proportioned evenly until the end of their growth spurt, it should come as no surprise that the most common sports injury for a teenager is a knee injury. Add the impetuosity of the age group, the lack of judgment about using the correct equipment, and the desire to hide an injury before their peers and you have the makings for significant injury.

Common among teens is Osgood-Schlatter disease, which affects the ligament that attaches the lower part of the knee to the tibial bone. In the disease, the part immediately below the knee is swollen and painful. If you could magnify the point of entry for the ligament, you would see microscopic fractures in the bone. As these small pieces of bones pull off, scars form on the bone, resulting in a bump that is visible, palpable, and tender. Since injuries usually occur during the third stage of sexual maturity while the teen is having a growth spurt, they are often referred to as "growing pains." X rays are often taken, not so much to diagnose this condition but rather to rule out a bone tumor. Often the coincidental finding on X ray may be osteochondritis dissecans in which there is a gradual separation of the bone at the lateral side of the kneecap.

Although it appears as if the kneecap will break, no treatment is needed as the lesion heals spontaneously. It is felt that the lesion is seldom the cause of any knee pain.

Although common, Osgood-Schlatter is still painful. One of the "reasons" for pain is to remind a person to stop what she is doing, and usually rest will result in an improved knee. Once the pain has subsided the teen should strengthen the quadriceps muscles of the thigh with special exercises. But the point of needing rest cannot be overemphasized since the disorder evolves because of overuse. Analgesics help but dulling the pain so that the teen can resume activities early is counterproductive and will lead to further damage.

Chondromalacia patella, or patellofemoral syndrome, is another common cause of knee pain in athletic teens. The difference in anatomy makes females more prone to this disorder, and as many as a third of female athletes will have chondromalacia patella at some point. The hallmark of the disorder is that both knees tend to be affected and the pain worsens *after* the exercise. A classic complaint is that the teen can climb stairs but when she stops her knees feel sore. No masses or swellings are evident. Typically, the knee will hurt when the examiner pushes the kneecap toward the inside. This diagnosis is made clinically, as routine X rays will be normal. In cases of doubt an arthroscopy may be needed, and it will reveal a softened cartilage supporting the patella.

Treatment of chondromalacia patella depends on the severity of the discomfort. Limiting the activity that elicits the pain and letting the joint rest may suffice. If the teen is an athlete this is not good news. Asking a runner to stop running and switch to a nonweight-bearing sport like swimming is ideal but impractical in many cases. Strengthening the muscles of the thigh and lower leg are recommended, but at times even this is insufficient. In extreme cases, surgery may be advised.

Some knee injuries require immediate attention. The knee can be fractured, its ligaments sprained or torn, its muscles strained or torn, and its cartilage damaged. Any teen who cannot bear weight should be evaluated for a tear of some kind. A knee with torn ligaments or cartilage may not be swollen. Knees that are damaged are difficult to assess properly and often your teen needs to see an orthopedist or sports-oriented physician.

One of the first questions a patient will be asked is whether a "pop" was heard at the time of injury. This indicates that a ligament or muscle tore. (The lack of the sound does not, however, preclude a tear.) If the injury occurred in a sport that requires a pivot or change of direction, a tear is common. Basketball and field sports, like soccer and football, are associated with torn ligaments. The anterior cruciate ligament (ACL) tear is by far the most common. Tearing an ACL in swimming, crew, or even track is unusual (unless the long jumper lands "off balance"). Other ligaments that support the knee can tear depending on the force exerted on them. Most of the time the ligament is only strained, and the teen will be able to support weight; with the tear, few can stand on the leg.

As with chondromalacia patella syndrome, an ACL tear is more common in the female athlete. The twisting forces on the knee place a strain on the quadriceps muscles, and girls are thought to place even greater stresses on these than their male counterparts. It is also speculated that females land more flat-footed. It is anatomy and not hormonal influences that are thought to be the reason for the increased injury rate among girls.

As with sprains, the treatment is to RICE (Rest, Ice, Compress, Elevate) the injury until further evaluation by a doctor. If a teen cannot bear weight on the leg, get crutches and keep the knee free of weight until the doctor examines the damage. An athlete with a damaged knee tends to keep the knee slightly flexed to prevent pressure. Not all tears are treated surgically. It depends on the tear and the individual's level of activity. A small tear can be treated conservatively with physical therapy and by temporarily avoiding the sport that caused the tear. If it is deemed necessary to have surgery, the type of surgery will depend on the amount of damage. An orthopedist may decide to repair a tear with arthroscopic surgery or advise more traditional surgery, depending on how badly the knee is damaged. The rehabilitation time is dramatically longer with the latter.

Amy, sixteen, is on *the high school varsity basketball team. While making a sharp cut toward the basket, she felt a sudden shooting pain in her right knee. She collapsed and immediately flexed the knee to her chest and held it in with both arms as she writhed in pain. She couldn't put weight on that leg as she was helped from the court. The trainer tried to examine the knee, but the pain was unbearable. Ice was placed on the knee, and it was wrapped with an elastic bandage, which provided some relief as the knee continued to swell. Because of the pain, she was taken to the orthopedist who asked her if she heard a snap sound as she was injured. Julie replied that it sounded like a rubber band being plucked. The doctor placed her knee in slight flexion, and as he examined it, he felt the looseness of the tibia being pulled forward. It became clear to him that Julie had an ACL tear. She was splinted, given crutches, and scheduled for surgery.*

Shin Splints

A common aliment, especially in novice athletes or in someone wearing improper shoes, is the "shin splint." The muscles that run down the knee to the ankle must be trained and balanced for the demands of running. An imbalance at the ankle or an improper stride when running may result in a misuse of these muscles, causing the tendons to become inflamed. This tendonitis results from an overuse without proper conditioning.

If an athlete has a tendency to get shin splints, heat should be applied before running and ice after. As with all tendonitis, the use of antiinflammatory medications such as ibuprofen may help. Long-term treatment requires a change of something; it may be as simple as changing shoes or running on a different surface. If the situation continues, a search for muscle imbalance, leg length discrepancy, or improper shoes should be undertaken. A change in running shoes or a course of physical therapy to strengthen leg muscles may be necessary.

Stress Fracture

A stress fracture can be confused with a shin splint. Here the athlete has so overused the muscles that minute fractures of the tibial bone (the long one running down the leg below the knee) have occurred. Both the tibia and the bones of the foot are prone to stress fractures since they bear the most weight. There is intense pain at the site of the fracture, and eventually there may be localized swelling. Because the fractures are so small, they are often missed on routine X rays, and a bone scan, which will show increased bone formation at the damaged site, may be required for diagnosis. With normal bone, a stress fracture will require rest and refraining from the sport for about two months.

A recent concern has been the increase in stress fractures in women. Girls with low ratios of body fat may have correspondingly lower amounts of estrogen, leading to lower bone density. The diminished bone density puts the female at higher risk for fracture. This condition has been labeled the "female athlete triad": low body fat leads to amenorrhea, and the resulting low estrogen causes osteoporosis. I have seen girls with anorexia nervosa ignore stress fractures and continue running! Putting such pressure on a slightly healed stress fracture may reinjure the bone to the point where it may never heal properly. It is important for families to get professional help for teens with eating disorders, while convincing the teenager to take a break and let her fracture heal.

Ankle Injuries

Almost all athletes will eventually sustain a sprained or strained ankle. In both, the foot is turned suddenly downward and inward and the muscle-ligament unit that attaches the muscle to the foot is damaged. The outside part of the ankle swells immediately and the ability to bear weight is compromised. Touching the outside part of the ankle is painful, and soon there may be discoloration.

As soon as the sprain-strain occurs RICE (Rest, Ice, Compress, Elevate) should be applied to limit swelling. An easy way to apply compression pressure is with an ace bandage; if the pain is significant, the ankle can be splinted with plastic splints sold in most drug stores. If a fracture is suspected and these splints are not available, stabilize the ankle with pieces of wood or with a magazine curled around the ankle. Tape the splint, get crutches and go to the doctor or ER for X rays.

Remembering What Is Important

Although this chapter is filled with descriptions of injuries, most teenagers who go out for sports will not come home with bandaged wounds and limping on crutches. Proper training and conditioning are the hallmarks of injury avoid-

Medical Care and Sports

If questions about your teen's health and a sport arises, you may be able to turn to a "sports medicine" doctor, if one practices in your community. These doctors are trained to diagnose and treat all types of sports-related problems. I routinely refer to a sports medicine doctor any patient who has a fracture that will not require surgery and for those athletes where I need a second opinion. This teamwork assures accurate diagnosis and speedy recovery for the teen athlete.

ance. Good equipment and solid teaching of proper sports techniques keeps players in the game and off the injury list. As parents, we need to listen to our kids' complaints about their bodies. Few who participate actively in athletics want to be on the sidelines; they want to play and be part of the team. If they complain about an injury, we have to assume that their concerns are founded. Take them seriously, and see a doctor.

By the same token if your child complains that the sport is taking too much time, or that she doesn't want to practice, then she may be having a problem. Perhaps it is the coach or other members of the team making her anxious. Sit down and listen. The important thing about athletics is keeping your teen moving; if she doesn't want to be on the tennis team, so be it. Maybe she just wants to play for fun. Give your teen the lifelong gift of understanding that physical activity is important, but stress that she has the right to select a sport or hobby that is just right for her.

Part Three

Teen Sexual Practices and Issues

Chapter 8

Sexuality and the Adolescent

A s teenagers undergo the changes of puberty, they have no choice but to see themselves in a sexual light. The hormonal surges change not only how they look but also how they *feel* and act. By the time breasts, pubic hair, and acne hit, teenagers are already looking at themselves in relation to the opposite sex. Note how the little girl's cute one-piece bathing suit has given way to the bikini. Think next of the teen male who, unsure at the beach unless surrounded by other similarly unsure males, moans as Mom says, "Oh look. There are some nice boys and girls. Maybe you can join them." He yearns to be noticed by the girls but at the same time would like to crawl into the hole that his younger brother is digging with his old beach pail. In a few years he will be aching to be seen as he "casually" preens and flexes on the beach.

Teenagers are sexual. Being sexual does not mean that you "have sex." It means that you are aware of yourself as a sexual entity that attracts and is attracted to others sexually. If Mary is Tom's friend and they are eight, then the two may appreciate the other's skill in running. If Mary and Tom are sixteen, each will have to put aside the intrinsic sexuality of the relationship in order to appreciate the other's running.

I recently gave a lecture to the parents of seventh and eighth graders at a coed school. I had gone over a list of questions, and we were in the midst of a discussion about pressures from school and peers. One mother, perhaps wanting to get down to the nitty gritty, asked, "What are the kids in the eighth grade doing sexually?" All heads turned in her direction and the fact that we were shifting gears did not seem to be a problem. "Does the group want to deal with this now?" I asked. A loud chorus of "yes" and we were into a discussion of oral sex, condoms, and drinking. (Parents first need to put aside memories of the sexual mores of their own teen years; these are the issues confronting kids today.) Some parents turned pale at this discussion, others nodded in painful agreement of the reality. It should not be a surprise that the parents of the girls were more vocal and upset at this data than the boys' parents. Some could not believe that they had to deal with such behavior so early.

What exactly is going on in this sexual world of the teenager? How do you apply what you read in the papers about teen sex to your own teen? What messages can you get by reading your own teen's behavior? These are the issues we'll explore in this chapter.

Sex and the Teen

Because statistics take years to collect, I cannot report to you exactly what this current crop of teens is doing; what I can do is provide you with the general trends in teen sexual behavior. What I am seeing in both private and clinic settings is a group of seventh, eighth, and ninth graders who are hurrying to become older. They want to dress older and see R-rated movies because they see little difference between that and what is on network television. For those who have cable access, there is an even greater world of sexual stimulation. All they need to do is stay up past ten o'clock and a movie that would have been rated "X" in theaters in the 1960s and 1970s will show up on cable television. We make it even easier by putting televisions in their rooms. (Many boys tell me about a popular midnight show that features strippers and frontal nudity. If it's any consolation, I think that few girls ever watch the show.) They also search sexual sites on the Internet.

Recently one of my fifteen-year-old patients (let's call him Joe) told me that he was concerned because of the difficulty he had with erections. I asked him if this happened when he read an erotic magazine. I was surprised and concerned by Joe's negative answer. He then added, perhaps to allay my visible apprehensions about organic pathology, "I have the Internet, doc. You don't need to buy magazines." When I further pursued the notion that one needed "adult" clearance to get on the porn web sites, he asked if I were hooked up to go "online," went over to the computer on my desk, and with three swift key strokes I was facing choices of sexual pornography that made the "girly" magazines of my youth seem innocent. He asked if I had any "preferences" and decided on his own to log on to "oral sex." There, without any need to address adult status, were very explicit photos. With more discussion, it became clear that Joe was a bit bored with sex and "normal" exposure with real girls had become tame. Only the Internet's buffet of choices provided the necessary stimulation.

Is it a wonder that this young age group knows about, and wants to participate in, sexual activity? Hormones will drive you to the feeling that you have new urges; accessibility will make activity happen. Our ads tell us to be sexy; the gorgeous girl walks into the bar and goes over to the hunk who is drinking the correct beer. Teens watch it and they want to replicate what they see.

Parents have asked how to solve the problem of television and Internet sex and pornography. While newer models of televisions have ways to block out certain channels, a problem here is that even the regular channels air questionable material late at night. Internet services also offer opportunities for parents to block access to certain sites, but teens still may have access at friends' houses, or they may simply know more than you do about computers, meaning they can find a way around the block. The bottom line is you will not be able to fully avoid teens' access to porn. If they want it, they will find it.

But What Are They *Doing*?

As early as the eighth grade kids feel the need to get into the sport of sex. They realize that there is an inherent danger in intercourse for it poses risks for STD. The big fear is not pregnancy but rather dying of HIV. So they have solved the problem easily; they invented the "hook-up." (Use the term "making out" and

---

Myths about Oral Sex

Teens comfort themselves with the following myths about oral sex:

1. It's safe. You don't have to worry about pregnancy and infection. *Only half right*, since infection is still a possible consequence.
2. It's no big deal, and you are "supposed" to do it anyway.
3. It's not "sex." I have pleaded with the kids in my practice to give me a new definition. They have failed.
4. I'm still a virgin! This is a natural consequence of the third premise and a truism.

you date yourself and your generation. Talk about "going steady" and you're back in the Stone Age.) Teenagers themselves have carefully explained to me about "hooking up." The concept is easy and simple. You meet someone that you like, and there is an understanding that a certain amount of sexual contact is acceptable. No one expects to "go all the way" (another term that will date you) but fondling, kissing, and partial, or even full, nudity is allowed. The girl may or may not have her genitals touched (remember "third base"?), but as you get older, according to the kids, that is a reasonable part of the encounter. Oral sex *for* but not necessarily *by* the boy is within hook-up rules. "Are you nuts?!" typifies the general tone of many boys when I ask if they reciprocate when it comes to oral sex. So we have kids who are having growth spurts, periods of acne, new suits for special events, and oral sex. It's as if we have a new rite of passage.

As the teen enters the later high school years, the practice of oral sex does not stop. If they have a "relationship" (a few weeks of "being together" can constitute a relationship), new parameters in the sexual encounter are allowed. Their world has established a new set of rules that condones intercourse because the "relationship" eliminates any sense of promiscuity or better put, "being a slut"—a term that has managed to survive generational language. Being in a "relationship" sanctions their behavior in their eyes and in the eyes of their peers. Guilt disappears. By senior year, it is estimated that anywhere from 50 percent to 60 percent of girls will have had intercourse. (Do not say "sex" to kids as they will say they have not had "sex" if they haven't had intercourse; anything short of that is certainly not sex—despite what most adults might think.) Add a few percentage points for the boys to estimate the number of nonvirginal male high school seniors. Ironically, the condom, although preventative for infection, has allowed a more casual sense of intercourse. And few teens are embarrassed to buy condoms. Years ago, I saw a need to have them in my office as a backup for the teen who "couldn't" buy them. For a while the boys (and the girls) would take them; now they all argue that "It's no big deal, doc. I have them. Thanks anyway."

As we see a rise in condom use, we are witnessing a fall in use of the Pill for this age group. The alleged weight gain from the Pill is the most often given reason. Large breasts and extra pounds are not attractive to girls in this age group. Telling a teenager that the weight gain from a pregnancy is even greater falls on deaf ears that believe that nothing will happen to her and anything that does can be "fixed." "I won't get pregnant. Not me!" After telling girls that the weight gain is negligible, most still fear the possibility of "getting fat."

Where does all this sexual activity take place? To my knowledge none of the kids go to motels or hotels. They still do it in the backseat of cars, but many just go to their rooms and close the doors. Parents may be asleep next door, comfortable knowing that their son or daughter is safe at home. It's okay if the boy (or girl) friend is there since they "trust" their teen. (What do they think will happen eventually if you put two sexually stimulated teens together?) I have had teens tell me that they had sex while in boarding school, in their own bedrooms, in their partner's room, in the park, and on the beach. One boasted of having it in a movie theater but I was skeptical.

There's also always the empty house. When parents leave a teen home while the rest of the family goes away on a trip, every teen within a radius of a few miles will hear about it. With or without parental approval, an impromptu "get together" of a few friends will find their way there, and soon couples sort out to different rooms.

"What Is Normal?"

Parents often ask me "What is normal?" as if I had some standard amount, type, and place for teenage sex. Many of us can recall the terms "good girls" and "bad girls," but today they don't apply. In the current climate, few teens will feel that they are having "promiscuous sex," a term that requires a value judgment as to when something is "promiscuous." They have heard the message about HIV, and they will tell you that they need to know their partner better (a few weeks might do) before they have intercourse. However, the hook-up solves the problem of the sexual urge. The new "hot" girl or guy who is introduced at a party (by a best friend) might do nicely for a hook-up, but not for intercourse.

This doctrine applies throughout most of high school but something changes in college. Most of the cases of "I did something stupid sexually" come from kids in college. At lease one college student a week calls to ask me about an STD, or when to test for one, or simply that they have one. All will admit either to impulsive or drunken behavior. The idea that this is a captive crowd of "clean kids" makes for the poor judgment, and the next morning, the reality sinks in that they put themselves in peril for a disease. Perhaps the ultimate question facing a parent is "Is this sexual activity okay for the teenager?" In answering that, a parent has to be honest about his or her feelings. What is the message that you are sending your teenager by your own conduct, by your dress, and by your attitudes? Is your own dress style one that is obviously sexual? Are you flirtatious? Do you ever comment on celebrities and their appearances in such a manner that your teen picks up from you that these are luminaries to be emulated? Do you guide your teen toward belonging to the "right crowd?" Have you permitted your pre-teen to dress in a sexual way so that a "norm" has already been set? Where exactly have you drawn the line and why? Or does your religion impose standards that make the boundaries very clear and rigid?

Parents have to let their teenagers find their own path to sexual expression, but they can guide them and send messages about what they believe is clear and proper.

My own role, and that of most doctors who work with this age group, is to guide and help parents deal with their teen's sexuality. I cannot dictate correct values to parents. I had to decide that for my daughter, you must do the same for yours.

Mr. and Mrs. Thompson *came to my office because they had discovered that their daughter had oral sex while in the ninth grade. Shocked and unable to deal with this information, they spoke to their pediatrician who suggested they call me. ("He deals with this all the time," they were told.) My first question for the parents was how they discovered so personal an act. Their answer? "We read her diary!" Clearly they must have been suspicious or they would not have violated their daughter's privacy. They admitted that they had been closing their eyes to lies and behavior that should have alerted them to their daughter's "secret life."*

Interestingly, both parents were dressed in a "sexy way," and they admitted to me that sexual discussions were fairly open in their home. They also wanted their daughter to socialize with the "popular" kids, so they had purchased the latest expensive shoes, bags, and clothes for her. Their daughter was a walking advertisement for a Madison Avenue sexy teen, properly positioned for being in the "right crowd" at school. It took little discussion for them to appreciate that they had sent a message that it was okay for their daughter to do "whatever it took" to belong. Later, as they discussed this with their daughter, she readily admitted that she didn't really want to have oral sex but "All the kids did, and I thought it would be okay."

As the teenager enters high school, parents have to confront the real possibility that their teen is having intercourse. To stick one's head in the sand and think that it "won't happen to my kid" is foolhardy. While many teens maintain their virginity into and throughout college, about 50 to 70 percent of teens will go beyond the "hook-up" and form a relationship that graduates to intercourse by senior year. Today, many kids will discuss intercourse as part of a relationship, and it is a planned-for activity for which they are "prepared." The boy will have a condom, and the girl will be an active participant in the decision.

Helping Teens Establish Their Own Sexuality

As teens move through adolescence, they are working hard to find a comfort level with their own sexuality. Here are some of the things parents can do to help guide them.

1. Remember that your "pre-teen" is actually a *child*. The "pre-teen" concept is a marketing invention, and fosters premature sexual expression. By encouraging this concept, we allow our kids to shortchange their childhood. From ages ten to twelve your child is still very much a child. There is plenty of time for her to evolve into a sexual being; don't rush the process. Dress them appropriately and parent them as one does a "child."

2. As parents you need to be aware of the impact that your own sexual expression has on your teenager. Whether or not teens are conscious of it, parents function as role models. If an adult dresses in a revealing style, the teen will internalize this as acceptable. In their desire to be seen as adults themselves, they will emulate this example.

3. "Keeping up with the neighbors" is a poor goal in life for either you or your teenager. The sense of being "accepted" at all costs is a dangerous concept to instill in a teenager. If a family finds that an acceptable tenet by which to live, then as parents, you are lost when your teen whines "But everyone else's parents said they could!"

4. Don't be afraid to tell your teenager that you disapprove of how he dresses. The rule is simple. You are under no obligation to accept his outfits. If you don't like his hat, his baggy pants, or his T-shirt with its crude message, don't make a big fuss. Simply tell him that you don't like it but you are not going to interfere because no one is being hurt, and you have the right to insist that his attire be improved when attending family events. On the other hand, piercing a belly button (see Chapter 6) or wearing a revealingly low-cut blouse to an after-school job are things worth deeming unacceptable. If you don't provide children with family guidelines, they have no way of knowing when they are about to go too far.

5. Talk with your teen about your own values and listen to hers. You do not have to know everything that is going on, but give her a sense that you are interested and caring. If your attitude is one of listening, she is more likely to come to you for advice.

They have no moral objection and no sense that intercourse is wrong. They view it as part of a relationship, and they and their peers feel it's okay. As I listen to kids talk about sex, it is clear that a "relationship" exonerates any sense of wrongdoing. No girl is a "slut" if she has sex while "seeing" a boy for a long time. The peer group simply accepts the reality that their friend is having intercourse with her boyfriend. As in previous generations, though, boys still get the benefit of the doubt and the double standard prevails.

Talking to Your Teen

You may be saying, "That's not my teen." I agree that some teens are not engaged in any sexual behavior. But, how do you know your teen is one of them? Is there a way of telling who is and who is not doing something sexual? Can you appreciate a tone, a gesture, a glow that is a telltale sign? Do you really believe that all kids will tell their parents "everything?"

To begin with, eliminate the notion that you are privy to all that is going on with your teen. If, in fact, you do know everything, you have a different problem. How do you expect your teen to grow and develop as an individual when a parent monitors every act and decision? Adolescents are entitled to a "private" life. Many parents think that being their teen's "best friend" is great, but it actually thwarts growth, because it ties the teen to the parent. A parent must risk popularity by setting limits. Once you appreciate the difference between being "friendly" and needing to be a "best friend," you can develop an objectivity that allows you to look rationally at your teen and his actions.

The process of thinking about your teen as a sexual being and and talking with her about sex has to begin before the seventh (maybe even the sixth) grade. (Before that most kids are in the latent stage of sexual development, and they aren't too concerned with these topics.) Your first conversation is really one that should ascertain that your pre-teen is aware of the mechanics of sex and to state your availability should there be any questions. Toward the end of middle school, or a bit later for a sexually less mature teenager, you will want to begin a conversation that lets you also reinforce family values.

Before opening a discussion, you and your spouse need to sit down and review the "silent words" listed in Chapter 2. You cannot effectively talk about sex with your teen if you are embarrassed. This is also a conversation where gender matters; mothers should talk to their daughters; fathers must take responsibility for their sons. If there is no same gender parent, then family relatives and your teen's physician can play an important role.

On the assumption that you are now comfortable with the silent words, find a good time to talk with your teen. It is another nonnegotiable rule that you do not ask any of his friends about what is going on in school, nor do you have a "talk" when his friends are around. The first sentences your teen hears have to imply that you respect two major points: first, that he may actually have a fair amount of sexual information, and second, that you are not there to pry into his private life. He is entitled to friends that you don't know about and thoughts that are all his. As a parent you cannot control whom he sees and what he thinks about. Rather than lecturing about friends and your concerns, your intent is to open with a discussion about something less personal. What is happening in the community (what's going on sexually among local school kids) is more neutral than discussing exactly what he is doing. Popular television shows or movies that depict a certain amount of teen sexual activity are also good conversational launch pads: "Does this show represent what's going on at school, or is this unrealistic?" As you talk, avoid the "When I was your age" trap. This only turns off most kids since this affirms that parents have no idea of what is going on today.

The timing of your conversation has to be appropriate and relaxed. Let's assume that you watched a movie with your twelve-year-old and there were sexual innuendoes throughout.

"Jane, that movie got me thinking. I know that kids in your school talk about sexual topics and about actually doing sexual things. I guess I come from a time when it was hard to discuss this with your parents, but I don't want that for us. You probably have been learning all about sex in health classes and I just want you to know that you and I, or you and Dad, for that matter, can always talk about this. I don't pretend to know all the answers, but I can listen and help. Okay?"

Don't try too much at once. If your twelve-year-old nods or says nothing for that matter, don't push it. And don't worry—it has sunk in. As an opening that is all you can hope for. Look for the next chance and follow up with something along the lines of, "I heard that, or I read that, or Mrs. Jones said that . . . the kids in your age group are experimenting with sex." Stop and wait a few beats and see if there is any comment. If there is no response (unlikely), follow up with, "Dad and I were talking about this, and we both feel that kids in your age group may be under a lot of pressure to do things that they are not ready for. Do you agree?"

The tone more than anything is critical. You want to open up dialogue, not close it with a tone of judgmental disapproval. Again, if nothing happens, leave it alone and don't force it. "Honey, if you ever have questions, ask me. I want you to feel you can talk to me about anything." With an open and nonjudgmental tone, you may soon find your teen approaching you with a question like, "Mom, can you get an infection from oral sex?" That's when you really will have to maintain composure. If you create the right atmosphere, you will likely find that the conversations will happen when you least expect them—but the important thing is that they happen.

When it comes to a topic like oral sex, you might say something like, "I guess I don't understand why it's done so easily. My generation felt that this was not something you did casually." Is there pressure to do it? Do the girls seem willing, or are they going along because of expectations? What happens if you don't want to? Do you have to know the boy for a while, or is this done simply because there is an opportunity? All of the questions need to have a sense of generality and should not be pointed at your teen. There is a major difference between, "Are there lots of kids actually having oral sex?" versus "Are you or your friends having oral sex?" The former is inquisitive; the latter is accusatory. "Mom!" is the appropriate response to the second inquiry. Admittedly one should have the same discussion with both boys and girls; however, the reality is that fellatio is more common with girls. By all means, one should explore the fact that boys are involved in oral sex, and that conversation ideally begins with the father.

Before fathers have the "sex discussion" with their sons, they should ask themselves how they feel about their son's likely sexual activity. Do you secretly feel a sense of pride that he is popular and sexy? Is there a sense of a "score" for your son? Do you harbor a double standard? Do you feel that he should treat the girls with the same dignity that you expect your daughter to be treated? Your personal expectations and biases change the tone of the discussion.

Do you want to be the father who addresses his teen with: "Hey son, I know what's happening. Just be sure you take care . . . if you know what I mean. Heh, heh!"? This father is giving tacit approval to his son's activities and demonstrating that there is no need to care for the girl's feelings. If we are trying to teach responsibility and caring to our teens, we cannot imply that one should "take all he can." The father's own value system must alter before he can send the correct message to his son. I doubt that this father will change soon enough for his son to get the right message.

In contrast, Tom's father opens the door for a more meaningful conversation with his son by saying: "Tom, I know that there is a lot of sexual activity among the kids at school. I don't want to pry into your affairs, but how do you feel about what I am hearing—about oral sex in the middle school?"

This father does not accuse or condone—he opens the discussion by giving his son the opportunity to lead the discussion.

Teaching or Reaffirming Values

Statistics about teen sexuality do not provide us with information about values. They only tell us what the kids are doing and at what age. How you feel about the issues is very important. Too many parents have the discussion about their feelings *after* their teen is sexually active. Take an early opportunity to discuss your feelings with your spouse and think about what you want for your teen. Do it before your child is in sixth grade if possible, and do it with a sense that you will eventually be discussing these feelings with your teen. Our society has accepted as inevitable the notion that teens will be sexually active, and there is no doubt that teens will be thinking about sex and worrying about their image with their peers. Your underlying feelings about what is going on can have a direct bearing on your teen's sexual behavior during these years. (Your acceptance of sexual activity does not have to mean there will be more of it, but it does, in general, mean that a teen will handle it more responsibly because she has access to adult help with questions and/or birth control.)

Teens receive a lot of their values from parents' daily actions. If teenagers see their parents treating each other with dignity and respect, they learn a lesson. If, alternatively, one parent berates the other and generally comes across as patronizing, then a different lesson is learned. We learn how to be males and females by how our parents behave. Instincts may be hormonal, but action is based on the style of the parents. It takes years to shed bad gender-role lessons, and few teens have the insight early enough to change during high school.

Gender bias also still exists when it comes to sexual activity. Girls who are sexually active still get a reputation if they engage in this activity outside of a "relationship," and even with "hooking up" the girl runs the risk of being viewed as a "slut" if she does it "too much." Boys still have the luxury of being sexually active and not being labeled. We, as parents, will do little to change this if we maintain the idea that "boys will be boys." Communicating responsible, respectful behavior to both genders is a very important parental obligation.

Parents must be knowledgeable and available to discuss values early and often. (If you have a comfortable relationship with your teen, you will find that this conversation is ongoing throughout the different ages and stages of adolescence.) No one, not your school, not your religious leader, and certainly not the government, is in a position to establish the values for your family. You and you alone can let kids know what you feel is "right."

A difficult part of discussing values with teenagers is their sense of what is "a lot." You will hear them say that it's okay for friends to have intercourse or drink, if they don't do it "a lot," or "often." When you try to pin down this vague number, you get shrugged shoulders and an "I don't know" response. At some ill-defined point, teens intuitively know that the line has been crossed, but they are hard-pressed to define it. One sixteen-year-old told me that it's okay for her friend to have several intercourse partners because they are all friends and they know each other. The fact that she has three partners would be "a lot" in my view, but my patient felt it was okay. She said that a "slut" is someone who "sleeps around a lot," yet the three guys in the picture were somehow acceptable. This hardly bodes well for the parent trying to instill a sense of values and perspective on behavior. Indeed, she may have learned this value system directly from her parents.

Another important message to convey to teens is that in addition to physical readiness for sex, there is also emotional readiness. The more strongly you can convey that meaningful intercourse is much more than a physical act, the more teens may listen to your reasons for recommending that they wait.

Perhaps parents whose religious values are strong will object to the idea that we are even raising the possibility of allowing sexual behavior. I have been privy to discussions about intercourse and missed periods with teens whose parents are ardently religious. Many of these kids are the ones who "tell everything to their parents," but for obvious reasons, do not share these particulars. These teens need to consider protection for birth control and sexually transmitted diseases as seriously as any other teen.

Teens whose parents advocate total abstinence can be left without any guidance, and this makes them more vulnerable than other teens. Abstinence is fine, but in a sexually laden society it gets harder to uphold this value. If your religion forbids premarital sex, then you should clearly communicate to your teen the level of abstinence expected (some simply want virginity; others want no sexual activity at all). You should give some thought to the following questions: Would you want your teen to tell you what is going on? Would you get her a gynecologist to aid in birth control if it is needed, or make sure your son knows he must use a condom? Should you share this with your spouse or do you keep this information to yourself? Can you preach abstinence to your teens yet still supply them with information? Can you let them know they can come to you if they have a problem?

I also feel strongly about the importance of teens having the guidance of both parents. If a mother is let in on a secret concerning sexual activity, sometimes mother and daughter will conspire to "keep it from Dad." In my observation this does no one any real good. Two heads really are better than one, and teens should have input and support from both parents.

> **Kristin called me from college** *to tell me that she was worried that she could be pregnant. She came home from school, and the test and her history confirmed the diagnosis. She wanted to terminate the pregnancy without telling anyone because her parents "would kill her," and besides, they were religious. I prevailed on Kristin to allow me to contact her mother, who within minutes of the call came into the office. There, Kristin told her about the pregnancy. It was the mother's decision to withhold the information from Dad because they had been going through some difficult times with Kristin and "This would only upset him more." She consoled Kristin, who cried in her arms, and asked me to call the doctor to arrange an abortion as soon as possible. Within three days Kristin had terminated the pregnancy, her mother paying cash so that the secret would not be found out. The only problem was that Kristin was miserable living with the guilt of having deceived her father. It took two years of therapy before she came to the realization that she needed to tell her father what had happened. She did, and fortunately the parents' marriage survived the deception.*

The possible outcome of any intercourse is pregnancy, and I can think of few more frightening or lonely moments than when a teenager finds out she is pregnant. Parents' support at this time is crucial.

The Homosexual Teen

Gender identity is a difficult issue for most parents, and yet it comes up more frequently than readers may think. In a doctor's office, the discussion presents itself in one of two ways: Either the parents (or the physician) see something in the teenager's behavior that prompts a call; or teens may confide that they feel they are gay and need help in dealing with their parents.

To begin this discussion, we need to define our terms.

The term homosexual defines someone whose sexual attraction is for the same sex. They are not confused as to their gender; they have a sexual preference for partners of the same sex. It is a conscious decision that often takes years for the individual to accept because it's not the "norm." She may have heterosexual encounters in an attempt to please parents and herself; but ultimately she realizes that there is an attraction that she can no longer hide. Homosexuals do not want to change their own sex as transsexuals do, nor do they wear the other gender's clothing, which is the desire of a transvestite.

There are two prevailing schools of thought about what causes homosexuality: one is based on a biological model, the other on a psychosocial model.

Biological Model

The biological model of homosexuality says that those who are gay are "born" that way; they have no choice. Studies on the biological model are clearly inconclusive to date, but there are a few pieces of information that a parent needs to know. First, there is no difference in the hormones of the homosexual; each gender has the normal amount. Second, no one has found a "gay gene." The possibility of the latter has caused a great deal of press excitement recently because it would end the discussion; however, careful study of the research has not proven the existence of such a gene. There is, however, some research that gives the biological model credibility.

Some researchers have found an "association" of a different *piece* of one chromosome in homosexuals. Yet, that has not been shown to be consistent in all cases. Twin studies have shown that it is statistically more probable that, if one identical twin is gay, the other is also. There is evidence that infants born with overly high levels of the opposite gender's sex hormone are more likely to perform as the hormone and not as the gender dictates. Hence, if the girl has high levels of testosterone, she behaves more "male" and less like her biological gender. This is an interesting argument for we have accepted the notion of a male and a female brain. We know that each gender has receptor sites for both hormones but in different locations of the brain! Even the most casual observer of human nature will quickly agree that women see things differently than men. They behave differently and nurture differently; they do as humans and they do as lower animals. Simply spend a half hour at any zoo and watch the animals behave. In no time, the gender behaviors will be apparent. Is it so different to observe the human? Is it so difficult to believe that there are different receptor sites, and in the right environment, we produce a "gay brain"? It is an interesting but unproven theory. How one accepts this theory is critical in how one counsels parents whose teen is "coming out."

Psychosocial Model

Others argue that the homosexual is made by a series of circumstances and parental dynamics. Each parent's actions help to shape a child's sexuality, and the child begins to drift in the direction of the homosexual mindset.

The problem with this model is that the psychology experts from Freud onward have widely differing theories. One argues passionately that a child becomes a homosexual when the mother is absent from the child or uninvolved; another study states unequivocally that the problem is one of an overpossessive mother. Fathers are also indicted with the same confusing model. The bottom line is that somehow parents confuse the child, so that the child thinks a same-gender preference is desirable.

A major problem with both arguments is that you are hard pressed to know which is the chicken and the egg. Proponents of the "nature" argument will argue that the intrinsically "less masculine" boy disturbs the father and thereby makes him less desirable as a son. The father becomes distant. Alternatively, the "nurture" proponents argue the other way around. The distant father fosters a need for males that eventually yields the homosexual feelings in the son. What is part of children's nature and what is created by their environment is hard to untangle.

Obviously which theory you believe would warrant a different approach to a therapeutic intervention for the gay teen. Proponents of the psychological model would have the child in psychotherapy with an expert in "turning" the gay into a functional and happy heterosexual. (The effectiveness of therapy in gender change identity is difficult to measure.) Alternatively, the biological model would necessitate therapy that is nonjudgmental and compassionate. The therapist's role is to make the teen and the family comfortable with the homosexuality, to discuss the impact of the teen's sexuality on the rest of the family, and to support the adolescent who may receive negative responses from peers and the school community. It is not the therapist's role to alter the decision but to help one live with it.

My own leaning is toward the biological model. Too many adults who "come out" argue "they always knew they were gay." The mental health community has, for the past twenty years, felt that homosexuality is neither deviant nor "abnormal." It is viewed as a continuum of sexual identity and has actually been eliminated from the DSM-IV book (the gold standard for diagnostic criteria for psychopathology). Our current thinking is that we need to blend the two theories a bit and say that there is a biological predisposition and a certain set of circumstances brings out the underlying gay potential. What we can be sure of is that teens who feel that they are homosexual need support, not chastisement. Most will need some psychotherapy to deal with the fact that there will be a bias against them for their sexual choice.

"Coming Out"

My experience is that many teens do not "come out" during their high school years but wait until college. During adolescence they struggle with their orientation and may even demonstrate "hatred" for gays in an attempt to deny their own feelings.

The acceptability of the gay and lesbian community by mainstream society has made the teenager's confusion, and her decision to "come out," both easier and harder. Forty years ago, it was easy to know what to do: you simply hid your preference from everyone. Today the more open climate that allows politicians, actors, and designers to "come out," makes this an issue that is now dealt with earlier. Parents are more aware of the possibility of a child being gay, or at least are more willing to consider it. Yet the atmosphere of the home today can still make this an impossible discussion.

I have seen both sides. Some teens are so horrified that they will be found out that they sink into a depression or run away or ponder suicide. Others, feeling a sense of parental and social acceptance, declare their feelings and go on with their lives.

My own experience and that reported in the literature is that girls who "come out" do so later than boys. Perhaps the intimacy that is allowed between girls throughout their childhood and teen years allows them to "hide" their feelings longer both from others and themselves. We seem to accept girls hugging and kissing each other as normal, so a girl may be able to disguise her true feelings.

One set of parents confessed to me that they feared their nineteen-year-old son was gay. They based this, not on any specific homosexual act, but rather on the fact that he was a "sissy" in the way he behaved and dressed. They said that they could recall this behavior as far back as kindergarten, and in contrast to his very athletic brother, it was evident to them that there was "something wrong." As the discussion continued, the father seemed to be saying that he could accept his son's decision to be gay with reservation, but he was convinced that his wife would never be willing to accept this. When I posed the rhetorical question, "Would you prefer that he were happy as a homosexual, or miserable as a heterosexual?" I was astonished at her response. She replied, "I would rather he were dead and a heterosexual, than alive and a homosexual!" Both the father and I looked on with amazement and had little to say for quite a while.

Unfortunately for this young man, he did "come out" in college, and mother and son became estranged. Most contact with the family was through the brother, since the mother refused to see her younger son.

In marked contrast, the following took place in my practice.

Paul became my patient *when he was fourteen. When he was seventeen, his parents called me because they were suspicious of Paul's behavior on the Internet. He had become secretive as he went on line, and the parents found that he had been on a porn site. I get this call quite frequently and was about to tell them that the Internet has replaced the porn magazine when they completed their concern. "It was a gay porn site, Doctor."*

As it turned out, I was scheduled to see him for an annual exam and took that opportunity to inquire a bit into his sexual life. He admitted that he was a virgin and that he had sexual thoughts but said that he "enjoyed girls." I saw nothing in his behavior, or his answer, that prompted suspicion of homosexuality. Over the next few years I would ask my usual questions about sexual activity; on one visit he admitted that he was "confused" about his sexual preference. I asked him directly if he thought he was gay, and he said he wasn't sure but he thought so. I offered an opportunity to discuss this further, but he was in therapy and felt that he was okay. I added that if he ever wanted to tell his parents but couldn't, he could do so in my office. A year later he came in with his parents; I thought the topic was a chronic medical problem from which Paul suffered. Instead, he looked at me and said, "You remember what you said about talking with my parents? I want to now." With that, he faced his parents and told them that he was gay. Neither flinched; his mother picked up the baton and simply said, "We thought so." The father chimed in and reassured Paul how much they both loved him, and they would support his decisions. He finished the session by gently reminding him that the "Gay community has to be careful about infection." Paul, realized how hard his father was trying and simply said, "I know."

What does a parent do next? First, and foremost, as Paul's father did, you tell your child that you love him and you are there for him. For teens to state that they are homosexual requires incredible courage. As a parent, the least helpful thing to do is to then treat your teen as a leper. Discussions about HIV should be no more than what you would discuss with a heterosexual teen. Don't belabor the point; odds are that your son or daughter is already well aware of the issue. No one turns from homosexuality because of a fear of AIDS, no more than the heterosexual avoids sex for fear of it.

Few families will handle this news so easily that nothing changes, but if parents remain loving and accepting, the family bonds can remain strong. If the therapy is begun but is predicated on the notion to "turn" the individual straight, proof of success is scant. I am well aware of the claims made by those who believe that being a homosexual is the result of a psychological error in upbringing and can be "fixed." However, in an atmosphere in which there is guilt and shame, the "turned" person may simply find it easier to say one thing and feel another.

Articles that point out a low incidence of homosexuality in a particular religious sect must also account for the secrecy that surrounds the homosexual person in that community. To be a member of a religious group that argues damnation for being gay is hardly an enticement to "come out."

So I leave you with an unanswered issue. Why? We just don't know the exact reasons why anyone is gay. Each side of the argument righteously claims the answer. Yet, I have no right to argue that I have any more of the answer than others. But does an answer really matter? All I can proffer is the argument that your teen is at higher risk for depression and suicide (it is estimated that the gay teen is twice as likely to commit suicide) if you, as a parent, don't accept him. If the mental health community as a whole has eliminated homosexuality as pathology, then parents have to begin to think about their sons and daughters in a different light.

Chapter 9

Birth Control

I n an age in which sex talk is prevalent and "safe sex" practices are preached in public service announcements on national television, it would be foolhardy to think that adolescents are not going to engage in some sexual activities, ranging from kissing to intercourse. (The teen who practices abstinence still needs to be informed, as do their parents.)

However, if you bring up this topic for discussion with your teen, you will find a variety of interpretations of sexual activities. If you ask teenagers if they have "had sex," you may be greeted with a resounding "NO." Most teenagers would consider that a valid answer as long as they did not have intercourse, despite the fact that they may have done everything short of that. If a teen is walking this "fine line," then it's time to think about birth control. If intercourse hasn't happened yet, it may soon.

One can divide birth control into four categories:

1. Abstinence, the rhythm method, and withdrawal
2. Intrauterine devices
3. Barrier methods (condom, spermicide, diaphragm, female condom)
4. Hormonal methods (the Pill, Depo-Provera, subcutaneous implants, mifepristone)

We'll begin with abstinence. At the end of the chapter there is information about the diagnosis of pregnancy and what parents should know about the "morning after" pill and abortion.

Abstinence, the Rhythm Method, and Withdrawal

Abstinence

With the vast amount of sexual information that is available to the teen, one would think that all kids are engaged in some sort of sexual activity. Parents ask about "abstinence" as an alternative and many schools have introduced this into their discussions about sex and birth control. I applaud, congratulate, and encourage all of my patients to be abstinent not only because of pregnancy and infection, but because I think that most are not emotionally ready for intercourse. Yet I want the reader to realistically consider the possibility that your daughter or son may engage in intercourse.

Almost all research on human sexuality concludes that so intimate an act has a profoundy emotional effect on the partners. Judging from what I hear in the office I concur. Yet, I still hear teens making light of it. All too often I get the impression that some of our teens view sex and intercourse as nothing more than a pastime or a sport. Particularly with teen boys, it's as if they say: "I'm doing basketball, track, and intercourse this year." One should not strive for a varsity letter in so delicate and important an act as intercourse.

Those kids who are willing to abstain need support to maintain their resolve. Your teenager's physician should encourage the decision, and those who have made the decision for religious reasons will feel the support of those who share their spiritual values. Your own guidance has likely gotten them to this point, and while you should feel pleased that they received your "message," don't be lulled into a false sense of security that you've "done enough." The sexual urges are so strong during this period of life that one must constantly struggle with one's decision. Be there for any discussion that may surface and learn to listen to and discuss your teen's anxieties and confusion with a soothing voice and an understanding tone. Guilt only works for a short time.

Rhythm Method

The rhythm method is highly impractical for teenagers. Though it can be an effective method, it is difficult to practice and for teenagers it is fraught with risk. For the rhythm method to work, the couple must abstain before and after ovulation, so the girl needs to have very regular cycles so she can keep track of when she is likely to be ovulating. This is most effectively determined by careful tracking of body temperature on a calendar. Teenage girls do not yet have an established cycle history, and sexually active teen couples have a hard time being cautious.

Withdrawal

This used to be a very popular method for the first time or two of teen intercourse. Today condoms are more easily available, and couples are more likely to use them even for first-time encounters. However, I still have a number of males who will brag about their skills in timing an ejaculation. I caution them that so far they may have been lucky, but that it is indeed luck and not skill that has kept the girl from getting pregnant. No one is that good.

Intrauterine Devices

IUDs are not an acceptable birth control method for teens and college students. The FDA does not recommend this method for women who have not had children and may desire to do so in the future. The problem with the IUD is the risk of pelvic inflammatory disease, which can lead to scarring the uterus and infertility.

Barrier Methods

As the name implies, these are barriers to the sperm's travel. Either gender can use a protective shield that in some way impedes the ability of the sperm to reach the egg.

Condoms

My generation knew the condom as something that you purchased with a whisper, usually from a little old lady behind the drugstore counter who would bellow across the room what you wanted. Inevitably the mark of bravado, most teenage boys carried a condom in their wallet as a way of demonstrating (to other guys) that they were always ready. The fact that the condom had been in the wallet for over a year and was probably too dried out to be useful was irrelevant. Few girls of that day would have purchased condoms during their teen years. Doing so would have implied that she was too "ready," too open to sexual intercourse.

Then came HIV and AIDS. Suddenly mothers and fathers were asking me to discuss condoms with their teens. And I knew we had reached a new milestone in teen birth control when I lectured to an all-girls' tenth grade class, and one girl asked, "Doctor, if I take my condom with me on a date, how can I make sure the boy uses it correctly?"

That young lady asked a good question. Birth control and infection prevention is a mutual responsibility. In today's climate it does not matter who buys the condom, or who brings it on the "date." I am happy to tell you that most teens have gotten the message, and the condom is now part of their culture. Kids talk about them easily and purchasing them is not a big deal. Most drugstores now have them right next to the shaving equipment in full display, and they can be purchased by anyone—no questions asked.

Quality control of condoms has been monitored by the FDA since the late 1980s, which is reassuring. After quality comes sales appeal (we hope in that order). In an effort to market the condoms as different, the consumer now has a choice of lubricated, spermicidal, colored, ribbed, extra tip, glow in the dark, and flavored. I am not making any of this up. (The information here refers to traditional—or male—condoms. The female condom, a fairly recent entry into the birth control market, is discussed later in the chapter.) Condoms are made either in latex or plastic, and there is a natural membrane condom made from lamb.

The latex condom is the most commonly used. Easily available and cheap ($6-$7 per package), the latex condom is also considered the most effective. Whether the partners engage in vaginal intercourse or in oral or anal sex, studies demonstrate that the latex condom will provide the best protection against pregnancy and infection, including the transmission of HIV.

Some people are allergic to latex, leading them to use the polyurethane condom or one of the "natural" condoms. Polyurethane condoms are effective in preventing both pregnancy and STDs and have the added advantage of being thinner and odorless. Yet they seem to break more often and they also tend to slip a bit more on withdrawal than the latex condoms. Since these concerns are critical in dealing with teens, I don't yet recommend the polyurethanes to my patients unless there is a latex allergy. If a polyurethane condom must be used, it should be coupled with a spermicide.

"Natural" condoms are made from lamb intestine. That alone is enough to make many teens avoid them. But there are other reasons also. As a birth control device they are as good, if not slightly better, than the latex. However, they are more porous than latex condoms and, as such, do not filter viruses as well. They are also considerably more costly.

One option for dealing with a latex allergy is to use the "natural" condom along with a latex one. This way the latex will only come in contact with the partner who is not allergic. Clearly the allergic male will use the latex over the natural one, reversing the order for the allergic female.

▪ The Importance of Proper Usage

The condom is, in theory, 100 percent effective in preventing pregnancy, but improper use changes the statistics. Over a six-month period the effective birth-control rate is actually about 93 to 95 percent. That means that there is a 5 to 7 percent failure rate as a means of birth control when the condom is used alone. (Some statistics show a failure rate as high as 15 percent.) Although the above are the national statistics for condom use and pregnancy rates, usage among teenagers may well yield higher failure rates because they simply don't use them properly. Teens' sense of risk-taking, and their willingness to believe that nothing bad will happen, puts them at higher risk of not using condoms even if they are available. They are also looking for spontaneity in most actions, and stopping to put on the condom is not spontaneous. They think that if they use the condom "most of the time," they will be okay. When I ask the kids if they are using condoms, I often get this "most of the time" answer. This is especially true if the girl is "on the pill." Another teen fallacy is that if they know their partner, they feel they needn't worry about infection.

Because condom usage is well covered in health education class, most kids know about, understand the need for, and can get condoms, so a parent's task is usually one of reinforcement. One serious discussion with your teen will go a long way; however, if questions should arise, here's what you should know:

How to Properly Use a Condom

1. The condom has to be intact. One has to be careful opening the sealed package so that it does not tear. (The packages have tear notches so that the user does not have to open the condom package with a scissor or with teeth.)
2. There should be no direct genital contact without the condom. This means that the condom must be part of most foreplay. Since teens tend to be impetuous, this is one of the key problems in preventing infection.
3. After ejaculation, one has to withdraw the condom slowly while holding on to the top part.
4. Each act of intercourse requires a new condom.
5. Since most condoms now have a lubricant that is also a spermicide, lubrication is usually not needed. If lubricant is desired, it is important to avoid any oil-based product, which will break down the latex. To make it simple, I tell kids that, if they must use a lubricant, a water-based one such as KY Jelly will do fine. Avoid Vaseline, body lotions, cold creams, etc.
5. Condoms, like milk, can expire. Few of us would drink from a carton of milk that is a few weeks old. The same instinct should prevail when noting a condom's expiration date (clearly labeled on the package). That means that the risk of a dry and damaged condom is quite high. Don't do it. Parenthood is much more expensive than a new condom. Condoms should be stored in a cool, dry place. The glove compartment of your car or your wallet or jeans pocket are not good places to store condoms.
7. As obvious as this sounds, do not use condoms more than once.

One of the most common calls I get on weekends is from a patient stating that "the condom broke." The couple should first use a spermicide (see below) as soon as possible, and then within seventy-two hours (the sooner the better) the girl should see a doctor for the "morning after pill." (This will be discussed in the abortion section later.)

For couples who engage in anal sex, two condoms are recommended as an extra protection against breakage and infection. The FDA has not approved condoms for this use, and therefore, the quality control of condoms does not meet any official test.

A fairly recent phenomenon in my office, and I suspect in other doctors' offices, are calls from patients coming in with their sex partner. They want to be tested for HIV and once proven negative, they feel sex is safe without a condom. They forget about how condoms also protect against gonorrhea, chlamydia, herpes, and syphilis (see Chapter 10). Tell your teen to keep using them, no matter how "safe" their partner is.

Spermicides

The leading chemical used in most spermicides is nonoxynol-9, which kills sperm by destroying the wall of the sperm. Thus, the condom that has nonoxynol-9 offers an extra barrier to pregnancy and STD transmission even if the condom breaks. Since it functions as a lubricant, a killer of sperm, and an STD protector, I recommend that the kids use condoms with this product built in. An important caveat is that nonoxynol-9 has not been proven to kill HIV. The Centers for Disease Control and Protection (CDC) recently sent a warning to physicians that "Nonoxynol-9 should not be recommended as an effective means of HIV prevention" (August 11, 2000, *Mortality and Morbidity*).*

Vaginal spermicides are not prescription items; these products are carried in most drugstores. For the female who wants an extra amount of protection and control in preventing pregnancy and STDs these afford both. Some teens find the foams and gels a bit messy but there are enough products on the market to suit everyone. It is vital to explain to teens that these provide only one hour of protection. She cannot insert it at home and feel that she will have protection after the dance or movie. These can be used alone, but using them with a condom is much safer.

These spermicides are sold in the following forms:

1. **Films.** Nonoxynol-9 is in a transparent film that looks like developed exposed photography film. Sold in a small package (about 3" square) VCF is easily inserted into the vagina and the spermicide is active within fifteen minutes.
2. **Suppositories.** Probably the most common one known is Encare (though there are other brands on the market), which looks like an

---

*The study has been criticized because the women who were included were at very high risk for HIV transmission. However, given the CDC warning, we can no longer recommend that nonoxynol-9 provides HIV protection.

oval suppository. It is inserted into the vagina (after removing the foil!) and it will begin to dissolve within ten to fifteen minutes.

3. **Gels, jelly, and foams.** Messy but effective. They come with an applicator so that there is no waiting time for the spermicide to work.

It is difficult to judge the real effectiveness of spermicides because they are rarely used alone. They should never be the only means of birth control, as they are not sufficient protection. Failures might result if the couple acted sooner than the required time for the spermicide to become effective. Also, the spermicide, in whatever form, must be inserted deep into the vagina so that it covers most of the cervical opening. (As absurd as it sounds when dealing with so sexual a population as teens, many girls are reluctant to insert anything into their vagina with their fingers, let alone deeply.) In addition, douching after using the spermicides will diminish their effectiveness. Douching is not something that teens do often so this is usually not an issue for this population.

Vaginal spermicides increase protection when used with condoms, and they provide the female with more control over the situation. The fact that there is no need to see a doctor and that they can be purchased over-the-counter for less than a dollar per usage also offers advantages. On the other hand, spermicides can be messy, are not foolproof as birth control if it is the only method used, and they do not enhance the spontaneous aspect of sex. Finally, since oral-genital sex is common as part of foreplay, one has to deal with the taste.

Diaphragm and Cervical Cap

The diaphragm looks like a small flexible rubber cup; it is designed to be bent and inserted in the vagina so that it rests under the pubic bone and covers the cervix. Adding a spermicide on either side of the rubber before insertion adds another layer of safety. To say that it requires some dexterity and positioning is a mild statement; it is also messy to put the spermicide jelly on and maneuver it into the correct position, and as a result, it is not popular with teens. The need for it to be initially fitted by a medical professional increases the cost and intimidation factor, and the fact that it needs to be left in place for more than six hours after sex further reduces its desirability. Its pregnancy failure rate in common use is also about 20 percent (because of improper use), making it highly inadequate for teen use. Lastly, a weight change of ten pounds or more may require a new fitting.

A variant of the diaphragm is the cervical cap, which is smaller and fits over the cervix. It also needs to be fitted by a medical professional. Its main advantage is that it can be kept in place for forty-eight hours and does not need repeated applications of spermicide. With typical use, the failure rate of the cap is 40 percent in the first year. With perfect use, the failure rate drops to 26 percent, which is still too high to recommend for use by a teenager.

Female Condom

This is a rather recent entry into the market, and most people are unaware of its existence. Also a one-time-use product, the design is like that of a large condom, about three inches wide by about seven inches long. It is made of polyurethane and therefore is quite strong. At either end there is a flexible ring to help keep it in place. The inner ring, at the closed end, is similar to the rim of the diaphragm and can be folded for insertion. The outer rim prevents it from slipping inside while providing some protection to the external genitalia of the female. Inside, the condom is lubricated with a silicone-based solution to simulate natural lubrication. Because it totally covers the vagina, spermicides are not needed if it is used properly.

The female condom does not require a prescription and can be inserted for up to eight hours before intercourse. It provides protection against pregnancy and against infection since the vagina is fully covered.

Failure rates are a bit hard to calculate since the female condom has only been on the market since 1993, but it is estimated to be similar to the effective use of the diaphragm for a failure rate of approximately 20 percent. I know of no statistics for teenage-use failure rates.

Of these methods, the male condom is probably the most effective, easiest to use, and most cost-effective method for preventing infection and, to some degree, pregnancy. However, the condom does not compare in birth control efficacy with the Pill so the ideal would be a combination of the two.

Hormonal Methods

The Birth Control Pill

In the 1960s, when "the Pill" became readily available, women could, for the first time in history, participate in sex without fear of pregnancy. Over the years the Pill has changed from a high-dose estrogen and progesterone combination to a more carefully calibrated and lower level estrogen and progesterone combination.

In most cases, teenagers have already started having intercourse before they decide to get the Pill as protection. In my practice, many girls have started with the condom, while deciding if they are "serious" about a particular boy before seeking the Pill.

■ How the Pill Works

In the discussion on menstruation (see p. 442), the impact on the ovary by the pituitary gland and two of its hormones, follicle stimulating hormone (FSH) and luteinizing hormone (LH) is discussed. Under the stimulation of these "message" hormones, the ovary will produce estrogen first and then in midcycle will produce progesterone. If the pituitary gland doesn't know that the necessary effect has taken place, it will continue to send its messages and too much hormone production from the ovary would result. However, the very release of the needed hormones is sufficient to send a "feedback signal" to the pituitary that "enough is enough." The Pill takes advantage of this feedback loop by providing just enough estrogen or progesterone (or both) to send a message to shut down FSH and LH production. Once that is accomplished there are no messages sent to the ovary to ovulate. The Pill literally fools the brain into thinking that ovulation has taken place.

At first, the amount of estrogen that was thought necessary to suppress the messenger hormones was quite high. Early pills contained 100 micrograms of the synthetic hormones ethinyl estradiol or mestranol, in contrast with today's pills, which contain as little as 20 micrograms. (Many of the pills also contain progesterone compounds so that the natural menstrual cycle is mimicked.) Your teen's doctor will be able to prescribe the dosage that is right for her. Because many of the health warnings regarding the Pill involved studies of women who took quite high doses, the original data is no longer applicable to most of the pills prescribed today.

Simply put, if you want your teen to use the birth control method that is most foolproof, then the Pill is the answer. It is nearly 99.9 percent effective;

efficacy drops when the Pill is not used properly (not taken daily). I have had only one patient get pregnant while on the Pill and that was during the first month of use, a time when it is recommended that another method of birth control be used along with the Pill. Some of the newer pills claim that there is no need for backup birth control even during the first month of use. However, I recommend that, since we are dealing with the teenage population where there is great risk of forgetting one or more pills before the "habit" is established, it is important to use another method of birth control in the first month. Since the Pill only protects against a pregnancy, the use of a condom with the Pill will give maximum protection against infection and should be used whenever the couple has sex.

■ Who Can Take the Pill?

The risk of complications from a pregnancy termination, or even a full-term pregnancy for a teen generally far outweigh the risks of the Pill. Most teenage girls are healthy enough that the use of the Pill is not a problem but that is a discussion your daughter needs to have with her doctor. However, there are a few things parents should consider and discuss with their daughter before she decides to go on the Pill.

■ Types of Birth Control Pills and Their Use

Since the cycle of most women is about twenty-eight days, most companies package the Pill with twenty-one days of hormones and seven days of a placebo to mimic the menstrual period (this pill will be a different color). This allows the girl to take a pill daily and not forget the rhythm she has started. I usually recommend taking the Pill with some daily activity such as brushing teeth.

For teenagers trying to hide the package from their parents, this may pose some complications, causing them to forget to take a pill. If you learn belatedly that your daughter is on the Pill, clear the air and let her know that whether or not you approve, she doesn't need to hide it from you. The risk of forgetting the Pill because she must hide it gives rise to the danger of getting pregnant— the exact thing she is trying to avoid. (In the event that a pill is forgotten, two pills can be taken the next day. However, if two or more days in a row are forgotten then one cannot rely on the Pill for that month, and another birth control method must be used for that time.) If I find that a teen does this repeatedly, I become concerned about whether the Pill is the correct birth control method for her.

Your doctor will decide which pill to use; however, understand the labeling on the Pill is helpful. There are usually two numbers on the package. The first represents the amount of progesterone and the second the amount of estrogen.

Points to Discuss with Your Daughter about the Pill

1. **Expense.** She should know that this will be an monthly cost, not a one-time expense. You may want to make her responsible for it. If we want to teach responsibility, the cost should be borne by the teen. There is a potentially damaging message in "You can have sex and Mommy will pay for the Pill." The estimated cost of the Pill is between $20 and $35 per month, plus the initial cost of seeing the doctor and getting a Pap smear. In many cities there are public clinics that will provide free or low-cost exams and that provide the Pill at much lower cost. At this time, some insurance companies provide coverage for birth control prescriptions.

2. **Responsibility.** Your daughter must assume responsibility for taking the Pill regularly. An undisciplined teen who forgets to brush her teeth, often sleeps at friends' instead of coming home, and isn't particularly diligent about anything in life is a poor candidate for the Pill. It must be impressed upon her that every aspect of sex is an adult privilege and an adult responsibility; especially emphasize the adult responsibility of having a baby. This takes us back to the need to have the girl pay for the Pill.

3. **No smoking.** The official recommendation is to caution against Pill use in smokers over thirty-five. If one looks at the overall statistics for risks, the teenage girl has an advantage from the point of view of her youth. If she smokes, it raises the risk and basically puts her in the same age range as a thirty-year-old in terms of risk factors. Yet, the concern about unwanted pregnancy is so great that even smokers can be put on the Pill. I use this as a deterrent to smoking.

4. **Risk factors.** The health of each teenager who contemplates going on the Pill needs to be evaluated, and no one should start this medication without knowing that there are risks involved:
   Possible blood clots. Since the Pill increases the risk of making the blood clot faster (this is an effect of the estrogen), it makes no sense to initiate this method if there is an existing risk.
   Artery blockage. While estrogen can cause clotting problems on the venous side of the system, some preexisting conditions might actually promote the rare problem of blockage of the arteries. Girls who are very heavy smokers, obese, or have previously damaged arteries from

kidney disease or diabetes mellitus may have so high a risk that the Pill is not an option.

Breast cancer. Girls with a very high familial risk factor for breast cancer may not be good candidates for the Pill. Although there is a lot of controversy about the risk factors, it does *not* appear that the Pill will greatly, if at all, alter the risk factors for breast cancer. The risk was greater for familial breast cancer with the high-dose pills and not the new low-dose ones. However, if the girl is reluctant because of fear of cancer, my concern is that she will unconsciously forget to take the Pill. I would prefer she not take the Pill when I am not convinced of compliance. The amount of unconscious anxiety associated with breast cancer and Pill use is almost certain to lead to "forgetting to take the Pill." Despite FDA approval of the Pill even with a breast cancer history in the family, I am concerned about compliance in this situation and with this age group.

Cervical cancer risk. While it is true that the woman who uses the Pill has a slightly higher risk of cervical cancer, statistics show that she must be a "long-term" user (more than five continuous years) and have had multiple partners. For teenagers, the Pill does not create an immediate risk. However, the teenager with multiple partners does run a higher risk of infection that can alter the cells of the cervix and lead to cancer. The bottom line to the data is that there is only an "incidental" relationship between the Pill and cervical cancer.

Other concerns. Other reasons that would preclude use of the Pill include severe headaches that suggest increase pressure in the brain, hypertension, advanced diabetes, disorders of liver or gallbladder function (hepatitis carriers *can* use the Pill), vaginal bleeding of unknown cause, and pregnancy (one usually waits until the girl gets a period before starting the Pill).

Some good news. The other side of the coin is that the Pill, by suppressing ovulation, diminishes the risk of ovarian and uterine cancer. One generally does not think about this with teenagers, as the risk for both is quite low. However, it is a factor if their is a family history of either disease.

Possible Side Effects from the Pill

Depending on the pill selected, a teen may suffer some mild side effects. Those associated with estrogen include:

- **Weight gain.** Society's infatuation with thinness sometimes makes a girl choose not to use a method that would make her "fat." She will, and often does, decline the Pill. She shouldn't. Studies have shown that weight gain is vastly over-stated, and most girls will not gain weight. One to two pounds, at most, may be due to the Pill; the rest belong to French fries, cookies, and cake.
- **Fluid retention.** Rarely severe.
- **Breast enlargement.** Although often met with gratitude by many girls, those who have very large breasts find this side effect troublesome. The doctor should be consulted if this is a problem.
- **Increased blood pressure.**
- **Increased coagulation effect.**

Progesterone side effects include:

- **Increased blood pressure.**
- **Headaches.**
- **Breast tenderness.** Most women are aware of this before their period when progesterone is high.
- **Depression.**

Hence, a pill like OrthoNovum 1/50/28 contains 1 milligram of progestin and 50 micrograms of estrogen; the 28 indicates that there are twenty-one days of "real pills" and seven days of placebo to allow the person ease of use on a daily basis. Some pills only contain progesterone.

There are a great many pills on the market, some with varying degrees of estrogen and progesterone. A teen should discuss with her doctor which pill is best for her and why it has been selected. Sometimes it takes a few attempts before the right one works for a particular woman.

With all of the pills that either have low amounts of estrogen, or have low amounts of progesterone in the first week, there is a risk of breakthrough bleed-

Pill Users Must Be Mindful of Warnings about Medicine Combinations

Teens often forget to view the Pill as medication. I often will ask a new patient who is in for a general examination what medication, if any, she is taking and I will get a "none" response. Later with questions about menstruation, the same patient will now tell me that she "is on the Pill" and that's why her period is regular. Since some medications do interfere with the efficacy of the Pill, it is critical that anyone who is on the Pill tell their physician. The following are of concern:

■ Anticonvulsant medications interfere with estrogen breakdown and actually lower the amount of estrogen for birth control efficacy.

■ Antibiotics. Prolonged use of antibiotics has been anecdotally implicated in lowering the Pill's effect. The premise is that the bacteria eliminated in the stomach will affect absorption of the Pill. This warning is particularly germane for the teenager, since the ampicillin group and the tetracyclines are often used for acne control. The hard data fail to support the concern about lowering the estrogen effect. I simply recommend that teenagers on the Pill use an alternative "backup" method, such as a condom, during antibiotic use.

ing. This often happens in the first month of use and doesn't require a change in the pill. However, in some girls, the constant breakthrough will necessitate a change to a higher dose estrogen or to one that contains a different progestin. Most pill takers will adjust after the first month and will be able to stay on the same pill without interruptions.

I am often asked if it is dangerous to start "too early," and if a girl is on the Pill how long can she use it. Currently the lower doses have made the Pill safer and many physicians will prescribe up to the age of thirty-five for a woman who does not smoke. In all cases your physician will advise as to safety and use of the Pill.

When a woman stops taking the Pill, she can presume she will be fertile. She may not become pregnant immediately, but after a few months off the Pill she should be ovulating and ready for pregnancy.

The "Morning After" Pill

Emergency contraception such as the "morning after" pill is considered under several types of circumstances:

■ The couple who finds themselves with a broken or leaking condom.
■ Teens who foolishly have unprotected intercourse. They have no recourse for prevention of sexually transmitted disease, but they can still do something about preventing pregnancy.
■ Anyone who misses several days of the Pill and has intercourse.
■ Rape.

The usual remedy under these circumstances is a high dose of the birth control pill. The one generally prescribed is Ovral, or its successor, Lo/Ovral, and its function is to prevent implantation of the egg. Because a high dose of hormones is involved, many women will complain of nausea and vomiting with the first dose. Because it would make no sense to take the pills and then throw them up, many physicians advise the use of an antiemetic (antinausea) medication one hour before taking the pills. Over-the-counter medicines that can help with vomiting include Benadryl and Dramamine. (Prescription medications such as a Tigan or Phenergan suppository can be used as well. However, I find that suppository use is a problem with many teens.) A recent prescription product that is packaged for single use is Preven, a combination estrogen and progesterone emergency kit. I have found that teens like the easy-to-use instructions. A new alternative to the combination pills is the progestin-only emergency pill (containing 0.75 mg of levonorgestrel). This new method is referred to as Plan B and has the advantage of causing less nausea.

A potential new method for emergency care involves the use of mifepristone (RU 486) within the same time frame. However, it is not a currently approved method. This drug blocks the progesterone effect and has fewer side effects. However, mifepristone is not without some risk, and most physicians tend to rely on the availability of "the Pill."

This "morning after" pill is effective up to seventy-two hours post-coital; however, ideally it should be used within forty-eight hours. Your teen should call her doctor, or if she is away from home, emergency rooms and walk-in clinics such as Planned Parenthood can prescribe the medication. There is also a national hotline that will direct teens to appropriate facilities or to doctors in their area who will help. The phone number is 1-800-NOT-2-LATE. Simple and clever.

Anyone who needs emergency contraception should be warned to do a pregnancy test in a few weeks if no menstrual flow is seen. Also, teens need to know that this is an "emergency" treatment and not a standard birth control method.

Depo-Provera

Depo-Provera (depot medroxyprogesterone acetate, DMPA) is a very effective means of birth control. It was a very popular method several years ago, and some physicians still use it for teens who are at risk for good compliance with other methods. It works by suppressing FSH and LH by means of an injection of long-acting progesterone. It has a low failure rate, but it has the disadvantage of needing a medical worker to inject the hormone, usually every three months. With the exception of some breakthrough bleeding and the need to continue to get shots, this is an effective and easy method of birth control. The problem is corralling the teenager for the shot.

The other potential issue is that the injection site is sometimes painful. However, for those who keep forgetting pills, condoms, and spermicides, the Depo shot may be the answer. It is important to also note that once the shots stop, the patient may not get her period for up to six months. Since there is no estrogen, patients who are only Depo are at risk for a lower bone density.

Norplant: Subcutaneous Implants

An even better method in terms of compliance and effectiveness is Norplant. This carries a nearly 100 percent success rate in preventing pregnancy. Once the implants of progesterone are placed under the skin of the inner part of the arm, the teen has nothing more to remember. Other than using a condom to prevent infection, this is ideal for teens who are unreliable Pill users. So why hasn't this become the method of choice?

To begin with, Norplant requires a "minor" surgical procedure with local anesthesia and a small incision through which the six implants are implanted. This is hardly something that is eagerly met by the teen population. Some clinics were very enthusiastic in the early 1990s about Norplant as a method for those patients who could not afford other methods, or who were not particularly compliant with the Pill or condoms. However, complications eventually made the Norplant less popular.

Aside from the same side effects of irregular bleeding and breast tenderness associated with progesterone, the site of the incisions can become infected and painful. Some women object to feeling the implants under the skin and many opt to remove them; a few have expelled them spontaneously. For the teen who is willing to put up with all this and who has a doctor who approves, the implants give effective protection for about five years.

In my practice and in talking to other physicians who work with teens, however, the drawbacks to this method of birth control make it unpopular with teens.

Newly Released Birth Control Methods

Recently, the FDA has approved some new products. Although they are not in general use and have not become part of the mainstream of birth control methods, they show promise and may serve teens' needs for effective control as they are not daily methods. Since they are all new, be sure to discuss their safety with your doctor.

1. **Lunelle**. This is the first monthly birth control (so named after the "lunar" calendar of the "once-a-month") method. Its immediate appeal is that the woman does not have to remember to take anything daily, nor insert anything vaginally or intrauterine, nor deal with painful subcutaneous implants. Instead a single, once-a-month injection of time-released hormones (estrogen and progestoerone) is given. The current data suggest effectiveness equal to the Pill.

   The immediate drawback of an injection for the teenager has to be weighed against its advantage of only requiring a single, once-a-month shot. Yet, it is too soon to know if we should be using this on teens as it has only recently been released. For this to work, Lunelle must be given at intervals of twenty-eight to thirty days (no later than thirty-three). Hence, compliance plays an important part.

2. **Birth Control Patch**. We have learned that many medications can be delivered through the skin (the nicotine patch and the testosterone patch are but a few examples). A patch that will deliver birth control hormones is now being made with the intention of substituting it for the Pill. Approval is pending, and one company is marketing it under the name Evra. The patch is about the size of a half-dollar and is applied on the arm, abdomen, or buttocks. We obviously have no experience with this, but one immediate drawback that I can envision

for a teenager is the visibility of the patch. Also, the teen who is very active and sweats will have a problem keeping on the patch.

3. **Vaginal Ring**. This has gotten recent FDA approval and is marketed for women who have difficulty remembering to take their pills daily. A flexible plastic ring, it releases continuous low-dose hormones while placed in the vagina for three weeks out of the month. As long as the ring is in place, the hormones necessary to prevent pregnancy are released and the woman has good protection. Marketed as NuvaRing, its effectiveness in preventing pregnancy is about 98 percent in preliminary stuudies. Since the woman inserts and removes the ring herself, we have to expect the teenager to be able to comply with the three-week rule.

4. **Mirena**. Although we have said that the IUD is not for teens, the reader should know that there is a new IUD being proposed that prevents pregnancy for up to five years. Mirena is expected to be released soon. Just as with all IUDs, it is inserted into the uterus, but this one releases progesterone directly onto the lining. Although effective for pregnancy prevention, I cannot see too many teens using this method. Again, for a woman who intends to get pregnant in the future, the IUD poses problems of infection and inflammation. Will Mirena do the same?

Pregnancy

As painful as it is to consider, some teens *will* get pregnant. Whether by birth control failure or recklessness, it happens. Some girls will call furtively and ask for help in deciding the next step while others will come with one or both parents to decide what to do next.

Most pregnancies are diagnosed by a measurement of HCG (the hormone made during pregnancy). The test used in doctors' offices is accurate to a very low level of HCG and the newer ones can detect within a week of implantation (when the fertilized egg attaches to the uterine lining). The over-the-counter test kits sold in pharmacies do not have the same degree of accuracy. Because of inexperience or doing the test too early, the test may yield a false negative; the person is pregnant but the test fails to detect the small amount of HCG present. The teen's best chance of correct and early analysis is to see her doctor for the test. When there is doubt, the physician can confirm the diagnosis with a pelvic exam or with a more accurate blood test that quantifies the amount of HCG present.

Some girls will opt to continue the pregnancy. At that point, she needs to select an obstetrician and establish a schedule for prenatal visits and care. These girls often have to drop out of school and rely on their parents for support. The statistics on successful marriages and teenage pregnancy are not encouraging. Many girls will feel that their lives would be altered for the worse and they feel that they cannot continue the pregnancy. On the assumption that the patient wants to terminate, what are her options?

Before further discussing abortion, I would like to say that the only personal opinion I am going to put forward as relevant here is this: I don't approve of abortion as a means of *birth control.* It represents a complete failure of the system, whether it is the method that failed or the message we have expressed to kids about sex. I have never seen a teen terminate a pregnancy casually. They may sound glib, but when you press a little you will hear the anxiety and the panic underneath.

Perhaps the first step is to realize that the teenager needs help. She is frightened and needs her parents and her doctor to support her. I have had parents whose first words were "What am I going to tell my friends?" I have always countered with "*Nothing!* Let's help your daughter first!"

When faced with the reality of an unwanted pregnancy, I have watched both sides agonize over what lies ahead. I have listened to the most ardent supporters of abortion, whether the girl or her parent, tell me that this is one of the most difficult steps they have ever taken. On the other side, I have confronted parents whose beliefs are such that they could never condone or support abortion. Yet, when it came to their own daughter they hesitated and realized that they were no longer dealing with an abstraction; we were talking about a real sixteen-year-old who was faced with delivering a baby. Moral issues change when they hit home, regardless of your position. The moral, ethical, and religious issues will be left to each individual. My role is to guide the teen and her family through the options.

Abortion

Currently U.S. law gives a teenager access to abortion and, in most states, she can do so without parental consent. In some states, parents have to be notified prior to the teenager getting the abortion. In some there is a mandatory waiting period, and others require counseling prior to the termination. Ask the doctor about your own state's law.

In my experience, most teenagers' first think about going through the abortion alone. They feel that it will be better if their parents don't know; they fear their parents' reaction and their disappointment. Some will argue that their boyfriend will pay for it and others say that a good friend will accompany them to the procedure. I keep expressing my view that she needs her parents there for her. I have failed twice in getting the girl to allow me to tell her parents. In both cases, the depression and guilt that later occurred made me sad that the girls didn't have their parents to help them through this difficult time. I have also had several situations where the decision was made by the girl to tell the mother only. That decision also worked out poorly, as the mother had to keep a secret from her husband. The ideal situation under these circumstances is for both parents to know what is happening. I say it's ideal, not easy or common. Some girls will emphatically not allow the parent to be told, and under most state laws she will be allowed to terminate without her parents knowing. I still believe that she will need some support, either in the form of friends, a caring relative, or certainly a compassionate and understanding physician.

Mifepristone (RU 486)

This is the infamous French pill that took the entire world by storm. It has recently been released in the United States, and the FDA has approved this pill for use in terminating pregnancies of seven weeks or less. Its use and effectiveness with teens is not known.

Administering RU 486 generally requires at least three office visits. In the first the patient is given the mifepristone vaginally (there is also a form that can be taken by mouth) and sent home. After forty-eight hours the patient must return to the doctor's office for further evaluation and possible treatment with Cytotec, another uterine stimulant that the doctor may use. She may have to stay several hours because of the potential for cramping and bleeding. Although some physicians will allow mature women to take these pills at home, my preference is not to do this with teenagers. Regardless of the outcome of the second visit, the patient is seen in two weeks to assess if the termination is complete. If there is a failure to terminate, then a traditional D & C (dilation and curettage) is done. For this reason, gynecologists are the proper physicians to see for this process.

> **Bethany is seventeen** *and a member of a religion that does not allow abortion. She is close to her parents and they would proudly say that Bethany "tells them everything." I knew from my confidential discussions with her that she had not told her mother everything and that she was close to having intercourse with her boyfriend. The amount of "sex" short of intercourse was such that I suggested she consider the Pill. She declined and said that she was okay with what was going on. Several months later I got a call*

from her therapist that she was pregnant, and he wanted to know if I knew someone who could help with an abortion. Both the therapist and I realized that the medications she was taking for depression and arthritis would pose a problem in terms of birth defects. The therapist received Bethany's permission to divulge her situation to the parents. I contacted a gynecologist whom I knew was sympathetic to this age group and to the situation.

Bethany wanted to terminate the pregnancy, but her parents were caught in an ethical dilemma. Having a baby would put going to college, indeed her whole future, in jeopardy. Furthermore, this pregnancy could yield major birth defects for the baby because of the medications. The parents were stunned and paralyzed in deciding what to do. Bethany did not need parental consent but the relationship with her parents almost mandated a unanimous decision. Though both parents felt terribly conflicted, they finally agreed to the decision to terminate. Bethany saw the gynecologist and mifepristone was administered in his office. Two days later he prescribed Cytotec, and Bethany began to bleed. But on her follow up visit ten days later, the gynecologist found the abortion was not complete. The gynecologist finished the termination with a D & C in the office.

The long-term effects of this ordeal may not be known for a while. At present, Bethany is in therapy and is dealing with the issues of her depression and her pregnancy. The parents have continued to be supportive of her but may bear their own scars.

Other Abortion Methods

Since not all teenagers have the support of parents, or even easy access to medical care, all too often the teen is pregnant and either doesn't know it or denies it for too long. She will then find her options more limited. The availability and advisability of abortion methods is determined by the number of weeks of gestation. Beyond the eighth week the options involve surgical intervention to terminate the pregnancy. As for all medical or surgical procedures, the girl's doctor will be able to advise about the best options. In the United States, most terminations may take place through the second trimester (technically through the twenty-seventh week of gestation). However, some states limit the time to twenty-four weeks.

Abortion Procedures

1. If the patient is more than eight weeks but less than twelve weeks pregnant, then a vacuum aspiration is available. The patient's uterine contents are literally suctioned out; the patient can have local anesthesia or general. One complication for teens is the expense, and whether the physician will want to do the procedure on an outpatient basis. I do know of some physicians who do the procedure in their offices, but the risk of anesthesia, bleeding, and surgery in general has made this an inpatient procedure.
2. Beyond twelve but before twenty weeks, a similar procedure is undertaken but with a dilatation of the cervix for better control. If the physician cleans out the uterus with curettage and nothing else, it is called a dilation and curettage, or D & C. If the uterine contents have to be removed with a forceps then it is called a Dilation and Evacuation (D & E).
3. For second trimester terminations (later than twelve weeks), hypertonic solutions are administered directly into the uterus, which induce miscarriage. These are still available.
4. For second trimester abortions, prostaglandins (as vaginal suppositories) are available. These chemicals stimulate uterine contractions, which induce abortion.

Complications of Abortion

1. Potential infection. Generalized chills and fever may indicate localized vaginal infection.
2. Cramps and abdominal pain may indicate infection or even possible rupture of the uterine wall. However, these may be the natural byproducts of the stimulation of the uterus required to expel its contents.
3. Vaginal bleeding, usually from part of the placenta remaining in the uterus.
4. Emotional. Not all teenagers will see a therapist to deal with post-abortion issues. However, all teens who terminate a pregnancy need to be watched for signs of depression that *may* ultimately lead back to the abortion.

Helping Your Teen
(Both Sons and Daughters)
"Do the Right Thing"

In summary, other than abstinence, the Pill provides the safest, most effective method of birth control for most girls. The responsible teenage girl can get the Pill in a confidential manner in most states. She does, however, need a gynecologic exam, and this may be the single most important deterrent. The cost and the need to schedule an appointment for the examination often make teenagers wary. I am frequently asked by my male patients how their girlfriends can get the Pill. My female patients ask if I'm going to tell their parents. In New York State, teenagers are allowed birth control and pelvic exams without parental consent, but physicians have different comfort levels. Check with your doctor regarding the law in your state. They may feel that the law is fine, but they will not prescribe the Pill to a teenager without the parents' knowledge. Teens often turn to public clinics for their exams and prescriptions. These facilities do provide safe and effective care, but as a rule they tend to be less personally involved with their patients.

Condoms are a must for kids even if they feel they "know" their partner and they have both tested negative for HIV. This ignores the other infections and reveals a naiveté that all will be fine because "bad things happen to others." When one of my patients comes in with a lesion, or a discharge, or pregnant, they are stunned that what they have been hearing in sex ed class has actually happened to them. They are no longer reading about teen statistics. They are now one of them.

As a parent of a girl you need to consider the following and how it applies to you:

■ If you find yourself in a situation in which your daughter asks for birth control, how do you feel about allowing her to have it? Can you even talk about it with her?
■ Will you allow a visit to the gynecologist and thus permit her to establish a relationship with a physician who will be there for all her questions?
■ How will you react if you find a package of pills or a diaphragm in your daughter's room?

I suggest that parents not yet in this situation take the time to discuss these feelings with their spouses. In an earlier chapter I had parents discuss the "silent words" as an exercise. It's time for another exercise. Talk to your spouse and your child about birth control. Talk about your real feelings now that she has reached a stage of sexual maturity in which intercourse is a possibility. Don't approach this from the point of view that "My child is not going to need it." If she doesn't become sexually active to the point of intercourse, bravo for her. If she does and you are prepared, bravo for you.

Sons raise a different set of responses and questions. If you found condoms in your son's room, you might be slightly surprised and then pleased at this "responsible" act of practicing safe sex. For many, the double standard still makes it easier to think of boys having sex. However, you should be equally concerned about your son's physical and emotional health.

If you are the parent of a boy, ask yourself the following:

■ How do you feel about him having sex? What do you want him to know about birth control, and can you really have a discussion with him?

■ Should Dad go into his room, smile, punch him in the arm and say "Way to go, son!"? Can you have a serious discussion with your son about responsibility and respect for himself and for the girl? Can you do this without making it sound as if it were nothing more than a rite of passage?

When you finish discussing your expectations and values, take a deep breath and get ready for an even harder discussion. We are about to deal with sexually transmitted diseases.

Chapter 10

Sexually Transmitted Diseases

The very thinking process that makes teens feel they are immune to disaster magnifies their risk of exposure to sexually transmitted diseases. Their risk-taking behavior (not using condoms), the typical youthful belief that nothing bad will happen to them, their naiveté in thinking they "know" their partner, and the reality that they will probably have multiple sexual partners all combine to pose large risks for this age group.

The average teen is bombarded with education about the use of condoms and the risk of HIV. That is all well and good, but there are other diseases, and a negative test for HIV cannot be the sole criteria for not using condoms. They want to be sexually spontaneous and they don't like condoms. Most feel if they aren't at risk for contracting HIV, then safety is no longer a concern. Despite admonitions about herpes, chlamydia, or other STDs, they will counter with "They don't kill you. Besides you can get treatment for them." This is a dangerous mistake. Some STDs, such as herpes, *cannot* be cured. Others, such as chlamydia, can permanently impair fertility if left untreated.

Sexually transmitted diseases can be classified as viral (herpes simplex, genital warts, molluscum contagiosum, HIV), bacterial (chlamydia, gonorrhea), fungal (candida), syphilis (caused by a spirochete, will be dealt with separately), and as parasites (pediculosis, scabies). We'll take a look at the individual diseases, how they are contracted, and their treatment.

How Prevalent Are STDs?

One of the problems in interpreting data on STDs is the demography of the sample. If one looks at an inner-city population with less access to medical care, the statistics are quite different from those of a middle-class population that goes to private doctors. Socioeconomic group, gender, race, and sexual practices will also slant the numbers, so it is difficult to give a statistic that is meaningful to parents. It is often quoted that 25 percent of all reported STDs in the United States are in the teenage population, and it is known that 45 percent of Caucasian girls aged fifteen to nineteen have had intercourse; in the other races, that statistic approaches 56 percent. Among boys, the statistics are higher for both races. If the national statistics tell us that one in eight women aged fifteen to nineteen get pregnant yearly, then we can conclude that at least this many girls are also at risk for STDs. When you consider girls who are using the Pill without condoms, this number obviously is higher.

As with other diseases, early diagnosis is helpful. The American Academy of Obstetrics and Gynecology has long recommended an annual gynecologic

Factors That Increase Risk of STDs

1. **Multiple partners**. Clearly, multiple partners increase exposure.
2. **Gender**. Females may be harder to diagnose and may be more prone to certain infections because of the vulnerability of vaginal lining.
3. **Smoking**. The teen smoker, particularly if smoking begins at a very early age, indicates a willingness to engage in risk-taking behavior.
4. **Alcohol**. Underage drinking is another sign of willingness to take risks; alcohol consumption also impairs judgment, increasing the likelihood of unsafe sex and exposure to STDs.
5. **Drug abuse**. Like alcohol consumption, substance abuse shows a willingness to take risks; judgment is similarly impaired.
6. **Lack of use of condoms**. They work, but only if worn!
7. **Unavailability of health care**. Early diagnosis and treatment helps prevent the spread of disease.
8. **Socioeconomic grouping**. (Refer to the statistics above.)
9. **Lack of circumcision**. The male's infection may be hard to spot if he is uncircumcised. On the other hand, the circumcised male may be at higher risk for penile warts.

exam and a Pap smear (sampling and analysis of cells from the cervix) for any-one who is sexually active. I have always had a problem with the "annual" Pap smear because this was predicated on monogamy. Frankly, it makes more sense to argue that if there is a new partner there is a new exposure and a new Pap smear should be done. Put another way, my female patients have all heard me say "new penis, new Pap."

Viral Infections

Herpes Simplex

When teens say they have "herpes" they would be more accurate if they announced they have herpes simplex, since there is more than one form of her-pes. (Herpes zoster causes chickenpox and shingles; see p. 334.)

Herpes simplex appears in two types in humans: herpes simplex virus 1 (HSV-1) and herpes simplex virus 2 (HSV-2). The first virus is less virulent and is associated with lesions of the mouth, often called "fever blisters" or "cold sores." The more aggressively invasive lesions of the genitalia are caused by the second virus. Unfortunately, current sexual practices make it impossible to diagnose simply by the location of a lesion. (Oral sex can lead to a type 2 infec-tion on the mouth.)

The only way to make a definitive diagnosis is by using a swab to obtain cells from the lesion and viewing the cells through a microscope or culturing directly for HSV. Unfortunately the latter takes time to yield an answer and by the time the results return the episode may be over. Hence, most physicians will treat on suspicion once it is established that the patient gets recurrent episodes.

With HSV-2, the initial lesion is usually on the genitalia, and the patient will experience a fairly painful, itchy area that, on inspection, may demonstrate a very small shallow ulcer. The lesion actually goes through a small blister stage that ruptures easily, and the patient often misses that phase. If the lesions are clustered in a group, it makes the visual diagnosis of herpes (regardless of type) easier. The first episode will last anywhere from ten to fourteen days, during which the virus can be transmitted. When the lesions dry up, the patient can-not assume she is no longer contagious. During the time that the lesions are not visibly present, the virus will lie dormant in the cervix, or labia, or on the skin of the penis waiting to erupt. Subsequent episodes tend not to last as long or be as painful. On average, future outbreaks will last about five days; inter-vals between episodes will vary.

About ten years ago a new antiviral medication, acyclovir, came on the market, offering the first safe, easy way to treat the virus. (Remember that antibiotics do nothing to keep a virus from spreading.) The drug changed the treatment of HSV. Given orally for five days at the first sign of an outbreak, this medicine, and newer ones, helps control lesions, and the patient feels better immediately. The same antiviral medicine is also available in an ointment form and helps relieve symptoms. However, the oral medicine is more effective at controlling outbreaks. In some cases, as with frequent outbreaks, the patient is put on a six-month course of these antiviral drugs. Currently HSV is treatable on an episode-by-episode basis, but we have yet to develop a true cure for the underlying virus. Teens are hard-pressed to believe that they got an infection that may be there for "life."

If a patient has herpes simplex, the disease is transmittable even when there are no visible lesions, so condoms should be used at all times. As discussed in the section on birth control, the latex ones afford some protection against the virus but only on areas covered by the condom. The patient who has an active lesion, whether it's a genital one or a "fever blister" around the mouth, should refrain from sexual contact—proper use of condoms is sometimes problematic for teens, and it's not worth taking a chance.

Hepatitis B Virus

This virus can be transmitted through all body fluids including blood. As such it clearly falls into the category of a "sexually transmitted disease." Every teen should receive the three-shot immunization series. (See p. 332 for a discussion of Hepatitis B.)

Genital Warts

Warts are viral infections. There are about seventy different types of the human papilloma virus (HPV), but only a few subtypes are involved in the premalignant genital wart. Sometimes they are referred to as venereal warts, or by their technical medical name, condylomata acuminata. (The type of wart that appears on our hands and feet is not caused by the same virus as warts that one finds on the genitalia.)

The warts of HPV are small flesh-colored lesions that look like cauliflower; they may be single or grouped, flat or raised. With that degree of variability it is sometimes hard to be sure that the lesion is HPV. In addition, the person may experience few symptoms. On females the warts appear on the cervix or inside the vagina, giving little indication of infection; other times, the warts may appear on the labia, and a patient may experience itchiness and discomfort. In severe cases the warts will spread to the anus, or this area can be infected by direct contact. On males the wart is usually on the tip of the penis but it can be found anywhere along the shaft and scrotum. Often the wart is found by chance, or on girls by Pap smear.

If the person seeks medical help because of exposure, there may not yet be a wart to diagnose. It may take weeks to months before the wart is visible. In an age in which the teenager wants to know "who gave it to them," this last may be difficult.

The virus needs skin-to-skin transmission, so the most common exposure is through unprotected intercourse. However, since a condom may not cover all the skin that can harbor the virus, it can offer no guarantee of protection. Oral transmission of this virus is possible but not very likely, a fact that many teens use to argue for the "safety" of oral sex.

Steven is a college sophomore *who called my office during a recent December break. He and his girlfriend had been "tested," and they decided that it would be safe to stop using condoms. His girlfriend was on the Pill, and they were assured that this would prevent pregnancy. Each was comfortable with the other's STD history.*

Because of an insurance physical for the girl, she subsequently had to get another pelvic and Pap smear. This Pap was positive, and she was told, "It was likely to be HPV." Somewhat panicked, Steven wanted to be sure that he did not have the wart. When he undressed, I could find no evidence of infection. Since I saw nothing, I told him that we now needed to know for sure if his girlfriend really had HPV (which would be confirmed by a colposcopy biopsy). He felt relieved again until he asked me if I was sure he didn't have it. My response that he could have a subclinical infection and that we would have to "wait and see" was less than reassuring.

HPV is felt to be a risk factor for cancer of the cervix, the vulva, the anus, and the penis. Hence, all HPV warts in this area need to be removed either with liquid nitrogen (freezing) or with a caustic acid agent. Some physicians will use an electrocautery device, and lately, laser surgery is being used. Obviously the fact that there may be subclinical warts makes definitive treatment problematic; follow-up visits to detect new warts are critical. Although it is possible that the warts will spontaneously disappear, no one should bank on that as treatment.

There is some hope for improved treatment. The FDA has recently approved a prescription cream (Aldara) that helps suppress the external wart's growth. Its major advantage is that it can be applied at home. Clinical trials are also currently being held to test an HPV vaccine.

Molluscum Contagiosum

This virus causes pearly bumps (warts) on the skin and is harmless. However, because genital warts can lead to malignancy, molluscum contagiosum causes concern until diagnosis is definitive. (The term *molluscum* refers to its pearl-like appearance: molluscum is Latin for oysters.)

The lesions often appear in clusters; each small bump has a thin milky fluid inside, giving it the pearl-like appearance. At the top of each bump, there is a dimple, or umbilicus. From their appearance alone, one can generally make the diagnosis. This virus belongs to the same family as the virus that causes chickenpox. Sometimes the two lesions will appear similar and one may need to examine the fluid contents under a microscope.

If the transmission occurs sexually, then the lesions tend to appear along the lower abdomen and pubic area. However, it isn't always passed through sexual contact, so its presence does not mean that the teenager is sexually active. There are reports of molluscum contagiosum outbreaks in children, in wrestlers, and in those who share gym equipment, which demonstrates that one can have the lesions without sexual contact. Often the person with the lesions may not even know that they have a contagious rash and take no protection against transmitting it. As such, one cannot realistically protect against getting these warts.

It takes anywhere from a week to a few months after contact before the lesions appear. In most cases the lesions are asymptomatic and may actually be on the body for some time before they are identified. Treatment is simple but tedious if there are many lesions: each one is opened, and the base is cauterized. As with HPV sometimes they spontaneously disappear.

Human Immunodeficiency Virus and Acquired Immune Deficiency Syndrome (HIV and AIDS)

I doubt that there is a person on the planet who has not heard of this virus. We have educated, lectured, preached, and frightened our teens to the point where they fear *only* this virus, ignoring the precautions necessary to avoid other STDs. But when death is the consequence of a sexual act, I suppose that makes sense.

At present, it is estimated that there are almost two million Americans infected with HIV. That does not mean that we have two million people with AIDS. The latter is a complex disease with many features that stem from the infection of the virus we call HIV, and it takes years for most HIV patients to develop AIDS. For that reason, the medical community does not see full-blown

Factors That Increase Risk of HIV

The specific factors that place a person at risk for contracting HIV are the following:

1. **Unprotected intercourse.**
2. **Injected drug use with shared needles.**
3. **Sexual contact with anyone who uses injected drugs.**
4. **Drug and alcohol abuse.** It is estimated that at least one-third of teens will have had unprotected sex while using drugs or alcohol.
5. **Body piercing.** Recent evidence suggests an increased risk of exposure. See Chapter 6, "The Teen Obsession: Skin."
6. **Sex with someone who has other STDs.** Whenever there is one STD, you must worry about others. If you got an STD, you probably didn't use a condom and therefore you are at a higher risk-taking behavior level.
7. **Rape.**
8. **Blood transfusions before 1985.** Before 1985, the blood supply was not screened for the virus.
9. **Accidental exposure to HIV.** For example, a health care worker who gets pricked by a needle after drawing blood is at risk.

AIDS in teens with any regularity. When a patient is tested, the purpose is to identify whether or not he is infected with HIV.

The fact that teens are sexually active and don't mind taking risks certainly makes HIV exposure a possibility. Unless a partner can guarantee virginity, even someone your teen knows well can pose a risk. Those who have multiple partners simply raise the stakes. As remarkable as it may sound, some teens do see prostitutes and the risks are obvious. (I have had more than one college student call me on Monday about stupid drunken behavior on Saturday.) If there is a history of injected drug use, the risk is even higher. This is why condom use is so important. The latex condom affords protection, and it is simply foolhardy to have intercourse without them.

As discussed in Chapter 8, the current trend with teenagers is to feel that "sex" does not include oral sex. It is important that they understand that oral sex carries some risks for various diseases including HIV. It is true that the risk is quite low and it is difficult to prove that oral sex alone gave someone HIV. Yet the ideal protection is a condom or a "dental dam" (a latex cover over the vagina). It is fair to say that most teens will use neither as they participate in oral sex.

If any of the above risks are present, one needs to have an HIV test. Fortunately this has become easier as many states have relaxed the laws about getting HIV tests from commercial labs. For a while only specialized centers in some states were doing the test. For example, in New York only the Board of Health could do an HIV test a few years ago, and I could not send a specimen to a commercial lab. Yet in New Jersey it was no problem. An argument could be made for testing anyone who is sexually active outside of a monogamous relationship with two partners who entered it as virgins, but it is impractical to test every teen who admits to intercourse. However, if any of the above factors are present the test should be done. In most medical offices, if a patient is diagnosed with one STD, then an HIV test is offered as a precaution.

Today the tests are commercially available, and teens do not need parental consent to be screened. In my own practice the blood test is always available but there are some constraints involved. The test involves drawing a separate blood vial and sending it to the lab in its own sealed envelope. Most labs will not "include" HIV as part of a group screening so one cannot "sneak" the test into routine blood tests. For example, if my patient is sexually active, I can easily have a syphilis test run simply by checking off a box on my order form, and the blood sample will be screened for it. The patient is tested for syphilis without fanfare and very little additional cost. Unfortunately, the HIV test requires a separate tube of blood, a separate requisition form, and a separate bill. How does the teen pay for this? Will she get the bill in the mail and pay before her parents see it? The test can cost as much as $70 or more. Will parents pay but object that she does not need it, or will they be pleased at her responsible behavior?

Newer tests are available for use with saliva or with urine but most experts still feel that the blood test is the gold standard. Even the tests that provide rapid screening and do not use blood suggest that a positive test be followed up with the traditional blood test. The Western blot (the confirmatory standard blood test that is done to confirm any positive sample) checks for the specific DNA of the virus and confirms the preliminary tests. In brief, we rarely have false positives with the current screening programs and most reputable labs will guarantee 99 percent accuracy.

Unfortunately, there is a "waiting" time between possible exposure and appearance of the virus. Most testing involves looking for the antibodies against the virus, and these develop over several months, not days; experts generally say a six-month wait is generally necessary. Imagine the anxiety when someone has to wait simply to do the test! Recently the validity of the test allows for testing within a three-month wait providing that the blood test and the Western blot is done. (The Western blot test is a confirmatory DNA test that is done on the sample to validate a positive test.)

Treatment for HIV has changed with the advent of newer drugs that prevent viral replication. Without going into details that are beyond this book, one needs to know that HIV identified early no longer necessary leads inexorably to AIDS and death. It is expensive and time-consuming to treat HIV but the current data suggests that the protocols are working. They are not felt to be cures as the virus remains at low levels; the question still remains about these low levels of virus and the fate of the infection. Will they suddenly act up or will they remain dormant and do nothing to the host? We don't yet know that critical answer.

Bacterial Infections

Chlamydia

Chlamydia trachomatis leads the list of possible infections in the group of bacterial STDs. Twenty years ago it was barely recognized; today it is the most commonly reported infection in the United States. This organism is unusual in that it has viral qualities in so far as it inhabits the cell; however, it is bacteria-like in that it responds to standard antibiotics.

For years chlamydia was called "non-gonococcal urethritis" as the patient had a penile or vaginal discharge similar to that in gonorrhea, but the symptoms were not as severe. It is a difficult organism to culture in both genders because it doesn't grow easily in culture media. For boys it is particularly difficult because it requires a penile swab, something to which adolescent males don't take kindly because it is painful. Since treatment requires very safe antibiotics that have few side effects (used commonly to treat acne), teens are often treated on suspicion alone. Certainly, if there is an infected partner, the "uninfected" partner should also be treated with the short course of doxycycline or even erythromycin.

The symptoms vary with gender. Since males use their penises both for urination and sexual activity they tend to have urinary tract symptoms if infected. Within one to two weeks of exposure they complain of a burning sensation on urination, or a white penile discharge, or a pain in the testicles if the infection has traveled. In a way they are "lucky" because diagnosis is easier to detect if they have early symptoms. Some males have a very mild, transient set of symptoms and may even be asymptomatic. They don't appreciate that they can infect their female partners and then wonder "how their girlfriend got infected." This scenario tends to lead to questions of fidelity.

Females are not as fortunate. Since their sexual tract is different, they may not have any discomfort on urination. Their infection can linger and increase inside the vagina and uterus without symptoms. Indeed, they may only be diagnosed during a routine pelvic exam. Since the infection can worsen without treatment, it can spread throughout the uterus and lead to pelvic inflammatory disease. With so virulent an infection, scar tissue may develop if not treated early, and the girl is at risk for infertility. The infection of the Bartholin ducts (ducts that line the labia and help with lubrication) is also frequently due to chlamydia, and Fitz-Hugh-Curtis syndrome (see p. 424) is possible. What we do know is that the girl who has unprotected sex with an infected male, has about a 70 percent chance of being asymptomatically infected. Condoms are effective protection against this infection.

James is in his senior year *of high school. He came for a consultation because he noted a painful nagging pain in his "groin." He wondered if it was a pulled muscle. I asked him in private if he had had intercourse, which he admitted easily. However, when pushed about unprotected intercourse, he answered a definite "No." When I examined him, there was no indication that he had a muscle strain but there was a very tender area on the top part of his testicle. I commented out loud that I felt this was the cause of the problem, but I was concerned how he had this in the absence of unprotected* *intercourse. He waited, and after a few "ah, ahems" said, "Well I didn't want to tell you but there was this one time a month ago. . . . But I knew this girl and I can't believe that's a problem." Since there was no discharge, no prostatic tenderness, and no other immediate explanation, I told him that it would be hard to culture for chlamydia but I would put him on antibiotics. He called forty-eight hours later to report a remarkable improvement, and by the following week the tenderness has disappeared. I suggested he contact the girl for diagnosis and treatment.*

Gonorrhea

Gonorrhea is still with us but not with the same level of occurrence that it was during the late 1960s, due primarily to concern over HIV and a greater acceptance of condoms. The CDC has reported an annual drop in the prevalence of gonorrhea since 1987. It is primarily seen in urban areas of high density population where unprotected sex is prevalent and multiple partners are common. This is a serious disease, which should not be ignored in the rush to focus on HIV and chlamydia.

Though the number of cases has declined, gonorrhea is still with us. Teens need to be aware that it is "out there"; statistically teens are more likely to be infected than older people, since they have more partners and take more risks.

It is not very hard to get gonorrhea if your partner is infected. This is especially true if the infected partner is male; the female will retain the infected ejaculate and is at higher risk. The incubation period averages three to five days after exposure but it can be as long as a month in some cases. It is also possible to have gonorrhea in another part of the body, and the sexual practice will determine the outcome: A sore throat may actually be a pharyngeal gonorrhea infection; a rectal itch with discharge may be due to gonorrheal proctitis; and joint pains and a rash may actually signal the spread of the bacteria into the joints.

Because an increasing number of teens are participating in oral sex, a doctor who sees a teen for a strange or persistent sore throat must always consider whether the teen is sexually active. They may be embarrassed to be asked about oral sex, but it is important to be thorough; the question itself becomes a way of instructing kids since they often ask, "Really, can you get that?!"

If the infection is in the penis, the patient will have a thick discharge that will stain his underwear. It is hard to miss, and it is unusual for the patient not to complain. (It is possible to be asymptomatic but that is usually because of a "missed" diagnosis in a mild case.) In females, about three-quarters will complain of abdominal pain, or a vaginal discharge. The rest are free of symptoms but become a reservoir for the bacteria and can easily transmit the disease. Girls with gonorrhea have a special problem because the symptoms may not present themselves early enough. By the time the diagnosis is made with a pelvic examination, scarring and possible infertility can occur.

Gonorrhea will spread if it is in the community. One person infects the other, and it is quckly transmitted to others. With teens this is a major problem, since intercourse tends to be integrated with the immediate social group. Random "hooking up" (see Chapter 8) doesn't happen outside of the immediate circle; this works either to the teen's advantage or disadvantage.

The diagnosis of gonorrhea involves taking a smear of the infected site and either examining the organisms under a microscope or culturing for it. The "old timers" will tell you that all medical students could identify this disease with one look at the microscope. The younger physicians will probably rely on cultures to be sure of their diagnosis. For legal reasons the latter is the preferred method. Treatment for gonorrhea now involves concomitant treatment for chlamydia since the two are often found together. An injection and several days of oral antibiotics is standard. A new single oral dose is quite effective in eradicating the organism. One advantage to the single oral dose is that it can be done in the doctor's office and the physician is assured that the medication is taken. One explanation for poorly treated gonorrhea has been patient compliance in taking medicine for several days. Your physician will advise which is the best method.

Susan, age fifteen, called on *a Tuesday complaining of sharp abdominal pains. She said that her lower abdomen felt "crampy" and she had trouble standing up. Since the possibility of a surgical emergency existed, I asked her to come to the office immediately; her mother took her right into the examination room. There was exquisite tenderness in both lower quadrants of her abdomen. She had a low-grade fever and she said her last period was three weeks ago. I was able to have mother leave us for a confidential discussion, and Susan admitted that she had been "picked up" by a boy during the weekend. She also admitted that she had unprotected intercourse. A pelvic examination soon revealed a yellow purulent discharge that was visible in the cervical opening. A gram stain (a series of dyes placed on the microscope slide) showed the classic organisms of gonorrhea. She allowed me to discuss the findings with her mother, who listened stupefied that her "intelligent daughter" was in this situation, but she stood up and hugged her daughter. Susan was treated right away.*

One last word on gonorrhea. The organism is very unstable outside of the body. In fact it is difficult to grow without the correct culture media. Hence, the old argument of "getting it from the toilet seat" is absurd. The bacteria would not last long on the seat or anywhere outside the body. As we used to say during my training, "If you got it on the toilet seat, it was a strange place to have sex."

Vaginosis

Often called "bacterial vaginosis," this disorder presents with a malodorous vaginal discharge. Classically identified because of its "fishy" odor and white purulent discharge it has to be differentiated from other discharges associated with STDs.

The organism has been identified as gardnerella vaginalis and is associated with sexual transmission. As such it can be classified in the STD family, but it has also been found in about 10 to 30 percent of sexually inexperienced girls. Hence, the presence of this infection in a teenager is not proof that she is having intercourse.

Treatment consists of intravaginal suppositories, gels, creams, or tablets containing the antibiotic metronidazole (sold as Flagyl; one cannot drink alcohol during its use as the combination causes severe vomiting) or clindamycin (another antibiotic) for three to seven days. Newer oral treatments are available either in one dose or extended over one week. Since there is no proof that the partner transmitted the organism, there is no current practice of also treating the male.

Syphilis

Known as the "great impostor," syphilis can give you anything from a rash to dementia and heart failure. Fortunately, standard blood tests identify patients easily, and our current teen population is not particularly prone to getting syphilis. Since I went into practice, I have not seen a single case, and my last case was at Bellevue Hospital in 1964. Other than through childbirth, it is only transmitted through sexual contact.

Yet this historically famous disease is not gone from our midst. There are reported outbreaks but they occur primarily in underdeveloping countries. Although we no longer require the "premarital test" in the United States as a prerequisite for a marriage license, we still see about 15 cases per 100,000, which is a far cry from the nearly 100 per 100,000 of the 1920s. However, because teens still fear syphilis and many parents grew up with the notion of the disease lurking behind every sexual encounter, it is worth explaining a little more about it. As you read, bear in mind the "great impostor" term that this infection bears.

There are three distinct phases of the disease. After contact the patient will soon develop a chancre, a painless ulceration at the site of exposure. Since the chancre is caused by contact, it can be anywhere on the body and it can look like an innocent nonsexual sore. The lesion is teeming with the syphilis organism and a swab taken will quickly yield the diagnosis.

Untreated, the patient progresses to the secondary stage during which a rash may be present, particularly on the hands and soles of the feet as well as the mouth. The rash may look like viral rashes, impetigo, psoriasis, or any of several fungal infections, and the patient may have a sore throat, swollen lymph glands, headache, and malaise. All of these are standard symptoms for many diseases, so again, we see the reason for the nickname "great imposter." As a result, syphilis, although rare, is always in the back of a physician's mind when dealing with these common complaints. It is during this stage that the patient may show fleshy, wartlike growths at the site of infection and may lose his hair.

If still untreated, the final stage of neurosyphilis, or cardiac syphilis, takes place. (Today only the most impoverished patient will reach this stage since simple antibiotics would have long aborted this progression.) Since this stage of syphilis takes ten to thirty years to develop, one would not see this in the teenager.

Syphilis is caused by a *treponeme,* a thread-like organism that is in the same family as the organism that causes Lyme disease. In testing for Lyme one can get a false positive test if syphilis is present and vice versa. Today laboratories do a confirmatory test for each that eliminates the confusion.

Fungal Infections

Candida

Either gender can have candida, and this fungal infection usually manifests itself with a thick white discharge and intense itching. (The same organism that is responsible for thrush in the infant is the offender in this infection.) In most cases this infection is *not* due to a sexual act but rather to the presence of antibiotics that alter the normal vaginal flora. With the change of normal bacteria, the opportunistic fungus (*Candida albicans*) takes over. The most common scenario is the teen who is on acne medication, or the one who is being treated for a prolonged sinus infection. However, sexual contact with someone who has candida will also transmit the fungus.

The affected male, after sexual contact, may complain of a rash on his penis that is very itchy. On inspection, a red excoriated area will be noted. The application of a topical antifungal cream will generally treat it. For the female, treatment used to consist of several days of antifungal creams or tablets. With the advent of a new oral medication, fluconazole, the woman takes one tablet and the infection is treated. As a precaution, I usually prescribe this when I anticipate a prolonged course of antibiotics in a teen girl.

> **Lori's dermatologist had started her** *on antibiotics for her acne. After she had been on the treatment for a few weeks, I got a call. She said that her vagina was so itchy that "I had to do something right away." She said that there was a white discharge from her vagina and that her labia were swollen, and they, too, itched. She described the discharge as thick and lumpy. When she arrived she was unable to sit still in the waiting room, and I took her into the examination room as soon as possible. Her labia were swollen to twice their normal size and very red. Trying to spread her labia was painful but once done, a thick discharge could be seen even without the speculum exam. Under the microscope, the classic strands of a fungal infection were easily seen. She was treated with the single-dose oral pills and topical fungal cream. By the next day she was vastly improved.*

Parasites

Pediculosis Pubis

I can safely say that everyone that I have ever diagnosed with pediculosis pubis (pubic lice or in slang, "crabs") greets the news with horror. Anyone with head lice feels dirty and "gross"; imagine the thought that a sexual partner left you small crabs clawing their way around your pubic area.

> **Paul had just started college.** *He called on a Monday morning to say that he saw "something crawling" on his pubic area and he was panicked that it could be "crabs." He asked me what else it could be, and since I could come up with little else that would be traveling around his pubic hair, I told him he was probably right. However, I needed to see him. Would it be pos-*

sible for him to come over in the afternoon? "Sure!" and he hung up. At three o'clock he sat with a smile in my waiting room; I gave him a quizzical look. As he undressed, I realized that he felt he had triumphed for in front of me was a nineteen-year-old male who had shaved every part of his body except for head and eyebrows. "Pretty cool, hey Doc? I couldn't wait for you to do something, so I shaved it all off!" He had indeed eliminated all signs of the adult parasites, but I still had to treat him for any leftover eggs. "No problem. As long as I don't have to see them crawling on me!"

Diagnosis of pubic lice is easy. By using a magnifying glass they become quite simple to spot. The adult louse has a slightly brownish hue, is a few millimeters long and wide, with little legs. What else could it be? Diagnosis can also be made by the eggs, or "nits." These look like dandruff flakes but they cling to the hair and cannot be easily pulled off the hair shaft. Under the microscope the egg-shaped appearance of the nit stuck on the hair is unmistakable. The adults will leave small bites and the area is very itchy so that one sees excoriations secondary to the scratching. When it is bad enough the whole area becomes red and swollen from the scratching.

As with head lice, treatment (using a pediculicide to kill the bugs) is not a one-shot deal. Kwell and RID are probably the best known for this treatment and involve specific instructions as to length of time the solution should be left on the area, which must be followed exactly. Treatment is repeated in seven to ten days to get any missed adults or eggs. The concern of too much absorption of these potentially neurotoxic chemicals is real for small children but should not be a consideration in the teenage body.

The next question posed by parents involves clothing and bedding. You do not have to throw them out and replace them—as tempting as it may sound. Just wash everything in hot water or send items out to be dry cleaned at the beginning of the first treatment. If the lice are still there in a week, wash again.

Sexual contacts falls into two groups: the giver of lice and the receiver. It's simple. If your teen has crabs, somebody gave them to her. In turn, she will pass them on unless treated.

Scabies

Like crabs, the itch mite (sarcoptes scabiei) also causes repulsion when diagnosed. The association of "scabies" with sexual promiscuity, poor hygiene, filth, and poverty is well grounded. Close personal contact is critical for the transmission, so if a teen picks up scabies it has to be from someone that got close enough for the mite to jump over. Sexual contact is a common way of spreading the mite. However, the mite's hypersensitivity has so long an incubation period (several weeks) that it is hard to tell when someone was exposed. Moreover, they are not like the lice, which can easily dive from one person's pubic hair to the other. The mite is very slow and deliberate in going from one person to the other. If the casual contact ends up with lice, the mite requires hours of close and intimate contact before it transfers. Don't blame a school if your teen gets scabies, unless he, or she, slept there overnight with someone that had it.

The infected patient will complain primarily of itchiness that is frequently worse at night. Close examination will reveal burrows (think of moles) that form irregular red lines on the penetrated skin. The usual sites occupied by the mites are the fingers, the underside of the wrist and arm, the elbows and the genitals. Patients are often misdiagnosed as having eczema, hives, contact dermatitis, impetigo, and a host of other disorders. By taking a small needle and exposing the tunnel, one can take scrapings and see the sarcoptes scabies under a microscope.

Because of the extensive burrowing, this infection is treated aggressively. Medications (Lindane, or Elmite Cream) similar to the ones used for lice are prescribed, but they must remain on the person for twelve hours to kill the parasite. After twenty-four hours, the mites are dead and the patient will not infect anyone. There are some medications (Eurax, sulfur medicines) that are perceived as less toxic but they require treatment for several nights to complete the job. However, the dead carcass of the mite will still cause itchy symptoms. I have seen more than one patient treated repeatedly while in college because of the persistent itching. Feeling that the patient did not do an adequate job, he may get treated again needlessly. Instead of another course of anti-mite medicines, place the patient on antihistamines for itch. In severe cases of hypersensitivity, a short course of steroids is indicated.

Teen Awareness

My practice has seen a recent shift of interest in STDs. Kids are now coming in alone or with their partners and asking to be tested for HIV, and "while you're at it, can you check for all of them, Doc?"

At least they are asking. Yet, the reality is that one cannot check for "all of them," and the teen is often disappointed to learn that he, or she, still has to be vigilant for sores, for discharges, and for discomfort. In the classic teen mindset they want a guarantee that they are free of disease so they can get back into the game. No one can give this reassurance as STD symptoms can be subtle or hidden from view. The solution of using a condom is heard over and over by kids at school. Most parents should not fear that the message has not been given about their effectiveness and their need. Yet, the magic of teen-think will always prevail, and their notion of "it won't happen here" is always a danger.

Condoms work, they are available, and they are cheap. Telling your kids that they are necessary often makes them feel that a lecture is coming on. Rest assured that they have heard the message; but tell them anyhow in a tone that says you are aware of what is happening. Maybe the best solution is to casually leave this page open in a visible location and hope they read it!

Part Four

Teen Substance Abuse

Chapter 11

What Parents Need to Know about Substance Abuse

hree years ago a colleague of mine, a pediatrician, called my office in August to ask me to see a patient of his, an eighteen-year-old male. I missed the call and ended up meeting the young man without any information as to the reason for the referral. A charming 6'3" two-hundred-and-forty-pound athlete sat opposite my desk and smiled a "hello" as we sat down to talk.

"How can I help?" I asked. "I know Dr. Jones sent you to meet me, but we played phone tag, and I missed his call."

"Well, I am scheduled to go to college in two weeks and I don't think I can make it," he said calmly. My immediate thoughts ranged from separation anxiety to missed learning disabilities to panic disorders but I let the interview unwind at its own pace. Bill continued: "I'm an alcoholic. If I go to college I know I will party to the point where I won't make it. I need help, and Dr. Jones wants to know if I should be admitted to a drug center."

"What makes you think you're an alcoholic? It takes a lot of drinking to use that term."

"I have been drinking beer for the past four years," Bill responded. "I get 'wasted' on weekends, and I've done a fair amount of drugs. I don't think that I can stop on my own. Is that enough?"

"But you're an athlete," I said. "How did you manage to compete?"

"I could have been a helluva lot better. I'm so big that I guess I could 'hold' my liquor and no one knew. But, to tell you the truth, I was sometimes out of it when I played. I drank all the time and no one knew."

"Have you told your parents?" I asked.

"Yep. But they're not sure what to think. I guess it's hard to accept that I have been doing this so long, right under everyone's nose. I think they're shocked right now. So what are we going to do?" Bill persisted.

"I think you're an incredible kid who just made my job easier," I said, getting up from my desk. "I can't think of a good reason not to send you to a rehab center right away. Let's get some more history, do an exam, and start things rolling. I have to call Dr. Jones and your parents. Is that okay?"

I will tell you that this story has a happy ending. While Bill's parents were very shaken by the news, they realized their son needed help and arranged for him to defer college for a year so that he could enter a rehabilitation center. At the rehab center, the level of his drinking and drug abuse history emerged. He got the help he needed and did go on to college.

The reasons for his drinking are not important at this time, but the story illustrates how a teen can hide his drug usage if he "does well enough." In retrospect, Bill left lots of clues. Still, his problem, like those of many teens, went unnoticed. Bill caught himself because he became fearful; others are finally rescued when a crisis occurs. To his enormous credit, Bill recognized that college would be his downfall and asked for help. He is the exception and not the rule.

Many teens who are involved with drugs are more like Susan. Susan had been a very good student, and then, inexplicably, her grades worsened, and she became surly and secretive about her activities. Her parents also noted that she was hanging out with a group of kids who were known marijuana users. I was asked to do a drug screen, and Susan complied. She acknowledged that there "might" be drugs, but she said she didn't do a lot and, perhaps, the test would be negative. I assured her that the test would likely pick up the drugs if she was doing them. She didn't seem upset. Susan could not see why her parents were making such a big deal about all of this, and complained to me that they were being a "real pain," yet, she complied so easily that I wondered if she wanted to get caught.

Her drug screen proved positive for THC (a component of marijuana), and her parents started her in therapy. It was also understood that she would undergo periodic and random drug screens. She had a couple of "clean specimens," but soon the tests started to show THC again. Susan was resistant to getting help; she even admitted to me that she wasn't telling her psychiatrist the entire truth, but she continued to go to keep her parents off her back. Her attitude continued to be one of defiance to any parental limits. She would sneak out at night after her parents had gone to bed and try to get back unnoticed. Then one night she came home very drunk. After that incident, her mother called me to tell me that she had arranged for Susan to be *taken* to a drug rehabilitation program. (Many programs begin with a wilderness program to get kids used to using their bodies in a "clean way.") Indeed, that Friday night two strong adults showed up in their home and, as arranged, they awoke Susan, told her to get dressed, and showed her a document from her parents giving them the right to do this. They told her to come with them right away. There was no time to pack anything, the three left directly for the airport, and Susan spent the next month on a wilderness trip learning about staying sober and not using drugs. She came back changed and grateful that someone had acted. She realized hanging out with her "old" friends would be counterproductive and she stopped seeing them. She is now finishing high school and getting therapy.

Learning about Alcohol and Drug Abuse

When I lecture to parents of teenagers almost every group wants a discussion about drugs and the adolescent. What are the prevalent drugs? When does drug use start? What do I do if we find that my son or daughter is drinking? Smoking pot? What about drug testing? Is it reliable, and when do we do it? What about issues of confidentiality: Can you tell me if my son/daughter is using drugs?

Drugs and alcohol are everywhere in the world of the adolescent. They are found in schools, in summer camps, at many parties (chaperoned or not), and certainly at clubs. In some homes, you need go no further than the parents' own rooms. In brief, if you are a teenager you will have to deal with the drug issue; if you are a parent of a teenager, you need to be informed about what is out there (see Chapters 12 to 16). However, knowledge is only part of the solution.

Your own attitude plays an enormous part in the message that you give your kids even before they reach adolescence. A great deal of honest soul searching on your part is in order if you are to understand your teenager's behavior. Do you smoke? Drink alcohol for recreation or to "loosen up" after a stressful day? Were you a product of the generation that did drugs and now have a particular perspective, pro or con, because of that experience? Does your spouse share your attitude so that there is a single message being sent to the teen? Lastly, do you or your spouse occasionally "light up a joint" just to relax?

Recognizing a Drug User

It is impossible to draw a specific profile of the teen drug user or to generalize as to gender, race, religion, or age. We know that experimentation may begin early, between the sixth and eighth grades in some communities, and we know that there seems to be a logical progression from cigarettes or alcohol to pot and, potentially, to other drugs. But if you think it is only the teenagers with the dyed red hair, the angry messages on their T-shirts, or the nose rings, you will miss the larger picture. I could bring kids into your home who dress well, speak politely, come from intact families, and are model citizens. Yet, they drink on weekends, or more often; they smoke when not around mom and dad; and, when possible, use pot. The face of the teenager who is using drugs may well be that of the kid sleeping down the hall from you. Forget that, and you may be lulled into complacency in your own home.

That does not mean that you need to accuse your teenager of using drugs because she looks normal. What it does mean is that you need to be aware of drug use in your community and in your teen's school environment. Don't expect your teenager to ignore the whole scene; that's asking too much. The good news is that many kids will try a cigarette, a drink, a puff of a "joint," and then walk away with a feeling of accomplishment. "I tried it and it's not for me."

Finding the Right Time

I don't think there is a good time to sit a teen, or pre-teen, down and discuss drugs and alcohol anymore than you'll find an "ideal" opportunity to talk about sex. You need to look for casual opportunities—and several of them; talking about drugs is not a one-time discussion. As you see a TV show, or read about a news story related to drugs, ask your teens how they feel about the story. Kids respond well to being asked their opinion. Probe gently and slowly; the point is to gradually sustain a conversation in which you can assess their knowledge and attitude.

If it turns into a lecture, or worse, into an accusation, you have lost an opportunity. Many parents are quite adept at talking; many have to learn to listen. If your kids express curiosity about drugs, don't start lecturing about how "drugs can kill you" and quoting statistics. Instead, you might try something along the following lines:

"I can understand your curiosity since so many kids try it, but drugs are still a serious problem. Some can cause a lot of damage with just one try. Let

Talking with Your Teen about Drug and Alcohol Abuse

We have a generation of parents who swore to be open with their kids—no topic would be too difficult and no subject taboo for discussion. However, one problem was ignored: These aren't easy discussions to have with teenagers. You can't help but be emotionally involved in how the discussion goes, and your teen senses the awkwardness of the moment—everyone ends up feeling ill at ease.

It's vital that you present your feelings on the subject, so talk you must and be prepared to listen. Don't buy the argument that they "don't care" how you feel. They do. Here are some general guidelines for the discussion:

Rule 1: Don't tell teens you understand them. Teens are trying to understand *themselves.* If you come along and in one sentence claim to be able to define them they won't believe you, and it will be destructive to your relationship. Let them have ownership of who they are and how they feel.

Rule 2: Don't say, "When I was your age . . ." You cannot relate your experiences to theirs. When you were growing up, there were different issues and different concerns.

Rule 3: Talk less and listen more. Approach your teens and express your concerns. Then keep quiet and listen. If you know what they are going to say, swell. Still keep quiet and listen. If you can appreciate the argument's conclusion as they develop it, terrific and good for you. Keep quiet some more. Even if there is a predictable outcome, your silence has allowed them to feel they got their point across. At the end of this enforced silence your reward may be teenagers who think you are someone who is willing to listen. It gets easier each time, and soon you are having a dialogue and not a haranguing yelling session about how you, the parent, know best.

Rule 4: You now have a chance to express concerns about the current drug scene in the school or in the community. (You cannot go to rule 4 without passing, with flying colors, rules 1 through 3.) A critical part of this rule is how you present your point of view. If you lecture, or pontificate, or if you ignore what they say, there is no point to this rule. Express yourself in a calm way. You *can* say, "I don't think that pot is safe, and Mom and I (or vice versa) are concerned if it gets to be more often than just trying it. Besides, if some of the kids are doing drugs, it gets hard to keep saying no to them, doesn't it?" That sounds much better than, "Listen here! I know what's happening. I read the papers and you can't tell me that Billy, that kid you hang around with, isn't on 'something.' Why he just looks like a druggie! What do you think we are, stupid or something?"

me know if I can answer any questions, although you may already know a lot about it. Didn't you cover some of this in health class?"

While your comments must be made in your own style, the suggested lines above accomplish several things: An appreciation that curiosity among teens is normal, a warning that drugs are a "problem," an acknowledgment that they are not ignorant on the topic. All this is then wrapped in your offer to be available if they need help or have questions. In brief, you discussed the topic with them; you did not lecture.

At this point, they may ask you about your own experience with drugs. If there is none, then it is easy.

"I never smoked pot. I may have thought about it since it was common in my college (high school), but I did steer clear."

However, if that's not the case and you have a history of using pot, now or then, you're faced with a dilemma. Some parents feel strongly that one should be honest with kids so that there is a reciprocal honesty on their parts. I am not one of those people. Do mothers tell sons, or fathers tell daughters, about their teenage sexual lives simply because they were asked? To me that information is private and not to be shared with anyone except perhaps a spouse. I see no difference with information about past parental drug use. If you decide to open up past history, where will you draw the line? Is saying, "I did pot at sixteen, honey," really so different from saying, "I lost my virginity at seventeen, sweetie"? Mine is often an unpopular view at lectures because it runs counter to the notion of "open communication" with teenagers.

Your job is to raise your children and to provide guidelines. You and your spouse are entitled to privacy. In general, I can think of few situations where you share your past drug use with your teenager. The major exception would be to illustrate a point that the family is vulnerable. For example, if you are an alcoholic, it is important to share this as it warns your child of the risk of alcohol use. Allowing that teen to use alcohol or drugs in a "recreational" manner is allowing that teenager to court danger. The addictive person is genetically prone to addiction. Chronic use and addiction are not something that "just happens." Even if parents are not alcoholics themselves, the presence of a strong family history (grandparents, uncles, siblings) poses risks for addiction in the teenager. Teenagers with a family history of addiction who use alcohol are lighting matches in a gasoline factory!

If your teen approaches you with the question about your past drug use, or your sex life, answer instead with,

"Why are you asking? Is there something you want to talk about?"

She may respond: "Well, no, not really. I'm just curious, that's all."

"That's a very personal question. I'm happy to answer any other questions on the topic, but I feel that what I did is very personal and private. Just as I'm sure you would want me to respect your privacy, I know you can understand why I won't give you an answer. But, maybe we can talk about the topic anyhow. What do you think?"

"Come on. You want me to tell *you* everything, don't you?"

"No, I don't. I want you to tell me about anything that is puzzling or a problem. Or, stuff that you *want* to tell me. If you told me everything, you would have no personal life. I'm here to listen, not to know everything you do."

You may initially disagree with me about a teens' right to privacy, but your goal as a parent is to help guide them in becoming adults who can manage their own public and private lives. Not knowing absolutely everything they say or do is a way of letting them grow up.

Unless you can come up with a terrific reason, perhaps a disaster that occurred because of your drug use, I see little to be gained by telling your teen about your past drug experience. This sets up a standard of acceptance that is not the message you want to give.

The Information Pipeline

To stay on top of what is happening, you have two dependable resources—your teen and your friends.

Share with your teen your ignorance and your knowledge. Words to the effect of "I heard that some of the kids go to XYZ after school and there is a lot of pot there. I don't want names, but is this true?" The tone is not accusatory but it implies to your teen that you are on top of this issue. You also acknowledge the code of ethics that you do not snitch on a friend—a time-honored teen code. You want her to know, however, that you have your ear to the ground and are not naïve. It will be the rare school that will be totally free of drugs so don't expect to hear a denial by your teenager.

Since you are already suspicious, or actually know what is happening in the school, your demeanor should be one of relief that she told you the truth. That is a major step in a trusting relationship. Next, try asking: "How do you feel about what's going on?" and let her answer. At the end of this, you do not judge her, scold her, or even tell her that she is not to spend time with the kids that are involved with the drug scene. That will only accomplish two results: It will notify her that telling you the truth has bad consequences (she told you honestly and now she is getting a lecture). Secondly, you have suggested that she cannot make judgments on her own and are now trying to dictate how she must spend her time. Try something along the lines of "Are those kids very pop-ular?" After that, ask her if she feels that she needs to spend time with them. Then, and only then, you can suggest that this may be a crowd to avoid. (I know of no way that a parent can enforce a rule of forbidding a teenager from seeing certain kids at school.)

You can also talk to other parents. You likely have a built-in network of parents, or you can reach out to the school's parents' association for help if this is a schoolwide problem. Don't just raise money for new band uniforms; tackle the hard issue of possible drugs on school grounds or nearby.

The Discovery: Your Teen Is Drinking or Using Drugs

What do you do if one day you discover that your teen has "used" pot. How do you react? What do you say?

No fireman goes into a fire without drills and practices, and no parent should be confronted with evidence of their child doing drugs or drinking without having prepared mentally beforehand. Ask yourself right now, how you would handle the above possibilities. Then talk to your spouse about what he or she would do. Discuss the way you would handle a son coming home drunk, a daughter caught smoking, or the reality that a child "tried pot." Do you agree with each other? Does one feel that the drinking is okay because it's a "first time" and a rite of passage? Do you have zero tolerance for alcohol or pot? Clear up any differences with your spouse, because the first step in helping your teen is to present a united front.

Let's suppose your teen comes home drunk for the first time. Is this a cri-sis? Frankly, if I were to get overwhelmingly concerned about every teen who tries a drink or pot once, I would have nothing else in my practice but parents bringing in their teens for a "problem." While you may not like the idea of experimentation, most teens are going to try *some*thing out of curiosity or just to be "cool." The first time is not the time to start scaring her with threats and with the picture of her becoming a heroin addict. She will only look at you and feel there is no sense of proportion to the argument. When she says, "It's no big deal," she genuinely means it.

I don't like having a discussion with kids when they come home with alco-hol on their breath or the smell of pot in their hair or on their clothing. Dis-cussions held at 2 A.M. inevitably become shouting matches and accomplish little since both parent and teen become so angry that even valid points in the argument are taken to extremes.

In the morning, sit the teen down after breakfast and, with both parents present, ask what happened last night. If you know she was drinking, say you know and that you are concerned. Whether your teen is an honors student or struggling with school, the discussion and possible consequences need to be the same. Since parents should have already established guidelines as to their rules on drinking and drugs, it should come as no surprise to the teen that you are upset. You can be understanding but you are also entitled to be upset.

Should you choose to punish the teen and ground her, do it because of something other than admitting she drank or tried pot. If she came home late, drove a car, went somewhere explicitly forbidden, those are reasonable behaviors to punish. To punish her because she told you she had a first drink is unreasonable, even in the face of a family history of alcoholism. Otherwise, your teen is learning that telling you the truth is worse than lying.

The discussion at this point should focus on reestablishing the family rules. Explain that if this happens again, you will not go as easy and future consequences will be significant. For example, automobiles are privileges and also deadly weapons. Taking keys from teens who violated family rules brings home your message. Once the meeting is over allow the rest of the day to proceed without further discussion. Harping on any subject is a guaranteed way to get kids to ignore you.

After dealing with the immediate infraction, look at the total picture to try to discern if there is a worrisome pattern. How is she doing in school? If she's capable of A's but is only doing getting C's, this should be noted. Also look for other signs of drug use. Has she become increasingly moody (more than expected from a teen)? Is there a constant cough, or runny nose, or red, watery eyes?

Lastly, look at the peer group your teen chooses. The peer group reflects a teen's world, and it may—or may not—provide you with answers. Dreads, piercings, tattoos, and a Motley Crue shirt are peacock signals of a culture that says pot is okay. It doesn't mean she's smoking pot, any more than a buttoned-down white oxford shirt and cuffed chino pants means that your son is playing golf. However, being aware of the group gives you another set of clues.

If your teen is doing mediocre work at school, appears tired and short-tempered at home, and attends concerts where pot is a "given," you can conclude that he *might* be doing pot. On the other hand, he could be a teen with a learning disability who has mono and a distinct taste in music and friends. Just be cautious about accepting the latter too easily.

Getting Additional Advice or Help

If you're at all concerned, call your physician and discuss the signs and symptoms of a particular drug. If your doctor sees a lot of teenagers, she should be able to give you an overview of what is going on in your town.

If the two of you concur that there may be a problem, ask your physician about drug testing. Most physicians will not do a drug screen unless the teenager is aware of the test beforehand. If the teen refuses the test, the physician is legally obligated to not do it. In order to allow teenagers to discuss drug concerns with physicians, most states give any information about drugs and alcohol regardless of patient age guaranteed confidentiality. This holds even if the teenager is a minor under the law. Therefore, the only way of effectively using a drug screen is to let the teen know you are doing it for whatever reason, and let him know ahead of time that the parent will be told the results. In other words, I may know that your son is doing pot but I am not allowed to tell you.

I am often asked why I can't just "sneak" in a drug screen. Some physicians may do it, but if the test is positive, and they tell the parents, they will need to find a new doctor. Few teens will ever trust that doctor again.

To me, there is only one situation in which the doctor can breach confidentiality, and that would be in an emergency where the patient is in danger. I had a seventeen-year-old girl who was losing weight, was irritable, had elevated blood pressure, and had a constant cold. I told her that all of this pointed to cocaine use, and she said I was right. A month later she was still using cocaine and her weight was slipping further. I warned her that she had to tell her mother or I would declare it an emergency and violate her confidentiality. She was furious with me and called me a few names that are not printable here. In the end, she told her mother and I was able to send her to a rehabilitation center. When she left the center she was told she needed medical follow up. Despite the anger she had expressed, she wanted to return to my practice. Eventually, kids will understand that you acted because they needed help at the time.

If one test is positive, parents have to be vigilant for drug-related behavior. Poor grades, surly behavior, disinterest in what is going on, secretiveness, and a poor attitude all suggest that the teen should be re-tested. Clearly, an increase of drugs in the subsequent urine warrants a conclusion that outpatient therapy is not working and a drug rehabilitation center may be in order.

But what of the teen who refuses a drug screen? He is essentially admitting to using something. This teen is in trouble, and a team is needed to help you decide the next step. Perhaps parents cannot convince the teen to submit to the drug screen, but they should make an appointment to see his physician and discuss the problem. A meeting with the doctor so that the family can, in front of the teenager, tell the physician their concerns is the next step. The physician can either deal with the problem directly, or call in a therapist as part of the team. The medical concerns of drugs need to be explored and the therapist will need to help the teenager open up the issues behind the drug use.

Finding a therapist may take some time because not all therapists are comfortable dealing with teenagers and their families, and not all therapists want to deal with drug and alcohol problems. Once family members are involved in the therapeutic process, issues around the family, drugs, and even drug screens can be resolved. If not, then one has to admit the teen to an inpatient facility.

Admitting your teenager to an inpatient rehabilitation center is a difficult step. (A "rehab" center is a mental health facility that helps people with drug and alcohol addictions. If your child has a secondary, or dual diagnosis, such as bipolar disorder, then a specialized rehabilitation center needs to be found.) Some communities have after-school programs to which the teen goes while attending his regular school. Many of these have a working relationship with different rehabilitation facilities and can help guide the family.

Many parents have a hard time doing "that" to their teenager. Actually, this line is often used by the kids themselves: "I can't believe you would do that to me! I'll never forgive you!" Parents have to understand that they are doing this *for* their teenager. At one point or another, all kids who go to rehab will acknowledge the fact that they needed inpatient care. In many cases, kids have a moment in their treatment when they confront their parents and admit this need and ask for forgiveness.

Rehab is very expensive, and without insurance few parents can afford to pay. If you have any concern about your teen using drugs, I would caution you to look immediately into your health coverage, because when the time comes to act you need to do it quickly and decisively. The time to purchase insurance is before a problem arises.

For those who face a crisis with no coverage, most local governments provide facilities in their communities. Search out the local hospital or use your religious leader as a resource. A priest, a minister, or a rabbi are in a position to guide families through the referral process.

Putting a Teen into a Rehabilitation Program

Some teens will go peacefully and willingly into treatment. Others just thumb their noses at the notion and leave the parents with little choice. As hard as the next step is, you need to get them into a community that is free of drugs and has professionals that can deal with denial, withdrawal, and anger. If need be, there are professionals who will provide "escort services." Two rather large, strong, and determined people show up at your son or daughter's bed and take the teenager, with your signed consent, to the program. All kids will complain, feel betrayed, cry, yell, scream, and curse their parents' existence. After being in these programs, most eventually realize the favor that was done to them. They understand that their parents probably saved their lives.

Is This an Emergency?

So one Saturday night your son comes home drunk. How do you know if he's "just drunk," or if this is an emergency situation where his stomach needs to be pumped? If he is breathing approximately 12 to 16 breaths per minute and is somewhat coherent, he can "sleep it off." If his breathing is slow, if he is throwing up constantly, or if he cannot be aroused or is in a stupor (the individual is incoherent; he makes no sense), he needs to be taken to the emergency room. If you can, call your doctor, but don't wait for a response. Tell the service to let the doctor know you are on your way to the emergency room, and he should contact you there. This is a time to act swiftly. If he seems to be "on something," let fear be your guide. If you are at all alarmed by his behavior, get him to the emergency room.

Suffice it to say, that when your child is in danger you need to act. In a hospital, they will have the proper testing laboratory (for drugs) and the proper equipment (for dehydration and medication) to assess his condition.

Improving Your Knowledge

Reading about drugs is difficult for parents because few ever expect drug problems to happen to their children. The next chapters concern the drugs that are abused most frequently and some specifics about each. All parents can read these pages for information. Some have to read them for action.

The most common "drugs" a teenager will encounter are alcohol, cigarettes, and marijuana, so these topics are given their own chapters. The fourth chapter focuses on a group of drugs that are classified as hallucinogens—LSD being the granddaddy of them all. The final chapter in this part covers all other drugs kids make use of, from inhalants to drugs used for date rape.

All parents need to familiarize themselves with the drugs in the teenager's world. They need to know their names and their properties. Some are inhaled, others smoked, and still others taken as pills. All are part of the teen world.

Chapter 12

Teens and Alcohol

Most teenagers (and many adults) accept the premise that there is a hierarchy of drugs. Some drugs are not perceived to be as bad as others, and alcohol is probably the top "drug" on that list. Parents and grandparents may have something to drink either at dinner or just to relax, any type of adult social gathering almost always involves alcohol, and beer is considered the perfect complement to pizza. If alcohol is a drug, why is this okay?

For any parent who thinks that alcohol is nothing more than a rite of passage and something that we must learn to use responsibly, I give you a sobering statistic. A sad reality when dealing with alcohol and teens is that the leading cause of death in this age group is automobile accidents caused by drunk driving. Teens' sense of invincibility and an even greater tendency to take risks when judgment is impaired by alcohol is a combination waiting for disaster. Alcohol both distorts judgment and can be addictive, especially in families where there is a propensity to alcoholism.

Alcohol as Part of the Teen Scene

In my practice I am constantly dealing with the argument that the party on Friday or Saturday needs alcohol. Without alcohol it can't be a good party and one cannot have fun.

I will hear teens argue eloquently, vociferously, and frequently that all their friends drink, or they'll say "What's the big deal?; I just 'had a couple.'" A classic retort of most teens and one that should be known by all parents is that "Pot is worse for you."

Because parents are aware that the party scene today involves alcohol, some ask my opinion on the appropriate age for teens to drink. The right age is the legal age. The fact that many teens are drinking does not excuse, condone, or make drinking alcohol acceptable. I cannot promise that the twenty-one-year-old, simply by virtue of age, is a more careful drinker, but there is a better chance of improved judgment than in the sixteen-year-old.

Is teenage drinking acceptable? No, but the teenage years are a time of experimentation and resistance to authority. As a parent, you need to do what you can to minimize the need for risky experimentation and be watchful for the moment when your teen's experimenting crosses over to regular drinking, heavy drinking, or both. If your son or daughter goes to a party or two and comes home having had a drink, you can consider that "experimentation." If your son or daughter "goes out drinking" or drinks every weekend, you should consider that a problem. The teenager with a DWI (driving while intoxicated) arrest, the teenager who gets dismissed from a boarding school because she had a bottle of alcohol in her room, the teenager who parties every weekend and has poor grades, or the teen who comes home after a night out and *consistently* smells of alcohol also has a problem and needs help.

Alcohol Effects

Alcohol is a depressant. Depending on how much you consume you alter your level of consciousness. With a small amount of alcohol, most individuals feel more socially outgoing and generally relaxed. The perceived euphoria is the direct result of a double negative. Since alcohol depresses the drinker's inhibitions, she is more likely to behave in an ebullient manner. However, in an attempt to maintain that feeling, she has more to drink, and she may soon feel its depressing effects on the brain.

With enough alcohol, and it takes little, the following functions are also affected:

Heart: The ability of the heart to beat forcefully and rhythmically may be altered. I have had several patients who noted unusual heartbeat because of alcohol. When the alcohol is out of the system, the heart resumes its normal pace and rhythm.

Liver: Alcohol is metabolized into lactic acid, which causes muscle pain, and acetaldehyde (a toxic chemical that can accumulate and make you feel sick). There is also interference in the metabolism of fatty acids, and they show up as elevated lipids in the blood and as fat in the liver. When you elevate lipids, your blood literally gets turbulent and damages the liver's ability to function.

Kidney: Since alcohol stimulates the production of urine, the drinker, ironically, can become dehydrated.

Digestive system: The most common effect is an irritation of the stomach leading to inflammation and nausea. Drink enough and you can also get diarrhea. A particularly dangerous situation can occur in some patients as their pancreas can become inflamed.

Skin: Sweating and broken capillaries.

Brain: As brain function is affected, the senses suffer, vision is somewhat diminished, and sense of taste and smell are lessened. Eventually, the drinker will act and feel depressed.

Sexual function: The myth that sex is improved with alcohol is *almost* not true. Teens often think that the secret to meeting the opposite sex is to begin with a few drinks, a perception that is shared by many adults. Since the first drink gives you a sense of loosened inhibitions, it is a bit easier to become social. One sixteen-year-old patient said it best when asked about drinking: "Doc, I'm so shy I can't even talk to the girl. So I have a couple and I feel better. With a few I always feel I can get an extra base with the girl!"

As we continued to talk, he finally admitted that as he drank more in an effort to maintain his euphoria, he noted a marked diminution in his sexual performance—he was unable to maintain an erection.

Although some parents will welcome the idea that alcohol will diminish sexual performance, and even see it as a potential deterrent to promiscuity, this is no rational argument for underage drinking. You cannot depend on a teen getting to the point of impotence before he attempts to have sex. In addition, alcohol and good sexual judgment just don't mix. Most teenagers see alcohol as a prelude to a sexual encounter, and because their judgment may be impaired, they are more likely to take the kinds of risks that lead to pregnancy and sexually transmitted diseases.

What Parents Should Know about Alcohol

Alcohol Content

Beer is probably the first alcoholic drink tried by teens. Depending on the label, beer contains between 3 and 6 percent alcohol. (Malts and ales contain twice the amount of alcohol per volume, while the distilled liquors contain 35 and 50 percent alcohol.) Obviously, a few drinks of hard distilled liquor can cause intoxication a lot faster.

If one considers that a single drink of two ounces of 50 percent proof whisky, gin, or rum, is the same as drinking 1 ounce of pure alcohol, then the equivalent amount of alcohol in beer would be a twelve-ounce bottle or a five-ounce glass of wine.

Measuring Alcohol Consumption

Since the brain's reaction to alcohol is not measured easily, we speak of blood levels to determine a person's status in relation to drinking. Since size and gender are critical in the body's processing of alcohol, it is hard to give firm numbers as to the amount of alcohol required to achieve certain levels. However, estimates here are based on four ounces of alcohol (two drinks) per hour.

Equivalent Volumes of Alcoholic Drinks

2 ounces of grain liquor
12 ounces of beer
6 ounces of wine
1 mixed drink with 1½ ounces of distillate

Blood Levels

First hour: blood-alcohol level is 50 mg/dl (milligram per deciliter). This is sometimes read as 0.05. Drinker will speak of feeling "great," "loose."

Second hour: 100 mg/dl (0.1). At this level, a person is "legally drunk" in most states but not necessarily *visibly* drunk. In some states, 80 mg/dl (0.08) is the legal level for intoxication. Someone who is good at "holding his liquor" may not show signs of inebriation but by legal standards he is drunk. Despite the fact that he does not appear drunk, he should not drive, nor should one believe him when he tells you he is "all right."

Third hour: 100–200 mg/dl (0.1–0.2). Now even the most experienced and seasoned drinkers will show toxicity. They stagger and slur their speech and generally demonstrate drunken behavior. It should be obvious that no one should let these teens drive or get in the car with them.

Fourth hour: Greater than 200 mg/dl (0.2). A danger point has been reached. Drinkers are so numb that they could tolerate a minor surgical procedure. Even *considering* driving is absurd, yet judgment is so impaired that driving seems easy to the person with so high a level of alcohol in his blood.

Fifth hour: Greater than 300 mg/dl (0.3). Potentially fatal. This level also results from the dangerous rite of binge drinking, in which a young person is asked to "chug-a-lug" a series of drinks, or even a bottle of alcohol, to prove his acceptance into a club or fraternity. With this action accomplished, it is quite conceivable that the teen will hit the toxic blood level.

One of my patients, fresh from a fraternity drinking party at a large school, went to his room and collapsed in his own vomit. He is alive today because his roommate returned to get a forgotten set of keys. The hospital report was that his blood alcohol level was above 320 mg/dl.

Breath analysis is the most common way of measuring alcohol levels. The breath analysis has become a standard for the courts to determine if a person is "legally" drunk. Another way of determining the alcohol level in an individual is through a blood test. The accuracy of the breath test, its ease of use, and its low cost have made the blood test less necessary. I recently saw a breath analyzer being sold at a local retailer as a tool to see who should be driving. Several of my parents have purchased these as a way of checking drinking in their teens.

Factors in Alcohol Absorption

Not all alcohol is absorbed equally. However, eventually it all "goes to your head"; it's just a matter of time. Nothing you can do, once you drink the alcohol, can change the inevitable fact that it will enter your bloodstream and do its natural damage. No matter how long the shower or how many cups of coffee, the blood level won't change until it has followed its natural path through the body.

The level of alcohol in the bloodstream is a result of several factors:

1. The type of alcohol (see previous chart). If you add carbonation to the drink, then the alcohol is absorbed faster. Champagne literally "goes to your head," and a vodka or gin with juice rather than soda will take longer to enter the bloodstream.
2. The amount consumed and the size of the person
   a. A 100-pound person will need two cocktails to achieve levels above 80 mg/dl within one hour. (Most people simply refer to the blood alcohol level as either "80" or "100" or as "0.8" or "point 8.")
   b. A 150-pound person will need three cocktails to achieve the same level.
   c. A 200-pound person will need four cocktails.
3. Food in the stomach slows absorption.
4. Gender. Alcohol is water soluble and not fat soluble (exactly the opposite of marijuana). Women, with their higher concentrations of body fat will attain a higher blood-alcohol level faster than men. A further problem for women is the presence of more stomach enzymes that allow alcohol to enter the bloodstream faster.

A girl who goes out to party and has not eaten well is clearly at risk for attaining high alcohol levels even with very little to drink. In fact, a single bottle of beer may put her at the legally drunk limit. On too many Mondays I have had girls come in for the "morning after pill" saying, "I only had a few drinks."

Weight Gain

It never even occurs to teens that they are consuming calories when they drink, and as a parent, this is one of your most potent weapons against drinking, particularly when talking to weight-conscious daughters. The teen who watches her weight all week may actually think twice about having a beer if she realizes how calorie-laden it is. The male athlete may also hear this argument.

Although alcohol has qualities similar to carbohydrates, alcohol actually behaves more like a fat. Each gram of alcohol has 7.1 calories; carbohydrates only have 4 calories per gram. Since the body has absolutely no use for alcohol, it represents pure excess caloric consumption. Someone who is "trying to lose weight" needs to consider the amount of alcohol she drinks, as well as her food intake.

The Number of Calories in Common Drinks

Alcoholic drink	Calories
Beer: regular	12 cal/oz: a 12-oz. beer has 144 calories
Beer: light	8 cal/oz: a 12-oz. light beer has 96 calories
Champagne	20 cal/oz: a 6-oz. glass has 120 calories
Gin, rum, vodka, scotch, whiskey	64 cal/oz if 80% proof; 74 cal if 90%: excluding mixer a drink has 128 and 148 calories, respectively
Wine	19 cal/oz: an 8-oz. glass has 152 calories
Pina colada	65 cal/ oz: an 8-oz. drink has 524 calories
Coffee and cream liquor	93 cal/oz: a 6-oz. drink has 558 calories
Nonalcoholic drink	Calories
Hot chocolate with milk	25 cal./oz.: a 6-oz. cup has 150 calories
Cream soda	15 cal./oz.: a 12-oz. glass has 180 calories
Capuccino	9 cal./oz.: an 8-oz. cup has 77 calories
Regular cola	12 cal./oz.: a 12-oz. glass has 145 calories
Diet cola	0.12 cal./oz.: a 12-oz. glass has 1.5 calories
Bottled iced tea	10 cal./oz.: a 12-oz. bottle has 120 calories

Teenagers who have cut out high-calorie foods may appreciate knowing what they are doing to their diets on Friday nights. And if your teen is putting on a "beer belly" without seeming to have increased his food intake at home, you might start checking on him when he arrives home on weekend nights.

Responsible Drinking

The key to teaching a healthy attitude toward alcohol is to model responsible drinking and be willing to discuss drinking with your teenager early on. Here's what won't work:

1. "It's illegal."
2. "It's bad for you. It can affect your liver." Liver toxicity is a weak argument with teens because it may take years before the alcohol will do its damage. Don't request a blood test for liver function; the normal result may backfire on you.
3. "Don't tell me everyone is doing it. If everyone jumped off the roof, would you follow them?" I think your grandparents' grandparents used this one.

More important than anything parents say is what they do. If there is a toast of wine on a special occasion or a glass of beer as part of a meal, then the child perceives the moderation of use and sees that alcohol can be part of socializing or a meal without being the sole point. On the other hand, if Dad or Mom comes home and quickly takes a drink "to relax," if the glass of wine at dinner turns into finishing the bottle during dessert, or if a parent encourages and laughs at the drunk relative, then the lesson is easily learned that drinking is recreational and an end in itself. Why, then, be surprised if the teen "gets wasted" as a part of going to parties?

I was once invited to give a lecture at a weekend resort. The adults had noted a particularly troublesome amount of drinking by their teenagers and I was asked to lecture on "Teen Drinking." I saw a great chance to combine sun, sea, sand, and a lecture. My wife and I were charmed by the hotel and found a note on our dresser inviting us "for drinks" before lunch. The lunch was a buffet in one of the local homes, and the gin and tonics, the margaritas, and the vodka fizz lasted far longer than the finger food. After lunch we rested, but we were reminded to come to the lobsterfest and clambake before the lecture. At six o'clock, the community had gathered at the beach to begin the consumption of lobsters. As we balanced our plates with the dangling lobster claws, we were directed to the makeshift table that held the beer. Surprise! The beer held out longer than the lobsters. The providers seemed to have found it more important to stock alcohol than food.

It was interesting to lecture to the gathered group on the problems of teen drinking while many of the adults in the audience were struggling with the full effects of their own day's imbibing. Their children were only following the example set at home.

During adolescence there is no greater lesson than "by example." The words of wisdom that once flowed, unquestioned and unchallenged, from the parent's lofty pedestal are now open to scrutiny and judgment by teens. If you have preached sobriety and driving, then it is time to demonstrate what you mean by refusing to drink if you plan on driving the family home. A simple, "No thank you, I have to drive," to the well-meaning host, within earshot of your child, is more valuable than any formal lecture. Moderate your alcohol consumption to a single drink at the restaurant and you teach your children that you mean what you say. Give the keys to your spouse and proclaim that you are not comfortable driving and you make another point.

Lastly, try to eliminate the sense that alcohol is needed to relax, to have fun, and to unwind. Comments that are sure to give a teen the wrong impression are: "Boy, do I need a drink"; "A drink would be perfect now"; "John sure is funny when he has a few. I never laughed so hard in my life"; "I'm fine! I only had a couple—I can still drive."

Of course, if there is a parental sense that all alcohol is to be banned for teens, then so be it. Just be clear that both spouses agree and are willing to enforce this rule. Also be clear what the consequences are for violating the house rule, that kids understand that you will enforce them, and do so whenever they are broken.

So You Think Your Teen's Been Drinking

What do you do if you find out that your son or daughter had a drink? It was his first drink with his friends and he came home slightly "buzzed."

Don't make a joke about it! Avoid any indication that an adult plateau has been reached by drinking. Have a conversation about alcohol, and do it by communicating that you understand the need for kids to experiment but that you are concerned. Listen to his arguments, and have your guard up for his actions over the year.

You can be fairly confident that most teens will try alcohol. There are few parties, or few small gatherings, where beer or hard liquor will not be present to some degree. Parents have to be sure of their own feelings about drinking in general and in particular how they feel about their teenager's drinking. In many families the use of beer is viewed as "a rite of passage." Since parents did it, and grandparents did it, why make a fuss? Most teens will have an episode of a "beer too many" and not like the sensation of being drunk and acting out of control. If, on the other hand, this is the only way a teen can enjoy herself the seeds for "needing" alcohol are being planted. Indeed, the fuss might only wake up the sleeping giant of the family's alcoholism. It won't work for parents to start talking to their kids about drinking "responsibly" when they themselves cannot go to a party and without coming home drunk, or come home and not have a "drink before dinner." We have to be honest with ourselves if we are to be honest with our children.

Let us, however, not use the example of the family that has the extra burden of alcoholism as a genetic time bomb. Consider instead parents who have no knowledge about alcoholism in their family and, therefore, cannot evoke the frightening specter of drinking as an addiction. This family has discovered that their teenager goes to parties and comes home drunk quite often. This teenager may show signs of poor concentration, poor judgment, missed assignments in school, and failing grades. The best approach is to discuss the situation with your teen's physician and, my own suggestion, is to go to an AA meeting for some help in dealing with this problem.

Some parents want to find an "acceptable level of teen drinking." Frankly, I know of none. If the family is comfortable with their teenager drinking at parties and he still is capable of getting good grades, functions within the family, and associates with a good peer group, then they will argue that this is acceptable. My own sense is that they are just closing our eyes to a situation that may escalate. I think that parents have to tell their kids that they are concerned and don't approve of their drinking behavior. Certainly, if grades slip, or attitudes change, these parents will have reached a point where the drinking is "unacceptable" and intervention is needed. Why wait until this point?

Parents are concerned that a confrontation may set up a sense of mistrust that will alter their relationship with their child, but if a teen is openly drinking, he has "put you on notice," and it is your obligation to let him know that you're monitoring the situation closely. If your teen continues drinking, you're going to have to do something. What are you watching for?

To begin with, school performance should be watched. School is a teenager's "work." Declining grades and a surly attitude about school and teachers should be noted.

It is to be hoped that you have kept your teenagers "tight" with the family. Though they may not be available for every family gathering, they should be expected to attend most, and they should certainly have some household chores. Allow for the fact that teens like some privacy, and then evaluate whether or not they have pulled away from the family in a drastic way (door-slamming, brief appearances at family meals, bad moods, etc.). Also consider the peer group. Do you know who they hang out with? Does their choice of friends worry you? Do they feel comfortable inviting their friends home? Try to keep in mind teens' normal moodiness and attempts to achieve their own "nonfamily" identity.

If you're beginning to suspect that alcohol is playing an important part in your teen's life, you have to take control of a dangerous situation. Continue your exploration with the most obvious questions: Where is the alcohol coming from? Check your liquor cabinet and see if there is some missing. I constantly see kids who simply go to the parents' supply and help themselves. Parents may not even be aware that a vodka or rum bottle is gone. If nothing is missing, get over the idea that they're too young to buy it. Kids can buy alcohol with fake IDs and from older friends. It is easier than parents realize.

Where is the money for alcohol coming from? Unwitting parents who dole out money as needed may actually be purchasing the very alcohol (or pot or cocaine) that is destructive. Consider the amount you've been giving your adolescents recently and what they have been spending it on. Does the money spent on items of which you're aware approximately match the money given? I have even had parents who painfully admitted "money was missing" from their wallet or purse but could not accept that their son or daughter was stealing from them. (Stealing from parents is, to my way of thinking, two problems. The first is a violation of trust and the second an admission that the money has to be used for something that parents would not approve.)

If you believe your teen is drinking, there are practical steps you can take. First, take away access to the car. A car is a privilege and no one is entitled to it if he shows poor judgment. Drinking is poor judgment. One of my patients lived in a suburb where the only way around was to drive. Despite the fact that she had a concussion following a drunk-driving incident, her parents were concerned that she could not get around without a car. It took a lot of arguing to convince them that she had not "earned" the right to drive a car.

Arrange your schedule so that you can be home at key times. Going out to dinner and leaving teenagers unattended is not unusual for modern parents. I can guarantee that the teenage grapevine will immediately broadcast whose house is empty for a particular night. Recognize this in your plans and make arrangements accordingly. Yes, it might mean that you must stay home if someone responsible cannot watch the house: it's called parenting. You can arrange for your teen to stay at a friend's house if you know the parents will be home, or you can limit the number of friends your teen can invite when unchaperoned to one or two whom you already know and trust. Remember, though, that the dynamics of a group of unattended teens is such that even the most "trustworthy" of kids may slip.

In dealing with your teen and alcohol abuse, avoid the bluffing game played by many families, "If you do this one more time, . . ."

One more time? You should only say this once. After that how many times will it take before you realize that the teen is in danger? She needs help now.

You don't give her an extra chance at hurting herself. You do something about it as soon as possible.

Consider purchasing a breath analyzer. While aware parents will be able to determine their teen is drinking by observing her actions and smelling her breath, arguments can be ended by breath analyzers. I caution that this is not for universal use with teens. Some element of trust is in order, but if you have repeated doubts, and his safety is an issue, I would not hesitate to use the analyzer.

One of my fifteen-year-old patients, who was well dressed and well spoken, slowly began slipping in school. He had begun to "dabble" in alcohol in the eighth grade when "lots of kids" in his group thought it was no big deal to have a few drinks on the weekends. Most parents who met him would not have suspected he had a secret life.

One day his parents received a call that their son had been caught drunk and had urinated on a lawn near the school. Dismissal from the school followed. The parents expressed the attitude that "boys will be boys" and seemed to view his drinking as a rite of passage. One day when I was trying to discuss the issue with him, he told me that his father was no one to talk because he had been quite the party animal while in college. The sense of pride was obvious. He actually could not understand why I was so intent on making his drinking an issue. It took a dismissal from another school before the parents acknowledged that they needed to act; then he was sent to a rehabilitation center.

If Your Teen Comes Home Drunk

If your teenager arrives home drunk, this is no time to talk. First, he is not functioning well enough to listen properly to the argument. Second, parents tend to be so angry that the wrong words are used. This is serious stuff and the discussion must be done calmly. At this point, breathe deeply and be glad that he is safely home. Then you and your spouse should discuss the situation in order to present a united front.

That night your first priority is making certain he is safe. Remember that no amount of coffee, no amount of walking him around will eliminate the alcohol from his system. There is no concoction that "has been in the family for years" that will sober him up. If he is throwing up, stay with him; if he is staggering, keep one eye on him at all times in case he falls or decides to leave home again. The teen who is incoherent, who is staggering and nearly falls over, or who is close to being unconscious belongs in the emergency room of the nearest hospital. He may need to have his stomach pumped. At the least, he needs monitoring and observation.

The normal respiratory rate is about sixteen full breaths per minute. We take this for granted. Yet, as a depressant, alcohol can lower that rate; if it starts to approach eight breaths per minute, the person is in danger. To let him "sleep it off" in a quiet room may only invite a disaster if he chokes on his own vomit or falls off the bed in an unconscious move and sustains a concussion.

More likely, he will show signs of slurred speech and appear slightly off balance. He is drunk but safe at home. Let him go to sleep. The next morning, after a calm breakfast, and what may have been a sleepless night for you, sit the teen down and say words to this effect: "We know that you were drinking last night and, in fact, were drunk. I think we have a problem, and we have to do something about it."

At this point, expect denial and arguments that you are overreacting. He may raise the ante by saying, "What? You think I'm an alcoholic! What's the big deal? I just had a beer or two. "

A good response here is the following: "In our family it is a big deal. A beer, especially two, is a problem for both of us. It can impair your judgment, and that's why we're concerned."

Or he may realize that the best defense is a good offense. This method often works because it throws parents off guard: "Are you staying up to spy on me?!" The answer should be a simple "Yes," followed by the statement that you are worried about his behavior. If you back down now, he has won the argument. I think that all teenagers have an inherent sense of courtroom drama. Their ability to hit the parent in the guilt zone is extraordinary.

Cleverly, he may try to split the two parents by pleading to the one who usually takes his side. Counter his argument calmly and say: "All we know is that you are drinking too much and we have to see someone about it. Your father and I [or vice versa] have talked about it, and we both agree."

The reader should note that I encourage the use of the word "we" at this point. "We" refers not only to you and your spouse, but to the entire family. True, it is the teen who is drinking, but it is the entire family that has a problem. I know of no way that a teenager who is drinking heavily does not have an impact on the entire family. His parents worry, his siblings suffer, his school work is endangered, and his life is in jeopardy. The teen's drinking is not isolated to the teen.

If the Shoe Fits

There's more work to be done if your teen lashes back with a family truth: "You drink!"

If the parents have done their homework and have come to the conclusion that this statement is justified, the next response will end the argument: "Yes, and watching you has helped us realize that we have not done anything about it. We need help, too. I think we should start as soon as possible."

I guarantee that the family will change with that statement.

I had a patient who was concerned that his father was an alcoholic. His mother agreed and suggested a family meeting to air things out. The father came to the meeting thinking we were going to discuss his son, who had been acting depressed. The father was shocked to be considered the problem, and he was adamant that he could not be an alcoholic because he "only" drank wine and expensive ones at that! That he was drunk afterwards mattered little to the man.

The image of the drunk, wallowing in filth, and disoriented on a street is not the norm. Many well-dressed, well-groomed, and affluent people of both genders, all ages, and all social groups have "a problem" with alcohol. Indeed, they could qualify as alcoholics, but the label takes a long time to appreciate and accept. The alcoholic has a progressive illness that involves excessive consumption of alcohol. Briefly put, he needs to drink. He will drink alone, in public, or in a social setting. He may drink to deal with his feelings, and his judgment about the appropriateness of his alcohol intake is impaired.

Most teens who drink heavily do not reach the stage of "alcoholism" during their adolescent years. Often they will argue that they may drink a bit, but they will adamantly deny that they "need" to drink. They argue that they can walk away from alcohol, proving that they are not alcoholics. To a degree they are correct. They would qualify as "alcohol abusers." This term implies that the amount of drinking impairs judgment and can cause physical damage. They fail to appreciate that this is step one on the road to alcoholism. The alcoholic is someone who is physically and emotionally *dependent* on alcohol. It is a complex syndrome that develops over years of abuse. Literally, a physical addiction to the drug develops and, if alcohol is stopped suddenly, the individual will experience withdrawal.

Yet, despite their protests, even teens can become alcoholics during their adolescent years. However, it's not just the teen alcoholic who should receive help.

The family of this teen also needs to get help to understand how to deal with the issues involved in drinking. One father confessed that he had not appreciated how hard it was for his son to stay sober until he casually ordered a "beer with the sandwich" and it so bothered his son that he had to leave the table. Parents and siblings of the teen alcoholic have to understand the pressures and the struggle to abstain. One cannot be an "enabler" by ignorance and expect the alcoholic to do well with their fight against drinking.

Helping Your Teen

If you find that your teen has a drinking problem, make an appointment with your teen's physician. If the doctor is sensitive, let the physician have a confidential session with your son or daughter. Both parents should go to the appointment. The mere fact that both parents are present alerts everyone as to the severity of the problem. If only one parent goes you imply that the issue isn't that important. If your physician isn't comfortable with alcohol intervention, ask for a referral to someone in adolescent medicine, or a therapist who specializes in drugs and alcohol.

Leave the room after the concerns are expressed to the physician and allow the teen to privately discuss issues with the doctor. You should discuss a game plan with your teen and the doctor. When do we return? Does she come back? Do we come back? Will there be a referral to someone else? All of these first steps put the teen on alert. If there is an escalation in the alcohol issue, then a referral to a drug therapist is indicated. Don't hesitate at this point! Many parents fear that this is too drastic a step. If you have gotten here, no step is too drastic to stop the problem.

The key at this point is to get help. Later, the pieces of the story will unfold, and who drinks and how much will soon be sorted out. In the alcoholic world, there is a term for someone who does nothing, or worse, someone who passively sees the problem and allows it to continue: The word used is "enabler." Standing by without taking any action makes you an enabler. Parents whose kids are drinking feel powerless to stop the problem. In many ways they are right; it will be up to the teen to stop himself, but it is up to you to demand that he be accountable for his actions.

Alcoholic Anonymous is another great place to get help. It is a self-help group for anyone with an alcohol problem. Meetings are run by members and are attended by people in all stages of recovery. One of its premises is that you can't fool someone who has been there before. Getting the teen to the meeting is only a step but it sends a powerful message. I have had some patients who felt that AA changed their lives and that it continues to provide the necessary lifeline to keep them from drinking. Others find the spirituality of the program not to their liking. It's still worth a try if there is doubt. Al-Anon and Alateen are companion programs that help the families of the alcoholic.

Fortunately most teens do not require such drastic steps. Many have to be reminded that their actions have consequences. Knowing that their parents are on the alert and that they are ready to do "something" is enough to get them to stop. The critical point is for parents to be vigilant and not assume that it can't happen to their family.

The Party Scene

As parents, you have an additional responsibility. Having established that your role is to make sure your adolescents are safe, it stands to reason that you cannot serve alcohol at a party. As cool as it may be, as much as your teenager's friends might appreciate your lax attitude, you just shouldn't, and legally cannot, do it.

You will meet with the objection that if you do not serve alcohol no one will come to your teen's party. Stand firm and be clear: "Then we can't have a party. We will not serve beer or any other alcohol to your friends." Expect a minor temper tantrum but know you are doing the right thing as a parent. Reiterate that you will gladly host parties with no alcohol, but stand firm on the no-alcohol policy regardless of how hard it is.

In many states, the law holds people who serve minors, or who serve someone who is visibly drunk, coresponsible for the actions of that person. In other words, the bartender who serves a minor, or someone who is staggering, shares liability if that person has an accident. If you serve alcohol to a minor in your house, you, too, may share responsibility and liability for his/her actions.

The Underage College Years

We tend to think of college students as adults, and colleges often treat them as such, but in truth they're just older kids, and as a result, they pose a special problem for parents. College students have been handed an enormous amount of freedom and, for some, this is their first taste of true responsibility. There is no more detention, and they are permitted latitude in their choice of classes, housing, and curfew. For the first time in their lives, they are also free of the watchful eyes of parents and teachers. In their social lives, they now have most of the privileges of adults: they don't have to answer to anyone about how they spend their leisure.

Statistics about college drinking are alarming. Nearly half of the students reporting academic problems are involved with drinking. Statistics gathered by the government point to the following:

1. Alcohol is implicated in 66 percent of college suicides.
2. Alcohol is involved with most rape cases on campus.
3. One-half to two-thirds of college students admitted to driving drunk or being in a car that was being driven by someone who had been drinking.
4. The lower the grades, the more likely it is that a student was drinking.

As a parent, your job of teaching independence, good judgment, and responsibility will now be put to the test. Yet, the eighteen- or nineteen-year-old going to college may feel a sense of freedom that is unparalleled in his experience. They no longer have to check in for a curfew, nor explain how they spend money. They have a credit card, in most cases for an "emergency," and are hundreds, or even thousands, of miles away from concerned parents. They now have to establish themselves amidst a new group of kids.

The temptation to "party" is overwhelming. Kids recognize that they need to study, to get good grades, but college is also perceived as part of a larger social process. They need to find a place to "fit in." Parties are important in this process, and the amount of alcohol consumed by college students is extraordinary.

In almost all colleges, one can assume that any student who is not a senior is probably violating the alcohol laws of the state. Yet, the college seldom enforces these laws. Everyone recognizes that the "party" has liquor, and no one does anything about it unless someone gets hurt. (This is changing as I write. Some states and colleges are enforcing "zero-tolerance laws," and the underage drinker is not given special consideration.) Despite being underage, it is not particularly difficult to obtain alcohol. Many simply order it without being "carded"; others have fake IDs. Where do you get a fake ID? Ask a teen to find out.

A further complication to the drinking issue is the "Greek system" of fraternities and sororities that welcomes the young collegian with open arms and open bottles. Alcohol and fraternities has long been a problem, and it begins with the pledge process itself. The pledges need to prove themselves to the brothers, and often a rite of passage is how much alcohol you can tolerate. Fortunately this is changing, but not fast enough. Some colleges outlaw fraternity "chug-a-lug" in which the pledge has to drink a pitcher of beer, or worse, an entire bottle of hard liquor. (If your teen expresses interest in pledging, discuss head-on your concerns about pledging and the overemphasis by frats on drinking.) A well-publicized national story told of a "clean-cut" young man who was a straight-A student and a model of teenage behavior, who died one night after trying to fit in with a fraternity crowd that demanded consumption of a bottle of alcohol as its freshman requirement. It took this level of tragedy to highlight what everyone knew: College students drink a lot.

As for parties, the movie *Animal House* serves as an example. The more liquor, the greater the fraternity, the greater the sex, the greater the fun. To many college students, the line between liquor and fun is direct. Although sororities tend not to use alcohol for pledging, they are usually linked to a "brother" fraternity and, as such, members participate in the frat's parties and the alcohol. More than one of my patients has complained of "going too far" with a guy because she had too much to drink.

What about college drinking in general? It would be nice if I could honestly tell you that you can do a lot about it as you leave your teenager in his new dorm room. You meet the new roommate, have a parting lunch before the long drive home, and, before you leave, you sit down with your child to discuss drinking and college. If this is the first time you've discussed this, don't expect this talk to have an effect. Your lessons are over; you were supposed to have done all of this in high school. Regretfully, if he never learned the lesson, or if you felt you didn't need to teach it, it's a bit too late.

Almost all colleges have drug and alcohol counselors and even chapters of AA on campus. The only drawback is that the student has to seek help; it won't come to her. With so much free time, with no supervision, and with long weekends, the college student is at high risk to drink. If you find that the situation is serious, take her out of college! A semester off in some treatment program beats a drunk driving accident or alcohol poisoning.

A second-year college student *of mine was lucky. Mike had attended a competitive high school and although his grades were not stellar, he had survived. Unknown to parents and to his doctors, he had been spending a fair amount of time smoking pot and drinking alcohol. Mike did well enough that he had generated little suspicion. Since he had "acceptable" grades in high school, little was expected of him in college, and he used the same skills to get by, barely passing his freshman year. In his sophomore year, he got drunk and the campus police were called. He lashed out and punched the policeman. Sometimes you hit the right person. This officer was an alcoholic and he recognized that Mike needed help, not prison. He took him to the Dean, who gave Mike the option of leaving immediately or entering a drug* *rehabilitation program. The option was generous. Although Mike entered the program with a cynical attitude, thinking he had gotten away with a con, he began to listen and understand that his drinking was consistent with being an alcoholic. He finally declared himself as such and his life began to change. A year later he was fully vested in AA and his return to college was successful. His grades improved and his entire perspective has changed.*

You may note a newfound sense of "maturity" when your college son or daughter comes home for Thanksgiving. The natural tendency on parents' part is to acknowledge the new status and offer her alcohol with the holiday meal. If you do it, then keep her home. (It would be preferable not to offer the alcohol at all, but we do not live in an ideal world.) But your effort to acknowledge her new status does not have to include allowing liquor. Just because she has finished a few exams in college and is now home, does not mean she is prepared for drinking. By serving alcohol at home you are saying, in effect, that she is free to drink at school. Don't try to be popular. Remember your job as parents.

Chapter 13

Teens and Smoking

In my office, I always address the issue of smoking, and here's what I can share with you: Most kids genuinely agree that cigarettes are bad for you, but not for *them* (they are invincible). The cigarette at the party or the one after school (smoked while hanging out) is viewed as "no big deal."

If I ask a teen "Do you smoke?" I often get a long pause and a hesitant "not really." This means that they might not smoke daily or are just at the beginning stages of the habit. Some answer: "I only smoke on weekends." The other frequent response I receive is, "I only have a couple. No big deal. I plan to quit." Teens genuinely believe they can "quit any time they want to."

Unfortunately, teenagers are wrong about this. They fail to appreciate that they are not immune from the addictive qualities of smoking, and that starting to smoke means having to face the prospect of quitting and withdrawal. Quitting is very difficult. Anyone who has ever tried can tell you so. Even people with lung disease or cardiovascular disorder still find it difficult, if not impossible, to give up after years of smoking. We can expect no less from the teenager who has begun to smoke. It is not impossible, but it is extraordinarily difficult. The hope is that kids never start so they never have to deal with quitting.

Alcohol is perceived as a rite of passage into the adult world where cocktails and drinking carry an air of sophistication. In sharp contrast, cigarettes would seem to be "out." They are banned in many restaurants, dentists tell you that they stain your teeth, doctors warn of the many dangers of smoking; clearly, cigarettes have lost some of their cool status. Yet, our teens are joining the ranks of smokers in numbers that are staggering. The current estimates are that at least four million teenagers are smoking, with an estimated three thousand teenagers starting each day.

Marketing to Teens

In the past, cigarette companies targeted young people with clever ads, cartoon characters (Joe Camel), coupons redeemable for merchandise, and a message that showed smoking as sexy, mature, and generally cool. The muscular rugged cowboy or the slim fashionable executive was the person you could be if you tried their brand. Today those companies are forbidden to have advertisements aimed directly at the youth market. There is hope.

Nonetheless, sales still rely on the fact that cigarettes are perceived as grown up. For teens, anything that is adult is a step in the right direction in establishing their identity. Smoking, long felt to be an adult habit, can accomplish this goal in one quick moment.

Until forty years ago, girls were left out of tobacco marketing. Then, starting in the 1960s, tobacco companies picked up on something that still works today. During the "sexual revolution," cigarettes that were long and thin became identified as a way of staying slim and sexy. In no time at all girls were buying cigarettes marketed expressly for women. A feminine cigarette! Girls heard the message that smoking can keep you slim. Even with current knowledge about how deadly cigarettes are, one of my patients who worried about her figure managed to smoke up to three packs per day!

Even if your teen manages to survive high school without smoking, both genders face a new hurdle in college. A study recently done by the Harvard College Alcohol group found that nearly half of college students had used tobacco products during the previous year. Many of the previous studies had failed to include cigars and smokeless tobacco. With this inclusive look, one-third of the nearly 14,000 students surveyed acknowledged tobacco use in the previous month, and over half admitted to some tobacco use over the past year. Once the campaign to lure teens was outlawed, the college student became the new target of the cigarette companies.

Why Teens Start

When parents find that their teen has taken up smoking, they often look for a scapegoat. Inevitably there is a "bad crowd" or a particular friend that they feel has led their teenager into smoking. This is only partially true. Studies on teenage drug use show that you need two obvious variables to encourage use: the drug itself must be available, and there is group acceptance of its use.

Rarely will someone in a group force a teen into trying a drug, including cigarettes. Cigarettes are simply available, and the group sanctions smoking by doing it. Put yourself in your teen's place: If you are accepted by a group of kids, and they do something, chances are you will be doing the same thing soon. Teens need acceptance, and they welcome being included in group activities. Many will be able to turn away from the dangerous and unacceptable, but it isn't easy. If your teen hangs out with a group of kids who smoke, chances are that she will take up smoking, too. It's just a matter of group dynamics. What can seem uncool, or even dangerous, takes on a totally different acceptance within a group.

The Effects of Nicotine

Once you start smoking, it takes very little time for the body to *need* nicotine. A single puff of a cigarette sends a message to the brain to release serotonin and dopamine, and within eight seconds of smoking, the brain feels the effects. Herein lies the problem. Since serotonin makes you feel good, makes you feel less hungry, and generally gives you an overall sense of pleasure, each puff of nicotine basically rewards you. When you don't smoke, your body craves the sensation that it has known and soon you are lighting up to reward the memory. Beyond this, the body becomes physically addicted to nicotine.

An extra problem for girls is the use of cigarettes and birth control pills (see Chapter 9). The Pill, combined with smoking, places a girl at increased risk for cardiovascular disease. The smoking teenager on the Pill is at the same risk for heart disease and blood clots as a mature woman in her thirties or forties. By smoking, the girl gives up the advantage of her age. Even with that information it is hard to get girls to give up cigarettes.

The Overall Effects of Smoking

Peripheral Nervous System.

Nicotine blocks the normal transmission of nerves in the vascular system.

Nicotine releases catecholamines (natural stimulants in the body) from the adrenal gland. This partially accounts for the "good" feeling from a cigarette.

Central Nervous System and the Brain.

The brain is stimulated. With enough nicotine you can precipitate muscle tremors.

Respiration increases.

Receptors that induce vomiting can be stimulated.

Urinary output is diminished by stimulating a brain hormone that concentrates urine.

Cardiovascular System.

Heart rate increases.

Blood pressure increases.

Blood vessels constrict.

Gastrointestinal Tract.

There is increased tone and motility of the bowels.

There is nausea, vomiting, and potentially diarrhea.

Lungs.

The bronchial tree is irritated (as anyone who has burnt leaves in the fall will understand).

Bad breath.

Cancer.

Other Means of Taking In Nicotine

Cigars

The use of cigars has been a recent trend among the younger set. The covers of magazines picture movie stars or financial moguls smiling and holding a cigar. Many major cities have "cigar bars."

I now get the occasional teen who proudly tells me that he and his dad know a great deal about cigars. One gets the impression that there is more than just knowledge going on. Cigars have become a symbol of power and success with the college and graduate crowd; it had always been there with the older, more established, male. Forget that image. Younger males and even females are buying cigars.

Cigars are not inhaled, as a rule, and hence there is less nicotine reaching the lungs. That does not mean smoking cigars is "safer." The high nicotine content is now pressed on the lips and on the lining of the mouth, so nicotine is still entering the system. Cancer of these areas is one of the main concerns with long-term cigar smoking.

Chewing Tobacco, or "Dip"

Whether because of the image of the virile American cowboy or our major league baseball players, adolescent males have come to perceive the chewing and spitting involved in "smokeless tobacco," also known as "dip," to be a sign of machismo. The cheek bulging with tobacco, followed by the "spit" of the professional athlete, is part of what sports success is all about. The admiring teen male has witnessed this marvelously disgusting process and decided that "cigarettes are bad for you" so he will chew tobacco instead. The market for smokeless tobacco gladly sells him the tobacco and he is "cool"; he is not like the other kids who smoke. No, his habit goes further. His breath is disgusting smelling. Girls hate it. Parents are shocked to discover that their son is doing it. Doctors warn of cancer of the lining of the mouth. Fortunately most teens give up dip early. Maybe the lack of available spittoons has helped. Those more obstinate chewers need to be reminded of the response that they elicit from all around and of the potential of cancer.

The Gateway Theory

A current concept regarding drug use in the teenager is the "gateway" theory. This theory argues that all drug usage begins with cigarettes. The proposal is that the cigarette is an "innocent" beginning, which will lead to alcohol or to marijuana. These in turn will not satisfy cravings for immediate gratification, and the teen will turn to cocaine and other drugs. Rarely will a teen start with cocaine; it's perceived as dangerous. He first starts on that road with more accessible, cheaper drugs. Nicotine is usually the starting point. Likewise, the pot smoker does not usually start with pot; a few cigarettes and learning how to inhale precede the first pot puffs.

Fortunately, most kids who smoke do not go down the inexorable path to harder drugs. The gateway concept simply argues that the first step into harder drugs begins with easier steps. How valid is this concept? I cannot recall too many pot smokers, cocaine users, or heroin users who did not also smoke. On the other hand, it will not work to confront your teen by saying that cigarette smoking is the beginning of the road to heroin. I promise you he will think you have read one article too many, or that your own brain is being influenced by drugs!

But you may want to keep these thoughts in mind as you ponder the seriousness of cigarette smoking.

Quitting

Anyone who says they "plan to quit" really won't. The New Year's resolution, the graduation pledge, the starting college resolve, or the birthday promise is usually little more than a wish. The good news is that with each attempt to quit the teenager will learn something about how hard it is, and each new "quit" tends to be more successful. My own experience with smoking is illustrative:

When we were thirteen, my friend Eddie and I went to the park with two stolen cigarettes (Camels, of course, and nonfiltered—filtered didn't exist) and tried our first puffs. After a few feeble attempts to light the cigarette on that windy fall day, we each took a deep lungful and waited seconds for the smile that we had witnessed so many times on smokers in advertisements. The smile never came; instead a wave of nausea overcame both of us and the only reason we didn't throw up our lunches was that the incessant cough prevented us.

I never appreciated breathing before this cigarette deprived me of air. What had I done wrong? Eddie concluded (correctly) that we just had to persevere and we would soon be smoking like adults. I looked at him and wondered if the single puff had eliminated air and his brains in one monumental moment. "Go ahead. I'll catch my breath for now. I'll have another try later." I had absolutely no intention of sticking that cigarette or any other in my mouth, now or for eternity. What could there possibly be in smoking that made people do it? Ah! I was so naive.

The story fast-forwards to my first year in college. Now, a full five years had gone by and no cigarette had ever again crossed my lips. I had watched one fallen friend after another succumb to the will of the advertisers who swore that we would look cool, be sexy, and feel relaxed. The first two promises seemed shallow. However, relaxation was something that a first-year premedical student could certainly use. The notion of addiction, of smelling funny, of expense seemed miniscule compared to the promise of "relaxation": a puff, a pause, and calmness. Some vague notion had been proposed that smoking might be bad for you; I, a budding scientist, had no definite proof of this allegation. And so, during a particularly difficult organic chemistry class I plotted to buy a pack of cigarettes.

I became a smoker on that day. Any attempts to tell me that cigarettes were bad for you were met with scorn, impatience, and denial. As I watched cancer patients die from lung disease, or as I listened to the lectures that suggested a linkage between cigarettes and poor health, or cancer, I simply went into more denial. By the time I became a navy lieutenant commander, my habit had climbed to *two packs* per day.

Wife, daughter, parents, and friends all wondered why I smoked. I seemed bright enough to equate the stupidity of smoking with poor health. Even the sides of the package of cigarettes mentioned that this was "dangerous to my health." Why did I smoke? Nonsmokers have a sense that smoking is silly, clearly bad for you, and logically, we smokers should just do something else. We-who-smoked did so because we had to.

Make no mistake about it; cigarettes are an addiction. I was addicted. When, and only when, I saw the need to quit did anything happen. My daughter had seen a commercial about a child imitating her Dad and reaching for the cigarette pack. When she asked if I was going to die from smoking, I naturally lied. But the truth, plainly put to me by a four-year-old, was devastating.

On October 2, 1972, at 12:20 P.M. in the officers' mess, I threw away my last six cigarettes and vowed to quit that day. I told the world (everyone at the mess table and all my friends) I had quit so that the humiliation of failure would be an incentive. Pride helps.

I am a smoker. Though I have not smoked a cigarette since 1972, I still feel, on occasion, the pangs of not having a cigarette to relax me.

I tell my story so that the parent of a teenager who wants his son or daughter to quit can understand the addictive nature of cigarettes. We have medications to help withdraw from many drugs, but the failure rate for cessation of smoking is still a problem. It is not a casual or easy process. Unless the teenager wants to quit, it will not happen. Entreaties to quit because "There is cancer in the family," or "You are breaking my heart, hurting yourself that way," or worse, "But you *know* they're bad for you" will have no impact.

Once I said to a patient that he had halitosis from cigarettes and that caught his attention. I pursued it with the notion that girls who kissed him would clearly notice the taste of cigarettes. His facial expression was tense, and I was winning. I thought I had discovered, at last, the clue to helping teens quit. Just tell them that their mouth has a great deal in common with the smell of yak droppings. That would do it. Alas, he finally countered with "My girl-friend smokes, too." I lost. And so did he.

Quitting Techniques

Once a teen decides that it is time to quit, it is important that you provide the support necessary, and don't expect him or her to succeed initially. It's not easy to quit, and few people succeed in quitting the first time around. When asked about quitting cigarettes, Mark Twain responded, "Quitting smoking is easy; I've done it a thousand times." There are a few "denial" games played by the smoker, and I will hear the following when someone comes in and is coughing, or has a sore throat:

1. "I've quit. Really. I haven't had a cigarette in four days, so it can't be the smoking that's the problem."

How to Help a Smoker Quit

1. Support her endeavor to quit. There are groups that can help smokers, not unlike AA. The American Cancer Society or the American Lung Association may be able to point you to a support program in your area.
2. The nicotine patch is a way of giving some nicotine so that the withdrawal is not as harsh. (Talk to your doctor before using this or any other method.)
3. Nicotine gum helps to stop the craving for nicotine and the need to put something in your mouth. Nasal sprays and inhalers can also help.
4. Alternative methods include acupuncture and hypnosis. Both, in my experience, have had little success.
5. In addition to craving nicotine, smokers find that one of the most difficult aspects of quitting is changing habits. To quit, anyone who smokes must learn to recognize the situations that particularly make him want a cigarette and avoid them if possible.

2. "I stopped smoking my brand. I switched to a mentholated one so my throat would feel better."
3. "I have been meaning to quit. Should I?"
4. "I don't really smoke. I just have one once in a while."
5. "I promise to quit, for my birthday!"

All of these are empty promises, and none of these kids will quit. However, the patients who say, "I need help quitting, Doc," are the ones who might succeed. How can we help?

Support

Because during these years, adolescents feel invincible, telling the teenager that cigarettes are bad won't change his mind. Nonetheless, it's important that he hears from a physician that it is a bad idea to smoke. Schedule an appointment with your teen's doctor. A nonscolding, direct approach filled with understanding is the best way of reaching the teen. I never regale the teen with facts about lung cancer, about heart disease, or about hypertension. They believe that none of this will happen to them during the immediate teenage years. Do you really think they worry about what their health will be like thirty years from now? Few do; most can't fathom the notion of their twenties, let alone their forties.

What I tell them is that it is very difficult to quit, and when they want to quit I will help if they ask. I discuss strategies such as avoiding situations that prompt smoking, or getting a friend to quit with them. Nicotine gum and nicotine patches help, and I try to have them consider using these as an adjunct to quitting. Usually you try one or the other at a time.

Parents who smoke have to recognize that they must quit if they are to have a smokefree home. The sheer hypocrisy of saying that "I'm too old to quit" will not be sufficient for the teen. Don't even try the "Do as I say and not as I do" line. On the other hand, parents who do not smoke have to present a concerned but appreciative attitude of how hard it is to quit. They must allow that their teen may be grumpy or moody during the process and not nag them about it. They must be supportive and offer words of encouragement along with an understanding of the difficulties.

Your teen should consult a doctor before using any of the following methods.

Nicotine Gum

Nicotine gum helps the smoker quit by satisfying the craving for nicotine in another form and gradually weaning the individual from it completely. The gum must be used *instead* of cigarettes; in other words, the patient must stop smoking cigarettes before using the gum. The gum is not chewed in the same manner as regular gum; it must be chewed slowly and thoroughly to get the full effect. I tell patients that the gum is to be chewed until there is a slightly bitter taste, a "peppery" taste according to the manufacturer; after that the gum rests between the cheek and gums for a period of about thirty minutes.

Because acid beverages can interfere with the absorption of the nicotine, coffee, acidic juices, and soft drinks are not allowed for fifteen minutes prior to and during chewing. I recommend banning all foods for the same fifteen minutes, because it gives the smoker one less thing to think about. Some people suffer a slightly upset stomach. This is transient in most cases and, frankly, there is little that can be done. It seems like a small price to pay if there is success with this method.

Now an over-the-counter product, nicotine gum is available in 2 mg strength for the person who smokes a pack per day or less and 4 mg strength for the heavier smoker. Nicotine gum should not be used by the person who may still smoke "occasionally." A combination of the gum and smoking could cause nicotine to reach toxic levels. The side effects of the gum can be divided into two major parts:

1. The withdrawal of nicotine itself can cause the individual to feel irritable, anxious, restless, and fatigued. There may be cravings and an increase in appetite leading to increased weight gain. Indeed, depending on the level of previous nicotine used, this withdrawal may actually manifest itself in a depression.
2. The second side effects are due to the effects of the nicotine in the gum itself. Nicotine can increase blood pressure, heart rate, cause heart palpitations, irritate the stomach, and because of its contact with the gums it can cause irritation of the gums. Pregnant women should contact their physicians as the nicotine can increase the fetal heart rate and nursing may also transmit the nicotine to the baby.

Your teen should contact a doctor for information on the advisability of using the gum, which to use, and for how long.

Nicotine Patch, Nasal Spray, and Inhaler

Nicotine can also be delivered "transdermally," or through the skin. The absorption is good enough that you can rely on sufficient medication without concern about taste or painful injections. A possible down side is a rash at the site of the patch. Nicotine patches are also sold over-the-counter now.

Patients are told to place the patch, starting with a full-strength one and gradually easing down to a lower dose patch, somewhere between their neck and their waist at the start of the day. To lessen the possibility of irritation, the patch should be rotated to different sites. One can use the patch for twenty-four hours or remove it during sleep. As with the gum, the idea is that the patch is a substitute for nicotine and one must not smoke while using it. Your physician can advise if you should use the patch and for how long.

Along with the transdermal delivery, we have found that the nose can absorb medication almost as fast as intravenous in some cases, so a nicotine nasal spray has been created. The nasal spray delivers a metered amount of nicotine, and the patient feels the effects immediately. The recommended dose is two sprays (one in each nostril), and within ten or so minutes the patient's blood-nicotine levels approximate that found after one cigarette. Each vial of the spray has enough for fifty doses (100 mg/bottle). Patients must be cautioned about the irritant effect on the nasal lining and of the fact that a cold will delay absorption of the nicotine. The spray has the same issues of dealing with withdrawal of nicotine and administering it. Since it is either inhaled through a pulmonary inhaler or a nasal spray, the respective routes of administration may be irritated along with the usual effects of nicotine. Although the insert recommends dosing, your doctor can tailor the doses to your needs and advise you. Some patients cannot use the spray at all.

The spray is recommended for a period of three months and the dose will vary between one to two doses per hour up to a maximum of five doses per hour. Since the spray is more expensive, cost is a factor in using the spray, especially if a maximum of forty doses per day is used.

The Nicotrol Inhaler is similar to the inhalers that the asthmatic patient uses daily. In this method the nicotine is delivered to the lungs and absorbed by the pulmonary tree. Ironically, asthmatic patients are the very ones who probably should not use this form of cessation since the nicotine itself may produce an asthmatic attack. For the patient who opts to use this method, the average dosage is six cartridges per day for a period of six to twelve weeks. The physician may want to tailor the dosage and period of use in a different way and should be consulted before starting on the inhaler.

Patients who opt to use nicotine replacement, regardless of the route of administration, have to recognize that this is a major commitment and that it is not a "quick fix" to quitting cigarettes.

Forming New Habits

Kids will smoke after school in groups as they gather in parks, in malls, in cars, and anywhere but school. Even that, for some, is not sacred. The sad conclusion is that kids will smoke if they have the opportunity. One cannot police them to the point where they cannot smoke. As soon as they are out of a parent's or school administrator's vigilant sight, they will light up. Once addicted, there is little to substitute the nicotine craving other than a tapering process.

It would be ideal if we could simply substitute one habit for another. Instead of smoking, do something else. Unfortunately, there is very little "else" that will satisfy the craving for nicotine. However, most smokers find that they need to be doing something with their hands when they are not smoking. It probably never occurred to them, but the holding of the cigarette is part of the ritual.

As silly as it may seem, I have bent a few hundred thousand paper clips. It started the day I quit, when I found myself putting the clip in my mouth and realized that, no matter how hard I sucked, no smoke would reach my lungs. Instead, I bent the clip into a straight line and played with the idea of putting it back into its original form. To date I have not been able to do it. Yet, this silly game is part of the way I have handled not smoking. I do find myself putting pencils and pens in between my teeth, too. I wonder why?

I have seen success with "make believe" porcelain cigarettes. The idea is to go around with this "cigarette" and pretend that you are still smoking. If it works, great. I even had one patient buy a pacifier and said it worked wonders. I think that probably would make most people quit sooner.

Each one of us has to find something to substitute for what we give up. If your teen finds something reasonably acceptable, go along with it. It's better than cancer.

Chapter 14

Marijuana

"How will I know if my teen is smoking pot?" is a question I hear frequently, followed by: "Can you just test him?"

All too often I receive calls such as this from a suspicious parent who wants to "sneak in" a urine test. The argument goes as follows:

"I don't know for sure but I am concerned that my daughter is doing drugs. Maybe pot. You're going to see her tomorrow for her camp exam. Do you think you can get a urine screen to test for this? She doesn't know I'm calling."

When I tell them that the only way I will do this is by confronting their daughter and letting her know that they are concerned, I may get the following:

"Well, I'm not sure she really is, but you can never tell with kids these days. Why can't we just do it, and if it is negative she doesn't need to know? What's wrong with that approach, doctor?"

A lot is wrong. Under most state laws the patient, even a minor, is protected in matters of drug use. That means that the teen and I can know the results of the drug screen, but not the parent. I would have to violate the law and my patient's trust in order to run a clandestine drug test.

Trust is the cornerstone for any good patient-doctor relationship. If I casually run a drug test on your son without his knowing, why would he discuss with me his concern about possibly having a sexually transmitted infection? If I run one on your daughter, without her knowing, I'll be the last person on her list of people to call if she thinks she's pregnant. Your teenager's doctor is there to help and support both of you, but this is best accomplished in the age-old way of creating an environment of mutual respect, trust, and understanding.

But you turned to this chapter to learn more about marijuana, likely because you're concerned that your teenager or his friends are using it. Before we get to the "testing" stage, there is a good deal that will be helpful to know.

First, a few statistics: The mean age of first-time pot use is approximately fourteen. That means that kids in the eighth and ninth grade are already at risk for trying pot. If you begin your vigilance in high school, you may be too late; statistically it is estimated that half of twelfth graders have already tried pot and about a quarter of the kids are actually using it on a regular basis.

A Few Definitions

Marijuana is not a single "drug." It actually is a composite of about sixty break-down products (metabolites) of cannabis, which are gathered from the flowering tops of the hemp plant. It is not a new drug that the flower children of the sixties discovered, but an ancient (well over five thousand years old) drug that has carried several names depending on the region of the world. The active ingredient is a compound called "delta-9-tetrahydrocannabinol," which is abbreviated as "THC" (derived from its chemical name). When THC reaches the blood, it immediately affects the brain and the central nervous system.

Hashish is the dried resin of the oily top of the plant. The term originated in the Middle East. Hashish usually contains a lot of psychoactive material. The same material is called charas in the Far East. If you remove the resin from the leaves you have *ganja*, a term that was made popular by the native Jamaican singer Bob Marley. Hash and ganja can be obtained in the United States, but the current marijuana sold in most cities contains so much THC that few need to get these today. During the 1960s, with a more diluted street pot, the need for the more powerful resins made them more desirable.

For the most part, marijuana is referred to as "pot," though you may also hear it referred to as grass, a joint, weed, herb, dope, cannabis, doob (or doobie), blunt, buds, bong, hookah, spliff, bowl, ganja, or reefer (not used too frequently, but made popular by the infamous movie *Reefer Madness*, which has become a cult classic). A "roach" refers to the last remaining puffs of a smoked joint, and the term itself refers to the clip ("roach clip") used to hold the joint so that you can get the remaining puffs from it without burning your fingers. If you hear discussion of "sens," they are talking about pot without seeds, which has about twice the amount of THC as does regular pot; "hash," contains about ten times the amount of THC as regular pot.

These are terms for your own knowledge. Don't use them with teens—they'll immediately sense you've been doing some research and know a lecture is coming.

Understanding the Chemistry of Pot

An understanding of the chemistry of pot is important to appreciate what happens once it enters your teen's body. If you put vinegar and olive oil into a glass, what happens? They don't mix, as any seasoned cook will tell you. Instead, there is a clearly defined level of vinegar and another of oil. We say they are "immiscible." Now let's put alcohol and pot into this glass. If we could see them dissolving, we would find the alcohol in the vinegar layer and the pot in the oil layer. Chemists speak of the alcohol as "water soluble" and the pot as "fat, or lipid soluble." This means that pot will dissolve in the "fat" or "lipid" layers of the body. Here's the problem: the brain is almost all lipid.

Pot is so soluble in lipid that it can stick to glass just the way a price sticker can gum up a glass. The brain normally has a protective barrier called the "blood-brain barrier" and this is not easily crossed. It is there as a shield against toxins easily entering the brain. However, the barrier is basically a cell membrane that is fat-soluble. To pot, this barrier is nothing more that a transparent sieve. It poses no obstacle to pot entering the brain, which it does rather quickly.

Because of the solubility of pot in the lipid portion of the body, it doesn't get cleared out right away. This explains why you may have heard that pot will stay in the body "for weeks." Actually, this is only part of the explanation; the rest depends on the amount that the person takes in, how often, and at what intervals.

Effects of Pot on the Body

■ The Brain
Probably the most important concern about pot is the effect that it has on the brain. No one can argue that the brain is in some way altered, since there are clearly changes in skills and thinking processes when you have THC in the body. We know that pot alters mood, energy level, and the ability to respond to stimuli. It alters time perception and can even lower body temperature.

We use our brains to think, to process information, to respond to stimuli, to remember, and to simply recognize reality, and since THC can invade the brain, there cannot be too much doubt that pot changes some of the brain chemistry. Since 1988, the scientific community has been aware that the brain even has receptors that can process cannabis. (Receptors are portions of the brain where a particular reaction occurs when a specific protein or hormone interacts with it.) If we look at all of the places in the brain that receptors for cannabinoids are located, it seems amazing that some people view pot as safe in all cases.

Brain Receptors That Process Cannabis

Brain Portion	Function	Abundant or Moderate Amounts of Receptors
Basal ganglia	Movement control	Abundant
Cerebellum	Movement coordination	Abundant
Hippocampus	Learning and Memory	Abundant
Cerebral cortex	Higher learning	Abundant
Nucleus accumbens	"Reward center"	Abundant
Hypothalamus	Temperature regulation; salt and water balance; reproductive function	Moderate
Amygdala	Emotional response; fear	Moderate
Spinal cord	Peripheral sensation	Moderate
Brain stem	Sleep and arousal	Moderate
Central gray matter	Analgesia	Moderate
Solitary tract nucleus	Visceral sensation; nausea and vomiting	Moderate

As you look at the center column, you can appreciate that marijuana can affect all of our body's functions. Some of the effects can be salutary. For example, we know the effects that pot has on patients who have chemotherapy: it can lessen nausea. Yet, if you look at the others, it becomes obvious that pot is not a harmless recreational drug.

■ The Heart

Marijuana can make the heart speed up and elevate blood pressure. In most cases this is not a major problem, but concerns about abnormal heart rates are appropriate. If there is a cardiac problem, or a blood pressure problem, the addition of marijuana may be of particular concern.

■ Lungs

A surprising comment I get from teens who smoke pot is that they cannot understand why they are coughing. Because they view pot as "natural," they don't consider that, like cigarettes, this type of burning leaf can also irritate the lungs and cause a cough. This reaction is particularly ironic since the way one smokes pot is by holding it in the lungs for as long as possible (the more time it is held, the more opportunity for it to irritate).

■ Endocrine System

By looking at the previous chart listing brain receptors, it is apparent that cannabis can interfere with the hypothalamus (the part of the brain that oversees the regulation and balance of bodily functions), and, hence, with the endocrine system. Poor nutrition tells the hypothalamus to slow down hormone production in the ovaries and testicles. The hypothalamus is so sensitive to our body changes that a shift in weight can alter our sexual hormones by deciding that the weight loss, or gain, would be injurious to a pregnancy. In other words, this portion of the brain makes "decisions" about the appropriateness of allowing us to procreate by monitoring what is going on in our body. The endocrine system produces our hormones. It is directly under the watchful eye of the hypothalamus since this portion of the brain decides to initiate puberty, halt it, turn on or off the thyroid hormones, and decide that a woman currently nursing should not immediately bear another child. Similarly, the presence of THC makes the hypothalamus think that something is not quite right, and in some cases, sperm count is lowered. (This is controversial and not verified yet. However, clinically, I have seen low testosterone levels in pot smokers.)

How Pot Is Used

The most common way of smoking is to make a rolled cigarette of the chopped up marijuana leaves. For ten dollars, a teen can get two or three joints. The paper used to roll the cigarette is fairly easy to get, although some states have outlawed "head shops," where the materials for pot smoking are obtained. Forget the image of some dubious store with darkness surrounding a mysterious character who asks for a password before he reaches into a deep drawer to complete the transaction. Think rather of a local candy store selling combs, magazines, gum, candy, and, oh yes, pot rolling paper. This homemade THC cigarette lacks a filter. Therefore, it rivals the old unfiltered cigarettes of my youth for tar content. Frankly most teens will, within a few days of the first day at a new school, be able to identify who will sell pot and where to get rolling papers.

Again, there is a mystical aura about pot that defies the logic of its simply being a burning leaf. It causes all of the problems of cigarettes: lung cancer, cough, irritability of the pulmonary tree, bad breath, stained teeth, and expense. Yet, most pot smokers believe that it's "not bad for you." It is estimated that each marijuana cigarette has more than four times the amount of tar as a standard cigarette. Not only is the tobacco not filtered, but the amount of time that the person holds the smoke against the bronchial tree is increased with pot. The bottom line for the pot smoker is that each joint is at least four times more likely to cause cancer than a comparable cigarette you buy at the store. The only good news is that a joint does not contain nicotine, which is addictive.

In the past few years it has become quite popular again to smoke a "bowl." This is nothing more than a pipe, and it is smoked the same way. The obvious advantage is that it doesn't require being rolled into a joint and is quickly available for a fast smoke. If you happen to find a pipe, usually a bit smaller than the one traditionally associated with college professors, be wary.

The pot community discovered that the heat of smoking THC pipes or cigarettes could be minimized if the smoke was "filtered" through water using a contraption much like what the caterpillar in *Alice's Adventures in Wonderland* uses. These "hookahs" (also called bongs or water pipes) do have the advantage of removing much of the tar from the smoke while it cools the inhaled pot as it travels through the water. Don't expect to find too many of these in your kid's room. They are hard to hide and expensive. Find one and beware. There is no earthly reason for owning one except for the intended purpose of smoking pot through it. I have not heard of anyone using it to further filter a Marlboro or a Parliament. Please don't accept the excuse that your teen is "starting a collection of these neat things."

The Mind-Altering Aspects of Pot

The evidence is strong that pot causes problems with thinking, with memory, and with judgment. Also remember that the pot currently available is estimated to be as much as ten times more potent than the pot in the 1960s. We really don't know what this will do to the current generation. Will they be "okay" in their later years? In the meantime, we do know that it has the following effects:

Reaction Time

One of the experiments with THC use involves the ability of the individual to perform a task efficiently. With pot, reaction time is slowed. Unfortunately, a difficult aspect of dealing with people who use pot is that they really believe that they did a task better. The fact that reaction time is delayed has a significant impact on such daily tasks as driving or just staying focused in school. The hard part is convincing smokers that this is happening; many would argue that they actually can drive better and that school is easier while on pot.

Short-Term Memory

One of the most consistent effects of marijuana is the disruption of short-term memory. Memory is divided into long-term and short-term memory. If you forget your birthday, you have a long-term memory deficit. If you forget where your keys are, your short-term memory is impaired. Doing homework after pot smoking is, therefore, asking for trouble. A teen may read about the battle of Little Big Horn and forget all about it before the next day.

Hunger

Hunger also often accompanies the use of marijuana. The sensation of being full comes partly from the stomach and mostly from the brain. THC alters this sense of being full. Marijuana smokers get "the munchies," a desire to eat after they smoke. Several of my patients lost weight by simply quitting pot!

Absorption of THC

Don't bother reading up on how much pot there is in a "joint" and trying to calculate how much will end up in your child's body. No two rolled cigarettes will contain the same amount of pot. However, the level of THC in most "commercial" grade pot is estimated to be ten times as strong as those of forty years ago. A single cigarette with a lot of pot, reaching the brain for full effect within ten to thirty minutes, can have quite an impact. The result will be felt for two to three hours.

On the other hand, pot that is eaten will take longer to have an effect and will reach peak effect in two or three hours, and will last for three to five hours. This may explain the lack of popularity of ingesting pot.

Jennifer is a fifteen-year-old *sophomore who attends a local private school. She gets "acceptable" grades and is on the state all-star soccer team. She had a boyfriend this summer but described the relationship as "nothing serious." Her medical history is not particularly significant although she is worried about her weight. The family is intact and there are no known problems.*

While cleaning up her daughter's room one day, Jennifer's mother found an unmarked envelope with what appeared to be oregano, although it did not smell quite like it. She was concerned and she and her husband called me. When I suggested that this was probably pot, since few kids collect oregano, I was countered with a dubious "Oh no, doctor! Not Jennifer." Nevertheless, I was able to convince them to confront their daughter with the incriminating envelope that evening. The next day I was told that Jennifer was incredibly upset that her mother had "searched" her room and told Mom that she had permanently damaged the relationship between them. As to the envelope, it belonged to a "friend" whom her mother did not know and whom Jennifer wouldn't tell on. Yes, it was pot, but she was only holding it because this friend's mother would search her room. Jennifer pouted and was indignant. The parents then left her alone in her room. The parents were relieved that Jennifer was not "doing" pot, and they did not want to further damage their relationship by requesting a drug screen.

When parents find pot, a teen's first line of defense is usually indignation about the intrusion into his privacy. He sums up all of his legal rights as a citizen and portrays himself as a victim of oppressive and intrusive parents. If you find pot, get ready for this reaction and then prepare to parent. Do not accept the argument that any pot you find in your teen's room is "not his." In the history of teen-dom, not one teen ever held pot that actually belonged to him. Really! Yet, when you happen to be fumbling through your teen's pockets (ahem!) before sending the pants to the cleaners, and you find a glassine envelope filled with pot, you need to accept something you can live with. The idea that it belongs to a friend becomes naively reassuring. "Thank God, it's not his! He is such a good friend."

The reality is painful. That pot, in those pants, in *your* hands, belongs to *your* teen. You need to speak to *your* spouse and have an immediate conference about *your* problem. This is not the time to start blaming your teen's friends. This is the time to confront your teen and make an appointment with his physician.

What happens then? Clearly the first step is to decide about a drug screen. You can safely assume he has "tried" pot but you may be unsure about two critical facts. How much is he smoking, and has he tried any other drugs? Both need to be answered with drug testing and with a professional who can help you sort out the objective facts.

I recommend that parents "go a bit overboard" by some standards and insist on the drug screening. In my experience, this shows teens that their parents are not naive and will not believe that "he only tried it once" and "will never do it again." If you find pot in your teen's room, this crosses the "tried it once" line. Why, if you tried it and intend never to use it again, do you still own it? I have yet to encounter an adolescent who "tried it" and decided to keep some as a souvenir. It is his pot, purchased with his money (or yours), and it is fully intended for further smoking. Ignore this and you are ignoring a present and future problem.

Drug Testing

THC is eliminated in the urine and in the stool. Urinalysis is the choice method of testing; hair and nail clipping tests are available but costly. There are home kits that give instant results and others that allow you to collect a specimen and send it to a commercial lab. What you cannot do is walk into a reputable lab and ask for a drug screen; you must have a doctor order that test, either in writing or verbally.

Blood can be used for drug screening as is evidenced when a patient arrives at a hospital comatose. However, the tests are more expensive and doing the blood test is not always easy on a teenager. In fact, even the urine test may not be easy. Collecting a urine specimen from an uncooperative teenager is not as simple as it sounds. I have had patients attempt to circumvent the process by bringing me someone else's urine!

One patient, who must have thought *me incredibly gullible, gave me a specimen on a cold January evening. She went into the bathroom and emerged a few minutes later with a vial of urine. "Here's your urine!" she snarled as she extended her hand. The problem with the ruse was that she neglected to warm the sample. It had traveled all afternoon in her backpack and it was as cold as the cold winter's day.*

"Either you're dead, or this urine belongs to someone else. It's too cold to have been freshly minted," I countered. We both smiled and I was most impressed with her final comment, "Oh, doc! Do you have any idea of how

many kids I had to talk to before I got a really clean specimen? Okay, you win." The new warm specimen proved to be filled with THC.

Parents may want to bring in a urine specimen collected at home. To be certain the urine actually belongs to your teenager, the same gender parent

What Can You Test For?

A standard "drug of abuse" panel can be obtained on a fresh urine specimen. Usually the following are screened if more than THC is suspected:

Amphetamines
Barbiturates
Benzodiazapines, including drugs like Valium
Cocaine
Marijuana (depending on the cutoff level) Each laboratory clearly prints out the drugs that a particular panel will screen and the level of "cut off" for each of the drugs. (This is the lowest amount that can be detected with the screening.) The lower the screening level the more likely you are to pick up any pot.
Methadone
Methaqualone (Quaaludes)
Opiates
Phencyclidine (PCP)
Propoxyphene (Darvon)

One can change the number of drugs in the panel to suit the situation. Each laboratory clearly prints out the drugs that a particular panel will screen for and the level of "cut off" for the THC. In some cases, such as for legal issues, you might want to order a "chain of custody" drug test. (If a court orders a test, or if there is a lawyer arguing with a school, these are legal issues and a chain of custody should be done.) In this case, every person involved in the collection, handling, and testing has to sign a document so that any potential tampering can be traced. In an everyday situation to assess the teenager's drug use, a chain of custody is not needed. However, if there is a legal concern (an arrest for driving under the influence of drugs, for example) then ask for, and insist on, the strict adherence of the policy of collection.

should witness the actual collection of the specimen (as embarrassing as it seems). This also will protect against any altering of the specimen that your teen might do. If you read one of the current magazines dedicated to the use of pot, you will discover kits designed to camouflage THC in the urine. The companies just about guarantee results. There are many sites on the Internet dedicated to selling the same kits. One enterprising product is urine, clean and free of all drugs. It struck me as an easy way of making a living. All you need to buy any of these products is a credit card and a computer.

Your teen may offer up this excuse: "I was with a bunch of kids doing pot. That must be why I tested positive." Sounds good on the surface, but let's examine this clever ploy. To begin with, the smoke exhaled by a pot smoker does not contain much, if any, pot since at least 50 percent has been absorbed by the smoker. Therefore, the only pot available for "passive" smoking is the one coming from the cigarette or bowl. Your clever teen would have had to stand directly in front of the cigarette and nearly covered his head with a towel to make sure that the cloud of smoke reached his nostrils. You need to try hard to get enough THC this way.

One notable exception of "passive smoking" is in order and that is the smoke at concerts. If your teen argues that he is only guilty of passive smoke because of going to a rock concert he had to be in a place where there was pot and a lot of it! And this excuse should be accepted on a limited basis. If there are too many excuses about "contact highs," then curtail his attendance at concerts for a time until you are assured that that is the *only* way he is getting high. Keep in mind that a contact high can never explain elevated urine levels of pot.

"How Can I Know What My Teen Is Doing?"

So how will you ever know whether or not your teenager should be tested for pot? By watching. Noting behavior, changes in behavior, school performance—all the normal benchmarks parents should be observing all the time to be certain their child is okay. And this *is* your responsibility—no teen is going to request her own drug test, and unless the situation is severe, a doctor may not pick up the signals. If you and your spouse determine that there is reason for concern, make an appointment to meet with the doctor in person. This type of discussion isn't easily done by phone.

In addition to the overzealous parents who want to test "just in case," I find there are those who are timid about asking that a drug test be run, fearing they will "upset" their son or daughter. My response is straightforward: If you believe that drugs are a possibility, then there should be sufficient incidents concerning behavior, school, friends, or attitude that are making you worried. If these are present, then you shouldn't hesitate to ask for a drug screen.

Above all, make sure that both parents are in agreement about the test and will follow up on the results. This requires a united front of both parents. Without this, it will only cause marital problems regardless of the result. If the test is negative, the spouse who hesitated may blame the other for ruining the relationship with the teenager. If positive, the spouse who wanted the test may blame the other for being so unaware. This is the time to have both parents compare notes and concerns and together decide on the appropriate action to take.

If parents are separated or divorced, they still must come together and deal with the issue of drugs and their teen. If the teen senses that one parent will oppose the parent who wants the screen, he will simply play one off against the other. The more acrimonious the reasons for the separation, the easier the manipulation is for the teen. Stepparents have a particularly difficult role in this scenario. They may be right in their assessment of the problem, but in many cases they cannot make demands about how to handle it. The rightful role of policing this problem lies with the parents. A stepparent who suggests that a stepchild is doing drugs, even if he is correct, risks escalating an already difficult family situation into a major power struggle. Stepparents need to support their spouse in their issues with the teen, not interfere or assume a parental role. Dealing with a drug-using teen is difficult enough, so parents must put aside their personal problems and agree on a common plan.

If the parents request it, and the patient agrees to the test, I make the teen fully aware that the results are going to be given to his parents. That way it is all aboveboard, and we can do something if the test is positive. I also tell the patient that the parents will interpret a refusal as proof that the test would be positive.

If you do a urine test on a teenager, have a game plan. A single test is insufficient. Do not agree on "just one test" but rather on as many, and as often, as it takes to make sure she is clean. Also, be sure you understand that a positive test requires you to do something about it. It makes no sense to screen "just to know." You may already know she is using drugs. A positive test only confirms that there is a problem Your teen needs someone to monitor her drug use, and you need to contact your physician for guidance.

It is also important to do the correct test. Ask for the quantitative test that measures the amount in the urine regardless of the level. It can measure down to a level of 25 mg/ml. The ideal number is "0," as in "zero amount in the urine."

If the number is above the two hundred mark, it's a problem no matter how you interpret it. I just tested two teens, both in their first year of college, and their levels were in the 400s. Each admitted to daily use, several joints per day. Each tried to explain the high numbers with the reminder that they had smoked heavily the night before. Both were angry that they were "caught," and both need to be in some drug treatment program rather than college.

Whatever the number, use it as a baseline test. Any further tests should be less than this baseline, since the pot level has to diminish if the person is not using. Ignore pleas that he "was around someone who smoked pot," or that she went to a "concert where there was a lot of pot around." One of the points of any game plan should include avoiding situations where pot is going to be present. That may have to include terminating relationships with kids who are part of the "pot group." Be sure you understand that this is hard for your teen; also be sure not to "blame" the group for the problem. Their role in your son or daughter's problem is in "allowing and encouraging" pot by bringing it into the group; they do not force its use.

If the test is positive, your family game plan for helping your teen should include some sort of counseling, both individual and group. Many communities have facilities where the teenager can go after school and participate in group therapy and drug-free activities. Drug screening is also part of that process, as is family therapy. Alternatively, a private therapist can help sort out personal issues.

A Family Plan for Dealing with Drug Use

A good family game plan for dealing with the problem will include:

1. Drug testing on a random and frequent basis.
2. Attendance at some individual and group therapy. This may involve after-school programs.
3. Family therapy if necessary.
4. Educational testing if there is an issue of a "learning disability."
5. Avoidance of "pot situations." Places such as concerts or after-school haunts like city parks are often temptations to smoke.
6. Repercussions for failure to quit: an inpatient facility. This is critical for teenagers to understand. Often they do not believe that you will take them out of school.

Long-Term Use of THC

In some homes, parents will turn a deaf ear to their teen's pot use because "It's only pot." They are pleased that "harder" drugs are not being used, and overall they feel that they have a "good kid." I agree with the last part of their analysis, but if pot has become a part of their teen's life something needs to be done. If they don't address the problem and feel that the B's and C's in school are sufficient, larger problems are looming. The excuses for being late for school and the ignored responsibilities will catch up with them. College is rarely the time to expect a miracle.

After smoking pot for a while, the person develops a need for more pot in order to get the same effects. This phenomenon is called tolerance, and it happens with many other drugs. As tolerance develops, the high is harder to reach unless greater quantities of pot are smoked.

This cycle can spiral into a syndrome that has been called the "amotivational syndrome." The person who has reached this stage is no longer interested in school, in social functions, in the opposite gender; she is perfectly content with the company of her pot. She has no goals and just wants to smoke. The problem is to ascertain that the THC itself is the problem. There well may be issues of depression, of learning disabilities, of problems at home that are underlying the teen's plight. THC then becomes a therapeutic drug for the patient. Once teens find themselves in this state, it is nearly impossible to treat them as outpatients. In most cases you have no choice but to have the teen placed in a "therapeutic community." (How to get her there is a separate problem. See Chapter 11 for more information about getting your teen into treatment.)

Pot Is Illegal, but That's a Small Deterrent

Pot is illegal. Although this would sound like a powerful deterrent, it tends to have little impact on the teenager. In fact, several patients in my practice have been arrested for "possession," and they actually spent a night in jail. These were kids who attended good schools and who, to the outside world, look like "nice kids"; we are not talking about the "typical" image of the druggie teen. Little happened to them and they were released to parents. In every case, this experience has only enhanced the mystique of these kids among many of their peers.

Telling kids that it is illegal to buy, to sell, or to possess is fine, but pressing the point is often futile. If coaches at school actually threw kids off teams if they found them using drugs, it would be great. However, many parents object to their kids being tested by a high school teacher, and I know of no school that has a drug-testing policy as part of its sports program. Don't even attempt the argument that colleges won't accept them with a "jail" record. Many teens are savvy enough to know that a single arrest as a juvenile is probably going to be erased after some community service. It seems cynical, but regretfully, it is only a realistic view.

Therapeutic Use of Marijuana

It should be briefly mentioned that there is a growing faction that sees marijuana as a useful tool in the medical care of such situations as controlling the nausea associated with chemotherapy and as a hunger stimulus for cancer patients and those with AIDS. It has also been used successfully with patients who have glaucoma.

I mention these facts both as a point of interest and thoroughness, but also to ward off the argument you might hear from teens that "Pot can be used as medicine." Yes, and quite well. Argue back that you are aware of this fact, but that the use is very narrow and only for cancer and AIDS patients. Tell them that it is prescribed to alleviate nausea and only by special permission from the government. Most physicians in practice cannot write a prescription for THC. This emphasizes the special and limited use. One doesn't use THC routinely.

Chapter 15

Hallucinogens and Stimulants

If your teen is involved with any of the hallucinogenic drugs, do not view it as merely experimenting or think that "it will go away." This is a troubled teen whose self-destructive behavior has to be tackled as soon as it is discovered. Not one of the hallucinogens, not one of the "speed" drugs, and not one of the "narcotics" can be considered safe. Death literally can be a result of this type of drug use.

While you would think that the "tripping" teen would be easy to spot, that isn't always the case. Seventeen-year-old David was a patient of mine for a time. He was a brilliant student, but family problems meant that in addition to his doctor, he was also being seen by a therapist. I saw him relatively frequently because he often complained of "feeling tired." I could find no medical reason for these feelings. All blood tests and routine urinalyses fell within normal limits.

When a new family crisis developed, his exhaustion was such that the parents asked me to see him again. I opened up the topic of drugs, and he seemed particularly interested in my comments that certain drugs could give him a feeling of being "down"; in particular he seemed interested in the effects of Ecstasy. Yet he denied any drug use and denied the need for any drug screening.

Finally on one occasion he came in fully panicked that he had "screwed up his brain." He was seeing flashing lights and these were coming on in intervals that made him think he was going crazy. When I asked him why he felt particularly responsible, he said that someone had probably spiked his drink one night and he feared that there could have been some acid in it. He wanted to know more about this, but he denied that he had actively participated in LSD use. Because of the unclear nature of his history, I ended up doing a full neurological evaluation for a possible seizure disorder, or even a possible brain tumor. Such was his concern that he agreed to all of these tests.

During the evaluation for these possible diagnoses, he sheepishly admitted that he had "tried" acid—but only a "few times." I suppose the notion of a brain tumor sparked a need for full disclosure. I told him that what he was describing might well be attributed to the effects of the drug. Though I could assure him that the symptoms would get better, I could not assure him they would disappear soon. He felt somewhat relieved; even more so when the brain scans and other tests came back normal. Recently, he called because he had had a flashback after a few months of not using acid. My first question was, had he used pot? Another sheepish "yes" followed, and David swore a new oath not to use any drugs.

He now has a new therapist who is working with him to deal with his "family issues" and to monitor his drug use. His LSD use was the main concern, but his slipping back into pot raises the notion that he "needs" some sort of drug. The diagnosis of "depression" is loud and clear, as is David's need for self-medication. The therapist has recommended an antidepressant to help David with his feelings and to help avoid the drug use. He undergoes urine tests on a random basis, and he is doing much better.

About Hallucinogens

After alcohol, cigarettes, and pot, your teen is most likely to experiment with one of the hallucinogens. The hallucinogens take the user on a mental journey; they see things, they experience sensations, and they can hear sounds that are not real but that seem so. Some of the hallucinogens come from plants and, frequently, have been used by native tribes as part of their spiritual rituals. Others are the result of creative chemistry. In this chapter we will cover the hallucinogens listed on the following page and the stimulants listed on p. 308. The order represents the level of hallucinogenic properties, from highest to lowest. It is not a ranking order of use among kids. Note that stimulants are not considered true hallucinogens. However, the rush they produce may seem hallucinogenic, and an overdose may produce hallucinations.

Hallucinogens

■ LSD
■ Phencyclidinine (PCP, or "angel dust")

■ Mescaline (peyote)
■ Psilocybin (mushrooms)

Hallucinogens

LSD (Lysergic Acid Diethylamide)

In the late seventeenth century, the witches of Salem were burned at the stake because of their visions. With no knowledge of chemistry there could be no other explanation for their behavior than demonic possession—a fair enough conclusion for its day. Today it has been postulated that a particular fungus grows periodically on the rye crops and the wild grasses in that part of New England. The fungus is ergot, and it is the basic ingredient of LSD. The witches of Salem were probably "tripping."

In 1938 a chemist, Dr. Albert Hofmann, working for the Sandoz pharmaceutical company, synthesized LSD from ergot. Some of the ergot derivative had been used to treat migraine (and still is) and to aid in uterine contractions. Nothing was done with the new drug, called LSD-25, as it didn't seem to have much medicinal value; in 1943 Hofmann synthesized it again. While working with the drug one day he began to feel ill and had to leave work. By the time he got home he was feeling restless, seeing flashing lights, and feeling "drunk." He saw an uninterrupted stream of colors and kaleidoscopic effects. He postulated that some of the LSD-25 must have accidentally entered his system.

His own account of his feelings and his fears illustrate a "bad" trip. The familiar furniture and walls of his home took on "grotesque" and "threatening" forms, and he felt that the entire room was moving. A neighbor, trying to soothe his anxiety, brought him some milk, and he imagined that she was trying to poison him. The caring neighbor became a "malevolent" witch wearing a colored mask. As for the inner effects, it is worth reading Dr. Hofmann's own words on the effects of LSD:

> *Even worse than these demonic transformations of the outer world, were the alterations that I perceived in myself, in my inner being. Every exertion of*

my will, every attempt to put an end to the disintegration of the outer world and the dissolution of my ego, seemed to be wasted effort. A demon had invaded me, had taken possession of my body, mind, and soul. I jumped and screamed, trying to free myself from him, but sank down again and lay helpless on the sofa. The substance, with which I had wanted to experiment, had vanquished me. It was the demon that scornfully triumphed over my will. I was seized with the dreadful fear of going insane.

Patients have told me about their trips, both good and bad ones. No one has spoken as eloquently, or as passionately, as the father of LSD.

Acid was used most frequently in the 1960s by hippies and others, and the heavy use of LSD has gone the way of the flower children. Regretfully, it is not completely gone from the teenage drug world. In 1993, the Drug Enforcement Agency (DEA) reported that 13.2 million Americans over the age of twelve admitted using acid at least once. This is in contrast with the 1985 number of 8.1 million. The Drug Abuse Warning Network data shows that the likely acid abuser will be a white male in his late teens or early twenties. This profile has not changed since the 1960s. A study of high school seniors in Indiana showed that 14 percent of the graduating class reported using acid at least once during 1997 and 1998.

I still see patients who "drop acid." Most of these have passed through cigarettes, alcohol, and perhaps pot on their way to this trip. They admit that the acid experience was weird and frightening. They don't always admit that they will stop. Although it would appear that something as scary as a "bad trip" would be sufficient reason not to trip again, it isn't. The acid user will claim

Getting Help

The teen with a drug problem needs help, and dealing with this will require a lot of time and effort by the family. He or she should be seeing a skilled therapist on an inpatient or outpatient basis. See Chapter 11 for more information on finding appropriate resources in your community. With any hallucinogen, a preexisting psychosis, not yet manifest, may be triggered by the experience—all the more reason why parents need outside help.

that the occasional bad experience isn't sufficient to offset the wonderful colors, the sensations, and the feelings that accompany an acid trip. The fact that there may be permanent damage or that anything bad will happen is not part of the rationale that precludes the trip.

Telling the acid user of others who have tried to fly or done dangerous stunts while tripping only lands on ears that do not want to hear the truth. It becomes part of a cult-like experience, and it is discussed with a fondness that belies the logic of it being dangerous. The acid user does not believe that she is in danger—she will argue that after each trip she feels fine. Those with flashbacks tend to be a little more cautious, but even these are not enough to stop them.

■ What LSD Does to the Body

LSD is consumed orally (it's usually administered as a microdot on a piece of paper), and it is absorbed quickly and easily. There are no needles; no snorting, no real paraphernalia is needed. The main effects are directly on the brain and these continue even after the drug is no longer measured in the body, meaning that LSD must trigger some biochemical reactions in the brain that are independent of the presence of the drug. Since all our thoughts and movements are biochemically mediated, the flashback sometimes generated by LSD has to be an altered chemical reaction in the brain. The current hypothesis is that there has been some change in the stimuli of brain chemistry that is "recalled" during the flashback. That alone should frighten the rational thinking person; it doesn't.

LSD is measured in micrograms; by contrast the dosages of other drugs are measured in milligrams (a thousand times larger). The estimates are that a human needs only 25 micrograms (0.025 milligrams—Hofmann's dose) to experience a "trip." The current estimates by the DEA are that the street acid is about 20 to 80 micrograms per dose.

Without much knowledge of the chemistry of the brain, it stands to reason that the effects on the brain must be significant. You don't have a temporary state of psychosis in which reality is distorted without realizing that the connections of brain neurons are altered. What always strikes me as absurd is the gamble taken by LSD users that their brains will be taken to "la la land" and will later be returned to their original station. Think about it! Let's do acid and take our brains on a trip. Let's also hope we come back to the same place from where we started.

The mechanisms of action of LSD are not clear. It is known that the serotonin and dopamine systems (the main neurotransmitters in the brain) are stimulated, which accounts for the psychic changes. What is clear is that not all experiences are pleasant. During the trip itself the patient exhibits dilated pupils, increased body temperature, elevated blood sugar, palpitations, sweating, blurred vision, slurred speech, and in some cases, a sense of panic. Some will argue that their trips are usually pleasant, but it all depends on the user's state of mind. A user's state of mind also affects the quality of the trip. The person surrounded by friends is more likely to have more pleasant hallucinations than the person who is feeling upset and troubled. In many cases, one person stays clean so as to guide the trip and keep the person safe. Dangerous behavior is quite possible during the trip, since, after all, reality is suspended. The user may not register distances and heights accurately, nor be able to respond appropriately to normal dangers like lit candles or swimming pools. Someone has to be there to protect the user from himself. The experience is so intense that the individual will rarely go back for "seconds" right away.

Some users will experience "flashbacks" for weeks or months; some for years. The argument is that there may have been some permanent damage to the visual centers of the brain; this is now called Hallucinogen Persisting Perceptual Disorder, or HPPD. These "mini" trips come on without warning, and the patient is usually alarmed by these intrusions. Other drugs may spur these flashbacks and, with teenagers, they create a great deal of anxiety.

Because LSD is metabolized in the liver and passed through the urine within twenty-four hours, urine drug screening is difficult. See Chapter 11 for more information about getting help.

■ What to Do for the Teen Who Is Tripping

Take him to the emergency room where he can be monitored. There is not much that can be done medically, but the hospital will provide a safe environment until enough of the acid is gone from his system. You want to avoid stress and excessive sensory stimulation when someone is already hallucinating.

Mescaline

Just as an innocent ergot fungus can cause hallucinations so, too, can the dried top portion of a small, spineless cactus called *Lophophora williamsii,* which grows wild in Mexico and the American Southwest. The natives of the New World would take the top of this cactus, dry it into a brownish "button," and chew it. As the chemical entered their system, they experienced some of the same effects as the user of LSD. Native Americans called these mystical cactii "peyotl" centuries before the Spanish Conquistadors translated it into "peyote."

The peyote plant yields many psychoactive drugs, and mescaline is felt to be the most potent of these. It has also been chemically synthesized since 1918. To take the drug, the user takes several "buttons" (the natural plant) and chews them. Though the mescaline contained in these plants is expensive and hard to get, it is the preferred hallucinogen for the teens whom I have seen. Many of these kids are actually getting a variant of weak LSD or PCP, although they believe that their experience was actually triggered by mescaline.

Besides the mind alteration, the heart rate is accelerated, the temperature of the body increases, as well as blood pressure, and the eyes dilate. Vomiting often follows the chewing. The full effects will be felt in a few hours and will last for as long as twelve. The patient becomes disoriented and often will feel itchy. Because it does not give as powerful an effect as LSD, some people who want to hallucinate prefer mescaline because it is "more manageable." The sense of panic that often accompanies LSD is not present. That is not to say that a bad trip isn't possible.

■ What If My Teenager Takes Mescaline?

As with the acid trip, you need to stay with her for the time that the hallucinations take place. Fortunately mescaline is about 4,000 times less powerful than LSD, so you can anticipate that your teen should have a "safer" trip. Even at that dilution mescaline can still give hallucinogenic experiences. If the patient becomes agitated, then an ER visit is in order and appropriate tranquilizers may be used. After you calm down and deal with the fact that your child took mescaline, a call to a therapist is in order (see Chapter 11).

Phencyclidine ("Angel Dust," or PCP)

This hallucinogen has gone by the street name of "angel dust" for years. Despite the fact that it was originally synthesized for use as a tranquilizer in the 1950s and used in animals, the street culture of the 1960s discovered it as a hallucinogen. Telling them that it could bring down a horse and that even the veterinarians stopped using it did little to dissuade them.

Available as a pure, white crystalline powder or as a tablet, PCP is ingested, snorted, smoked (not uncommonly dusted on a marijuana cigarette), or even injected—further running the risk of infection with bacteria, HIV, or hepatitis B virus. As with other hallucinogens it is often impossible to be sure that the person has actually taken PCP, since a mild amount of the cheaper LSD sometimes is substituted for it.

The patient will experience an increase in heart rate and blood pressure, flushing, dizziness, and sweating. Actually most of the effects of PCP are quite unpleasant and few users go back for more. As with acid, there is a potential for flashbacks that can occur for weeks to months after the event. The safety issue with PCP is critical. Because of poor judgment, illogical thinking, and potential violent behavior, the abuser puts himself and others at risk. Even the calm, normally nonviolent person can demonstrate behavior that is threatening. It is no accident that this drug is considered dangerous even among users.

Mushrooms (Psilocybin)

This naturally occurring hallucinogen is found in some mushrooms. Use of it is not as common because it is not readily available. You will hear of patients doing "mushrooms" or "shrooms" when actually they may have done a "watered down" version of LSD.

After ingestion, the patient will experience hallucinations as quickly as within ten minutes, and they can last as long as twelve hours. The patient will seem giddy and restless, as if "drunk"; he may also experience nausea, muscle aches, and abdominal pain. When the experience is over, typically patients fall into a deep sleep and may manifest deep depression.

Although the effects on the brain are much less than the effects of mescaline or LSD, the patient doing psilocybin may injure himself because of disorientation. Fatalities have been recorded as a result of head trauma or car accidents.

▪ The Teen Who Has Taken "Mushrooms"

Try to find out exactly what he took. Most of the mushrooms on the illegal market are not psilocybin, but some other adulterant. This complicates the manifestations and the treatment. If there is evidence that the ingestion was recent, it will probably be necessary to pump the stomach to remove any remaining drugs, so go to an emergency room. In addition, supportive care by medical personnel is necessary until the drug is out of the system.

Stimulants

■ Amphetamines   ■ MDMA (Ecstasy)
■ Methamphetamine (speed)   ■ Cocaine

Stimulants

Amphetamines

Although amphetamines are not considered "hallucinogens," they do produce mind-altering experiences. Most users will take an amphetamine for the "rush" or exhilaration that the drug produces. The mind races with flashing thoughts and the heart pounds as the amphetamine increases the heart rate. The "high" that is produced with the right amount of amphetamine can be so pleasurable that the user will want to use more. As the street name "speed" implies, the entire body feels like it is moving faster, and indeed it is. With enough amphetamine the euphoric state will disappear and one can enter a full-blown psychosis, complete with paranoid feelings and delusions, including hallucinations.

Today amphetamines are not as commonly abused as they were in the 1960s, although the current prescription use of amphetamines and derivatives for Attention Deficit Disorder has triggered a resurgence of abuse, such as the snorting of methylphenidate (Ritalin) and the abuse of other similar stimulant medications. Interestingly, it is usually not the ADD patient who is abusing, though he may be hoarding and selling. (If your teen has been diagnosed with ADD and is on "stimulant" medication, check the supply periodically, and consider if his behavior indicates whether or not he is taking his medication.) With the recent resurgence of the diagnosis of ADD these prescription pills are present in all schools, and they have often supplanted the amphetamines of the black market. Today's amphetamine may come via a friend's prescription pills.

A new version of amphetamine is "methamphetamine," which has the capability of being smoked. It is sold on the street as "crystal meth" or sometimes referred to as "ice." The effect of this drug is to release more dopamine on the central nervous system than amphetamine. Over time, however, it is toxic to the nerves, as the dopamine-containing cells are overstimulated.

Although "ice" is particularly strong and available, it is not a commonly used drug. Yet, according to the National Household Survey on Drug Abuse (NHSDA), nearly five million people age twelve or older had tried methamphetamine at least once in their lifetime. Another study (Monitoring the Future Study, or MFS) estimated that in 1997 4.4 percent of high school seniors had used crystal methamphetamine at least once in their lifetime. One has to be fairly involved in the drug scene to engage in crystal meth use.

Both high school and college students will abuse amphetamines to pull "all nighters." A friend's supply of Ritalin or Adderall (a new prescription stimulant for ADD) is usually available and little is thought of taking this prescription medication by mouth. After all, they logically argue, it's not an illegal drug, and it's prescribed to help my friend study—why can't it help me? Clearly the idea is that the patient with ADD needs this medication to allow concentration; it is not to be used for the student who simply wants to make his studying easier. When Adderall or Ritalin are not available, students often will take a lot of caffeine and will manifest symptoms similar to amphetamine use. The over-the-counter product "No Doz" is actually a caffeine product that stimulates in a similar fashion to Ritalin but not as powerfully. Each tablet contains 200 milligrams of caffeine. For comparison, a strong cup of coffee contains about the same amount, while a can of cola has about 75 to 110 milligrams. No one can compare caffeine with amphetamines, but both are going to produce increased heart rate, insomnia, diminished appetite, and headaches.

■ Effects of Amphetamine Use

All amphetamines act as adrenaline. People who take any of the amphetamines will experience a sense of euphoria. Rarely, they may actually get to the point of hallucinations. They feel bold and daring. Nothing daunts them during the time that the adrenaline rush is happening. After the "speed jag" the user crashes and wants to sleep. If taken in sufficient quantity, amphetamines will cause an increase in heart rate and respiratory rate, an elevation in blood pressure and body temperature, the pupils will dilate, and the bladder muscles will relax (potentially to the point of losing bladder control). If stimulated enough, the person can experience diarrhea and lose bowel control. Hunger is suppressed and insomnia develops. Taken to the extreme, he can experience a psychotic episode.

One of my patients, having taken a fair amount of speed, was driving too fast on a motorcycle, and the police started to chase him. He suddenly saw it as a game and was thoroughly enjoying the experience. When he saw a patrol car blocking his path, he thought, as in the movies, he would simply jump over it. Fortunately, the cycle got caught in the side of the patrol car, and my patient went flying, landing safely (breaking an arm) on a lawn. When I spoke to him in the hospital he remembered that he sincerely thought he could make his bike vault over the car.

▪ The Teen on Speed

All of the user's bodily functions and behavior appear to be on "fast forward." Aside from the physical symptoms, she may be exhibiting poor judgment, and someone needs to stay with her. In most cases, all that is required is for the drug to work through the body, at which point the teen will long for sleep. Sometimes the increased activity is so great that tranquilizers are in order, but that is a judgment to be made in the emergency room.

Withdrawal from both amphetamines and caffeine includes a feeling of depression. The patient will complain of "crashing" or feeling depressed. His claim then is that he needs to take caffeine or amphetamine to feel better, thus starting the cycle all over. Amphetamine withdrawal is difficult. The depression that sets in after the drug wears off often requires treatment with antidepressants, which should be prescribed by a psycho-pharmacologist.

MDMA, or Ecstasy (methylene-dioxymethamphetamine)

There is no question that the current drug of choice among the teenage and college population is Ecstasy (sometimes written as "X" or "XTC"), a cross between mescaline and amphetamine in its effect. Kids often argue that it is a "safe stimulant," partly because it originated with therapists using it in their practices. Ecstasy has not yet gotten the true reputation that it deserves—it is dangerous. Studies have linked the use of Ecstasy with problems of attention and memory. When compared to non-Ecstasy users on performance tests, there was a clear decline in memory skills and in tasks measuring alertness. Certainly at very high doses it can kill just as amphetamines can. The question, currently being studied, is whether repeated doses, even at low levels, can cause the same brain damage. There is strong evidence from animal experiments that there is damage to the brain but, as yet, there is no specific data on what dose is toxic to the human brain.

Similar to the history of acid, use of this drug started in California with doctors using it in psychotherapy. Patients taking the drug were supposed to gain insight and clarity of thinking in their sessions. As it traveled east in the early 1980s, it became more prevalent as a street level drug, and soon it became the "party" drug of choice. Normally a pill will contain about 100 mg of

MDMA (this acronym explains another of its street names, "ADAM."). At a 100 mg dose, patients will experience the "good" effects (the euphoria). At doses of 200 mg, patients can experience an acid-like trip. Ecstasy is almost always taken by mouth in the form of a pill that may carry a label such as Nike or Calvin Klein or some other corporate brand. Of concern is that the Ecstasy sold, also called "E" or "X", may not be MDMA but rather a mixture of other chemicals. Amphetamine, caffeine, PCP, or even ketamine (more in Chapter 16) mimic the effects of Ecstasy and may be substituted easily. It's bad enough to use an illegal drug; one should at least know what one is taking.

Users of Ecstasy seek the euphoria that begins about a half hour after ingestion. Since the drug acts on the serotonin system, users will feel a tremendous sense of well-being for about two hours. Tactile sensation is heightened and, as a tremendous advantage over other drugs, users are fairly alert and aware of their surroundings. After coming down, they then feel tired and this may last for a few days. I have had many patients whose exhaustion on Monday or Tuesday can be traced to Ecstasy use during the weekend. So great is the euphoric effect for some that they are more than willing to put up with the rebound aftereffects.

As with all amphetamines, Ecstasy elevates blood pressure, increases heart rate, and dilates pupils. Anxiety, disturbance of motor coordination, and appetite suppression are some of the side effects. Ecstasy can cause, in sufficient amounts, hallucinations, and there is some new concern about its damaging short-term memory. A particular myth that surrounds the use of Ecstasy is that it can cause sexual arousal. I have heard both that the use of Ecstasy made users more willing to participate, while others have told me they felt too much anxiety to perform.

As I talk to my patients, this is the one drug that keeps coming up among both high school and college students. It is particularly popular in "rave" clubs, where loud electronic music is played, usually in a nondescript location (a garage, a warehouse, or basement will do) and where drugs are readily available. Pot and Ecstasy abound at raves. (Few people go to raves "for the music" only. If your teenager mentions raves as a place that "the kids are going tonight," watch out for a problem.)

The widespread use of Ecstasy among the party crowd, and the rich and beautiful crowd has given Ecstasy a cult following. The message that cocaine is bad for you seems to have taken hold; we now need a new message that Ecstasy is equally bad. Ecstasy has left the rave clubs and the college campuses and is traveling into mainstream society, where it is currently quite easy for most kids to get. It is in city schools and in suburbia; it crosses cultural and racial boundaries and the only deterrent at present is economics. At roughly $20 or more per pill (the powder is bitter) not everyone can afford it; clearly, Ecstasy is more common among the affluent. However, I am impressed with the argument from many college women that guys are more than willing to buy Ecstasy for them.

The final chapter on the safety of Ecstasy is not yet written. Because it does not seem to cause addiction, people don't think of it as a "hard" drug. Yet I think there should be real concern about its depressive aftereffects. What will happen with frequent use? Are we producing a generation that eventually will pay the price in the years to come for using Ecstasy? Will this alteration of the serotonin system today result in patients whose adult depressions are rooted in the drug use of their adolescent years? I await the next chapter, being written by our young people as we speak, on Ecstasy. I anticipate a horror novel.

Cocaine

Cocaine has had a rather colorful history during the past century. It is the extracted chemical from the leaves of a South American plant, *E. coca*. Grown high in the Andes mountains, it had religious significance to the Indians of Bolivia and Peru. As with peyote, it was carefully guarded as a tool for religious experiences; it was a considered a royal gift from the gods.

The extract was synthesized in the middle of the nineteenth century and soon it was being used for a variety of medical purposes, especially as a topical anesthetic. Because of its stimulant effect, in 1886 it even found its way into Coca Cola. Until the formula was altered, people literally were drinking cocaine and giving it to their children.

The list of famous people who were intrigued and captivated by cocaine is impressive. Sir Arthur Conan Doyle, Jules Verne, Sigmund Freud, and Robert Louis Stevenson all experimented with cocaine. Stevenson's classic *Dr. Jekyll and Mr. Hyde* described a brilliant scientist who takes a mysterious potion and becomes the menacing Mr. Hyde. No doubt Stevenson's personal experiences with cocaine gave him the creative image of Mr. Hyde; the mysterious potion is no more than a metaphor for cocaine.

In the 1970s, cocaine emerged as a drug of choice, and as the price of cocaine soared it took on an allure that only made it more popular. People who never would have thought of doing drugs, saw cocaine as clean, safe, powerful, and trendy.

Because of the rapid absorption through the nasal lining, the most popular way of using cocaine is to snort it. Within a few seconds of a single dose, the person experiences the full effects of the cocaine. Depending on dosage, the effects will wane in minutes to hours. During the high, the person's movements, speech, and behavior are all accelerated. It's an amphetamine high, pure and simple. One of the most common side effects is a runny nose because of the irritant effects of the cocaine on the nasal membranes. Weight loss, diarrhea, muscle aches, nausea, and exhaustion are other complaints.

In order to counter the "unsmokability" of cocaine, some chemist found that by adding the correct amount of baking soda and altering the pH of the cocaine, you could create a base that could be smoked. Enter "crack," a cheaper cocaine available for the pipe that made a "crackling" noise as it was heated. With the appearance of crack the luster of cocaine was lost. Now anyone could afford it, and cocaine became less attractive.

■ Cocaine Effects

Think of all of the effects of speed, and you replicate the effects of cocaine. The one major problem with cocaine is the crash afterwards. This makes it the ideal drug to sell. The user feels terrible when the cocaine is out of her system and then needs more to get back the good feeling. The cycle continues and soon you have someone who is highly dependent on cocaine. Enough cocaine can trigger an amphetamine psychosis. The person appears hyperactive and paranoid. Interest in food, sex, and one's surroundings disappear.

An attractive young female patient *of mine was the epitome of poise, elegance, and style. Inside she felt unsuccessful. In a moment of weakness, she agreed to try some cocaine. It made her feel powerful and gave her the confidence to put herself forward. It took very little for her to wander back to the place where she tried her first cocaine. Soon it became her favorite haunt, and in no time she was a "cokehead." An interesting benefit (to her) was the suppression of her appetite. She could feel good and lose weight at the same time. Only a moment of shame over some of her behavior caused her to realize that she had become a variant of Mr. Hyde. She began to appreciate that she had a problem and she started to work out the issues in therapy that had brought her to use cocaine in the first place. Months went by and she admitted that, while not using, there were few days that went by without her thinking of going back to her old "cocaine haunts" to snort. The need for instant gratification was still there, and it took antidepressants and therapy for her cocaine need to wane. Today, two years after the last snort, she still thinks of using, but hasn't. She avoided an inpatient drug rehabilitation by agreeing to therapy and working hard at the process.*

Another patient had done so much cocaine that he was able to whistle through his nose. He had literally burned a hole through the nasal septum.

This is one of the drugs that is routinely detectable in a urine screening. Most tests do not directly measure cocaine, but rather its breakdown products. As such, it is possible to pick up traces in the urine for several days after the actual use. Naturally, this is dependent on the amount that was consumed.

■ If Your Teen Is Taking Cocaine

Since most users cannot easily forget the euphoria of cocaine, failure in treatment is common. Patients in therapy have to give up the friends with whom they did cocaine and not go to places where it's available. Both of these appear intolerable at the beginning and sometimes the only prescription that works is an inpatient facility that clears the air of the drug and the "friends." There is a Cocaine Anonymous program in which people who have been through cocaine addiction support one another (also see Chapter 11) .

Chapter 16

Other Frequently Used Drugs

A ny parent who reads the newspapers knows about the existence of "date rape drugs" or that kids are taking everything from "Vitamin K" to "roofies." This chapter will bring you up-to-date on the drugs of choice for today's teen generation:

- Inhalants
- Amyl Nitrate, or "Poppers"
- Ketamine, or "Vitamin K"
- GHB
- "Roofies"
- Klonopin
- Opiates
- Barbiturates and Quaaludes

Inhalants

Before the government banned them or restricted their sale, kids could easily go to a hardware store or craft shop and leave with products that would get them high. (Sometimes it is hard to believe what people will do to experience a high.) Below is a list of the inhalants that are often used:

- Model glue (the hobby glue used for building models)
- Nail polish remover

- Cleaning fluids
- Aerosol sprays in cans, including hair sprays and fabric protectors
- The small canisters used to propel the aerosol in canned whipped cream; hence the term "whippets"
- Gasoline
- Freon, from air conditioning

To protect kids from themselves, products with fluorocarbons and butane gas have been made illegal. The original solvents used in dry cleaning were banned because of their toxicity and potential for abuse and new, safer products are available. This does not stop the ingenious, however.

The profile of the "glue sniffer" has long been the young male, who may be as young as twelve with few pubertal changes. He cannot buy cigarettes easily and the thought of injecting anything is absurd to him; alcohol is hard to get and a fake ID at this age is ludicrous. It seems so easy to imitate his older siblings and get intoxicated by sniffing something as "harmless" as model airplane glue. So the hobby store unwittingly becomes a "head shop."

The inhalant is sniffed directly, or a sock or paper towel is soaked with the material and the fumes are "huffed." Some kids intensify the experience by using the inhalant with a plastic bag over their heads. Kids must have gotten word that sometimes suffocation occurred, so now smaller plastic bags are used and placed just over the mouth and nose. Users experience a stimulant effect, but with some inhalants, they can lose consciousness. (This is how they suffocated.) The user may feel tingling, nausea, loss of coordination, weakness, and light-headedness.

Since the nose and lungs are an excellent way of absorbing chemicals, these inhalants take effect almost immediately, but the concentrations are low enough that the effects are short lived. To counter this, the die-hard users simply keep repeating the inhalations and perpetuate the intoxication.

A teen using inhalants will show the normal signs of drug abuse: a lack of interest in school and little social interaction, either at home or with peers. Because of the irritant effect, parents may notice teary eyes, stuffy nose (irritated even to the point of bleeding), and the appearance of drunkenness. Speech will be slurred and he will be uncoordinated and disoriented. The telltale smell of the inhalant may tip you off. If your son is staggering and it smells like he just used hair spray, be suspicious. The underlying reasons for glue sniffing have to be addressed if the sniffing is to stop. A therapist will have to help the family and teen understand the motivation behind this.

Amyl Nitrate, or "Poppers"

In the last decade, many physicians routinely kept a small yellow box filled with ampules of amyl nitrite, which can be crushed and used as a "lifeline" drug for angina by dilating the critical blood vessels to the heart. One side effect was a pleasant euphoria that resulted from the dilation of the blood vessels in the brain. As the rush of blood flowed into the brain, patients experienced a warm feeling.

It didn't take long to realize that, even without a heart condition, this drug could cause a person to experience euphoria. There is an intense exhilaration that in some people crosses the line into nausea, dizziness, and headache. Ampules of amyl are a prescription-only medication. Clearly these are not the ones that are usually obtained by kids. Its street form is a liquid (Liquid Gold) that is clear and straw colored. The vapors are inhaled through the nose directly from a small bottle. The rush sensation is immediate and will fade within minutes; most will complain of a headache after the event. Amyl nitrate is not addictive—the danger lies in the fact that the drug lowers blood pressure and, if swallowed, can be fatal. With repeated inhalations, there can be nasal congestion and irritation.

A less potent version of amyl nitrite is sold as butyl nitrite, which is more commonly seen in England.

A side note on amyl nitrites is in order. For a while these were felt to be the province of the homosexual community. This is no longer the case. Finding these in your teenager's bag should first raise the concern of drug use and not one of sexual identity issues.

Ketamine, or "Vitamin K"

The term "Vitamin K" is slang for a relative of PCP that is quite dangerous. It is actually a prescription medicine called Ketalar, an intramuscularly injected anesthetic. In competent medical hands it is a safe, rapid-acting anesthetic. On the street, this white powder is a central nervous system depressant capable of eliciting hallucinations that are so bizarre that they are referred to as a "K hole." People talk about "out of body experiences" while on ketamine.

The powder (it's actually a liquid that is heated to form a powder) can be snorted or smoked alone, or it can be sprinkled on marijuana or even mixed with cocaine. As with any central nervous system depressant, the possibility of respiratory failure is quite real. Not too surprisingly the effects vary from nau-

The Price of Drugged Date Rape

In 1996, the federal government established a law, the Drug-Induced Rape Prevention and Punishment Act, that makes the use of a controlled substance, such as a "date rape drug," punishable by up to twenty years in prison. It is now a federal crime to use any controlled substance to assist in a sexual assault. [The Drug-Induced Rape Prevention and Punishment Act of 1996 (ACT), 21 U.S.C. Sec 841(b)(7)]

sea and vomiting to convulsions and death. Other street names are "Special K" and "Ketaject." Ketamine is also known as one of the "date rape drugs" that cause loss of consciousness.

In my practice, I do not see too many teenagers doing ketamine. The few who have admitted to its use were clearly into a heavy drug scene and already in treatment for drug-related problems.

If you find ketamine in your teenager's room, or suspect that it is being used, call your doctor for an immediate appointment. Your teen is in danger.

GHB

GHB (gamma-hydroxybutyrate), also known as a "date rape drug," is another central nervous system depressant, but this one is capable of being concocted at home by a reasonably good chemist. The point is that, like LSD in the 1960s, GHB is not only dangerous, but the quality will vary with the maker of the drug.

It is available in a clear liquid, a white powder, or in a tablet. Since it is odorless, tasteless, and colorless, it is the "ideal" date rape drug. When you hear about a "date rape drug" chances are that it is GHB or "roofies," rather than ketamine. It takes only a few drops of concentrated GHB to do the job. It is commonly called "GHB," "liquid ecstasy," or plain "G."

At low doses it can act like a sedative, and the patient feels relaxed but in control. At higher doses, it elicits nausea and respiratory depression. At very high levels the patient can fall into a deep sleep or even coma.

"Roofies"

Rohypnol (say it out loud and you understand the street name) is the pharmaceutical name for a powerful depressant. It is in the same family of drugs as the benzodiazapines (Valium is the most well known); it causes sedation and is used for insomnia. Despite an American ban on this drug, flunitrazepam (its generic name) is available in some countries in Europe and South America without a prescription.

It is available as a pill that is either swallowed whole or dissolved in a drink. Since it has powerful depressive effects (about tenfold the effect of Valium), it acts as a quick "drunk." These pills are often combined with alcohol and the effect of depression is magnified. "Roofies" also have the reputation of being a "date rape drug" since they are tasteless and odorless and act within ten minutes of ingestion.

There are several reports in the media of women who felt suddenly disoriented, unable to speak, complained of passing out, and had absolutely no memory of what happened. It was postulated that a "roofie" had been dropped into their drinks. Rapes could have occurred, and if they were given "roofies," the victims will be unable to recall any details.

Klonopin

To be complete, the reader should know that a perfectly legal prescription drug, Klonopin (clonazepam), which is used for anxiety disorders, has now started to appear as a drug of abuse. It has a similar effect as "roofies," and emergency rooms are beginning to report patients who are using this drug to enhance the effects of other opiates.

Opiates

All the drugs in this group have a sedative effect, and all are derived from the beautiful but deadly poppy plant. When the liquid extract of the plant is dried it becomes opium, a complex powder that contains several important medicinal products. Morphine, synthesized in 1803, and codeine (its derivative) were eventually isolated, and with the introduction of the hypodermic needle in 1853, the two medicines were transformed into painkillers. During the Civil War we welcomed the ability of morphine to relieve the pain of battle wounds. We cursed the addiction years later.

The Various Forms of Opiates

1. *Opium.* This is rarely used in the United States. It can be smoked, eaten, or injected.
2. *Morphine.* The most popular derivative of opium, it is used after major surgeries as a painkiller.
3. *Heroin.* A modified form of morphine, which gets into the brain faster.
4. *Codeine.* Both a painkiller and a cough suppressant. No general cough medicines today contain codeine; instead a mild derivative, dextromethrophan, is added to suppress a cough. However, doctors can prescribe Tylenol with codeine as a painkiller.
5. *Methadone.* Used as an oral substitute for opiate addiction. Has the advantage of avoiding a needle.

The effects of all the opiates are the same. They suppress the body's perception of pain, lower the respiratory rate, stimulate vomiting, and lower intestinal motility. Because the pupils contract, doctors commonly look at the eyes if they suspect a patient of opiate use. Another sign is the flushing that occurs on the skin (due to capillary dilatation); patients also complain of an "itchy," sweaty feeling as their bodies release histamine. The small nerves on the skin that control hair are stimulated and "goose flesh" is visible.

Once the body relies on the external opiates (there are internal, naturally occurring opiates, known as endorphins, that are released by sexual orgasm and exercise), repeated use of opiates becomes necessary because the body stops producing them. When the next opiate dose is due, the body craves it. Without further doses, the body goes into withdrawal. If you fail to take the next opium dose on schedule, you feel pain; your body literally craves the external opiate.

During my years at Bellevue I saw many opiate addicts. Often they presented the picture of the disheveled and downtrodden. They were dirty and malnourished; they had infections where they had injected themselves. Their abused and hardened veins were a testimony to frequent injections of heroin. That was the picture of poverty and drugs. However, the middle and upper classes are not immune. Now it's a teenager from a comfortable family who ends up being referred to my practice for heroin addiction by a disbelieving family physician. The idea that one of this doctor's patients is doing heroin is as implausible to him as it is to the family.

A colleague referred an *eighteen-year-old patient to me to evaluate medically what drugs had done to her body. Despite the fact that she was a brilliant student, she had crossed the line from alcohol and pot to "harder* *drugs." Her psychiatrist believed that she was using heroin. On taking her history it was clear that she was telling me both the truth and a story filled with bravado and shock. She came from a wealthy family, and she was enjoying the fact that she was able to get me to raise my eyebrows in disbelief as she told me about her heroin injections "on the weekends." None of what she told me was particularly new, only sad. I managed to keep my eyebrows directly in place but failed at one point when she told me, a week later, that she had tried to inject herself with a "cough medicine." There is a mild opiate in certain cough suppressants, but I never even thought of injection as an option. When my eyebrows did go up, so did my hand for the phone to tell the psychiatrist that I felt an inpatient hospitalization was immediately in order. A full year later, a lovely, calm, and very different young woman came in to have a physical and to thank all of the people who had assisted her in getting help.*

The Teen Addict

If teens are morphine or heroin users, and none is available or they don't have enough money, then any opiate will do. They will try to convince their physician that they are in pain, from a tooth if need be, so as to get some—any—pain medication. Their next option is to steal to get the drug.

Initially, the treatment for opiates requires a decision about detoxification. If there is sufficient opiate use (of any kind), the teen must go to a detoxification center. Because of legal issues, you can hospitalize teens against their wishes if they are minors. After the age of majority (eighteen in most states), you will need a legal commitment to admit them to a detox center.

Often a dangerous or criminal act will bring the police into play. Ironically, this may not be as unwelcome as it sounds. Teens who are legally adults and refuse help may be dangerous enough to warrant the call to the police. Do it! At that point, police procedure usually requires that the drug abuser be taken to a hospital for evaluation. They may then need a detox center and the hospital has the right to admit for a few days of observation, even against the will of the patient. (Not all hospitals are equipped to detoxify an addict. They may stabilize the patient for immediate care but they do not deal with the withdrawal. If the patient is admitted to a hospital that has both immediate care and detox capabilities, then it is done in one place.)

After the detox is over, then a period of inpatient drug and alcohol care is in order. After that period (usually months), the care usually shifts to a "halfway" program, in which there is residential care and patients are integrated back into society. Lastly, they go home to ongoing therapy. Short-stepping the process is rarely successful.

Barbiturates and Quaaludes

All barbiturates are depressants (downers) and are generally used to calm or sedate anxious or psychotic individuals. Most illegal downers are actually obtained through legal prescriptions that have found their way into the abuser's hands.

Today, physicians prescribe barbiturates less frequently than in the past, and the amount of abuse has accordingly lessened. I rarely see teens abusing this group of drugs. The only users who venture into barbiturate abuse are those who have already exhausted alcohol and pot and are seeking new territories.

The person who uses barbiturates acts like she is drunk on alcohol. Both substances depress the central nervous system. That is the appeal of this pill—it is a quick drunk, and loosens inhibitions. All of the precautions that one would render with alcohol apply here. Hence, driving a car or doing anything that requires full and competent judgment is foolhardy. (That includes sex.)

There are other well-known sedatives that do not belong in the barbiturate family. The most popular of these is methaqualone, or Quaalude. "Ludes" are a powerful and dangerous substitute for the barbiturates. While I have not seen much of this in the high school age group, it still is making the rounds on some college campuses.

Unfortunately, the user of barbiturates acts just like the person who is drunk. Short of measuring blood levels or urine samples, it may be quite difficult to tell them apart.

Besides the obvious problems of safe judgment while using these sedative drugs, the extra concern of addiction is also present. Withdrawal is quite painful and the casual use of these medications for "pain management" has taught us the importance of using them properly. The barbiturate street user does not appreciate this lesson.

It is obvious that the teenager who is using barbiturates needs help both medically and emotionally. She has passed by the experimentation stage and is demonstrating a great deal of internal turmoil. The use of barbiturates may represent an attempt to "self-medicate," but this only addresses the fact that there is a great need for the parents to act quickly upon discovery.

Withdrawal from barbiturates depends on how much has been used and for how long. A slow tapering process can be done as an outpatient with or without antidepressants. However, those whose use has been substantial may require the monitoring of a hospital or a detox center.

Over the years we have seen the drug scene change. Today's parents may have lived through the "turbulent" sixties and the STP, LSD, and THC of their day. For them, it may seem impossible that their own kids would view these as passé. Parents of teenagers will always be behind the "latest" information on drugs. Despite the new drugs that are discussed in this chapter, parents must stay vigilant as the news media or the community informs us of the latest drug being abused by kids. The first step for a parent is to be aware of what is out there. Ignorance is dangerous when it comes to the drug scene, as the parent who is not informed will miss the critical signs of his own child's abuse. These kids are in trouble and need help.

For guidance on managing all issues pertaining to getting a teen off drugs, please refer to Chapter 11.

Part Five

The Adolescent, Head to Toe: Common Ailments

Introduction

As children become teenagers there are unique health needs and concerns that arise because of age and because of the monumental changes occurring in their bodies. Understanding these adolescent health issues is vital for any family, because teenagers often don't know how to communicate their concerns properly. In addition to changes in their relationship with parents, teens seek an increasing amount of privacy, and many find it difficult to talk about personal health concerns. Some sensitive teens keep their symptoms hidden from parents and doctors because they fear that a headache may signal a brain tumor; that a mild limp could mean a bone malignancy. (Usually the headache is from stress or eye strain, and the limp is from a sports injury.) Others vocally dramatize every complaint so that it becomes a theatrical opening night. A patient who visited me for a sore throat is a good example of how some teens get around to dealing with health concerns.

A young man arrived in my office *complaining of a sore throat, but I could find little in the way of redness or infection during the examination. However, I remembered that he had mentioned initially that he had "another thing" to discuss with me, and I inquired about what it was. He had been doing "a lot of sit-ups" and had been having some back pain. When I examined his back I found an egg-sized lump over his spine. No, mom and dad didn't know about this, and he figured it "could be handled here when he came for the sore throat." You can imagine his parents' surprise when I told them I needed to do a magnetic resonance imaging (MRI) of* *his back, when they'd sent their son in complaining of a sore throat. Like this fellow, other teens also find it hard to approach their concerns directly.*

Some teens are worriers, and their parents, upon hearing about yet another stomachache or headache, often conclude that the health concern of the moment is actually psychosomatic. The teenager may, indeed, be feeling anxious or depressed, and the manifestations of the symptoms appear as abdominal pains, back pains, a sore throat, fatigue, etc. But it is far too easy, and potentially dangerous, to ascribe a problem to mental health problems, without first looking for organic explanations.

Sometimes, miscellaneous health complaints are attributed to "growing pains." Since teens are growing and since they have pains, this becomes a catch-all explanation; I do not like this term as it tells us nothing, and its use may lead to a complacency that misses something important.

Parents should know their kids well enough to appreciate when a complaint is out of the ordinary, and the teen's physician should be someone who is willing to listen to the teen's history and take it seriously. For parent or physician to judge that a teen health complaint is "nothing" is, at the least, insulting, and at worst, negligent. Teens with a cough may have bronchitis or a malignancy, and those who complain about abdominal pains may have ulcers. Organic causes of any health complaints need to be eliminated before a doctor can reach the conclusion that the cause may not be physical.

In order to help you decipher the complaints of your teenager, we will cover the usual complaints from head to toe. I will present a description of the complaint and a reasonable approach. If you suspect something specific, such as mononucleosis, find the information quickly by using the book's index; if your teen simply complains of a stomachache, turn to the section on the abdomen and the digestive system, which is designed to help you consider the symptoms and come up with some general possibilities of what the problem might be.

This information is also helpful after a doctor's visit. When you arrive home and realize you still don't really understand your teen's thyroid problem, turn to the appropriate section and read about how the thyroid functions and exactly what is happening to a teen who has "hypothyroidism."

To make it easier to look up your teen's ailments, I have divided this section into the following general areas:

■ Whole Body Issues: Immunizations and Fatigue
■ The Head
■ The Neck Area

- The Spine and Back
- The Shoulders, Chest, and Heart
- The Abdomen and Digestive System
- The Urinary Tract
- The Female Reproductive System
- The Male Reproductive System
- The Hips, Legs, and Feet

While having an understanding of what the possibilities are is very important to a parent, *it is vital that you check with your teen's physician for a definite diagnosis*. Then turn again to this book for an explanation of what you learn from the doctor.

Whole Body Issues

Immunizations

Immunizations are most strongly associated with the first six years of life, as a child is vaccinated against many of the most serious diseases. However, teenagers and college students still need their fair share of shots, as there are certain vaccination requirements for most schools, camps, colleges, postgraduate schooling, some jobs, and certain travel plans. Though my practice is limited to adolescents, I still hear the plaintive wail that echoes through any pediatrician's examining room: "Do you have to give me any shots?" I have had more than one teen think of cancelling a trip instead of getting "all those shots."

Immunizations Relevant to Teens

The idea behind immunization is simple: give teens protection by giving them the specific antibody necessary to kill a particular organism, or give them something that is so close to the organism's structure that patients will make the antibody themselves. When you take the antibody directly it is called *passive* immunization; when you force your immune system to work and make the antibody it is called *active* immunization. This difference in protection is important in understanding the risks and benefits of the process.

Passive immunity is used only rarely and then in a hospital setting or in special situations. The immunizations given to the normal population are active immunizations, meaning that either an attenuated, or mild, version of the virus is given, and the patient's own immune system makes the antibody. Because the immunity can wane, it is necessary to give "booster" shots along the way.

The following are immunizations that your teen may need:

DPT

The DPT (diphtheria, pertussis, and tetanus) series is probably the one that most parents recognize. Though the bulk of these vaccinations are given to young children, it is recommended by the American Academy of Pediatrics that the adolescent be immunized with the dT adult shot every ten years (immunization against pertussis is not needed in later years). If there is an injury that, in the opinion of the doctor, could result in tetanus, then the interval is five years. There can be side effects to the shot (generally pain at the site and fever), so it is important to maintain the proper and recommended intervals between shots.

Polio

In the adolescent it is not generally necessary to give polio vaccines. However, the one exception is a teen who travels to some of the third world countries. Since immunity is not consistent in the peoples of these areas, the teen should be given the IPV form (Inactivated Polio Vaccine) in a shot.

HIB

A common bacteria called *Hemophilus influenza (H. influenza)* can cause ear infections and a severe bacterial meningitis in the young child. I frequently get calls about this immunization, but it is for children only and is not repeated for the adolescent.

MMR

Measles, mumps, and rubella (German measles) were common infections before immunizations were developed. By 1970, a vaccine (MMR) was being given in combined form that made it easier to administer. A decline in these illnesses resulted. Then in 1989–90, we began to see cases of measles in teenagers and college students. Either we had vaccinated our kids at the wrong time, or there had been something wrong with the original vaccines. Adjustments were made both in the timing and in the vaccine: Children born after 1990 are now given two vaccines: one at twelve to fifteen months of age and a booster at least one month later, but preferably at four to six years old, prior to school entry. Most schools will not accept a student without these two vaccines, but I still get the occasional teenager who was "missed" for various reasons. Today most kids have gotten their proper shots, but if your son or daughter was born before 1990 check to see that they have received both MMR vaccines.

By way of reminder, these diseases are nothing to fool around with. Mumps can cause infertility by invading the testicles or the ovaries; rubella, an illness that for children is nothing more than a rash and an annoyance, can cause serious birth defects if a mother contracts it during the first trimester of a pregnancy. As for measles, it's a miserable illness featuring high fevers, cough, and a terrible rash.

Hepatitis

Any inflammation of a part of our bodies has the suffix "-itis" attached to the name of the organ. In medicine, we refer to our liver as a "hepar." Any inflammation of the liver is referred to as "hepatitis," including Hepatitis A, B, C, and some newer ones. There are only vaccines for Hepatitis A and B. Since the B vaccine came out first, let's start with it.

■ Hepatitis B

This virus is transmitted through all bodily fluids and, therefore, is certainly transmitted through the intimacy of sex, or through the natural process of birth if the mother is infected. In the late 1980s a vaccine became available for widespread use that gives protection against Hepatitis B. Getting this vaccine is particularly important because, with Hepatitis B, the patient does not become ill immediately but can be contagious long before there are symptoms. Without the vaccine, numerous innocent people can be exposed to the virus.

Hepatitis B can cause chronic liver dysfunction and may lead, in later life, to a form of cancer of the liver called primary hepatocellular carcinoma.

Since blood and body fluids are transmitting agents, it means that any wound exudate (pus or ooze), semen, vaginal secretions, or saliva is capable of carrying and transmitting the virus. It becomes immediately clear why blood transfusions are screened for the virus, why we are concerned with needle-sharing, or accidental needle-pricking from a patient to health care provider. From a parent's point of view it should also be clear why this is a vaccine that should be given to teenagers, before they become sexually active.

In the United States, the group most at risk for getting Hepatitis B is the adolescent population because of risk-taking sexual practices. The risk attendant to unsafe sexual practices and any drug activity that involves the use of needles raises the concern dramatically. For a while there was a stigma that only homosexuals were at risk because of their "promiscuity." This loaded word was actually used as a guideline for judging who should receive the vaccine. Yet it became clear that an equally active heterosexual was at risk if he or she were equally "promiscuous."

When the vaccines first became available for the general public, parents were concerned that administration of the Hepatitis B vaccine was a stigma. The thinking was that the teens who needed it were identifying themselves as sexually active. Many teens in my office faced the dilemma of agreeing to the recommended vaccine with their parents looking to them for some sign of confession about sexual activity. Finally, better logic has prevailed as the notion of vaccines as preventive care has sunk in. You want to immunize before the person is at risk, so the American Academy of Pediatrics first moved their recommendation to the immunization of "pre-teens" and has since changed it to infants, permitting the parental world to breathe a sigh of relief.

Today the three shots can be given to infants. If your child was not immunized as a baby, then certainly the vaccine should be given before the twelfth birthday (the second shot follows the first by a month; the third is given at least five months after that). Because many pre-teens miss the third shot ("We forgot . . . "), there are many teens out there with only two shots of Hepatitis B. The current recommendation is to simply give the third when you can. You need not start all over again.

■ Hepatitis A

For years we could not distinguish the different types of hepatitis other than to appreciate that the viruses acted differently. One type seemed to be quite virulent and the patient became rather dramatically jaundiced. Fever, chills, nausea, vomiting, and a general malaise were seen. The patient was sick for a short while and in a matter of weeks he was back to normal; his liver studies showed evidence of significant inflammation. This used to be called "infectious hepatitis" and later was called Hepatitis A. It is primarily transmitted through the fecal-oral route; that is, from eating contaminated foods. Because of concerns about foreign travel and improper food handling as well as sewage problems, this was the hepatitis that we worried about most.

Hepatitis A is not a currently recommended routine vaccine for teenagers unless travel or exposure is involved. However, some college forms are beginning to ask for it as a standard vaccine before college. The exception for routine Hepatitis A vaccine occurs where there are "pockets" of outbreaks. At that point, your doctor may recommend that everyone in the family receive it as well.

The Hepatitis A vaccine allows active immunity for exposed persons as well as prophylaxis for travelers. There are two vaccines on the market—Havrix and Vaqta—but they are only a few years old and information as to duration of protection is not yet clear. Children are given the Havrix vaccine at between ages two and eighteen. (The initial shot is followed by a second one six to twelve months later.) The teenager gets the shots on the same schedule but the dose is higher.

The Vaqta vaccine is not as common and is given to children between ages two and 18 in two doses six to eighteen months apart.

The key points to consider for the Hepatitis A vaccine are as follows:

1. It is estimated that it will take two to three weeks after the first dose to acquire any antibodies. Nearly full protection will be acquired after the second dose. However, it is important to note that the vaccine has to be administered at least *three* weeks prior to travel or the protection will not be available for the trip!
2. If the booster is given, current estimates are that the patient will have some immunity for three to four years. Most would recommend a booster after four years if the patient were to travel into an area where Hepatitis A is common, although new data suggests there may be longer immunity. Speak to your doctor if you travel often. If not, you can always get the vaccine prior to the next trip.

Varicella (Chickenpox)

The medical term for chickenpox is varicella, but the virus itself is known as herpes zoster. This virus, activated in a primary infection, causes the classic chickenpox lesions and symptoms (headache, fever, malaise). Generally, the older the person, the worse the infection.

Before the available vaccine (Varivax), all you could do was hope for the infection to strike a child early. Mothers would actually take their children to someone infected in the hopes of "getting it over with" before school. In most cases, this highly contagious virus gladly accommodated and the susceptible child came home infected.

However, those who have been infected as children have another problem. Since the virus doesn't just go away but stays latent, or asleep, in the nerve roots, it could act up again one day. First, a small itch and then a full-blown crop of small blisters will appear along a nerve on the side of the body—the chickenpox has reappeared as "shingles."

With the advent of the vaccine, a teenager who has not had chickenpox can be immunized. The current vaccine is given to teenagers in two doses four to eight weeks apart.

Because the vaccine is a relatively new one, we do not yet know the duration of immunity provided. Although we know that we can expect close to ten years of immunity, further research is necessary to more clearly establish it. If your teen has received the vaccine, your physician will keep you advised as to changes in the current recommendation.

Meningococcal Vaccine

The term "meningitis" refers to an inflammation of the coverings of the brain. There are several "Saran Wrap" linings that contain the brain called meninges, and if these are inflamed we speak of "meningitis."

Neisseria meningitis is a bacteria that can cause a virulent type of meningitis. It is so potentially lethal that patients diagnosed in the morning but left untreated may well be dead by the evening. The patient presents with fever, chills, malaise, and may have an initial rash. If properly diagnosed with a lumbar puncture (spinal tap) and cultures of stool and blood, treatment can be started immediately and generally has a good outcome. But, if treatment is delayed the outcome is poor.

We have known for some time that outbreaks occur in semi-enclosed communities. Child-care centers, schools, and colleges are in this category, as are military bases. For years, the recommendation had been that anyone with intimate exposure should get the vaccine. The only group that consistently warranted the vaccine prophylactically were new military recruits. Up to 1999, college students were not routinely included. Every year my office would receive a call from a distraught parent that "someone came down with meningitis" at her son or daughter's college. What to do?

The first question I would ask would never get an answer: namely, what kind of meningitis? Most of the time the response was that the college didn't know, and they suggested parents "call their doctor." The second question was how "intimate" was the contact? Being at the same college does not warrant action; being in the same classroom, maybe. Being a roommate, likely; being a boyfriend, definitely. For those where intimate exposure was an issue, an antibiotic as well as the meningococcal vaccine (Menomune) should be administered.

In 1999, many college forms began to recommend the vaccine for entering freshman. None I have seen mandate it yet. The current practice is to immunize entering freshman. Since the immunity should last for three to four years, it is hoped that over the next few years the campuses of America will have students protected against this dreaded disease. However, the vaccine only protects against some strains and cannot be taken as a universal protection against all *N. meningitis* strains. However, some protection is better than none in so lethal an infection.

Flu Shots

If someone is diagnosed with the "flu," or influenza, she will be very ill with a high fever and a bronchial cough. Once a flu epidemic gets started, it can lead to millions of dollars spent on doctors' appointments and absences from work or school. As a result, the Centers for Disease Control and Prevention (CDC) creates a new vaccine annually to counter what they anticipate will be the virus that will appear in the United States in the coming year. Ideally the shots are given in late October or November and enough time passes for the patient to develop antibodies before flu season hits. Any teens who have chronic respiratory diseases or any immune deficiency should talk to their doctors about vaccination.

Tuberculosis

Rather than vaccinate against the disease, U.S. medical practice is to screen for possible cases of tuberculosis through a skin test (the Mantoux test, which consists of a intradermal injection that is later examined for swelling). Currently, the recommendation in the United States is to test all teens every two years, and just as certain vaccines are required by middle and high schools and colleges,

Summary of the Vaccines Your Teen May Need

1. A dT booster (adult diphtheria-tetanus) or T (tetanus): Given every ten years or in case of injury
2. Mumps, measles, rubella: two doses
3. Hepatitis B shots: Three doses, formerly given to preadolescents and now usually given during infancy
4. Varicella vaccine for chickenpox: If the patient is over thirteen, a booster is given four to eight weeks after the first shot
5. Polio: the injectable form
6. Meningococcal vaccine against meningitis: for the college-bound
7. Tuberculosis screening test
8. Hepatitis A: for certain travel destinations

so, too, is the Mantoux test. Your doctor will have to account for the testing on all school forms, and most colleges require that it be administered within three months to a year of admission. If a teen has a positive result, an X ray is ordered and treatment is prescribed for a period of at least six months. If the X ray is positive for tuberculosis, then a different program is followed, which your teen's doctor will explain to you.

The vaccine against tuberculosis is used in other countries and becomes significant to teens in the United States if they have lived in a country where the vaccine is given as a regular part of medical care. Anyone who has been vaccinated against TB in another country may have a slight reaction at the site of the tuberculin test. If the reaction is greater than 10 ml, a health professional should interpret the test directly. A physician will recommend treatment.

Vaccines for Overseas Travel

In preparation for traveling abroad, teens should see a doctor well in advance of the trip to find out if any special immunizations are needed. These are the main ones that may be considered:

1. **Cholera.** The vaccine is not very effective and most tourists seldom contract cholera during short stays in a country.

2. **Yellow fever**. This is an attenuated viral vaccine. Its use is for travel to rural areas in tropical South America and most of Africa. It requires administration about two weeks before travel and is seldom available in a private physician's office. Only specially designated facilities are licensed to administer the vaccine. You must contact your state or city health department for information.

3. **Typhoid**. The injection for typhoid is useful if traveling to rural areas of tropical countries. There is also an oral vaccine available, but it is difficult to get, so check with your pharmacy.

4. **Rabies**. Only recommended in extreme cases of exposure, or if entering an area of high likelihood of rabid animals, it is seldom used. Some forms for traveling teens will list this as a requirement. Before starting on this regimen, have your doctor check with the CDC or with the foreign government. Only in specific cases will the teen need the vaccine.

5. **Japanese encephalitis.** This is a mosquito-borne infection and can be fatal. It occurs in rural Asia, and the Near and Far East. Only if traveling to rural parts should this be considered; the attack rate is very low for travelers.

Fatigue

Unquestionably, the most common complaint I hear from patients in my office is that they are "tired." Or parents call, worried that their teen is "exhausted" all the time or is sleeping an inordinate amount. They want to know if "there is something going around" or if there is something uniquely wrong with their teenager.

Reasons for being tired range from the obvious and easy to diagnose to the obscure and complicated. For that reason, if a teen complains regularly about being tired, it is worth bringing him in for a checkup. Each teen has his own sense of "tired" (as does anyone). If the teen is falling asleep in class or is consistently unable to get up in the morning, something may be wrong.

One can divide the reasons for being "tired" into three general categories:

1. Physical activity. Is he simply worn out?
2. Emotional issues. What are the stresses that the teen is experiencing?
3. Organic illness. Is there a medical cause responsible for the fatigue?

Physical Activity

Those who try to "burn the candle at both ends" should not be surprised that they are tired, and this applies to teenagers as well as adults. The young teen puts in a full day's work at school, participates in extracurricular activities, does homework, stays up late to "relax," and then commences the routine again the next day. The athlete, the yearbook editor, the debater who attends meets, and the teen who adds a job to her day are so overscheduled that "one more thing" can push her to the point that she is so tired that she just can't manage well. This pattern is not unique, and the consequence is that the general teenage population is overtired.

A teen should be getting eight hours of sleep a night and have a consistent waking and sleeping schedule. Ideally, he could also use an earlier bedtime and a later hour for the start of school, neither of which are going to happen soon. Most teens think that sleeping all day Saturday can make up their sleep deficit. Nope! Additional rest needs to be spaced out over a number of days in order to let the body recover its energy. (Also see Chapter 4, "The Sleep-Deprived Teen.")

Emotional Causes

Stress-related exhaustion is quite real. A patient who is anxious uses a great deal of energy in worrying. Patients who are tired because of emotional reasons have to be approached gently. The doctor who says, "This is all in your head," will probably lose a patient. It's bad enough for the teen to be dealing with emotional difficulties. It's worse to have them dismissed by the physician as being trivial.

To fully appreciate what a teen is experiencing, adults need to understand stress at a teen's level. What may not seem particularly worrisome to an older person may be genuinely monumental in the life of a teenager. The teen whose peers are taunting him may worry about going to school; the one who didn't make the field hockey team may feel she is doomed to a life of failure—these feelings are very strong in the teenager and should not be dismissed lightly. Other issues—school difficulties, parental divorce, or moving to a new community—are more readily understood to cause stress. Any of these issues can lead to emotional fatigue or even depression.

Depression in the adolescent is hard to appreciate since many of the features—withdrawal, isolation, and mood shifts—are normal behaviors during this time of life. Parents often will have to consult a professional who has worked closely with teenagers to assess the situation. Individual therapy with the teen, family therapy, and when warranted, medication, are the methods used to help a teen overcome depression. If medication for depression is prescribed, be sure to ask about side effects. Some antidepressants and antianxiety medications can ease the problem but the side effects may exact a high cost.

Organic Illness

As part of an examination for "fatigue," your doctor will want to rule out organic causes that might be making your teen tired.

■ Allergies

The patient with allergies will often complain of being tired. Allergy medication can cause drowsiness, or the patient's symptoms (runny nose, congestion) may be keeping her awake at night. Some of the prescription antihistamines are supposed to be less sedating, but they are not 100 percent free of the ingredients that cause sleepiness. Many teens, however, will be able to take prescription allergy medications and not experience drowsiness. This is not an exact science, and you may have to try several medications before finding one that will work for your teen.

If you suspect your teen has allergies, it makes sense to have an allergy workup to identify what is causing the allergic symptoms. In addition to identifying and treating for a specific allergen, the household can also be modified to lessen exposure. For example, if a teen has an allergy to feathers, the family should get rid of all down comforters and pillows. Complete information will be available from any allergist, once the cause of the allergy has been identified.

■ Anemia

The person who is seriously anemic is tired and low on energy. Anemia is the result of insufficient red blood cells or weakened red blood cells, which are incapable of carrying enough oxygen to the body tissues, resulting in tiredness. In iron-deficiency anemia, it can take as long as six months for a patient to become so low in iron that she is actually anemic. During that time, signs of tiredness will gradually increase.

A lack of iron (one of the raw ingredients bone marrow needs in order to make new red blood cells) is a common cause of anemia. In teenage girls, it may be as simple as not keeping up with iron consumption to compensate for the iron lost in the monthly menstrual cycle. In males, it is unusual to find iron deficiency unless there is a dietary problem. Teens who are anemic can generally overcome the problem simply by increasing the consumption of iron to replace the deficit. Fortunately, supplements and many foods can help increase iron stores in the body. The highest amount of absorbable iron is obtained from eating red meat, with pork liver also near the top of the list. Clams and oysters are other good sources of iron.

During the teen years, some opt to become vegetarians. It is crucial that the vegetarian eat the kinds of foods that are rich in the necessary nutrients. Plant foods contain iron, but it is much less than what is found in meat and it is absorbed differently. In cases where the iron level is low and the patient objects to red meat, then grains and iron-enriched foods can add iron to the diet. Often, iron supplements may be necessary for the vegetarian teen. For a more thorough discussion of different foods and iron absorption see Chapter 5.

Occasionally, a teen will be anemic from loss of blood somewhere, usually in the gastrointestinal tract (from ulcers, intestinal polyps, or cancer); the blood loss is often undetectable except by a test for "occult" blood in the stool (see p. 419 in the section on the abdomen). If your teen's anemia is not from a lack of iron in his diet, an assessment of the gastrointestinal tract is in order.

A deficit of folic acid and Vitamin B_{12} can also cause anemia. These are much less common than iron-deficiency anemia, though folic acid deficiency in teens generally signals an eating disorder. This problem is picked up in the "CBC" (complete blood count) that is done routinely at medical checkups. Folic acid pills and B_{12} (by injection) are the usual treatments (see Chapter 5, "Teens, Nutrition, and Eating Disorders").

▪ Chronic Fatigue Syndrome

Chronic Fatigue Syndrome (CFS) is a vague but distressing illness that has puzzled physicians for some time. In the 1980s, a group of patients suffered extreme fatigue and had such subtle symptoms as swollen glands, headache, muscle aches, and pains. They all had one thing in common: They had all previously had infectious mononucleosis as measured by antibodies. Infectious mononucleosis is caused by Epstein-Barr virus (a herpes virus). This report caused a split in the medical profession and the lay press. There was no scientific evidence that mono *caused* Chronic Fatigue Syndrome, and though the link between the two diseases is compelling, scientists feel other factors are involved. As a result, there currently is no explanation for CFS.

Over the years, I have seen several patients who fit the profile. One girl could barely keep her head off the desk during class. She had antibodies against Epstein-Barr virus, and they were elevated for quite a while; but this proved nothing in the long run. With no clear diagnosis or treatment that proved helpful, she finally had to have home tutoring for an entire year and has not fully recovered.

The CDC has acknowledged the existence of CFS by establishing criteria for the diagnosis. Four or more of the following symptoms should be present to make the diagnosis.

1. Unexplained fatigue for more than six months; the fatigue must be severe and of recent onset
2. Short-term memory loss or inability to concentrate
3. Sore throat
4. Neck lymph glands swollen
5. Muscle pain
6. Joint pains without accompanied swelling
7. Headaches
8. Trouble sleeping: "unrefreshing" sleep
9. After exertion, exhaustion for days

A word of caution is in order when applying this to teenagers. If you look at this list, many teenagers would easily have several of these symptoms on an ongoing basis. Also there are some illnesses that mimic these symptoms. For example, Lyme disease and thyroid disorders also have the symptoms of poor memory, headaches, sleep problems, and exhaustion.

Just as little is known about the cause of CFS, not much information is available as to treatment. What we do know is that the patient who is diagnosed with CFS should get *some* exercise or they will get worse. Diet is important, and currently it is suggested that a diet high in fiber and low in fat is helpful. A higher intake of salt is useful for those who feel dizzy from low blood pressure. Lastly, stress reduction has been useful. Biofeedback, meditation, and massage therapy have been used in an effort to help alleviate the muscle discomfort associated with CFS. Few medications have had great success although patients who are depressed may benefit from antidepressant therapy. It is, however, important to emphasize that depression is not the *cause* of CFS but rather is one of its by-products.

Although there is mounting evidence that CFS is diagnosed too late in many cases, I caution against too quick a diagnosis in teenagers. Normally one expects adolescents to be tired; they are growing rapidly and their lifestyle and the demands on their time would exhaust even the most energetic person. The diagnosis of CFS made too readily may create an environment that is not conducive to letting the teen do as much as she is capable of. For example, if a teen has been told she has CFS, it becomes more difficult to judge whether or not she should go to school, participate in extracurricular sports, or go to camp for the summer. Parents may view her as "vulnerable," and this may interfere with the independence that she is entitled to by her age. It is better if the diagnosis is not made until there has been a period of six months of extreme exhaustion. Also, be wary of the physician who promises quick results with the "latest" treatment. To date, none are proven effective.

■ Drugs

Any teen abusing drugs, including pot, will be fatigued. Stimulants provide an "up" for a while, but there is an inevitable crash. "Downers," such as Valium, Quaaludes, or barbiturates, are designed to sedate.

How will you know if fatigue is caused by drugs? There will be other signs and symptoms, such as changes in mood, patterns of friendship, activities, etc. For more information, refer to Chapters 11 through 16 in Part Four of the book.

■ Lyme Disease

Called one of the "great masqueraders" because it parades as many other maladies, Lyme disease was first diagnosed in the Northeast, and most patients were mistakenly thought to have juvenile rheumatoid arthritis. It took a while to sort out the fact that this is an infection from a spirochete (a type of bacteria) carried by deer ticks. A tick infected with the Lyme spirochete bites a human, and the person develops Lyme disease. *The infected person cannot transmit the disease to another; each person needs to be bitten by the tick.* (I am frequently asked if Lyme disease can be transmitted sexually, and the answer is, no, it can't.) The symptoms of the illness are so varied that this disease often needs to be considered when there is no other definitive diagnosis, but the patient is clearly suffering from something.

Ticks predominate in woody and high-grass areas, and spend part of their life cycle living on deer. Anyone in areas inhabited by deer are at higher risk for Lyme disease. If you live in such an area (or your teen has been at camp or traveling in an area known to have a high tick population), and there is a strong history of fatigue, especially if accompanied by joint pains or headaches, the diagnosis of Lyme disease should be considered.

If you or your teen find a tick on your skin, it should be removed with tweezers and saved. Not all ticks carry Lyme, so the easiest way to evaluate whether or not to treat is to have a doctor send the tick for analysis. If the tick is not a carrier, no treatment is necessary; if it is infected, then your teen can be treated.

Your teen may not realize she was bitten, but may eventually develop the trademark "bull's-eye" rash: this is a large red spot that expands to six inches in diameter, with a clearing in its center. However, not all patients exhibit the rash. Otherwise, the Lyme sufferer will present with a variety of symptoms. The disease has three phases: In the first phase, the patient may develop the rash a few days after the bite. Some may complain of fever, chills, malaise, stiffness of the neck muscles, headache, and muscle and joint aches. Many patients are not diagnosed at this stage because of the vagueness of symptoms, so they move on to the next phase. At this stage the patient complains of a stiff neck, headache, fatigue, and may present with a Bell's palsy (inflammation of a facial nerve that paralyzes half of the face). Later, untreated patients may demonstrate neurological problems as a result of inflammation of the brain. Others may manifest myocarditis, which is an inflammation of the heart muscles. Fortunately, heart defects are not common at this point. Some untreated patients may develop recurrent arthritis or further neurological damage leading to memory loss. The cardiac manifestations will range from persistent pericarditis to a heart block in which the conduction system of the heart is damaged.

Early diagnosis is key, since these very serious complications are preventable by adequate and early treatment. Currently the tests for Lyme are markedly improved in their accuracy, and if diagnosed early, Lyme can generally be treated successfully with a few weeks of oral antibiotics.

Getting teens to take responsibility for themselves in areas such as tick-bite prevention is an important step toward maturity. Walking in woody areas with shorts is an open invitation to ticks. Teens should be taught to wear long pants tucked into socks while strolling through woods and high-grassed areas. Checking for ticks after being outdoors is also important.

■ Medications

Many medications, both prescription and over-the-counter, may cause fatigue. If your teenager is on any type of medication, be sure to include this information when you are discussing his fatigue with a doctor. The most common medications that cause fatigue are antihistamines, but even medications that are purported to not be sleep-inducing may still cause a slight drowsiness in some people. Check with your teen's physician about this if you are concerned.

■ Mononucleosis

Most people who've had it remember their bout with "mono." Who could forget a sore throat so painful you are willing to have surgery to "cut out the pain" and exhaustion so profound you can hardly move?

Because it is teenagers who usually get the classic symptoms of this horrible sore throat, everyone assumes that the infamous "kissing disease" is the price for "fooling around." However, because the virus replicates in the cells (lymphocytes) in the back of the throat, a good cough or sneeze by someone infected with the virus may also leave you with the gift of mono. (However, it is not passed by sharing a glass.) As for transmission within the family, estimates are that siblings have a 20 percent chance of getting mono from an ailing brother or sister. The good news is that many people, including teens and pre-teens, have already had mono, and don't even know it. This may be the reason why intrafamily transmission is low.

Although the "classic" symptoms of mono are sore throat, fever, swollen lymph nodes, and exhaustion, many patients have so mild a case that it can be missed. A "cold" may in fact have been mono. It is possible to have mono with very subtle symptoms, which is responsible for a teen's feeling tired. Routine tests may not pick this up. To diagnose the disease in a patient with subtle mono, it may be necessary to measure a battery of antibodies against the Epstein-Barr virus. Several other infections, cytomegalovirus for example, can give you "mono-like" symptoms and, they too, need special tests to determine their presence.

> **Seventeen-year-old Ken,** *who complained of being "exhausted," is a good example of how the illness sometimes progresses. Ken noted that in January he returned to school and was falling asleep in class. There was nothing I could find that was different in his schedule and no immediate stresses had been recently added to his life. His pediatrician had evaluated him in late January, and new blood work done by my office in February failed to reveal anything; an office mono test was negative, and the physical examination was completely normal except for a few not very significant swollen neck glands. An Epstein-Barr virus profile was ordered to see if he had ever had mono. A few days later the tests revealed the presence of antibodies against EBV. This told us that Ken had had the virus at least six or eight weeks ago. The presence of this antibody was waning but it provided the evidence needed that his EBV contact was fairly recent. It permitted me to make the hypothesis that he had been ill in December, and we were seeing the remnants of the mono infection.*
>
> *Since each patient takes his or her own time to recover, there was nothing to give us a clue when Ken would be over the exhaustion. Because Ken was already recovering on his own, all I could do was monitor his illness until he made a full recovery a couple of months later.*

During the acute phase, there is no specific treatment for mono. The sore throat and exhaustion are due to viral infection and, therefore, antibiotics are of no use. However, a short course of prednisone (a steroid similar to hydro-cortisone) given in a tapering dose over one week will often alleviate some of the sore throat symptoms and allow the patient to swallow more easily. Some physicians (and parents) prefer not to treat with steroids because of their side effects, but I consider it no different than the tapering dose of steroids used with a bad case of poison ivy. Check with your doctor to see if this is recommended. During this acute phase the spleen is often swollen. Since a swollen spleen could be subject to rupture, it is vital that anyone with acute mononucleosis not play contact sports. Drinking alcohol during the acute phase is also dangerous. Inflammation of the liver and mild hepatitis often accompanies mono. It will go away in almost all cases but during the acute phase alcohol will only aggravate the situation. Since each teen will recover at his own pace, consult with your physician as to when recovery is complete enough to resume normal activities.

Each case of mono is unique. The lucky will get better in a few weeks, while others may take a few months to get back to their usual activity level.

■ Thyroid

This gland will be discussed in detail on p. 371 in the section concerning the neck area. However, for now I will mention that both an excess of thyroid hormone and a deficiency of it can cause patients to be tired. A routine thyroid test is often a part of an assessment for someone who is complaining of fatigue.

The Head

Headaches

Though some patients and their parents fear that the complaint of recurring headaches may signal a brain tumor or some mysterious malady, most headaches signal nothing more complicated than a misuse of the facial and head muscles.

Frequently, headaches signal muscle contracture headaches. In this type, facial muscles will be overused as the person clenches her facial muscles—sometimes this comes from grinding her teeth, or as a result of an imbalance of jaw growth. Since the top and bottom of the jaw grows unevenly, the chance of muscle imbalance during adolescence is quite great. The term "tension" headache is applicable, but it refers to muscle tension and not emotional tension.

As the child becomes a teenager, the possibility of migraine is also considered. Children don't generally suffer migraines, and those who are destined to have them one day may occasionally have head pain, but more frequently have inexplicable bouts of stomachache or a frequent history of motion sickness.

For proper diagnosis, your teen's physician must take a "headache history": How long has the teen been suffering this type of headache, which part of the head is involved, is it constant or pulsating, how long does it last, is there nausea, vomiting, or dizziness, and does the patient see or hear anything unusual before or during the ache? Lastly, is there fever or any congestion associated with the headache?

Although laboratory data helps, a solid history and a few key parts of the physical exam will yield the information needed for the doctor to make a correct diagnosis.

■ Migraine

A migraine headache is due to spasms and contractions of blood vessels in the brain. This headache is triggered in two phases; the first is a dilation (expansion) of arteries, the second is a spastic occlusion of the arteries, which is what produces the headache. These headaches are often described as pounding or throbbing. Generally one set of arteries is involved in the brain and the patient complains of a headache that is localized to that side of the head.

In the classic migraine, the patient complains of an "aura," during which time unusual lights, or flashes, can be seen. Strange noises may be heard, and a feeling of nausea and dizziness may be experienced. The sufferer has difficulty focusing, and he may even appear confused, sometimes to the point that parents may suspect drug use. (Lewis Carroll's description of Alice getting larger and smaller is believed to stem from the fact that he was a migraine sufferer.)

If the headache sufferer describes an aura, then diagnosis is easy. However, not all migraines have an aura, and tension headaches can also be very severe.

Most patients start treatment with over-the-counter analgesics such as ibuprofen and acetaminophen, which are usually ineffective for this type of headache. Today we have a whole new group of medications that are injected, taken by mouth, or inhaled through the nose, and these can prevent migraine if taken soon enough, permitting the sufferer to function at school or work. This is a major breakthrough in treatment since previously patients who had migraines would be unable to attend classes, go to work, and generally had to stay in a dark room to alleviate symptoms. Most physicians use a drug that blocks the effects of 5-hydroxytryptamine, which is felt to be the chemical release that ultimately is responsible for the pain. One of the first of this group to contain sumatriptan (the blocking compound) is Imitrex. Some newer medications are now on the market. Clearly the correct diagnosis needs to be made and treatment monitored, since the more powerful migraine drugs carry the risk of serious side effects.

One last factor to keep in mind: Some migraine attacks are triggered by certain foods. The standard ones are chocolate, wines containing sulfites (even with teens!), and strong-smelling cheeses. To identify which ones may be affecting your teen, have her jot down what she ate the day of the headache. Eventually a profile of some "trigger" foods will be revealed.

■ Muscle Contraction, or "Tension Headaches"

Fortunately, the most commonly occurring headache is one due to the misuse or overuse of muscles. This is no different than a runner who runs a marathon or runs a mile using a poor gait. The former runner can expect pain from "overuse" of the muscles; the latter from "misuse" of the muscles. Both yield similar results, and muscle contraction headaches are no different.

The face, head, and back of the neck are covered with muscles. The teen who frequently clenches his teeth, or who chews a lot of gum, or who grinds his teeth at night (called bruxism) is both misusing and overusing the muscles of the jaw. Aches along the temple and sides of the face will be perceived as a "headache."

Although muscle relaxants like ibuprofen or acetaminophen are therapeutic, the key is to stop the muscle misuse. For example, bite plates worn at night may be necessary for the tooth-grinding patient, but simply stopping gum-chewing may suffice if that is suspected as the cause of the headaches.

Pains along the back of the neck may come from sleeping in such a way that the neck muscles are placed at an awkward angle. Consider whether your teen sleeps with too many or too thick a pillow. Neck pain can also result from "slouching" and walking with bad posture that throws the neck forward. A similar phenomenon may occur from computer use. Kids spend hours and hours at their computers, and if the monitor is not positioned correctly, it can cause head pain. If I think that the problem is the computer, I ask the teen to sit at the computer in my office to show me how he types and where his monitor is. Laptops on a lap are a particular problem because the monitor is too low in relation to the keyboard. Check your setup at home to make sure it is comfortable for your teen (and other family members!).

Eye strain can also cause headaches. The teen who is struggling to see the blackboard, constantly using a computer, or straining the eyes for any other reason will have headaches. If you have any concern, an eye examination by an ophthalmologist is in order (also see "The Eyes," p. 352).

Temporomandibular joint syndrome (TMJ) frequently starts during puberty. Teens may have a slight malocclusion (the top and bottom jaw do not yet meet evenly) and may complain of a sudden, sharp and often piercing pain in the ear, pointing to a spot just in front of the small part of the ear lobe that covers the opening to the ear canal. An examination generally proves that it is not an ear infection, but rather a temporary inflammation of the temporal mandibular joint. The patient may hear a small "click" that occurs in the affected area when he opens and closes his mouth. This, along with the pain, is TMJ syndrome. A common treatment (but one that teens hate) is the use of a nightguard. This device is specifically fitted by the orthodontist to prevent the tension on the joint by altering the bite.

Another common headache complaint related to the jaw is the facial headache that occurs after a visit to the orthodontist for an "adjustment." The shifting of the teeth by the appliance causes temporary discomfort.

While these are all generally referred to as "tension headaches," I try not to use this term because it implies to many teens that the headaches are due to emotional instead of physical tension and therefore that the headache is not real. When I have a patient who has been diagnosed with "tension headache," I make sure she understands that it is muscle tension that is causing the headache and that I know that the pain is quite real.

Regardless of the reason for the muscle aches, the treatment remains the same. Muscle relaxation exercises, heat, and muscle relaxant medications are the treatment of choice. While treating the muscles, it is critical to search for clues as to the teenager's "stress" level overall. The tension of the day may be translated into the tension of the face, and without appreciating the underlying stress you never fully treat the tension headache.

■ Sinus Headaches

Like a drainpipe from your kitchen sink, the sinuses are intracranial drainage systems that create trouble if blocked. Children do not have fully developed sinuses, since we are not born with them; for that reason, it takes until puberty before they can cause trouble and get infected. Allergy patients with frequent runny noses, patients who have a significant nasal deviation or break, and patients who have an obstruction in the nose, such as a polyp, all will be particularly prone to "sinus infections."

Sinuses are located in several areas of the head—above the nose and between the eyes (ethmoid), toward the back of the head (sphenoid), and on either side of the nose and under the eyes (maxillary). The location of the infected sinus will determine the whereabouts of the head pain. Infection of the frontal sinuses above the nose can give the patient pain over the eyes, while infection of the ones further back, which are located quite close to the brain, can lead to brain infection. Commonly, the teen will complain of pain under the eyes and on either side of the nose, if the maxillary sinuses are infected. Since the floor of these sinuses touches the roof of the top teeth, a patient may complain of dental pain but really be suffering from a sinus infection.

The usual signs of a sinus infection are pressure over the area affected, nasal congestion, and a foul smell or taste. The nasal discharge is generally thick and yellow or greenish. Heavy post-nasal drip can also be a major symptom. The patient will experience a bad taste, will smell bad to others, and may have a diminished sense of smell and taste.

A patient with a sinus infection requires antibiotics to kill the bacteria and treatment to improve drainage (such as inhaling steam) or a nasal spray your doctor will prescribe. A true case of sinusitis may require at least a month of treatment. It is vital to take the full course of medicine required, even if the teen feels better before having taken it all. Very rarely an infection requires surgical drainage.

Sometimes, because of repeated throat infections, the tonsils and the adenoids get so enlarged that the patient has trouble draining mucous. Surgical removal is the only way of "shrinking" the adenoids or tonsils. Patients with "palatal speech" need to have their adenoids checked for enlargement, as the large tissue prevents clear speech. "Palatal speech" comes from closing the glottis, which is effectively done with large adenoids. The speech seems to be coming just from the mouth with little from the vocal box.

■ Systemic Diseases

In some cases, headache is the result of a metabolic problem and only a part of the issue. For example, the diabetic patient, the patient with elevated thyroid levels, or the patient with renal problems may complain of headaches. Often, treating the disease treats the headache. Even a simple cold can cause a headache. When the cold is gone, so are the headaches.

■ Trauma

After a concussion, patients may suffer from headaches that may last for weeks. Although some patients have migraine-like symptoms, usually there is nothing distinctive about these headaches, and they get better. In most situations, the pain lessens each day and the interval between headaches begins to get longer. However, if headaches worsen, you should contact your teen's doctor immediately.

It is not unusual for a teen to get headaches after some type of head trauma while playing football or another physical contact sport. If the trauma is severe, a doctor should be consulted right away, but if relief is obtained with analgesics, the likelihood of anything serious is very low. However, if the headache is accompanied by nausea, or vomiting, *regardless of the severity of trauma*, you need to contact your doctor. Those headaches may actually represent increased pressure on the brain, and the physician needs to check your teen. (For additional information on concussions, see Chapter 7, "Teens and Sports: Sports-Related Injuries.")

■ Tumors

Headaches may very rarely be the presenting symptom for a brain tumor. In most cases, there are other clues before the headache, but it may happen that the reason a patient finally sees a doctor is due to headaches. The patient with a brain tumor tends to have symptoms related to the area of the brain that contains the tumor. There may be a personality change, visual or auditory disturbances, some hormonal disruption, if the tumor is in the hormone message area, or any of a host of speech or movement abnormalities. The other symptoms give the physician a clue as to the tumor's location.

Often the headache is not severe, and it may be intermittent. The examination may reveal an increase in blood pressure, and on examination of the eye, the doctor may see signs of increased pressure in the brain. To rule out a brain mass, an MRI (magnetic resonance imaging) may be required.

> **One of my patients** *had had a normal physical prior to leaving for college, so I was surprised when I got a call from her reporting that she had begun having terrible headaches. When she called she was in severe pain, crying because the left side "hurt so much." She had also noted episodes of dizziness. What was particularly unusual was the new ringing sounds that she heard in her left ear. Because of this last symptom, I asked her to come home for an evaluation. On examination the most notable finding was diminished hearing in the left ear. I scheduled an MRI, which showed a mass sitting on a nerve in her inner ear. A neurosurgeon removed the mass and today the young woman is applying to medical school. The clue to the early diagnosis was the combination of the sudden headache, unrelenting ringing, the dizziness, and the hearing loss. (Ringing in the ear, called tinnitus, generally does not indicate a brain tumor; it usually indicates a transient inflammation of the inner ear.)*

The Eyes

As part of a physical exam, the doctor checks a teen's eyes to assess general health as well as the health of the eye. The exam begins by checking the color of the white part and the color of the iris. The eye should appear clear and free of any signs of infection. A red, teary eye may signal an inflammation due to an infection or an allergic attack. The obvious runny nose and post-nasal drip with fever may indicate an infection is brewing; the sneezing and itchy nose make allergy more likely. The iris has a central hole, or pupil, and the iris should appear to be even on both sides. The eyes should move in both directions evenly and symmetrically. If one side pulls too much, there is a muscle misalignment. While most of these have been detected in childhood, occasionally one is missed. Either corrective lenses or surgery to correct the muscle imbalance can fix this problem.

Teenagers will often need glasses for the first time. As the eyes grow during puberty, the ability to see distant objects like blackboards may become a problem. Occasionally, the young teen will complain of trouble seeing close objects; she tires easily as she strains to see the written word. The eyestrain of both situations may cause headaches. In both cases, glasses are needed; not that all will wear them. More comfortable contacts and disposables encourage even the most self-conscious teen to have her vision corrected.

The latest correction with laser surgery needs to be approached with caution as it is too new for any long-term studies on the growing eye. Most ophthalmologists will defer laser surgery for teens and wait until the eye has been stable for about three years. It makes no sense to have the procedure only to have the eye change through growth.

Because a general screening in a doctor's office will miss some things, take it seriously if your teen complains of blurred vision. A visit to an ophthalmologist for a thorough exam and to measure the pressure in the eye is recommended.

Allergies

Patients with allergies have chronic swelling under the eyes due to the swelling of the nasal passages. If the teen has frequent congestion, the veins under the eyes will slowly swell and "bags under the eyes" or "allergic shiners" with a purplish hue will result. The treatment is to deal with the allergy and congestion (see p. 355).

Infections

Infections of the eye are fairly common. Conjunctivitis (pink eye) is is an infection of the sclera (white part of the eye), and the eye will be red and itchy with a thick white or creamy discharge. If the infection occurs during sleep a teen may have trouble opening the lids as the discharge causes them to stick together. Warm water compresses loosen the lids and medication can be applied. Teens are no more prone to this than anyone else; however, because they tend to ignore early symptoms, the infection often progresses further than if they had gotten help right away. If the infection is bacterial, antibiotic ointment or drops may be prescribed. If the cause is viral or allergic, antibiotics do not work, but at times it will be difficult to tell if the infection is *not* bacterial. If one can be sure that it is allergic, topical eye drops for allergy or oral antihistamines will help. Viral infections of the eye can be very serious and spread rapidly. These are usually treated by ophthalmologists since proper tools are needed for an accurate diagnosis. Because conjunctivitis is highly contagious, teens should be instructed to wash their hands before and after treatment, to avoid touching the eye, and not to share towels.

A hordeolum, or sty, is an inflammation of one of the eyelid glands, usually from an infection, in which a small, tender round bump may appear. A warm compress applied to the area may help the sty rupture and drain, and antibiotics for the eyelid are sometimes prescribed.

A chalazion is a small lump, or cyst, at the base of the eyelid, which may at first be mistaken for a sty. However, symptoms will disappear while a painless lump remains. They are benign and may be removed by an ophthalmologist if they persist. The lacrimal gland drains through the nose and sometimes a severe nasal congestion will back up the gland, and it will get infected.

Trauma to the Eye

When the eye is hit, a teen may develop a classic "black eye," with its blue-purple coloring caused by blood infiltrating the soft tissue around the eye. As long as the cornea is not scratched and the eye can move in all directions, about all that can be done is to wait for the swelling to subside. Cold compresses will halt the spread of the blood, and this is a useful first line of treatment. If the teen complains of double vision, he needs immediate assessment by an eye doctor.

A scratched cornea is so painful that a visit to the ophthalmologist is inevitable. Medication to lessen the inflammation will be applied, and the doctor is likely to close the eye for a few days with an eye patch.

A much more dangerous and devastating injury is a hyphema, in which the trauma causes bleeding into the anterior (front) chamber of the eye. The patient will complain of not being able to see clearly or of double vision. All hyphema need to be assessed by an eye doctor to determine if surgical correction is needed. Sometimes a period of quiet waiting will be the only treatment, but this is a judgment call to be made by the ophthalmologist.

In all cases of swelling the principal concern is to check if the socket is damaged. A fracture of the zygomatic arch, the bone under the eye, may require surgery to lift the bone.

The Nose

The nose, in addition to its function as the organ of smell and main airway, serves as the major drainage area for the tear ducts, the sinuses, and the ear. The common problems that confront the teenager's nose are infections, trauma, and allergies, any of which can also cause inflammation and blockages.

Allergies

Allergy testing is not always done but should be considered for any teenager who has frequent "colds." Each allergic patient has his own combination of irritants that trigger allergic attacks, but the most frequent ones are dust, pollen, grasses, feathers, cat and dog hair, and ragweed.

The best method for managing allergies is preventive, but this requires that the allergen be identified. The family with a teen who sneezes whenever she visits a home with a cat should be able to avoid her allergen. If there is no obvious cause, you may need to take your teen to an allergist to identify what is triggering the attacks.

Avoidance becomes difficult if the allergens are dust, molds, and ragweed. The ideal bedroom in such cases is one with no carpet, no stuffed animals, no throw pillows, and as little clutter as possible—almost impossible in a teenager's room! Your best bet is to remove the carpet, use a hypoallergenic cover over the mattress, and remove whatever other dust catchers your teen lets you. If he sees some relief, the two of you may be able to work together to clear away a little more clutter.

One of my patients had *relatively good health, despite a history of occasional asthma attacks. She knew that certain foods, dust, and birds were particularly problematic, and her parents had "allergy-proofed" the house. Carpets had been removed and mattresses covered with plastic to minimize dust, there were no pets, and she was careful to watch her diet. She went to college and, inexplicably, her allergy attacks began again. The dorm room was free of carpets and not particularly dusty. However, a detailed examination of her belongings revealed that her new comforter was the culprit.*

She was allergic to the real down feathers in it. Once she replaced the comforter, her allergies became manageable again.

Mold is also a common irritant. Look in the bathroom—if there is a black or brown accumulation along the grouting of the tiles or on the shower curtain, you have mold. By cleaning with the appropriate mildew remover, you can lessen one allergen. Humidifiers are also a breeding ground for molds. These are great for increasing humidity during the winter, but they must be cleaned thoroughly and often.

Grasses and trees pose a problem since even the desert-like climate of Arizona contains vegetation that produces pollen. Frankly, all I can suggest as preventive is to not keep flowers indoors and to not ask your teen to mow the lawn if he has a strong grass allergy. (Watch, suddenly a whole group of teens caught grass allergy!)

■ Prophylacatic Treatments

Prophylactic methods of staving off allergies take two forms. There are medications that coat the nasal lining, the eyes, or the lungs and prevent the allergic attack from taking place. The cromolyn medications, such as Intal inhaler, are used *before* an attack, but require diligence and motivation since the patient has to remember to take the medicine even when not suffering allergic symptoms. Many teens find it difficult to stay with this treatment.

Allergy shots are another form of preventive care. The patient can have a vial of his allergens mixed into a solution to be injected weekly, and eventually monthly, to build up a tolerance to the offending allergens. Time, cost, and dedication are also factors in this method's success.

■ Medications

Antihistamines do exactly what they say: they fight histamine (the chemical responsible for the patient's allergic symptoms). Unfortunately, with many of these medications, primarily the over-the-counter ones, sedation is a side effect. Benadryl, a classic antihistamine, works well, but produces significant drowsiness. Breathing will improve and the rash will get better, but your child will fall asleep in class. There is a better solution. A new class of prescription medications that alter the release of histamine but do not cause sedation are now available. Allegra, Claritin, Zyrtec, and Hismanal are the current standards for allergy relief without drowsiness. They are not 100 percent free of sedative effects but they are certainly an improvement.

For some patients the inflammation from the allergic reaction is so great that corticosteroids are prescribed. Previously, the only way of taking steroids was to use orally dispensed medication. Clearly this had all of the side effects of ongoing steroid use. If your allergy was only in your nose, you took oral steroids that affected the whole body. Today you can target the nose directly and not have the systemic effects of the steroids. The new class of steroid nasal drops and sprays makes the delivery of the steroid easier and safer. The patient usually takes two sprays in each nostril once a day, which is effective for twenty-four hours. These sprays have few adverse side effects.

■ Side Effects of Allergies

Repeated allergy attacks cause more and more swelling of the lining of the nose, which in some patients may become a polyp. If the patient is repeatedly blocked on one side, the otorhinolaryngologist (ear, nose, and throat physician) needs to examine the patient with a flexible scope to see what is causing the block. The procedure is simple, can be done in the doctor's office, and yields a great deal of information. A polyp may need to be removed surgically if it blocks airflow. Sometimes corticosteroid sprays can shrink the polyp. Allergies in patients with deviated septums can also impede airflow and may require, depending on severity, a corrective surgical procedure.

Infections

Infections of the nose are usually viral. The common cold is an example of a viral infection; it requires only symptomatic relief, and antibiotics will be of no use since viruses do not respond to antibiotics. Thick, yellow-green, foul-smelling nasal discharge is usually a sign of sinusitis (a sinus infection), particularly if the phlegm is discharged from one nostril only. (Allergies usually involve both sides.) Pressure over the sinus, a sense of dizziness, and postnasal drip also provide the clue that you are dealing with sinusitis.

If the nasal passage is inflamed, and there is no reason to suspect allergies, then something else is causing the irritation. Smoking is one of the first suspects. Being in very dusty rooms, in rooms undergoing construction, or around some environmental irritant (burning leaves in the back yard) can also cause the nose to discharge. Unfortunately, as wonderful as these explanations may be for the runny nose, you may also have to think of cocaine use (see Chapter 15 in Part Four).

Trauma

Trauma to the nose comes from two sources: foreign objects (including fingers!) in the nostril and blows to the nose. The area immediately inside the nose is filled with blood vessels and can be easily traumatized. The result is a nosebleed from one side. This generally responds to local pressure, usually pinching the nose for five minutes is sufficient. If the bleeding persists, try applying the same pressure with an ice pack over the nose. If that fails, then the physician may have to cauterize (burn) the area to stop the bleeding.

Patients with a history of allergy, patients who have overused over-the-counter nasal sprays, or patients with very sensitive responses to dry air will show the same redness and even bleeding. The bleeding needs to be stopped in the same way, but the underlying reason for the bleeding should also be addressed. Treating the allergy, stopping the sprays, or increasing the humidity in the environment may prevent occurrences.

Blows to the nose can result in swelling or a broken nose. Broken noses most commonly occur on the athletic field or after a fight. If the nose looks like the number "7," it is probably fractured. Go to the emergency room or to your physician, and get an X ray to be certain. In most cases, the nose will have to be reset, but only after the swelling has gone down. On some occasions, the physician can simply pop the nose back into place if the alignment is just right. In either case, the nostrils are packed with cotton and a splint is applied to immobilize the nose while the bone heals. If the septum (the hard membrane separating the nostrils) is broken, it must be repaired surgically.

Some patients have a slight deviation of the nasal septum. It could have been broken slightly at some point and overlooked, or it could be a congenital abnormality. Unless the deviation is significant and impedes air flow or causes repeated infection, it doesn't need to be repaired. If the deviation is so great as to create breathing problems, then surgery may be required to correct this.

The Ears

The ear is divided into three areas. The outer ear consists of the visible portion of the ear as well as the ear canal that leads to the tympanic membrane, or eardrum. The middle ear contains three bones that transmit the vibration from the drum to the nerves. (This site is the one most frequently infected as fluid can be trapped here and become infected.) Lastly, the inner ear contains the cochlea, which is the organ of hearing, and the semicircular canals, which let us maintain our equilibrium.

Teenagers are prone to infections of all three areas: The outer ear is subject to the bacteria that causes acne, trauma from sports, and cosmetic piercing. The childhood malady of frequent ear infections are actually middle ear problems, which improve as the teen's face gets larger and the eustachian tube enlarges. If the inner ear is infected (as it often is with a viral infection), the patient will complain of dizziness and nausea as her normal equilibrium is disrupted. When this occurs, the teenager will complain of a sudden bout of vertigo.

The most common complaint of the ear are the little lumps that are present in the fleshy part of the earlobe, which can be painful. These are oily sebaceous cysts (arising from hair follicles: see Chapter 6, "The Teen Obsession: Skin"), and they are filled with a material similar to that of a pimple. These have a very small opening that is barely noticeable. These should be left alone but teens seem to find it irresistible to pop the lesion, sometimes leaving a small scar or leading to an infection. Naturally the more you play with the cyst the more it hurts.

Cleaning the Ear

While the external ear canal is meant to have some wax as a natural protective, many people feel the need to clean this by inserting cotton swabs in the ear canal. When I tell a teen that his canal is filled with hard obstructing wax that will have to be removed, he is often puzzled: "But I cleaned it, Doc." Yes, but the probing swab basically acted like a cannon rod, pushing the wax further back into the canal. The wax is stripped from the sides of the canal and neatly packed into the back of the canal, close to the eardrum. It has to be removed with an ear curette, which can hurt, or by washing and suctioning by an otorhinolaryngologist (ear, nose, and throat doctor). The external canal is remarkably sensitive and touching it can cause great pain. One curette cleaning, and it's the last time a cotton swab sees that area!

As for the teen who is self-conscious about visible wax in the outer ear, explain that some kids simply make a lot of wax, that it is protective, and that there is little that can be done. (This is exactly the teen who should not use a cotton swab, since there is an excess of wax just waiting to be packed.) Tell him to clean only the outside ear with a cotton swab or a wet washcloth (which has the advantage of being too large to get into the canal). Also explain that as he showers some water will naturally get into the canal and clean away some of the wax. Your physician may prescribe a wax thinner such as Debrox to help eliminate some of wax. This medication works by causing the wax to foam, making it possible to flush and clean the ear with warm water and a small bulb syringe. Even with this treatment, not all of the wax is removed. Teens who have a lot of wax should use audio earphones that cover the ear rather than plug into it; the latter causes even more wax to form.

Ear Infections

"Otitis media," or infection of the middle ear, is the scourge of some children. Frequent doctor visits, antibiotics, tubes in the eardrum, and missed school are part of their daily life. By the teenage years the frequent *middle* ear infections tend to lessen: as the growing teen's eustachian tube elongates, there is better drainage from the ear.

Treatment for middle ear infections aims to promote drainage. Steroid nasal drops or sprays diminish inflammation, salt water sprays moisturize, and antibiotics clear the infection. During the time that the patient has an infection, hearing may be impaired and it's a good idea to go back to the doctor for a hearing check after the full round of antibiotics has been taken. If a teenager gets an ear infection right before a plane trip, she should see her doctor. Fortunately, most physicians allow air travel since the likelihood of a ruptured drum is low; however, it is important to follow the advice of your own doctor. If a rupture does occur, the patient will complain of pain that is suddenly relieved as the drum ruptures and the pressured fluid behind the eardrum is released. She will note two things at once: relief and ooze from the affected ear. Until the drum heals, and it does by itself in most cases, hearing in the lower register is impaired as the drum does not move well until fully healed. In the meantime, contact your physician to have it checked out.

If a full and pressured drum is causing severe pain, or the patient doesn't want to risk a rupture during a plane trip, a physician can rupture the drum in the office. This is a safe, fast, and relatively painless procedure. Doctors now use a laser to make a small hole in the drum to release the pressure.

A teen with a pressured or punctured eardrum must not swim or dive without a doctor's permission. The pressure of deep sea-diving presents the risk of rupturing the eardrum and potential infection. Prior to any dive the nose of the diver has to be cleared of mucous and obstruction or else there will be no way of equilibrating both sides of the eardrum. Anyone with a chronic nasal congestion is advised not to dive. I have had several patients who calmly came in to "get cleared" for diving and also asked for "something for the cold." If there is a doubt, do not dive.

Swimmer's Ear

Swimming in chlorinated pools is unnatural. The waters of nature were not meant to be filled with chlorine. Oceans are a natural byproduct of the earth, filled with salt water and fish; swimming pools are created by some guy digging a hole and pouring chemicals into the water. The external canal is so sensitive that these chemicals can irritate it, causing it to be more easily infected with bacteria: the result is "swimmer's ear." In this condition the canal becomes very red and there is a white-yellow discharge. Just moving the pinna (the earlobe) can elicit pain. The treatment is to clear the canal of infected matter and then apply antibiotic drops into the canal and avoid swimming until it clears up.

Ear Cosmetics and Piercings

Teenagers rarely overlook their ears as they stare in the mirror. Some are quite happy with the result of nature, others feel that their ears stick out too far. These "Dumbo" ears can cause great anxiety and several of my patients have undergone plastic surgery to bring the ears closer to the head. General anesthesia is involved, so it is not a casual procedure. One needs to be sure of the emotional toll that the ears are taking before allowing the surgery.

Others, driven by the latest trend, will put one, two, or more earrings in the ear. Please advise your teen that the upper portion of the ear is cartilage and has little in the way of blood supply. Hence, an infection in that area is hard to treat because antibiotics work poorly if there is a poor blood supply. If you must pierce, avoid the cartilage (the "hard" part) as much as possible. I have had to take out several studs from that area because, once infected, all foreign bodies have to be removed in order for the infection to heal. Not all of the piercings can be unscrewed and removed easily; some have to be cut out.

The only "safe" piercing is the one in the soft fleshy part of the lobe. These can be done by competent jewelers or by doctors who have purchased an "ear piercing" kit. Once the number of holes goes beyond one, the chances of infection increase proportionally. Even a simple earring in the fleshy bottom portion can cause a problem for people if their scars become keloids (large, fleshy scars). If a piercing causes a keloid to form, the keloid generally has to be carefully excised, usually by a plastic surgeon. If you remove it incorrectly, you simply make a new keloid. (For more information on piercings, see Chapter 6, "The Teen Obsession: Skin.")

The Mouth

Although trauma to the mouth is not unique to teenagers, their world of sports, automobiles, and violence raises the likelihood of injury. Infections and trauma of the mouth probably account for most doctor visits for mouth problems. Sports injury, auto accidents, and "horsing around" account for the vast majority of injuries resulting in broken teeth and lacerated lips and gums. Punches to the jaw or falling face first seem more common than most parents appreciate. Sometimes trauma to the jaw will result in mouth pain from the hard shock to the muscles and teeth.

Muscle relaxants are indicated for the pain; ice for the swelling. If bleeding is present then acetaminophen is preferred since aspirin promotes bleeding. If the lip is lacerated and swollen, X rays of the mouth can discern if the patient has any broken teeth. I generally refer these patients to a dental surgeon who can do the X rays and treat the problem immediately.

Braces

Sometimes I think that braces have become part of the process of puberty. More teenagers than ever before wear braces. Part of this is medically necessary; crowded teeth and a poor bite will lead to serious jaw pain later in life, when surgery will be required to correct what could have been taken care of during the teen years. Yet, there is no question that a great deal of the orthodontic care is driven by cosmetics. We are a society that appreciates "perfection," and sometimes parents push their teen into an expensive and time-consuming process in an effort to correct something minor. However, before dismissing your teen's need for orthodontia, get a professional opinion. The number of adults who have orthodontic work done for cosmetic and medical reasons indicate that if you can afford to let your teen get braces during these years, it is a good investment in how he looks, and perhaps in how he feels, in later years.

By the time a child is in sixth grade (and sometimes earlier), most families are trying to decide if she will "need" braces. (Since girls will go through puberty and facial changes earlier than boys, they are the first candidates.) The timing of the braces should coincide with the growth of the mouth, which is undergoing major changes during these years. Braces applied too early may only aggravate a normal process and an unnecessary orthodontic treatment may result in costly corrections later. Check with your own dentist for names of well-respected orthodontists and talk to other families. Then get more than one opinion before deciding what path to follow.

Remember that at each visit, your teen's orthodontist will adjust the braces, which may cause the teeth to shift. Your teen may complain of facial pain or a headache a few hours later, and the pain may last for a few days. In most cases, a muscle relaxant or pain reliever such as ibuprofen or acetaminophen will help. If the headache is severe, the orthodontist should be informed so that future adjustments can be modified. Unfortunately, the medical physician may be called upon to treat the aftermath of the adjustment, and the information may not be relayed to the orthodontist.

Our society has so many teenagers wearing braces that they have now become a badge of pride. Small colored rubber bands are worn by kids without as much as a whimper if all their friends are doing it. Yet, as the teenager gets into the fifteen- or sixteen-year-old range, she can't wait to get them off. This is another good reason for starting at the proper time.

Dental Care

Teens should go to the dentist twice a year. Aside from the obvious need to check for cavities, the teeth should be cleaned and the gums assessed. Sometimes a sharp-eyed dentist will note that the patient is missing enamel and will raise the concern that the patient has been throwing up. A bulimic patient who vomits frequently will show damage to her teeth and absence of some of the tooth enamel due to stomach acid. More than one patient has been "caught" this way.

As teens approach their college years, the "wisdom teeth" can become a problem. Many teenagers have mouths that simply cannot accommodate the new teeth. These third molars come in about the time of the twenty-first birthday and are so named because of the "wisdom" that is supposed to come with age. What use are they? Actually none, and we can do without them (though if they come in properly and do not cause pain they can be kept). Some come in crooked; some don't want to leave their bone "nest" and get "impacted." Just about the time that college bills are due, you may get the notice that the wisdom teeth have to come out. Some dentists prefer a single operation where all four come out at once; others go for a two-step procedure and remove left and then right. All that matters is that they be removed in pairs so that you do not leave one wisdom tooth unopposed. For example, if you remove the top right and not the bottom right, you leave the bottom right at risk for bone decay because there is no stimulation by an opposing tooth.

Lesions

■ Canker Sores

These lesions occur in younger children, but they get worse during puberty. Often confused with herpes simplex (see below), canker sores form inside the mouth. These small white ulcers are unbelievably painful. They, by definition, do not involve the outside of the mouth. Patients who get them will complain of recurrences, often for life, as no one knows what causes them or exactly how to treat them. Nor is it possible to anticipate when they will reemerge.

Left alone, the lesions will resolve spontaneously in about a week. In the meantime, your teen can be made more comfortable by avoiding anything that irritates the area such as orange juice or acid foods like vinegar or pickles. Using a special toothpaste for sensitive gums alleviates the discomfort of brushing daily, and an over-the-counter wash called Glyoxide is useful but it is only a way of cleaning the area. The best that can be done is to alleviate the pain until the sores heal on their own. Cautery of the lesions, use of amino acids and acidophilus have all failed to actually heal the lesions.

Coxsackie Virus

Another ulcerative lesion that teenagers can get, especially during the summer months, is a condition caused by a virus called coxsackie virus. "Herpangina," as this is called, has gray white ulcerations, but they are confined to the back of the throat along the soft palate and tonsils. This painful condition is self-limiting and antibiotics are not required. It is important to be sure of this diagnosis, since the ailment closely resembles herpes. The key is the distribution of the lesions.

Herpes Simplex

Along the border of the colored portion of lip and the juncture with the skin, patients may develop "fever blisters." In fact, these "fever blisters" are actually herpes simplex. Generally the herpes simplex of the mouth is less virulent than that of the genital area, but it still warrants treatment with one of the new antiviral drugs. The lesions are passed on by direct contact and outbreaks are difficult, if not impossible, to prevent. Not all patients are aware that they are about to have an outbreak and the innocent kiss can become a mode of transmission. Clearly one avoids someone with an active sore but that is just common sense. The antiviral cream that is available helps, but it is not usually enough. Patients with recurrent herpes simplex of the lip should have an available supply of the antiviral drug so that at first sign of infection, they can start the medication and avert or lessen a major attack. In some cases, the outbreaks occur so frequently that the patient needs to be on these antiviral drugs for six months. If I think this is the case, I make sure that the lesion is culture-proven as herpes simplex. If needed, I will have a dermatologist consult before undertaking a six-month course of antiviral drugs.

Occasionally, a patient will have a full-blown herpetic attack covering his entire mouth. The mouth is covered from front to back with small ulcers; the patient may be feverish and in great discomfort. Use of hydrogen peroxide mouthwashes and oral topical anesthetics help, but essentially you need to treat the herpetic lesion. (Also refer to Chapter 6, "The Teen Obsession: Skin," and Chapter 10, "Sexually Transmitted Diseases.")

The Tongue

The tongue is filled with small taste buds neatly arranged along the sides and the front and back. A common condition in children is "thrush," but by adolescence teens generally become immune to it. One exception is the teen who is taking antibiotics for acne or for any chronic infection. The daily use of the antibiotic alters the balance of the bacterial-fungal system and coating of the tongue with unusual fungi or bacteria will result. Often it will be difficult to diagnose the organism without the aid of a culture. This is commonly treated with antifungal drugs applied topically.

The Throat

When you look at the back of the throat you see tonsils and a dangling central bell called the "uvula," which should be centrally located. Just behind the uvula is an area that communicates with the nose and is the site of the "postnasal drip" that accompanies so many colds. Sore throats can be caused by a variety of infections.

Many sore throats are actually due to infected phlegm and can easily be treated with antibiotics. Most sore throats are uncomfortable but will go away on their own. However, you need to make sure your teen does not have strep throat (caused by streptococcal Group A bacteria), which needs to be treated with antibiotics. The reason we treat with antibiotics if a patient has streptococcal A infection is to prevent rheumatic heart disease, which may be a consequence of untreated streptococcal A.

Now that "rapid" strep tests are available, the physician can check for strep A in the office. Although not 100 percent reliable, these tests are generally accurate. In some situations, the physician may treat empirically, or order a culture of the throat to be sure of the strep. The culture will take about forty-eight hours to yield results.

One further complication when dealing with a teenager and a "sore throat" is that it may be infectious mononucleosis. There may be pus-like material on the tonsils and the rapid strep test is negative. Since mono presents in the same way as strep, your doctor may order a test to rule out infectious mononucleosis. Keep in mind that not all patients will have a positive test at the beginning of their mono. I always tell patients that, even with a negative mono test, we have to be on the alert. A second test, at least forty-eight hours later, may prove positive (see "Mononucleosis," p. 344).

Tonsillitis

Infection of the tonsils are easy to diagnose because of the amount of pus-like material present. Antibiotics are indicated but not a tonsillectomy. In some cases, the infection of the tonsil is not "on" the tonsil but rather behind it. Then, we speak of a "peri-tonsillar abscess," which will require aggressive management.

Sam came to see me *with a sore throat. I saw that he had an obvious tonsil infection and one side of the soft palate appeared slightly swollen. He was started on antibiotics immediately, and they worked for a few days. However, on the sixth day he came in, and his tonsil was swollen and infected again. Sheepishly he admitted he had gotten better and had forgotten to take his antibiotics. He started again on the same drug since he had improved before. A week later he was significantly better, but forty-eight hours after his last dose, he complained of his tonsil "killing him." I told him that I* *thought he had developed an abscess and asked him to see an otorhino-laryngologist immediately.*

When he arrived at the doctor's office, he could hardly open his mouth and was unable to swallow his own saliva. The doctor inserted a needle into the soft tissue surrounding the tonsil and removed some pus from the area. Sam had immediate relief and was given a full course of antibiotics. When the infection subsided, his tonsils were removed. If Sam hadn't had surgery, he would have had another bout of tonsillitis in a week or so.

One indication for removal of a tonsil is the case just cited. Simply having an infection, or several, is not sufficient reason for a tonsillectomy. However, if you treat a patient, and he improves only to get worse a few days after the antibiotics are discontinued, and this pattern is repeated again, then the patient has a chronic infection and a tonsillectomy is usually warranted.

The Neck Area

Neck Pain

Pinched Nerves

Occasionally a teenager will have a deformity of the cervical spine that was not picked up when she was a child. She may complain of weakness in the arms and shoulders and a "tingling" sensation migrating down from the neck. A referral to a neurologist or orthopedist may be in order, or your teen's doctor may order appropriate X rays (including an MRI of the neck) to detect a pinched nerve, possibly from a deformed disc. The same procedure would take place if a teen had a "burner" (a pinched nerve that causes a "burning" sensation) while playing sports (see Chapter 7: Teens and Sports: Sports-Related Injuries).

Sports Injuries

The muscles of the neck are incredibly complex since they control the head and allow it to flex and extend, to move side to side, and to rotate clockwise and counterclockwise. All of these muscles are prone to injury. Sports and auto injuries account for most neck strains (see Chapter 7).

"Wryneck"

Great neck pain can also result from sleeping "wrong," often by using too many pillows. Doctors call this a torticollis, literally a "twisted neck in spasm," or more commonly, "wryneck." Treatment requires muscle relaxants and heat to the area. Most of the prescription muscle relaxants that are strong enough may relax the whole patient to the point of feeling dizzy and tired, so this type of medication should be taken only at night. This may be welcomed relief since the pain may prevent sleep.

The Glands

There are four types of glands in the neck area: the lymphatic, the salivary, the thyroid, and the parathyroid glands. Each has a very specific function in the body, and bodily symptoms as well as a physical examination of any gland that is suspect is important in assessing what is wrong.

Lymph Glands

When someone says "My glands are swollen," she is are generally referring to the lymph glands (or lymph nodes). These glands, filled with lymphocytes, or white cells, serve as a local filtration system responsible for helping fight off infection. If the area that the gland filters is infected, then the gland swells as part of the defense system. If your tooth is infected or you have a sore throat or a cut on your chin, the glands in the neck will respond to the infection. If the thigh is infected, the glands in the groin will be swollen.

The normal lymph gland feels rubbery and is freely movable from the surrounding tissue. Its location is less important than its consistency. However, the fact that these glands are present requires careful examination, and most doctors will order an occasional white cell count and differential count to see the types of cells that the body is making for a complete diagnosis.

The infected gland, once it does its job, does not return to its normal size immediately. It took some doing to swell and it will take some time for the swelling to go down. Since kids with ongoing postnasal drip, infected acne, infected facial hair follicles, infected ear lobes, and frequent sore throats get swollen glands, it is not unusual for parents to be concerned about the seemingly constant presence of swollen neck glands. Swollen glands that do not go down and that do not seem to stem from a localized infection merit further investigation.

There are two major types of cancer related to the lymphatic system: lymphoma and leukemia. A lymphoma is a malignant mass of lymph tissue. Though lymph glands throughout the body will contain malignant cells once the disease begins, the mass itself is separate from the swollen lymph glands. A common place for the mass is in the mid-portion of the chest, and it may be found during a chest X ray.

One of the better-known lymphomas is Hodgkin's disease, named after the physician who identified specific cells in the tumor mass. Hodgkin's lymphoma may be diagnosed as a result of swollen glands that do not go away. It is a particularly important disease during the teen years, since 60 percent of the cases are seen in ten- to fifteen-year-olds.

As part of any checkup, the doctor inspects the glands in your teen's body. If the glands do not feel as they should, a chest X ray and a white-cell count may be ordered; the doctor will also check for a swollen spleen and liver, since these can harbor cancerous lymphocytes. If all of these are positive, then the patient most likely has a lymphoma. A biopsy of the gland usually follows, followed by MRIs of the abdomen. The earlier the diagnosis, the better the prognosis. Today the disease is highly treatable with medication (chemotherapy), radiation, or a combination depending on the patient's age, the stage of the disease, and "tumor burden" (how much lymphoma is present).

Other lymphomas, represented by different lymphocytic cancer cells, can present in the adolescent years and they, too, will start with "swollen glands." The type of lymphoma will be determined by biopsy and the protocol for treatment depends on the type.

Sometimes the "swollen glands" are the first symptom for another type of cancer, called leukemia. The difference here is that there is no mass involved. The cancer does not accumulate in one area, such as the chest, but rather affects the white cells directly. The bone marrow, which produces blood cells, becomes filled with these abnormal cells and soon the total production of *all* cells from the marrow is compromised. The patient is unable to make normal white cells, red cells, and the small cells that help in clotting, the thrombocytes. Hence, the teen with leukemia may bleed and be susceptible to infections, and therefore run inexplicable fevers; he may complain of pains that are deep inside (bone pain); and he may even show nothing more than "swollen glands."

Parents should understand that most cases of "swollen glands" end up being nothing more than intermittent viral or bacterial infections. Only the rare teenager has a malignancy.

Salivary Glands

Swollen salivary glands in a teenager may signal a patient with an eating disorder, or the swelling may be due to frequent dehydration. Teens who do not drink enough water after participating in sports, or those who vomit frequently, as would a bulimic, may create thick saliva that can lead to small calcium stones that block drainage of the glands. These painful swollen glands can mimic the swelling of lymph glands but they are identified by their location at the angle of the jaw and directly beneath the jaw. The teen will complain of a bad taste and pain at the site of the gland. The otorhinolaryngologist (ear, nose, and throat doctor) will have to probe the duct to remove the stone.

The Thyroid Gland

Almost every patient who comes into my office with a weight problem or depression will ask, "Could it be my thyroid?" Either they have read an article in a current magazine about someone who was "missed" as having a thyroid problem, or they inevitably know someone whose doctor just diagnosed thyroid as the cause of their problem. The thyroid gland is sometimes overrated in what it can and cannot do. In order to appreciate the importance of the thyroid, we need to review its function and location.

The thyroid is located on either side of the trachea just at the Adam's apple level. It has a smooth, slightly pebbly consistency and there is a lobe of thyroid tissue sitting on each side of the trachea. The thyroid gland is the central thermal regulator in the body. It is responsible for setting the body's metabolic rate, which is the rate at which the body consumes calories. If the rate is high, the patient needs more calories in order to function; the person with a lower rate needs fewer calories. The patient who has *hyper*thyroidism (too much thyroid hormone) will complain that he eats and finds it difficult to gain weight. The patient who has *hypo*thyroidism (too little thyroid hormone) has a long way to go before he "needs" to eat, so unfortunately, this teen gains weight with very little food going in.

To examine the thyroid, the doctor stands in front or behind the patient, puts her fingers on either side of the gland, and has the patient swallow. As the swallowing takes place, the doctor can feel the thyroid and can determine that the lobe is present, whether it is enlarged, and whether there is a mass inside the thyroid.

If there is normal growth and, in girls, regular menstrual cycles, testing for thyroid function needn't be a part of a teenager's regular physical. However, if there is an indication of a problem, the physician will be looking for the following possibilities: thyroiditis, hypothyroidism, or hypothyroidism.

Hashimoto's thyroiditis is an autoimmune condition in which the body produces antibodies that work against the thyroid gland, causing inflammation. The disease is four times more common in girls than it is in boys and occurs quite frequently during the teen years. This is a challenging condition to diagnose because the blood work may appear to be normal and the thyroid may be only slightly enlarged, or in a patient who is overweight, it can simply be difficult to perform the exam adequately. In the meantime, the patient will tell you that she is exhausted beyond reason, and her periods may be irregular. She is struggling with weight, and she may be exercising without losing weight. This condition can only be definitively diagnosed if the physician orders the tests for antibodies against the thyroid gland.

> **Nancy complained that she** *could not lose weight, was falling asleep in class, and was moody. Her periods were on time but scant; she was on the Pill, thus further confusing the issue. At eighteen, she felt miserable and "knew something was wrong." Her other doctor had done blood work, and the results were normal. Since she'd had mononucleosis a few months earlier, he attributed her fatigue to the lingering effects of mono. The only finding was a slight enlargement of her thyroid, and based on that clue I ordered a thyroid scan. The scan proved the gland to be enlarged and her thyroid antibodies were markedly elevated. Ironically it may well have been the mono virus that caused the autoimmune production of the thyroid antibodies in the first place.*
>
> *Prescribing a thyroid replacement pill to be taken daily made all the difference in the world to Nancy. She needs to take the medication for life, but she didn't mind once the beneficial results of the thyroid pill were evident. In some rare cases, the gland can return to normal function.*

In hypothyroidism, not enough thyroid hormone is being produced, and the patient has the following symptoms:

1. Sluggish, weak, or tired. The patient constantly complains of not being able to keep up physically. She may have trouble staying alert and awake. The simplest daily activity takes an inordinate toll in exhaustion.
2. Weight gain

3. Growth interruption
4. Myxedema, characterized by a thickening of the skin
5. Cold intolerance. While everyone else is walking around in short sleeves, the individual is covered up with a long-sleeved shirt or sweater.
6. Slow heart rate
7. Constipation
8. Hair thinning or falling out
9. Irregular to absent menstrual cycles
10. Low blood sugar
11. Muscle cramps
12. Husky voice
13. Occasionally because of an accumulation of carotene (the yellow color in squash, pumpkins, and carrots), the patient may take on a yellow hue.

Once diagnosed, hypothyroidism is easily treated with hormone replacement pills taken daily.

Marsha had been a little late *in her development, but she was growing the appropriate amount yearly. Her menses had started at thirteen and she was doing well in school. Suddenly, at 5'3", she stopped growing, began to gain weight, and her menses stopped. At first her parents were not concerned about the height since her mother was not particularly tall. Yet when we examined Marsha's growth curve, she clearly was projected to grow beyond her mother's height. Moreover, the suddenness with which she stopped growing and the increase in her weight made it suspicious. Indeed, a blood test revealed her thyroid count was off. Further tests were conducted, which resulted in Marsha being placed on a daily synthetic thyroid replacement pill. She soon started to grow, lose weight, and feel more energetic. By the end of high school, she had grown to 5'7" and, to date, is still taking thyroid replacement pills.*

The hypothalamus in the brain makes critical decisions for the individual. If a patient is starving, either deliberately or due to dire circumstances, the hypothalamus decreases the metabolic rate so that what little food the body gets can go a long way. This may result in hypothalamic hypothyroidism. Teens with anorexia nervosa manifest this disorder. If there is a lack of food being taken in, the hypothalamus decides that it is important to prevent pregnancy and lowers specific hormone levels, such as estrogen and progesterone. Other symptoms of hypothalamic hypothyroidism are similar to those of a nonfunctioning thyroid gland with little or no production of thyroid hormones.

Hyperthyroidism occurs when the thyroid malfunctions, putting the body in "overdrive." It is less common but has the following symptoms:

1. Weight loss, despite increased appetite
2. Elevated heart rate and blood pressure
3. Diarrhea
4. Menstrual irregularity
5. Rapid growth
6. Eye abnormalities. With Graves' disease (see below), the eyes may bulge.
7. Increased sweating
8. Anxiety
9. Tremor
10. Sleep problems

With such a myriad of symptoms, one would guess that the diagnosis is fairly easy. However, the patient may experience symptoms before the laboratory data can confirm the diagnosis. Test results for thyroid function may show subtle abnormalities in the first phase of the disorder, and serial testing may be needed before the diagnosis is confirmed.

In hyperthyroidism, the thyroid gland has ceased to respond to the pituitary and is independently producing hormones. This is exactly what happens in two diseases: Graves' disease and thyroid cancer.

In Graves' disease, the thyroid is overstimulated, and treatment is aimed at blocking the overproduction of thyroid hormone. The symptoms include all those of hyperthyroidism; the bulging eyes are often a clue to making a proper diagnosis.

The younger the patient, the more likely it is that she will respond to antithyroid medication. Your physician will choose between propylthiouracil and methimazole as first-line treatments. Because of the increased agitation experienced by these patients, attempts to block some of the adrenaline-like effects of the excess hormone are met by using a beta-blocker such as propranolol to calm the increased anxiety, sweating, and fast pulse. Along with medication, a course of radioactive iodine treatment is used to further suppress the gland's production of hormone. Occasionally, when other methods don't work, some physicians advocate surgical removal of the gland. Although rare, Graves' is seen in the adolescent population and accounts for the most common reason one would have elevated thyroid levels.

Elsa, now twenty-two, *has been my patient since she was twelve. She had been healthy all her life, but she suddenly started to notice that she was "very anxious" all the time. She had episodes where she would feel her heart racing so fast that she thought it would "pop out of her chest." Her weight had started to drop, and she noted intermittent diarrhea. All this happened during a stressful period when she had started a new job. At first all of this was ascribed to the job, poor and intermittent eating, and anxiety. Friends suggested she was having "panic attacks," and she was so nervous that she agreed with them, until finally she decided to check in with me.*

Her examination revealed that she had lost weight; she had a slight increase in her blood pressure, and a marked increase in her heart rate. Her hands trembled, and she had a general air of anxiety throughout the examination. She was drenched with sweat despite the air conditioning in the office. Her neck examination revealed a slight increase in the size of her thyroid and her eyes were slightly bulged. The laboratory tests confirmed high thyroid levels. She was seen by an endocrinologist who started her on propylthiouracil and a course of iodine radiotherapy was scheduled. Within one week of medication, she started to feel significantly better.

If a patient has a tumor, experienced hands may be able to locate a nodule on the thyroid. The nodule itself is not diagnostic of a cancer but it needs to be checked out. If there is a doubt as to the malignancy of a nodule, a thyroid scan will show whether the nodule is functioning (cancerous nodules tend to be nonfunctioning). The scan should reveal either a cystic lesion (a noncancerous condition) or a malignancy. Thyroid cancers have a very high cure rate.

Erika, twenty-one, called *to ask if a "lump" she had found in her neck was important. She felt fine, but while stroking her neck she felt "something hard" in the right side. Her examination, with the exception of some increased weight, was negative. However, there was a firm half-inch mass sitting in the left lobe of the thyroid. A sonogram was conclusive that there was a mass in the area. A surgeon who specializes in thyroid disorders was called and he performed a needle biopsy. This procedure removes a small piece of the mass for testing and allows for a definitive diagnosis. Erika was found to have thyroid cancer, which is highly treatable and has a high cure rate. Her thyroid was removed; she was placed on thyroid replacement pills and resumed her normal life.*

Parathyroid Glands

Sitting next to the thyroid are two sets of small glands called the parathyroid glands, which produce a unique hormone to control calcium. These four glands are difficult to examine by hand, and normalcy is assumed if the calcium-blood levels are within the acceptable range. The gland is rarely thought of for pathology in this age group. However, occasionally the calcium level will be very high and an investigation is in order. In most cases it turns out that the patient has been increasing calcium intake by drinking a lot of dairy products or taking supplements.

The Spine and Back

The Spine

Scoliosis

Every teenager must be screened for curvature of the spine (scoliosis). It is required on almost every school or sports form that is filled out by a doctor. Some patients with curves will complain of back pain, screening is particularly critical in this age group. Girls are more likely to suffer scoliosis and the only pathological explanation seems to be that "it runs in the family." Most of the curves will be noted as pubertal changes occur and growth is accelerated. By age ten, girls should be screened carefully.

With scoliosis, there is an abnormal curve along the thoracolumbar (the chest and lower back, or lumbar area) spine that causes some rotation to the back as the teen bends forward. In being screened for scoliosis, the teenager stands straight with arms at the side and then bends forward while the doctor observes from behind. (It is best if the patient is dressed only in underpants; girls are best observed with no bra so that there are no impediments to seeing the shoulder blades, the spine, and the natural curve of the back.) A slight difference in shoulder height may be a clue that there is a mild difference in alignment, or a constant lower back pain may signal the improper balance of the muscles of the back. Sometimes, as seen from the front, girls may appear to have a discrepancy of breast height. Or, the doctor may observe that one side of the back is higher (rotated) than the other. In obvious cases the space normally present between the trunk and the arms will be different from left side to right; the height of the shoulder blades may also be on different planes.

If a curvature is diagnosed, the teen should be sent to an orthopedist for assessment and X rays should be ordered. Time is important with curvatures, and it is important that a parent make sure that the proper steps are taken. Both scoliosis and kyphosis (see below) can progress dramatically during the teen's growth spurt. What was a minor curve in the five-foot-tall teen may become quite dramatic when she reaches five-four.

A popular misunderstanding is that book bags and poor posture cause scoliosis. This is not the case. A teen inherits this problem; he or she does not create it. However, kids with book bags may also have scoliosis, so the lower back pain should not be dismissed easily.

On an X ray scoliosis reveals an "S" shape of the spine, usually in the lower portion, as well as a rotation of the vertebra. (After X rays are taken, ask to keep them yourself. Succeeding doctors may want to compare X rays taken at different ages, and you will simplify your life by holding on to them rather than expecting the hospital to do it for you.)

If the scoliosis is mild, then physical therapy to strengthen the back muscles is usually prescribed, but the physical therapy will not correct the curve. However, the teenager should be monitored every six months until growth stops to be sure that the curve is not progressing. In fact, some kids who are growing exceptionally fast may need monitoring in three-month intervals.

The critical time for monitoring scoliosis is during the adolescent growth period. Since boys eventually will grow more dramatically per year, a male teen with scoliosis warrants very careful and frequent monitoring.

If the scoliosis approaches a curve of 25 degrees, then the teen may need a back brace. (Clearly, discussion about bracing starts before one reaches this number, and the decision is a difficult one to make.) A brace must be molded for each individual, and its purpose is to force the patient's back into a straighter position. Most teens will be expected to wear it both day and night. Success depends greatly on the compliance of the teenager. To say that the wearing of a brace is difficult just at a time when a teen wants so badly to be "normal" is an understatement. The brace immediately sets a teen apart from her peers, and some activities are impossible while wearing it. Yet, I am amazed at how well some kids will adapt to the need for this appliance. The conflict of what you want to do and what you need to do is usually an "adult" behavior. These kids demonstrate that daily by simply wearing this mold.

Unfortunately, some others rebel and refuse to wear it; they suffer in the end as the curve progresses.

If the curve gets beyond 30 to 40 degrees and the teen is still growing, the orthopedist may recommend a spinal fusion to prevent a further continuation of the curve. Stainless steel rods are inserted on the side of the spine and the vertebrae are hooked onto these supporting braces. When the spine is straightened there are now open spaces where the bones had touched with the curve. These are filled with bone grafts so that the wedges of bone maintain the straight back. Only the fused part of the spine, which contained the curve, is immobile; the remainder maintains its flexibility. Despite the seriousness and extent of this surgery, it is not the type that can be postponed until the teen "is older." The very nature of the progress of the scoliosis demands critical timing in those cases where surgery appears inevitable. If one waits too long, the curvature only progresses and eventually it gets harder to correct.

During an examination for camp, *Leslie's pediatrician noted that she had a curve in her spine. She was thirteen at the time and measured a bit less than five feet; she had no complaints of back pain. Leslie had started puberty but had not yet had her first menses. The orthopedist measured a curve of 26 degrees involving the lower thoracic and upper lumbar vertebrae. At this degree she was close to needing a brace but it was decided to wait three months and reassess the curve. When the new X rays were taken, they showed that her curve had increased to 32 degrees. With a lot of growing left, Leslie was measured for a brace that went from the back of her neck to the top of the hips. She was to wear it full time. Three months later X rays taken of Leslie while in the brace revealed a curve of 12 degrees. Leslie's compliance was exceptional. Three months later, and still no menses, her measurements in the brace had improved to 8 degrees and she was allowed a few hours out of the brace on a daily basis. Six months went by and the degree had fallen to 6 in the brace, and she was 61½ inches tall. Nearly two years after the brace was started, she is 63 inches tall and her brace curve is approximately 10 degrees. With the onset of her menses, Leslie is almost at her full height, and X rays show that her bones are fusing. With this new information, Leslie is allowed more time out of the brace for the next few months. It is expected that as her bones finally fuse within the next year, the bracing will stop, and treatment will have been a success. Without the brace, and without Leslie's compliance, she was on a course destined for spinal surgery.*

Philip is the other extreme. *At twelve years of age, I had to do a camp exam and noted a subtle rotation of his chest as I checked for scoliosis. At 5'6", he still had a lot of growing left and I referred him to an orthopedist. He had no back pain, no neurological signs, and he essentially viewed a visit to the orthopedist with curiosity. His mother was surprised as she viewed him as having normal posture. When the orthopedist examined Philip he estimated a rotation of 7 degrees. X rays were surprising in that Philip measured a thoracic curve of 25 degrees! Three months later his curve had progressed to 36 degrees as he continue to grow dramatically; by now his shoulders were no longer on the same plane and even his parents could see the discrepancy. He still had no symptoms affecting his back or spine. Because of the high degree of scoliosis, he was given a brace. With the brace the curve was reduced to 24 degrees, which, although encouraging, was still quite pronounced. Because Philip is still growing with no signs of stopping soon, he may need surgery to halt the progression of the curve. What is in his favor is that he is incredibly compliant about using the brace.*

Despite his compliance, which was remarkable, the progression of the curvature continued and he eventually had the spinal surgery. Now, several months later, it is felt that the curve has stabilized with the rod.

The marked difference between Philip and Leslie is the amount of growth that Philip is still having. With each inch of growth he magnifies his rotation and his curve. Also of note is that each patient did not manifest any symptoms despite the magnitudes of their curves. Lastly, the two were referred on suspicion, not definitive diagnosis. It is far better to have an extra X ray than to miss the curvature.

Some medical professionals have tried using electrical stimulation of the muscles to promote strengthening of the back muscles and thus reduce the curve. Although promising and although some physicians are still using it, the data is inconclusive as to the results. My own experience is limited to a few patients who opted for this and ultimately had to use a brace.

Kyphosis

Sometimes the natural rounding of the upper back is exaggerated by a slight curvature of the spine in the thoracic region; this is called a kyphosis. As with scoliosis, this is a condition in which either there may be no symptoms or the patient may complain of back pain. Many parents will note a rounding of the upper back and bring it to the physician's attention. If the teen can correct the problem by standing straighter, then this is a postural problem and not a structural one. A true kyphosis that affects the bones is usually due to disease.

With a condition called Scheuermann's disease, seen more often in boys, the top and bottom of the vertebra grow more bone than is necessary. As a result, the vertebra at that part of the spine bend forward, and the exaggerated kyphosis develops. An X ray of the patient's vertebra shows the extra density of the bone and the diagnosis is confirmed. Treatment depends on the degree of the problem. In most cases the treatment consists of physical therapy to maintain the necessary flexibility of the area. In extreme cases, bracing or surgery will be indicated.

The Back

Lower Back Pain

In adults a common cause of lower back pain is a herniated disc. However, with teenagers the most frequent cause is misuse of their bodies. They seldom go out and warm up with stretching exercises before running, and they expect their youthful bodies to always be ready to perform, no matter what they want to do. Teens run, jump, climb, stretch, tackle, slide, lift, and twist, and then they come in complaining that their back "is killing them," forgetting all of the activities that preceded the pain. After most examinations of teens' lower backs, the conclusion is a muscle pull or a strained ligament.

Some teens actually will herniate a disc, but that usually requires some trauma. The symptoms of an out of place disc will include back pain as well as tingling feelings down the back and buttocks, which are associated with nerve compression. A thorough examination of the back and lower extremities will demonstrate the results of the herniated disc; a referral should be made to a back specialist. This becomes a bit of a problem at times since neurologists, orthopedists, neurosurgeons, and physiatrists all claim some responsibility and territoriality for this area. My own preference is to refer to a neurologist, since I am generally more concerned about possible nerve damage. He, in turn, can call in whoever is appropriate to deal with the herniation.

Spondylolysis and Spondylolisthesis

These two terms are important to distinguish when dealing with the adolescent with lower back pain. Growing teens are susceptible to these two conditions,

Slouching and Backpacks

Many parents have questions about "slouching" and about backpacks. Most want to know if their teen's slouching will cause the back to curve permanently. In fact, it's the other way around. If you have a curvature, your posture will follow the direction of the curve. Poor posture alone will not cause the problem. As for backpacks, yes, heavy books can strain the muscles of the neck and back; but no, the book bag will not cause permanent curvature. Asking the teenager to "clean out" the bookbag sometimes is met with the incredulous look that implies how little the parent understands. He "needs" these books and everything that is in there. Actually, if the teen is not complaining, why get involved? In most cases, the parent is more concerned than the teen.

Mark is a thin 5'8" high school junior and, by his own admission, is not "into" sports. He proudly will tell you that he is interested in the stock market and in computer programming, and he spends hours sitting in front of a computer screen. On his annual examination date I got a call from his mother that I "had to do something about Mark's posture." Sure enough, he stood like a slumping elderly man with his knees forward, his neck leaning, and his belly out. Technically, there was nothing structurally wrong with him that could not be fixed by simply standing properly. He saw no problem with his posture and saw his mother's complaints as nothing more than a "typical mom's complaining." There was no specific treatment other than a recommendation for some physical therapy to strengthen back muscles. He declined the offer.

This year Mark started to complain of pains in the back of his head that migrated down his neck. I suggested that this was all due to muscle imbalance from his poor posture and computer use. His parents insisted on a neurologist's consultation; he told Mark to "stand up straight" and the pain would get better. Somehow, when the neurologist said it, it made sense to Mark; when mother said it, she was being "obnoxious."

which often occur together. Not only are the terms confusing but often the X ray will reveal both in the teenager. A clue to figuring out which is which is to remember that "spondyl" means "back" in Greek and "lysis" means to dissolve. Hence, spondylolysis is a condition in which there is erosion of the bony part of the spine. Spondylolisthesis means slippage of the spine.

Teens who do a lot of bending and put stress on their backs are at risk for spondylolisthesis. Football players and gymnasts fit the bill nicely. Three hypotheses as to the reason for this ailment are proposed. It may be the result of direct trauma to the back portion of the vertebral disc, or it may be a congenital lesion, since it is found in about 7 percent of the adult population. Not all of these patients, despite the presence of the lesion, will complain, adding credibility to the hypothesis that it has been there all along. The third thesis is that the problem arises from undue overuse, and the problem is really a result of a stress fracture. A stress fracture is a type of trauma but it results from small repeated injuries rather than a direct blow.

When the vertebrae is eroded in spondylosis, this paves the way for spondylolisthesis, in which one vertebra slides forward on the other. Since the most common site for this lesion is the lower fifth lumbar vertebra, the patient may complain of pain in the lower portion of the back.

The diagnosis for both conditions can be made with standard X rays or with an MRI, which is preferable since this gives a better picture of a possible herniation of the intravertebral disc. In most cases physical therapy will suffice to improve the muscles of the back. A course of antiinflammatory medications and pain suppressors may be indicated. Rest is important and, sometimes to force the rest, the teenager is given a lower back brace. Contact sports are not permitted during this time. If the back pain is severe or you notice your teenager assuming unusual positions in an attempt to find a comfortable position, surgery to fuse the vertebra may be necessary.

The Shoulders, Chest, and Heart

The Shoulders

The shoulder is a shallow socket that is kept intact by a series of muscles surrounding the joint. These muscles are fastened to the bones by long rubber band–like strings called tendons, which give the muscle an anchor-point against which to flex. The muscle fibers, the tendons, the socket and joint, and the bones are susceptible to injuries and disease. When an injury occurs, the damage is usually to the muscles or tendons of the deltoid, the trapezius, or to the sternocleidomastoid muscle.

Trauma

For the adolescent, trauma is the primary cause of problems in the shoulder area, and most teens who suffer a shoulder injury come in after injuring themselves on the football field, falling off a skateboard, or on a ski slope. For this reason, you should refer to Chapter 7, "Teens and Sports: Sports-Related Injuries." However, even the nonathlete can fall and hurt his shoulder. If the injury results in a bruise, or hematoma, then all that is needed is to rest the area and do some physical therapy to bring the muscle back to its old form. The trauma will cause the blood to clot in the fibers of the damaged muscle, and it will take some time for the body to reabsorb the blood and for the bruise to fade.

If your teen cannot raise her arm above her head, if there is pain while the arm is not being moved, or if she feels "tingling" down the arm, then a doctor needs to assess the damage. The arm should be able to rotate fully (in a wind-mill motion) without pain, but if the arm is slightly out of the socket, such a maneuver will cause a great deal of pain. Any impingement of nerves will cause a sense of weakness, while any entrapment of blood vessels will change the color of the extremity.

Shoulder injury also happens to the teen looking for more "muscle defini-tion," who overestimates his strength. If he can lift twenty-five pounds, why not fifty? After fifty pounds is lifted, it makes even more sense to try one hun-dred. The only problem is that he may not have enough muscle mass for so strenuous a lift, and in the process, he overstretches the muscle and fibers tear. Now the injury must heal. Tell the teen that he may not lift for about a week, and that rest and over-the-counter antiinflammatory drugs will bring the mus-cle back. It requires patience. If the injury does not improve after a few days, a doctor's visit is in order.

Dislocated Shoulder

The fact that the shoulder is held in place with only muscles and tendons makes this injury much more common than is appreciated. I have had patients who had partial dislocations after falling down a few steps and landing on the shoulder. A full dislocation can occur if the blow is hard enough. The patient will find it impossible to lift the arm above the shoulder, as there is no full rota-tion capability if the head of the bone is out of the joint itself. All teens who have a dislocation, even a partial one, need to be seen by a physician to be sure of the diagnosis and treatment.

To correct a dislocated shoulder, the orthopedist can usually snap the shoulder back, but if the injury is recurrent, surgery to repair the torn muscles is in order. For a less serious tear, the surgery can actually be done through a small tubular scope called an arthroscope. Three or four small incisions are made around the shoulder and the surgeon can insert the narrow scope into the shoulder socket for the repair. Recovery is remarkably quick, since the surgical invasion of the shoulder is limited.

The Chest

The chest cavity is protected by a series of bones and muscles holding those bones in place. The arm and shoulder are anchored to the chest wall with large muscles, and there are also a series of small joints at the point where each rib meets the chest plate or sternum. In between each rib, there are small intercostal muscles that attach one rib to the other. The area is vulnerable to damage from a variety of sources, ranging from sports injuries to pain from frequent coughing.

The "Pecs"

One of the largest muscles of the body is the pectoralis major, or the "pecs." This is the one that boys usually try to build up in the weight room using barbells. Obviously women's "pecs" are covered by their breasts but they, too, can sustain injury. The usual injuries are sports-related and are included in Chapter 7, but any sudden forceful pulling back of the arms can tear the pectoralis major muscle. Chin-ups, push-ups, and rowing-type motions can all result in injuries to this muscle group.

These same activities may also cause injury to the sternum (breast plate). Since the rib-to-sternum joint has to move with each of these movements, it can become inflamed. This inflammation is no different than that of any other joint. Movement causes pain, the joint is tender to the touch, and the patient has trouble even putting on a shirt. This condition is called Tietze's syndrome, or costochondritis. The area will heal after about a week of rest and anti-inflammatory medication.

Rib Trauma

Rib trauma is unmistakable, as the patient cannot take a deep breath without pain. If you ask the patient to cough or sneeze, he will only do it once as it causes so much discomfort that he won't want to demonstrate again. This type of problem may come from a hard, persistent cough or from an injury. If the patient has a bad cough, repeated trauma to the area eventually causes damage. With each hard cough, the ribs expand and the muscles strain under the force of the cough. In time, they will hurt as much as any muscle that is overused.

If there is blunt trauma injury from being punched or injured in a bicycle or auto accident, the area around the ribs may bleed, or the small tissue covering the rib itself (the periosteum, or "lining around the bone") may be injured. The teen will splint (hold) his side, trying not to fully expand the side that is injured since the expansion of the wall muscles hurts so much. Over-the-counter antiinflammatory agents are the first line of treatment, and a chest bandage similar to a tight tank top will help to prevent full expansion of the chest wall. If the pain is not alleviated, a short course of stronger pain relievers, such as codeine, is given.

Misshapen Chest Wall (Pectus Excavatum and Carinatum)

One can have varying degrees of a sunken chest wall (excavatum) or a keel-shape to the chest wall, in which the chest comes to a pigeon-like point (carinatum). Both are found during childhood but the promise is usually made to "wait until adolescence" to see how the chest develops. In a way this is a fair promise because there is no point in doing cosmetic repair on a chest wall that is still growing. Yet, the promise implies that there will be some correction as the child grows older. Regretfully, change rarely comes on its own. Boys have a slight advantage if chest hair develops and partially covers the deformity. Girls will not have the same advantage and the breasts may turn in.

Surgical correction involves cracking the wall of the chest and resetting the bones. The scar tissue will be considerable. I have several patients who underwent the procedure and are less than satisfied. They traded the caved in, or pointed chest, for a scar that runs along the center of the chest and is very visible. The fact that the solution is imperfect makes having surgery a difficult decision. Appreciate that your teen is uncomfortable about the chest and reassure him that this will not interfere with his health. Teenagers do not always want solutions; they do want understanding.

Lungs

Most teenage complaints about the lungs have to do with coughing and phlegm production. For every true infection I have seen, I would estimate there are a few thousand mundane coughs due to environmental irritants. Yet it is important to figure out what is causing the cough in order to treat properly.

■ Asthma

Asthma occurs when there is a spasm of the smallest part of the bronchial tree. The effect is similar to pinching a straw and blowing through it, which produces a whistling sound as the air passes through the pinched area. In asthma we call this sound a "wheeze" and it happens when the patient exhales. Small children get asthma more easily because it takes little to clog their small bronchial tree; by puberty it gets better simply because the size of the tubes have enlarged.

Teenagers may still have asthma, although it usually improves as they grow older. The teenager who suddenly develops asthma requires a thorough assessment including a chest X ray to look for an obstruction as the cause of the wheeze. If asthma is the diagnosis, then the treatment plan consists of two medications: inhalers that will stop the spasm and inhalers containing steroids that will limit the amount of swelling at the pinched bronchial area.

Depending on a doctor's recommendation, asthma can be treated preventively, or on an attack-by-attack basis. If the patient has severe asthma, it makes sense to prescribe a type of steroid to use prophylactically or one of the newer family of asthma pills to avoid an attack. Teens need to manage their own care, and they will need to learn the difference between the inhalers used during an attack and those used on a daily basis.

Patients with asthma have very sensitive bronchial trees. Dust, temperature change, or infections (even mild ones) may trigger an attack. Cigarettes and pot clearly fall into this category, yet even the asthmatic teen may turn a deaf ear to the argument that she needs to stop using these substances.

One problem that frequently develops with asthma in teenagers is that parents may be reluctant to give them the full measure of freedom that would normally be allowed. Anytime a teenager gets a chronic disease, the normal dynamic of independence is thrown off balance. Parents of chronically ill teens need to periodically step back and look at how they are handling the disease and their child's independence.

■ Exercise-Induced Asthma

Exercise-induced asthma (EIA) is seen frequently in the teenager. It actually is incorrect to call this "asthma," since there is no allergic component and no "spasm" of the bronchial tree. Rather the effect of swelling at the small bronchial level occurs because of the difference between the internal lung temperature and the temperature of the ambient air in the exercise area. The cold air that the outdoor athlete breathes causes the swelling, which, in turn, causes wheezing. This type of wheezing is usually seen in outdoor sports during late fall and early spring. As the temperature warms up, or as the events move indoors, the problem improves.

Lung

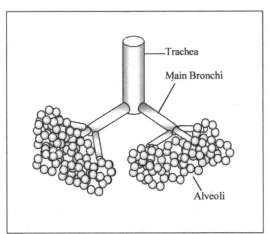

The EIA patient is pretreated with the same "asthmatic" inhaler that causes a spasm to go down. By taking two puffs of the inhalant fifteen minutes before exercise, the athlete can prevent the swelling from taking place.

■ Bronchitis versus Pneumonia

Think of the lungs as a bunch of grapes still attached to stems. The stems can be compared to the bronchial tubes that bring in air, and the grapes then represent the alveoli or lung tissue. It is at the grape level that the oxygen and carbon dioxide exchange takes place; it is through the stems (bronchial tubes) that the gases are transported. With this in mind, consider phlegm in the stems as "bronchitis," while phlegm in the grapes is "pneumonia." Using a stethoscope, a physician learns to identify the difference between bronchitis and pneumonia by the quality of the sounds that are made, which depend on the location of the infection. The distinction is not easy, and sometimes a doctor will need to order a chest X ray to confirm a diagnosis.

The deep rattling cough complete with phlegm is the classic manifestation of bronchitis. An expectorant is the first and best method of treatment. Most of these infections are due to viruses and do not respond to antibiotics, despite their frequent use. Both parents and physicians are guilty of asking for an antibiotic when it is not indicated, and the patient is needlessly given something that over time may yield antibiotic-resistant organisms.

If the cough is constant or the patient has a high fever over 101 degrees, a physician should listen to the chest to decide a proper course of action. The doctor may feel that there is so much thick phlegm that it has become infected with a bacterial organism and an antibiotic is now in order, or pneumonia may be diagnosed.

Pneumonia, although infrequent, is always a possibility and it's a good rule of thumb that if the cough persists, or if there is doubt about the diagnosis, a chest X ray should be done. The persistent cough may actually be pneumonia, even without much of a fever. The so-called "walking pneumonia" is more common than is appreciated. It is due to a particular organism called a *Mycoplasma pneumonia,* which doesn't quite fall into a traditional bacterial category and is, therefore, not responsive to traditional antibacterial antibiotics. It does, however, respond to the erythromycin and tetracycline antibiotic families, and your physician may prescribe one of these or their newer derivatives. Walking pneumonia is no different than other pneumonias; it's just less aggressive. While a serious condition, parents need not panic at the sound of "pneumonia," since most are amenable to antibiotic treatment and clear up over a few weeks time with medicine and rest.

Coughs

Though coughing is annoying, it actually serves an important purpose. If the bronchial tubes, the lungs, or the back of the throat become irritated, a message is sent to the brain that the body needs to rid itself of a noxious agent, and a cough is produced to try to dislodge the irritant. It doesn't matter whether the item to be dislodged is phlegm, a piece of chicken, or a fish bone, the cough does its best to free the area.

One of the problems with treating a cough with over-the-counter medications is that many seem to want to be all things to all infections. They stop a cough, they prevent runny noses, they stop itchy eyes, and in seconds you feel great and are sleeping like a baby! Instead, the cough has to be evaluated and the proper remedy given.

If the cough is productive (brings up lots of mucous), then it makes *no* sense to use anything that would suppress it—the person actually needs to keep coughing in order to get rid of the phlegm. A mucous thinner such as guaifenesin (an expectorant) makes sense. Buy plain guaifenesin, which is listed as glyceryl guaiacolate in many over-the-counter products (look for over-the-counter products that don't have letters after them, so Product X is different than Product X-DM, containing dextromethorphan, or Product X-C, a codeine derivative) if you are trying to bring up phlegm.

If the cough is not productive (not bringing up phlegm, just annoying everyone and keeping the cougher up at night), then buy a medicine containing either dextromethorphan or the codeine derivatives. In this case there is no need to "bring up phlegm" since there is none. Most of the suppressants are mild derivatives of codeine or morphine, and the patient may become drowsy. One of the common components is dextromethorphan, which makes up the DM postscript in many of the medications.

Be sure to clean out your medicine cabinet regularly. Old cough and cold medicines—even those that haven't expired—may still contain phenyl-propanolamine hydrochloride, an ingredient that is no longer permitted in these medications. Toss the old, and when you need them, purchase the new reformulated versions.

Dry air can cause or contribute to a cough. Extremely dry air irritates the bronchial tree or the nasal passages, so air conditioning or a dry heating system can actually cause a cough. A constant temperature and relatively normal humidity helps keep the bronchial tree moist and lessens the chance of it being irritated. Some people are particularly sensitive to the dryness of the air, and so they need increased humidity. Saline nose drops can help increase humidity in a person's nose without having to alter the air in the entire household. (Remember that humidifiers for winter use can be a breeding ground for bacteria and molds and must be cleaned frequently.)

■ Coughs Due to Allergies

Dust can also lead to an ever-present cough. The teenager's room may be a museum of life's accumulations—old sports equipment, hanging airplane models, balding dolls, fading photographs on walls and bulletin boards, books, CDs, television, VCR, computer, stuffed animals, clothes in various degrees of cleanliness. Unless parents make a cry for change, this room will stay this way as if to be preserved in a time capsule. Your physician may advise you to remove carpets, change blinds into shades, and eliminate as much of the memorabilia as possible. This is sound advice, but it will not be easy to enforce. You are asking your teen to change his "inner sanctum," and a simple directive will not do. Be prepared for the argument that he would rather keep the cough than change the room.

There is a difference between being allergic to dust and being irritated by dust. The net result is the same; you have phlegm. However, the distinction is important in that the *allergic* patient will need antihistamines *and* the removal of the dust—and sometimes, and with more difficulty, pets.

Some teens have such severe allergies that cleaning up their rooms is not enough. They may need allergy shots or some other type of prescriptive program to deal with their frequent runny nose and cough.

■ Coughs Due to Lymphoma

The one major concern for a cough that lingers in the teenager is that it may be caused by a malignancy in the lung. Any cough that continues beyond a couple of weeks for no discernable reason warrants a chest X ray. The incidence of lymphoma is low in the first place, but early diagnosis is key. This is more fully discussed in "The Neck Area " section under "Lymph Glands" (p. 369).

■ Coughs Due to Smoking

Aside from the obvious tell-tale aroma of cigarette smoke on clothing and stained teeth (some start smoking as early as age twelve, and staining may appear by middle adolescence), a constant cough may be a clue that the teen is smoking cigarettes or pot. "I plan to quit, Doc," is the ever-present line I get when kids come in coughing. As soon as the cough is better, they forget their vow. (See Chapter 13, "Teens and Smoking.")

Breast Enlargement in Boys

We mentioned the fact that boys go through a period of gynecomastia (breast development) during the third stage of puberty and, in most cases, this disappears. (The normal development of the breast is covered in Chapter 2, "Puberty: Your Developing Child, Your Developing Teen.") However, in some cases it lingers, and the psychological effect can be devastating. What appears to be a minor swelling is viewed by the teenage male as visible to the entire world. The mere thought of the school gym or showerroom can cause the teen not to attend school that day. Also, watch for the boy who, on a stifling hot day, wears a shirt poolside or refuses to go into the water. He may be telling us that the wet clinging shirt will reveal too much. This may only be due to modesty, but it may also signal embarrassment about his chest.

In such cases, the medical evaluation is quite simple, consisting of a physical examination to measure testicular size and blood tests to determine thyroid, liver function, and male hormone levels. One has to assess the amount of circulating testosterone and the amount of prolactin (the hormone responsible for lactation) that is present.

The testicles are evaluated to see if the relationship between the hormone it produces and the stimulation from the brain is normal. If the amount of testosterone is abnormal, then we can assume that neither testicle is working, and further tests are needed. (Even with only one functioning testicle, the body can make enough hormone and produce sperm.) Hence, the low hormone level is of concern and the doctor will need to order more blood tests, including a chromosome analysis. In this case, the breast increase is the clue to an underlying problem.

However, most patients have normal testosterone levels, normal-sized testes, and normal prolactin levels; they are normal except for the presence of the breast tissue. For cosmetic reasons or for psychological reasons, a patient may elect to have a plastic surgeon remove the excess breast tissue. The procedure is not complicated but should be done in as lean a patient as possible and in one who is not in the midst of a growth spurt.

Glen is a thin, *normal seventeen-year-old who has visible breast tissue. His hormone evaluation is normal and his testicles are nearly adult-sized. Despite the fact that his parents did not perceive the amount of breast tissue as excessive, they had promised the surgery "if it is necessary." Glen wanted to enter his senior year of high school without the problem of the breasts; he was tired of wearing shirts during the summer to hide his chest. In March, he went for a consultation and was told that two procedures were possible. He could have a "smile" incision made under each areola and have the breast tissue removed by flipping the areola and accessing the tissue. Or, to hide scars even further, a small incision could be made under his arm, below the armpit, and the surgeon could snake a cut under the skin from which to remove the breast tissue. He jumped at the idea of no visible scar and the surgery was set for April. By the end of spring break the scars were healed and he had a whole summer ahead of him.*

Although his post-surgical chest doesn't seem very different, the greater change is internal as Glen now feels a confidence that was clearly missing, as he perceived the breast tissue as the focal point of his body and identity.

This story is illustrative of the way teenagers view themselves. The teen could be a gorgeous, bright kid, who on the surface seems to have it all, but one pimple, one scar, one physical blemish produces a self-image that parents and adults wouldn't recognize. To understand, you need to remember how self-conscious you were when you were seventeen.

When tested, a rare patient will have an elevated prolactin level, a surprising finding since it is produced for the express purpose of lactation. Clearly, it has no business in the male's hormone profile. The physician will order an MRI of the pituitary gland to look for a small tumor (prolactinoma) that is secreting abnormal amounts of this hormone. Not only is it difficult to find the small tumor, but the solution involves its removal. Medications—some of the anti-depressants and hypertension medications, as well as cocaine and marijuana—can also raise the level of prolactin. Before starting on a complex and costly assessment of prolactin, be sure your teenager has been forthcoming about his personal history.

There are several genetic and congenital situations that may cause gyneco-mastia. There may be a chromosomal abnormality in which there is an extra X, or female, chromosome. The normal XY male now becomes the XXY male with a condition known as Klinefelter's syndrome. This, although quite rare, may be considered if the boy is tall, has small testicles, increased amount of breast tissue, and a delay in secondary sexual characteristics. Some of the puber-tal changes will take place, and pubic hair may well be present, but the breast tissue and the small testicles are the clue.

> **A six-foot patient of mine** *had complained of his breasts to another physi-*
> *cian. At the time he was fifteen, and it was felt that he had the normal*
> *gynecomastia of adolescence, so he was advised to "wait it out." Yet when I*
> *saw him at seventeen his breasts not only persisted, but he had continued to*
> *grow and was now at least 6'4". On routine examination it was evident*
> *that he had small testicles despite the presence of pubic hair. He had a sex-*
> *ual staging consistent with a much younger adolescent. In private consulta-*
> *tion with the parents, I requested that I be allowed to do a chromosome*
> *analysis. The eventual results confirmed the diagnosis that he had an extra*
> *X chromosome. He was started on monthly shots of testosterone and,*
> *although there was some shrinkage of the breast tissue, ultimately a surgical*
> *procedure was undertaken to remove the remainder. As rare as this condi-*
> *tion is, it is worth considering it in any male with large breast tissue.*

Extra Nipples

A common finding during a physical examination in both genders is the pres-ence of auxiliary nipples. Although present in childhood, they may enlarge dur-ing puberty and become noticeable to the teen and to others for the first time. They are benign, but at this age of incredible self-consciousness, this may be difficult to accept. The only treatment is assurance and acceptance; if that fails, then a plastic surgeon can remove them.

Girls' Breasts

■ Breast Hair

It is not unusual for a girl to have hair localized to the areola. Nothing is wrong, but she will almost certainly want to know how to remove it. If she plucks it, an inflammation can occur at the site; generally it is best to simply cut the hair at the base if the girl absolutely insists on "doing something."

Hair on the chest may warrant more concern. Some girls have too much testosterone (the male hormone), and need to be evaluated for an endocrine abnormality (see the discussion of the ovary and adrenal glands, p. 454).

■ Breast Lumps

Breast examination should begin during the later phase of puberty. Although this examination is critical, I think that telling the young girl who is dealing with her new body that she needs to be on the alert for lumps is too much. Once the breast reaches Tanner Stage Four (see Chapter 2, "Puberty: Your Developing Child, Your Developing Teen"), there should be enough emotional maturity to understand what is being done and why.

Most breast lumps are benign. However, the discovery of a mass causes a great deal of apprehension in the family. For this discussion we will divide breast lumps into three categories: fibrocystic breasts, benign masses, malignant masses.

The most common "lump" found in the teenage girl is a benign cyst that presents as a tender area. Because these cysts have fluid that fluctuates as a function of the monthly hormones, the cysts will change in size throughout the cycle. The closer to the time of menstrual flow, the greater the size and discomfort. Since teenagers have very dense breast tissue, some of the cysts have a fibrous covering. We speak of these cysts as "fibrocystic disease," but "disease" is really a misnomer: it is not a disease and it is not cancer. It happens so frequently, that despite the term, it is better to think of this as just a variation from the norm. Most physicians will advise a patient to wait and see if the cysts change and get smaller with the next menstrual cycle.

Parents will sometimes ask for a mammogram when this situation occurs. However, the fact that the adolescent has such a dense breast makes the reading of a mammogram problematic. Sonograms can help distinguish cysts from solid masses, and that is the recommended X-ray procedure if a cyst is suspected. In most cases the cyst will disappear with time. If not, then the surgeon will perform a needle biopsy to determine if the mass is cystic and benign. Treatment generally consists of prudent waiting and, if necessary, the birth control pill can be used to stabilize the girl's estrogen and progesterone levels.

Although this is a benign condition, the painful cyst and the concerns generated are generally put to a rest with this hormone regulation. Occasionally, it is worth draining the cyst to prevent recurrence.

Clare is a fourteen-year-old *who is almost fully developed. She has menstruated for about a year, and she came in because of tenderness in her breast. She pointed to a spot above the areola that she said had a "lump." I was able to discern a discrete area that, although tender, was movable and was not hot to the touch. She was expecting her period in a few days. I told her to take acetaminophen and not to touch the area. I asked to see her after she started her period. As expected, the lump was gone, and no tenderness was noted in the area. However, as she approached her menses again she called with the same concern. I sent her to a surgeon who did a needle biopsy. Clear fluid was obtained and the cyst was drained at the time. There have been no recurrences in over a year.*

In this age group, benign masses of the breast are usually fibroadenomas. These are firm, movable, usually nontender solitary masses that are present without any nipple discharge. The mass is often discovered by accident and often is located in the outside portion of the breast. Waiting a few weeks does not change the size, as the mass is independent of estrogen fluctuations. Few physicians are comfortable giving a conclusive answer without a needle aspiration. Under local anesthesia, a needle is inserted directly into the mass. By examining the tissue directly, the doctor can confirm it as a fibroadenoma. Alternatively, the surgeon may remove the mass because of its size during the biopsy.

Although most fibroadenomas are small enough that they can be observed, most patients "want it out." They feel, with justification, that the mass shouldn't be there, and though the adenoma is not likely to lead to cancer, it is easier to remove than to worry about it. In competent hands the scar that is left is about one to two inches, and generally it is on the outside part of the breast.

If the patient has a discharge from the nipple then a different diagnosis will be considered. A bloody discharge may indicate a block in one of the ducts that leads out to the nipple. A mass near the nipple will be palpable and possibly tender. One can culture the discharge and send it for cell examination. In all cases, a surgeon should be consulted as some of these discharges, though rarely so, may be malignant.

A nipple discharge that is not bloody may be due to inappropriate production of the hormone prolactin. The discharge may also be a clue that the patient was recently pregnant and hid the fact from her parents. Repeated stimulation of the breast by the patient can also cause excess prolactin. The brain releases prolactin as the infant nurses; the more he suckles the more prolactin. Frequent nipple manipulation can fool the brain into thinking that it is an infant's mouth that is stimulating it. Also some illicit drugs (amphetamines, pot, and some of the opiates) as well as some prescription drugs (oral contraceptives and some antidepressants) may cause the discharge. However, if there is no explanation then blood studies should include thyroid tests and measurements of the reproductive hormones, including a pregnancy test, and the doctor may order CAT scans and MRIs of the pituitary to make sure it is not malfunctioning.

A foul-smelling discharge is consistent with an infection or with a malignancy. The infected breast will not only have a discharge, which can be cultured for bacterial growth, but there will also be redness and tenderness around the nipple. A rare infection gets localized and an abscess can grow inside the breast. As with all abscesses they must be drained for adequate treatment. To test for infection, all the doctor needs to do is check the discharge on a slide, and then medication can be prescribed.

The likelihood of a malignant mass in a teenager is rare. The malignant mass is firm and nontender, which is also common with benign lesions; but in contrast, this malignancy tends to be hard to move. Despite statistics being on the teen's side, any breast lesion that does not regress after a few months of observation should be checked out. The prognosis for the adolescent is directly related to the time of diagnosis.

■ Breast Pain

In girls with large breasts, the very act of running can be sufficient to cause pain. Sports bras are available to make this less of a problem, but it is not always possible to eliminate the discomfort if the breasts are very large.

Transient swelling during the menstrual cycle contributes to breast discomfort, as does the use of caffeine.

■ Breast Trauma

Breast trauma is common now that more girls are involved in contact sports. The breast that has been traumatized by a blow or a fall may develop a tender mass that will take weeks or months to resolve. Indeed, the injured area may scar, and the area may never return to the "normal" state.

■ Breast Size

Breast development in girls is a very sensitive issue. Understandably, any "imperfections" in so apparent a part of the body are quite unsettling to a teen, but true deformities (such as an absent breast) are very rare. Many girls, however, will have a slight difference in the size of the two breasts. In fact it is more common than most girls appreciate and it is imperative that they understand that normal variation exists, and "normal" can mean breasts that are almost a full cup-size in difference.

Occasionally, the difference is marked beyond one cup size and questions about "corrections" immediately arise. Since girls develop at a relatively young age, the issue confronts the teen girl and her parents by tenth grade. Do you subject the girl to an augmentation or to a reduction at so young an age? Moreover, the girls seem so desperate for the surgery that they forget, or don't take into account, the degree of scar tissue that occurs.

Augmentation surgery is hard to recommend in an age when we have seen problems with breast implants. Admittedly, the newer saline implants boast of safer guidelines, but we are still talking about a teenager. Her impetuous need for fast results has to be tempered by full disclosure of the side effects. Parents who are heavily into plastic surgery may see no problem in rushing into the procedure. Why not fix the problem with a "simple" procedure? This argues that "small" is inherently abnormal and that the teen, therefore, looks bad.

My advice is to wait until the teenage girl is more comfortable with her body. She has just begun to see herself in a new light (a sexual one) and needs to wait, preferably years, before she interferes with so important an aspect of her body. A damaged breast, an infected breast, or scarred breasts are all potential outcomes of an operation. Let the girl wait until she is sure that the A cup—or unequally-sized breasts—is a problem that *she* cannot deal with. It should not be the mother who sees an A cup as an issue.

The reverse is also true. Very large breasts can become an issue for a girl and her parents, and breast reduction then becomes a topic of discussion. There are two likely situations where this occurs: The girl may have large breasts in the D cup range. She is unhappy with her breasts because of physical discomfort (particularly when exercising) and because of teasing from peers. Most observers will argue that a D cup is not a pathology; however, she may still feel quite uncomfortable. She should be advised that her decision to reduce her breast should wait until she is older and more comfortable with her body. As she matures, she may find her D size attractive.

Alternatively, a young girl may have what is known as "benign virginal mammary hyperplasia," in which there is no specific pathology and the girl has never been pregnant, but she has extremely large breasts. I have seen girls whose breasts reached their laps when they sat down, and their bra straps chafed their shoulders because of the weight. Some doctors have worked with anti-estrogen medication in an effort to halt the estrogen stimulation of the breast. However, the usual "cure" is to remove tissue surgically.

The surgery must be handled carefully by a plastic surgeon with experience in this procedure in order to maintain sensation and save the breast for future lactation, while leaving a minimum amount of scars. The scar from the surgery is traditionally called an "anchor" because it goes down from the areola and across the bottom of the breast. It looks like this:

Breast Reduction Incision

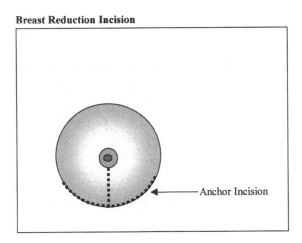

The surgeon usually lifts the areola and nipple from the breast by an incision around it and salvages the nerve and blood supplies. The visibility of the remaining scars depends on the skill of the surgeon and the healing ability of the teen. If your daughter has a tendency to scar, choose the surgeon even more carefully.

I have seen successful outcomes as well as unhappy ones as a result of breast reduction. One girl decided that she had had enough of boys making comments, having to wear clothes that made her look matronly, and uncomfortable bras. She underwent the procedure just after high school graduation and entered college with a new outlook and a new set of clothes. I also can think of several girls who welcomed the new size but had to undergo several plastic surgical procedures to correct the scar tissue that "they never realized would be so big."

This surgical decision is a major one as the process is not simple, so wait as long as possible to be sure it's the right thing to do, and then choose the surgeon carefully.

The Heart

Most heart problems are detected and dealt with prior to the teen years, so we will focus on the "normal teen" who is in the office for a routine examination.

The heart is a very simple pump consisting of four chambers and an incredibly sophisticated conduction system. When the teen is evaluated for any heart pathology, the physician needs to identify abnormalities of rate, of sound, and of electrical conduction. Rarely will "chest pain" be due to a cardiac abnormality, but teens often think of that first. Most chest pains have non-heart-related explanations. As part of the assessment of cardiac function the blood pressure is also evaluated.

The drawing below illustrates the blood's path through the heart.

Blood Pressure

Blood pressure measurement should be part of every annual exam. As the teen goes through puberty, the blood pressure approximates the adult's. Children have much lower blood pressure, and a chart is sometimes needed to compare

Heart

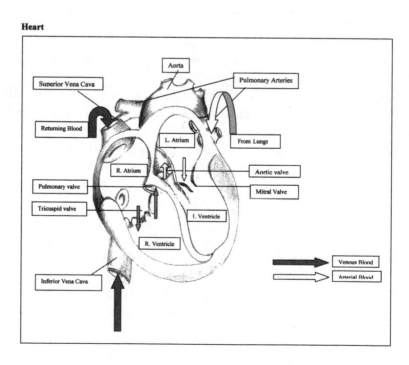

values with ages. High blood pressure is not a major issue for the adolescent, but occasionally it will be the clue to a problem with the kidney or part of a family profile that needs to be monitored. As with the heart rate, sometimes the very act of measuring the pressure will raise the numbers. I usually leave the cuff on, say nothing, and repeat it in a few minutes.

There are two numbers that are stated when blood pressure is read. The top number, or systolic pressure, is indicative of how much the heart has to work to push the blood through the vessels. The bottom number, or diastolic pressure, is the pressure that the heart maintains at rest. Most kids ask how the machine works and what the doctor is listening to when he places the stethoscope on the arm. The idea is to block all blood flow and, as the pressure is slowly lowered, the doctor listens to the first sound made as blood suddenly rushes past the obstruction of the cuff. That first sound is close enough to the pressure needed to push the blood through, and it constitutes the systolic number. As the sound finally disappears, we note the diastolic number. A rule of thumb is that the more important number is the diastolic number, since it represents the resting pressure in the heart.

A high systolic often is due to an adrenaline release when a person feels anxious. Elevated thyroid levels can also raise the top number, as can any stimulants in the blood stream. High blood pressure is not defined by one reading. If the pressure is elevated at one visit, the rule is to have it monitored for a few months before declaring that the teen has "elevated blood pressure." At this point, blood tests are done, urine is obtained, and every effort is made to be sure that there is no kidney pathology to account for the blood pressure reading.

In one condition called "labile (unstable) hypertension," the very act of taking the pressure may raise it way beyond normal. In that case it is worth considering using a small portable device to get twenty-four-hour monitoring of blood pressure. I have several teens who have blood pressure readings above 140 systolic almost every time I see them. With the monitor it is clear that they walk around with numbers in the 100 range all the time; when stressed slightly, their pressure shoots up immediately. If the blood pressure is constantly elevated during office visits, the only way around the issue is to monitor; otherwise, you will label and medicate incorrectly, offer unnecessary cautions about sports, and place insurance and military service in jeopardy.

One patient, who had the *monitor because of persistently elevated readings, fell on a ski slope. Since elevated blood pressure readings can be a sign of intracranial pressure, the ski patrol was anxious about head trauma. I got a call from a very concerned physician in Aspen that my patient had sustained minor trauma to his arm but his blood pressure reading was so high* *they were about to do an MRI to ascertain bleeding. He was confused because of the clarity of my patient's responses. "Call my doctor, he'll tell you I'm fine!" Indeed, without the monitor I would not have been as comfortable saying that Seth was okay. "That's normal for him" was my contribution.*

Heart Rate

The normal heart rate at rest varies with conditioning. A good ballpark number is about 70 to 75 beats per minute. The athlete who is in great shape can have a lower rate as she has developed an efficient muscle. With a strong heart you can pump harder and slower, which basically makes for an efficient system.

■ Rapid Heart Beat Problems

A fast heart rate is called tachycardia. One of the ironies in examining a heart rate is that the examination itself can produce enough anxiety to make the heart race. If the rate is too fast, the physician should check it again toward the end of the physical to see if it has slowed down. In most cases, this will suffice. If this doesn't work, the patient should be checked for other causes.

Illicit drugs can also affect the heart rate. I have seen many teens experience anxiety attacks after heavy marijuana use. They claim that they are experienced smokers and seem appalled at the idea that their favorite "harmless" drug is a problem. I usually prevail on the kids to allow me to disclose the information to their parents so that the situation is clear to all involved.

Cocaine use can also result in fast heart rate. Indeed, on one occasion I told the patient that either she would have to tell her parents or I would, as I believed her life was in danger. She did.

Jenna is a sixteen-year-old smoker *and her parents are aware of this. For the past few years she has tried the patch and nicotine gum to no avail. All of the entreaties of her family and physician to quit smoking were also useless. Over the weekend, her parents were alarmed when she complained that her heart was "going fast." I was paged and was able to calm down the parents who, in turn, took Jenna's pulse. Her heart rate was 130 beats per minute and she seemed "agitated." She was not hyperventilating, and I asked them not to appear panicked themselves. No immediate reason for the heart rate could be gotten from Jenna, and she said that the previous night had progressed in a normal way. I saw her the next day in the office, and her heart rate had settled into a comfortable 80 beats per minute. With the* *exception of a constant postnasal drip from smoking, her examination was normal. The one new piece of information was that she had been smoking pot over the weekend. She was unaware of anyone else having had a problem because she left when she began to feel ill. I told her that the most likely cause for her racing heart was the pot. It was either high in THC content or it was laced with something that had caused the problem. I told her that her parents needed some sort of an explanation. Jenna's immediate concern was that her parents would "kill her on the spot." I promised her they wouldn't, and she agreed, on condition that I tell them what had happened. She now gets monitored for pot periodically at her parents' request. To date there have been no further tachycardia episodes.*

It's not a bad idea to remember this story in the event of an unexplained rapid heart rate—it may be necessary to raise the issue of drug use.

An increasing number of teenagers are being diagnosed with anxiety or "panic" attacks, and the medical community is beginning to appreciate them as a biologically inherited disorder. A panic attack goes beyond feeling worried: the person may feel as if he is about to die, and because the teen is unaware of this as being relatively common, he may have difficulty expressing what is happening to his doctor or parents. A teenager may notice that his heart is racing and that he feels sweaty and clammy, and as if he is about to vomit. He may also have a sense of weakness and feel faint. By the time he sees a doctor, he is very likely to have normal cardiac rate and sounds, because most panic attacks are not long-lasting.

This type of experience is consistent with a panic attack, though because biological causes may be involved, it is important to consult a doctor. The diagnosis may be impossible to confirm through physical tests alone because the electrocardiogram is often normal. The doctor needs a thorough history and the cooperation of the teenager, who may prefer to speak privately with the doctor. The attack can be triggered by stress or emotional problems.

In most cases these attacks seem to run in families, so it is also important to get information from the parents about their own history with panic attacks. They should be asked about any undue pressure on their child as well. If the teen is diagnosed with anxiety attacks, she can be treated with benzodiazepines such as Xanax, which can be used as needed and will calm the adrenaline rush. However, because they can result in physical dependence, they must be used with caution. If the attacks occur with frequency, then daily antianxiety medication may be in order and a psychiatrist should be consulted. I usually treat the attacks for about one to two weeks before I make a referral to a therapist or psychiatrist. I preface this with a discussion that a therapist might be needed but "We'll see how it goes," because most teens and parents need time to get used to the idea of seeing a therapist.

The ultimate goal is to help patients function in life. Some patients need temporary relief and a couple of weeks to months of medication might suffice. Others may be paralyzed by anxiety and may require years of medication and therapy.

Since some patients only have anxiety in very specific situations, they should need medication only as the need arises. For example, the patient who has anxiety flying or speaking in front of an audience might do well with medication just before the event. Patients may slowly confront their anxiety situation with the guidance of a therapist, and eventually be able to get on a plane or enter an elevator. An exciting new development is the world of "virtual reality," which helps patients conquer anxiety through computer simulation. They don a helmet with a monitor inside and enter a world of virtual reality, as if they were in a computer game. The difference is that the "game" is tailored for them. If they fear handling a pet, the "game" takes them into a backyard with a virtual dog. Eventually, patients conquer their fears in virtual space by "touching" this unreal dog. In time, a real dog is brought in and the anxiety of touching the dog has been lessened by the game. It's too early to tell the full results, but recent reports are encouraging.

Andrew had gone through school *with no problems and had been on the varsity tennis team. Then over the course of a year, he was mugged while going home and broke a leg in a car accident. Andrew felt that "bad things were happening," and he just couldn't get over his bad luck. He was unable to play tennis while he mended. In the meantime, he met a terrific girl from Greece, and she invited him to her home in Athens. I got a call that he was now "terrified" at the thought of the trip. He had just been on a plane to visit a family member and throughout the flight all he could feel was a sense of anxiety and dread. He was literally sweating in his seat. He was fearful that the plane would crash, that a terrorist would hijack it and fly it to some unknown land, or that a wheel would fall off. He didn't understand that these fears stemmed from his feelings that he'd lost control over his life, but he did know that something was wrong and he needed help. We tried Xanax and it sedated him enough that he got on the plane and slept until he landed in Athens. On his return, he saw a therapist who worked with his sense of "loss of control" during a flight. He still took his medication on future flights but each time he flew he noted less anxiety. He finally asked to have the medication "in case he needed it." Eventually, he got to the point* *where he got on the airplane without taking the Xanax, but had it within easy reach.*

The one cardiac abnormality that causes fast heart rate and closely resembles panic attacks is a condition called paroxysmal atrial tachycardia, or PAT, in which the heart's upper portion rapidly sends out electrical signals, making the heart beat too fast to be effective. Children will rarely present with this, but as they enter puberty this condition becomes possible.

This condition is generally diagnosed and monitored by a small portable EKG machine that can be attached to a belt. After twenty-four hours any abnormality can be noted by running the tape through a computer. A cardiologist is needed for comprehensive evaluation and, if the episodes occur often enough, medication is in order to block the abnormal electrical signals. In most cases, after a period of several months, the medication can be stopped to see if the tachycardia reoccurs.

If your teen's heart rate is high, it may be caused by a high caffeine intake. Most teens don't realize that the sixteen-ounce Grande coffee they order at Starbucks actually contains 550 mg of caffeine. (In contrast, an eight-ounce mug of regular coffee has anywhere from 80 to 200 mg of caffeine, depending on strength.) Nor do kids consider the caffeine they consume in sodas—these range from 35 to 110 mg of caffeine per twelve-to-sixteen-ounce container. Even "decaffeinated" coffee isn't 100 percent free of caffeine; it is just lower in amount. Even some pain relievers, such as Excedrin, have 65 mg of caffeine per pill. We are surrounded by stimulants.

Ask your teen to keep track of any coffee, tea, or sodas she drinks each day, and this may provide the doctor with the explanation for her rapid heart beat.

▪ Slow Heart Beat Problems

The slow heart beat, called "bradycardia," can occur quite normally in the athlete. Rates of forty beats per minute can be seen in the slim well-conditioned runner or swimmer who has a strenuous aerobic workout.

There are two other conditions in which a slow heartbeat can be noted. Perhaps the most common is the patient with an eating disorder who has lost so much weight that she basically is slowing down all body functions. I had a patient whose heart rate was in the thirty beats per minute range and had to be hospitalized immediately (see Chapter 5, "Teens, Nutrition, and Eating Disorders").

A block in the electrical conduction between the top part of the heart (atria) and the bottom (ventricles) can also slow the heart rate. This is rare in teenagers, and most of the time a previous history of cardiac surgery can be found. The surgery in some way interfered with the conduction system of the heart resulting in the block.

We register our pulse (at the wrist of neck) from the pulsation that arises as the blood leaves the lower chamber, the ventircle. The top, or atrial pulse, should be synchronous and equal to the ventricular pulse. In a situation in which the top part of the heart is beating normally, at say seventy beats per minute, but not all of the electrical signals are conducted to the ventricle, a different rate is registered at the wrist or neck. This is a "cardiac block," or an "atrial ventricular block."

■ Extra Heart Beats

Occasionally a teen will come in and complain that his heart feels like it is skipping inside. What is happening is that an extra beat or more is escaping out of turn. The normal "lub-dub" becomes "lub-**da**-dub" or "lub-**da-da**-dub" and, if the "**da**" is hard enough, the patient will note the jump. If it is a soft "da," it may not be noted unless the doctor happens to hear it at the very moment he is listening to the heart rate.

> **Melissa is a tall, lanky, athletic teen** *in the tenth grade. She drinks a fair amount of coffee and soda and basically is in good health. She came in for her annual examination and, in the course of listening to her heart, I noted an extra beat for every four to six normal beats, which was confirmed by an electrocardiogram. I assured her that this was treatable, but before we did anything she had to cut out the coffee and soda. That was more of a problem for her than the abnormal beats, but she complied. A week later she was almost cleared of all the extra beats, but after monitoring with a twenty-four-hour monitoring system, it was proven that the problem remained, but was not serious enought to warrant medication. As long as she cut down on the caffeine, she was fine.*

Some patients simply walk around with these extra beats, and nothing needs to be done if they are not causing clinical symptoms. Still, the situation does need to be checked out by a doctor. If the beats arise from the ventricle or cause uncomfortable symptoms such as dizziness, medicine can be prescribed. (Generally speaking, abnormal beats arising from the ventricle are more likely to denote a problem in the conduction of the heart than if the extra beats are generated in the atria.) All sports clearance physicals that detect an abnormally beating heart should be referred to a cardiologist.

■ Murmurs

The illustration of the heart shown on page 400 shows that blood goes through the four chambers, the lungs, and through four different valves with every cycle. At any one point the blood can meet a slight obstruction that causes turbulence. Whenever a fluid hits turbulence you get a sound; in medicine we call these heart-related sounds "murmurs." Lots of people walk around with murmurs that are not significant, while other murmurs hold the key to major cardiac pathology. My own small murmur was discovered on a routine physical at the age of twenty-five.

For the sake of universal language, murmurs are graded 1 to 6, and each number implies something very specific to any doctor who hears that the patient has a Grade X murmur.

Aside from the murmurs that have continued from childhood in patients with congenital heart lesions, one of the most common in teenagers is the murmur of mitral valve prolapse (MVP). This is a fairly frequent condition, and it may be that one only hears the murmur for the first time in the growing teenager. Unless the physician listens to the heart with the patient sitting, lying down, or perhaps standing, it is possible to miss the murmur. Interestingly, once found, you will often get a parent volunteering that he or she also has "a murmur." The murmur of MVP is one in which the valve between the left atrium and the left ventricle has a minor defect, which may cause a small amount of blood to back-flow into the atrium. The regurgitation is partially responsible for the murmer, and occasionally the delayed closure of the back part of the valve can be heard as part of the MVP murmer.

Usually, the only way to definitively make the diagnosis is to obtain an echocardiogram (a fancy sonogram that sends sound waves to the heart to illustrate the heart's anatomy) from a cardiologist. If the amount of blood flow back through the valve is large, then the patient has MVP with "reflux" and that accounts for the murmur. In such a case, the patient is advised to take antibiotics prior to any dental or other potentially invasive procedure. The idea is to prevent any seeding of bacteria to the heart and, specifically, to any area in which there is a turbulent flow. Frankly, there is a controversy about needing to treat with antibiotics in *all* cases, and often the cardiologist will recommend that only those cases with significant reflux need to be treated. In my opinion, it is wise to treat, even if there is some doubt; it's a little antibiotic to prevent a potentially serious problem.

If I discover a murmur for the first time, I usually refer the patient to a cardiologist even if I feel that the murmur is not a problem. The reason is actually a practical one. If the teen has to go for a surgical procedure, an insurance physical, or needs to go to the emergency room, that murmur may become a huge issue. If medical personnel note the murmur, no physician will do surgery or possibly treat another problem until a cardiologist has been consulted. I want the cardiologist to see my patient when all is calm, and I usually send a copy of the report to the parent so they have it in hand for an emergency. In an age where everyone is overcautious about treating a new patient, it is reassuring if the murmur has already been evaluated.

Michael is a twenty-four-year-old *who is applying to the navy intelligence school. During his first visit at seventeen, he had a murmur that I thought was a Grade 2, which had never been brought to his or his parent's attention. I thought this was an innocent murmur, but because it had not been evaluated, and because he was a varsity athlete, I asked the parents to take him to a cardiologist. Interestingly enough, his mother told me she had a murmur and another son, soon to be my patient, also had a murmur. Michael went to the cardiologist who agreed that the murmur was there; his clinical impression was that Michael had mitral valve prolapse. However, the echocardiogram showed normal valves, and the final interpretation was that of a normal exam.*

Because he was moving around, he didn't come to see me for three years, but then I got a call from him that the "navy had temporarily failed him because of a murmur." When I reminded him that we had done the evaluation and he had a report, he was ecstatic. I faxed him a copy of the cardiologist's findings, which he took to navy intelligence. Without the previous evaluation, his indoctrination into the navy would have been jeopardized.

The Abdomen and Digestive System

The Esophageal Area

Heartburn

The esophagus is a slender tube of thin muscles that runs behind the bronchial tree. Its main job is to transport chewed food from the mouth into the stomach with access being granted by the gastroesophageal valve. The lining of the esophagus is incredibly thin and sensitive, and as a result, some chest pains actually emanate from this area. In contrast, the stomach's lining is as tough as the lining of a hard basketball. If it were not tough, the stomach would literally erode under the burn of the high acid load required to continue digestion (digestion actually begins in the mouth with saliva).

On a weekly basis, I see teenagers doubled over with pain "in the stomach" or "in the chest," with burning that "won't go away." These pains generally come from a high acidic content in the stomach that backs up into the esophagus, causing heartburn. If the acid content of the stomach is too high, or if there is increase in the amount of stomach pressure, then the gastroesophageal valve may open improperly and the contents of the stomach will go back up into the esophagus. Since the lining is so weak and sensitive, it takes little to "burn" the esophagus. We call it "reflux esophagitis" but "heartburn" will do nicely.

Coffee, tea, caffeinated soda, cigarettes, alcohol, orange juice, grapefruit juice, or vinegar (which is acetic acid) increases the acid load of the teen stomach. Some teens down a quart of orange juice at breakfast and then develop stomachaches. (It is called citric *acid* for a good reason.) Both eating quickly and not eating often enough also contribute to acidic buildup. A buildup of pressure in the stomach also can cause heartburn. Chewing gum and smoking contribute to the problem because when air is inhaled, some of it is swallowed and stomach pressure is increased; the same holds true for drinking soda (if a teen drinks a carbonated soda, where do the bubbles go?). All of these possibilities are a part of the life of the teenager, so it is small wonder that they suffer gastric distress.

Janet was a healthy sixteen-year-old *who had had several bouts of stomach pains. When they occurred she doubled over to find a position in which she could withstand the sharp, sudden, and excruciating pains that were "up here." She pointed to a spot just under the breastbone and above the belly button. Her urine was normal and there were no red cells. (This was important since kidney stones sometimes present as severe abdominal pains.) As for diet, she'd had "a few sodas" and "some Chinese food" just before the pains started. The time of her last bowel movement was unknown. Janet's stomach was tender throughout but what was most noticeable was the amount of gas I heard with the stethoscope. I had her listen to the "plink, plonk, plush, puusch, plink" of her stomach, and she was surprised at how much it gurgled. Her eyes opened wide, she smiled, and then went back to the reality that she was in a lot of pain. "Make it go away!" she wailed.*

Her parents requested a specialist referral, since the pains were so bad and not even antacids made her more comfortable. The gastroenterologist ran a myriad of tests to rule out inflammatory disease, sprue, and ulcers. The diagnosis was finally confirmed: "She drank too much Coca Cola and had too much caffeine. She had gastritis and some reflux." Rather than admit to her poor eating habits and her plentiful consumption of soda, she underwent an extensive (and expensive) evaluation that told us she needed to eat more wisely. Quite an expensive soda!

Dietary changes, antacids, and some types of medication (see "Duodenitis" below) will help with heartburn.

The Stomach

Duodenal Ulcers

The notions that ulcers are due to stress or that they do not occur in teenagers are both wrong. While stomach ulcers are rare in teens, duodenal ulcers do occur with some frequency. A bacteria called *Helicobacter pylori* (*H. Pylori*) is responsible for ulcers. We used to think that the bacteria were present because of the high acid medium associated with an ulcer. Now we recognize that this organism is actually responsible for the ulcer. People who are stressed tend to produce acid, aggravating the situation. Now that we understand that ulcers are an infection, it makes no sense to believe that teenagers won't get it.

To diagnose an ulcer, a culture must be taken from the duodenum (just beyond the stomach). This can be done in the gastroenterologist's office using an endoscope. The physician passes a tube down the throat, into the esophagus, across the stomach, and then into the duodenum to look for the ulcer. Once the ulcer is spotted, the diagnosis is made, and cultures and biopsies are easily obtained. While the process sounds uncomfortable, Valium is usually administered to help the patient relax. In order to halt the gag reflex, an anesthetic is sprayed in the back of the throat to take away any sensation. Another way of diagnosing the presence of the bacteria is to obtain blood for the presence of antibodies against the *H. pylori*.

Once an ulcer is diagnosed, the patient is treated with appropriate antibiotics and antacid medication. Early treatment of ulcers can catch the problem before it becomes even more painful.

Duodenitis

A burning sensation can also come from the duodenum, or the first portion of the small intestine. In this condition, increased acid has moved past the stomach and into the first twelve inches (Latin for "twelve" is "duodenum") of the small intestine. The main function of this portion of the tract is to accept bile from the liver and gallbladder and begin the neutralization of the acidity of the stomach contents. If all goes well, the acidity will diminish and not burn the rest of the tract and digestion will continue uneventfully. As with the esophagus, if too much acid enters the duodenum, it cannot be fully neutralized, and a burning pain in the center of the abdomen can occur. Some patients describe the pain as a "knife stab."

The treatment for this is exactly the same as with gastritis (too much acid in the stomach), the acidic environment needs to be neutralized. This can be accomplished by using antacids or other types of medication. The prescription medicines, Pepcid and Tagamet, for example, are mainstays in the treatment of hyperacidity and are now available without prescription in weaker doses. If the problem persists, your teen should see a doctor so that no other condition is overlooked.

Next, you need to discuss diet with your teenager. Begin with the consumption of soda. Soda has no nutritional value, but it does have artificial flavor, artificial sweetener or pure sugar, maybe caffeine, and, lastly, gas. Not one of these belongs in the normal food pyramid, yet teens often live on the stuff. If an adolescent has heartburn, gastritis, or duodenitis, it will be aggravated by soda: the caffeine will produce acid, the gas will create pressure, and the sugar may make you gain weight or give a "sugar high." Yet I am a realist. Encourage your teen to reduce soda intake if you can't get her to give it up. Sometimes I think teens have never heard of water.

Along those lines, one of the other tricks that teenagers often do is swallow pills without water. Every once in a while a pill gets stuck in the esophagus and the patient complains of severe pain. One of the boys in my practice took a pill in the tetracycline family that was prescribed for acne and simply swallowed it in a gulp. He went to bed and in an hour was calling me with the complaint that his chest was on fire. The tetracycline capsule was dissolving and releasing the contents onto the thin lining of the esophagus. Bad move. I asked him what possessed him to swallow the pill without water. His reply boasted, "I always do that, Doc!" Lots and lots of water later, he got some relief and a lesson.

Food Poisoning

Teenagers are not known for their discrimination when it comes to choosing places to eat. Their tendency to eat in fast food places and to grab whatever is available in the refrigerator makes them more susceptible to food poisoning.

If there is an inflammation of the stomach we speak of gastritis, and this is what occurs when a person has "food poisoning." As the toxin from the bacteria is released, more acid is produced and causes the nausea and the vomiting that is part of the infection. Treatment actually occurs when the person vomits because she is eliminating some of the offending bacteria and acid. When a patient is vomiting, it is reassuring if there is also diarrhea. This means that the entire gastrointestinal tract is irritated and should clear itself within about twelve hours. If a patient suffers vomiting or nausea alone, this may indicate a whole host of possibilities that include neurological problems and obstructions to the intestinal tract. Once diarrhea is part of the picture, you know that there is "food poisoning" or a viral poisoning of some type. It is unlikely that you would have both vomiting and diarrhea without something irritating the entire digestive tract.

Parents are often quite worried about their teen's food poisoning since they are often unaware of the reason for the sickness. Once told, they are reassured, as they themselves have usually had it before. Often the offending food is poultry because of its high bacterial content of *Salmonella*. Patients infected with this bacteria do not always have a high fever and there is little to do except be patient and wait for it to "go away." In general, antibiotics are not used to treat most diarrheal infections unless they are severe or bloody. Your physician will advise if antibiotics are appropriate. If there is a high fever, then the possibility of another bacteria, *Campylobacter*, is raised. If symptoms are severe or last more than a few days, you should call your doctor. Antibiotics can be used effectively with *Campylobacter*.

Dehydration and the loss of necessary body salts is a concern with any stomach illness that produces vomiting or diarrhea. During the acute phase of the illness, many teenagers try to drink water because they feel very thirsty. Unfortunately, the use of pure water may actually aggravate the situation as it further dilutes the sodium (salt) content in the blood, which then causes more vomiting, headache, and dizziness because of fluid shifts. The best types of fluid for rehydrating are bouillon soups (easily made with water and bouillon cubes) or Gatorade, which contains a balance of salt and glucose. It is similar in composition to the intravenous fluids that are used in the hospital for dehydration. Avoid acidic drinks (orange juice), which will irritate the stomach, or any drink with caffeine since that will also irritate the stomach as well as stimulate a need to urinate, which is counterproductive when you are trying to rehydrate.

Remember, too, that any large volume of fluid introduced into an irritated stomach will only come right up. I ask the teen to drink a tablespoon at a time and to do it slowly. Lastly, even though the teenager may ache all over, do not use the ibuprofen family of drugs, or aspirin, as they will only upset the stomach further.

Lactose Intolerance

Lactose intolerance may first manifest itself during the teen years. Lactose is the sugar that is present in most dairy products, including powdered ones. Through a chemical process, the body transforms the lactose into glucose, which is then absorbed into the body. If someone is "lactose intolerant," it means that the body does not process the lactose properly (usually because of a lack of the enzyme lactase). The extra lactose hangs around, and the bacteria in the gut then tackles this remaining sugar with gusto. The result is that the sugar becomes fermented. Fermentation produces gas, which can cause painful bloating, flatulance, and nausea.

When dealing with lactose intolerance in teenagers, it is worth remembering that the cheese in pizza has lactose. Most teens respond to this news by moaning that you are taking away their favorite meal. To overcome this tragedy, a doctor can recommend over-the-counter lactase pills that will make it possible for a teen to continue eating some dairy foods. Some lactase comes in a powder so that you can sprinkle the lactase on the food, which breaks down the lactase before you eat it. You need to decide how many pills per slice; or in the case of teens, how many handfuls per whole pizza! A lactose-free milk is also marketed. Be forewarned: It tastes different.

It is important to recognize that this is a genetically transmitted disorder, albeit a recessive one. In order for the teen to develop severe intolerance, she needs to get the gene from both parents. If it is inherited from only one side, she might have a milder intolerance and be able to eat one slice of pizza but not two.

Parasites

Every once in a while a teenager will complain of frequent and vague abdominal pains that have persisted for "months." These pains don't have the quality nor the severity to warrant a visit, but over time, the parent becomes concerned. The examination and blood tests may be normal, but the patient feels persistent discomfort with possible nausea and gas. Particularly if the teen has traveled outside the country, the doctor may order an analysis of the stool for parasites. However, I frequently see patients who have not traveled abroad, live in "nice" areas, and only eat in "safe" restaurants, yet they have picked up a parasite. There are a few parasites that simply live anywhere, and you can get infected a lot more easily than you think.

To get a definitive diagnosis, the stool sample should be fresh. Don't do your teenager a favor and collect it at home, bring it to the lab, and have the test done on a slightly dried-out specimen. The best way to assure accurate diagnosis is to have the patient produce the specimen at the testing site. Take the teen to the lab, and prepare him for the fact that he may have to get an enema to produce a "good" specimen. If a parasite is identified, the doctor will prescribe an appropriate antibiotic.

The Abdomen

"Abdominal pains" are one of the most common complaints in a practice of adolescent medicine. Most pain is a direct result of diet. Forgetting that they are subject to the laws of nature, teenagers will consume huge amounts of food, junk or otherwise, and then complain that they have a stomachache. The fact that they ate two hamburgers and two Cokes with French fries and a cheesecake is ignored. The teenager feels that there is nothing wrong with this choice of combustible mixtures.

Teens also don't always make the connection between diet and gas eruptions from either end. The teen also appears disinterested in occasionally making room for something new. Bowel movements are often parenthetical, as some, often girls, will literally forget when their last one took place. Below are some of the more common causes of pain and what can be done about them. Ultimately, any pain in the abdomen should be taken seriously; though the cause in many teenagers can be found in assessing their diet, and particularly, their last meal.

Appendicitis

Perhaps the most common concern when the teenager has abdominal pain is the possibility of appendicitis. This surgical emergency is a justified cause for worry as an incorrect diagnosis and treatment delay can have dire consequences.

Contrary to popular opinion, the first symptoms of appendicitis rarely begin in the lower right side; instead, they start as a pain around the belly button. At first it is no different than the pain of a nonspecific bellyache from eating too many potato chips and soda. However, the pain will get progressively worse, and soon the patient will develop a low-grade fever. She may feel nauseated and even vomit. (If at this point, or soon thereafter, the patient has a loose bowel movement, the diagnosis of food poisoning, or gastroenteritis, becomes more likely.) At some point the pain will migrate to the lower right side of the body. If you imagine a line from the belly button to the top part of the right hipbone the point in the middle is where the appendix is located. If, when you press this area, your teen winces with pain, *call your doctor and leave for the hospital immediately.*

It is important to get to the hospital before the appendix ruptures. A ruptured appendix releases bacteria into the abdominal cavity. Since the abdominal contents are surrounded by a thin membrane called the peritoneal lining, this results in peritonitis. The result is a painful, rigid abdomen that may prove fatal because of the infection. Don't waste time going to the doctor's office; get your teen to the hospital where X rays and blood tests can be done quickly, and if necessary, surgery can be performed. If the appendix ruptures, the pain is exquisite and the patient will develop a high fever. There is a great danger of an overwhelming sepsis, a blood-borne infection that travels throughout the body.

To confirm the diagnosis of appendicitis, a urine specimen and a blood test will be taken at the hospital. The few white cells in the urine come from the irritation of the appendix against the ureter. The blood count will show an elevation of the white cells, indicating that an infection is brewing.

Today surgery is done quickly, and if there are no complications, the patient will likely be in the operating room for no more than an hour. Recovery is also rapid. The incision is small, and the patient will be in the hospital for about two days. After two weeks many patients will feel fully recovered with an occasional wince of discomfort if the muscles around the incision are stressed.

Bowel Problems and Disease

Most bowel problems in teens have to do with constipation or hemorrhoids; however, bleeding in either case can indicate an underlying disease, so if your teen's problem doesn't resolve itself quickly, check with your doctor and also refer to the section below on gastrointestinal bleeding, p. 419.

■ Constipation

After so many years of seeing teenagers, I am no longer amazed at the ability of some teenagers to defy nature and go for days, indeed a week, without a bowel movement. They have a movement every few days as a norm, and can even forget to go. It makes a lot of sense to go daily as you tend to eat daily and you need to make some room for the new occupants. Yet I will settle for twice a week with my patient population. Arguing that daily movements are reasonable inevitably meets with incredulous expressions from teens and parents: "I don't have time" or "*I* don't have them daily, Doctor," says the mother who may have taught the daughter.

Constipation occurs in several situations, but the leading cause is poor eating habits, insufficient water, and poor bowel hygiene. In order to have a normal painless stool you need enough fluid in the large intestine to make the stool soft enough to pass. The purpose of the large intestine is to mold the digested material and to dehydrate it into a normal stool. If the digested material goes through too quickly you have diarrhea, as enough water could not be extracted.

If it goes through too slowly, the intestine continues to take water out and the stool become larger and harder. This makes it more difficult to pass, and the cycle continues.

Some teens will note blood on the toilet paper, which is usually caused by an anal tear, or fissure. The anus has a series of circular folds that allow it to stretch, but a large stool can stretch the anal mucosa beyond its capability. The examination will show small cuts along the folds. (For more information on blood in the stools, see "Gastrointestinal Bleeding," p. 419.)

Stool softeners are often given, but remember that they only work on stools being made, not on the stool already formed in the intestine. A suppository may stimulate the rectum, but there will still be pain as the large stool is passed. Enemas will help or, in order to lubricate the colon, you may need to drink mineral oil. It tastes terrible but it works in a few hours. I take it back; it tastes horrible but the relief is worth it.

Once the constipation is over, the teenager needs to revise the diet that caused the problem. First, more water needs to be added to the diet and "roughage" or fiber has to be added as well. Most of the fiber we need can come from spinach, lettuce, fruits, and bran cereals. I tell kids that eating raw vegetables and fruits will do the trick. It sometimes takes severe constipation to make the teenage male eat raw vegetables. Teenage girls seem to be better at the raw vegetable part, and the bottled water trend encourages fluid intake.

Occasionally an obstruction will be the cause for the constipation. Some children have a condition called Hirschsprung's disease, in which the intestinal nerves are not fully developed. These children present with constipation and carry the condition into adolescence.

There are also other causes for obstruction, and anyone with severe, ongoing constipation warrants a sonogram, abdominal X rays, or a CAT scan to reveal a possible obstruction. In girls, a large enough ovarian cyst can compress the intestine to the point of constipation. In boys, an enlarged prostate, although extremely rare, may be responsible for the obstruction. Both of these are difficult to diagnose on physical examination without doing a rectal exam. This is a very easy examination to do, yet it is met with resistance both from the teenager and, often, from the parents of teenage girls. In that case, sonograms or X rays will be necessary.

Very occasionally, a patient will have a partial obstruction that requires surgery to remove the damaged piece of bowel and prevent an emergency obstruction.

■ Hemorrhoids
Visible blood may appear as a result of hemorrhoids—a horrifying thought to the teenager. Actually parents don't do well with the news either. Hemor-

rhoids are anal veins that are dilated and can't drain because they are surrounded by swollen tissue. Any abdominal pressure that interferes with anal vein drainage will dilate the veins and give you hemorrhoids. (Think of a tourniquet.) Straining from coughing, from constipation, from urinary problems can cause enough pressure to block the anal veins. Long hours spent pondering magazines on the toilet will eventually take its toll. As the teen sits on the toilet in the "Thinker's" position, there is an increase in abdominal pressure that can lead to hemorrhoids.

A teen may report blood on the toilet tissue or say, "I just saw blood in my stool." A doctor's examination, as humiliating as it is for all teens, will reveal a grapelike, or hopefully a raisinlike, vein that is tender. It is hard to miss the dilated vein as the anus is stretched out. If blood is present and no hemorrhoid is visible, the patient will need to have a colonoscopy to establish if there is an internal hemorrhoid.

Treatment involves two phases. First, one has to treat the hemorrhoid directly with over-the-counter preparations. The classic, Preparation-H, works quite well as an initial treatment; it comes in a suppository and in an ointment. At the same time, a medicated pad (Tucks, or an equivalent brand) is recommended as a cleaner to soothe the inflamed area. If the Preparation-H is not working, your doctor may prescribe a cream or ointment that contains a steroid to help shrink the hemorrhoid. Second, the reason for the hemorrhoid has to be addressed. The prolonged sitting on the toilet, the cough, or the straining have to be cured or the cycle will perpetuate.

■ Inflammatory Bowel Disease

Most abdominal pains have easy explanations. Occasionally a teen will complain of pains, and it signals the beginning of inflammatory bowel disease or, more rarely, Crohn's disease (see below). In almost all cases one or more of the following will be present: abdominal pain, diarrhea, fever, loss of appetite, or blood in the stool. If the disease occurs during the pubertal growth spurt, the poor absorption of nutrients may cause growth and pubertal development to be compromised.

The two main inflammatory bowel diseases are ulcerative colitis, which tends to involve the large intestine, and Crohn's disease, which can involve the patient's gastrointestinal tract from mouth to anus.

The diagnosis is made with blood tests that signal the inflammation, and X rays that may show some strictures. A gastroenterologist should see these teens since treatment is quite complicated. In many cases, it may be necessary to obtain biopsies. Since the treatment for inflammatory disease uses many powerful drugs with side effects, it is crucial to make a correct diagnosis. The teenager needs to be carefully monitored for growth and pubertal changes as well as for the discomfort associated with these disorders.

The most common site for Crohn's disease is the first portion of the ileum, the point just before the small intestine joins the large intestine near the appendix. Before the diagnosis is made, there is a period of vague pains and potential bleeding that has gone unnoted.

Patients with Crohn's are often treated with steroids that slow down bowel motility and with special sulfa medications that treat inflammation. Antibiotics are also used to treat bacteria in the intestine, and in order to prevent vitamin deficiency, most patients also receive generous amounts of supplementary vitamins, including folic acid and iron. All of this takes a toll on the teenager in terms of compliance. Yet, if done properly, the teen will achieve maximal growth and physical maturity. The complications of steroids have to be carefully monitored for their many side effects, too numerous to mention here.

Gastrointestinal Bleeding

Patients who have abdominal pains, even mild ones, are possible candidates for internal bleeding. Your physician may feel that the symptoms are consistent with several possible diagnoses and order a guaiac test. This test, which requires the patient to place a small amount of stool on paper, is a fairly standard test in adults. It relies on the fact that occult bleeding is visible when an additive is placed on the stool sample. A positive test requires a thorough search for the source of bleeding, which could be due to an ulcer or to several other conditions in which the gastrointestinal tract becomes irritated.

If teenagers have bleeding gums, a recent nosebleed, or a cut tongue, they should wait to do the test. All will have some swallowed blood and the test will be positive. Also, if a girl has her period, it is important that the specimen be carefully isolated so that there is no menstrual blood on the stool specimen. "Occult" blood can also be noted if there are black stools. (Any time blood is present in the gastrointestinal tract above the large intestines, stools tend to look black, but Pepto Bismol has the same effect. Before you become alarmed at black stools, be certain your teen hasn't taken any Pepto.) All this signifies is that there is bleeding with a cause yet to be determined. The physician may order X rays or scans or refer the patient to a gastroenterologist for a direct visualization of the intestinal tract with a flexible scope.

There are several possibilities with gastrointestinal bleeding, so in addition to the topics discussed below, also refer to "Bowel Problems and Disease," p. 416.

If there is blood in vomit, the likely causes are a bleeding ulcer (see "Duodenal Ulcers," p. 411) or a rupture of the blood vessels in the esophagus. With violent vomiting the thin lining and muscles of the esophagus can tear and the patient will vomit blood. With teenagers, the likely cause is too much ibuprofen that causes bleeding from ulcerations, or he or she might be bulimic (see Chapter 5, "Teens, Nutrition, and Eating Disorders").

If the blood is from an ulcer, it may no longer look fresh. The acidity of the stomach breaks down the blood, and the vomit will contain broken down coagulated blood. It has the appearance of "coffee grounds." The broken down blood only tells you that there is bleeding; the diagnosis is found with an endoscopy. Even if the patient is believed to have a duodenal ulcer because of the presence of antibodies (see "Duodenal Ulcers," p. 411), the endoscopy should be done if there is active bleeding.

Bleeding from the rectum may signal one of several diagnoses, but most often is a sign of hemorrhoids, even in teens (see above). Fresh blood may sometimes signal an internal polyp. Since some polyps are malignant, this is another reason for the surgeon to scope the teenager who has fresh blood from the rectum if no other causes are found.

The Liver

A Malfunctioning Liver

The liver is responsible for so many detoxifications of what we put into our body that it is impossible to cover them all here. However, the recycling of our blood is one of the detoxifications that is worth understanding as it may affect your teen.

In a rather clever recycling system, "old" blood goes through a process to re-use part of it as new red cells. Part of the process causes bilirubin, a byproduct of the recycled red cells, to pass through the liver. There, an enzyme called glucuronyl transferase changes the bilirubin from fat soluble to water soluble before passing it into the gastrointestinal tract. Through a series of conversions the bilirubin is transformed from a yellow-orange color into green and then into brown. Therefore, the brown color of a bowel movement is dependent on bilirubin, and ultimately on normal liver function.

To understand the symptoms of a malfunctioning liver, this basic physiology is important. A high concentration of bilirubin in the bloodstream turns the skin yellow or "jaundiced." If there is an excessive amount that is not cleared by the liver, the patient may look yellow—even the whites of his eyes may take on a yellow hue. (Note that some people are yellow because they eat unusually large amounts of squash, pumpkin, or carrots, which are high in carotene.) The bilirubin, which is yellow, is actually deposited on the skin and on the eyes.

If you look at the drawing below, it explains why a patient whose stools are moving rapidly through the gastrointestinal tract will have "greenish" stools. The bacteria in the tract did not have enough time to convert the green to brown. In hepatitis, the stools of the patient may be light colored because the bilirubin never gets into the stool due to the malfunction of the liver.

Liver Function

As a result of the routine blood test I perform at a first visit, it is possible to find occasional elevated liver enzymes in otherwise normal teens. An abnormal liver study with elevated liver enzymes could indicate many things. Your physician will consider everything from the benign Gilbert's syndrome to hepatitis (see p. 422), or even possibly a lymphoma (see the discussion of lymphoma on p. 370). It also may indicate overeating or drinking more alcohol than the body can metabolize. Fat in and around the liver can be seen on a sonogram, and this will clear as the patient loses weight or stops drinking.

Parents may be relieved to learn that because one of the liver enzymes is also found in muscles, the athletic teenager or one who is lifting weights may have an abnormal liver study from nothing more serious than muscle use. Yet, in this case it will be the only enzyme elevated, indicating muscle and not liver damage.

Gilbert's syndrome is not unusual among older teenagers. This is not really an illness; the liver does not have a normal amount of glucuronyl transferase enzyme and the result is a slight increase in the unconjugated (or not water soluble) bilirubin found in the blood. If the blood is drawn when the teen has not eaten recently, the results are particularly notable. Patients are not jaundiced, and there are no other "abnormalities" of liver function in Gilbert's. I have lost track of the number of kids with Gilbert's who, once in college, called me with alarming reports from visiting the infirmary with a minor illness. When blood tests were run for their current malady, the slight increase in bilirubin showed up. A concern about early "hepatitis" and college contagion, with the threat of an "epidemic" worried the doctor they were seeing. I was able to reassure the doctor of the previous Gilbert's diagnosis, and nothing needed to be done except to note its presence.

If, however, they are elevated liver enzymes, then an investigation as to a possible infectious hepatitis is in order. A bacteria, a parasite, or a toxic agent can cause the problem; however, in an adolescent, infection by a virus is the most likely cause. Some of these hepatitis infections are so mild and symptom-free that the only way they are picked up is by chance.

If it is a mild infection, all that needs to be done is to monitor the blood until the enzymes of the liver return to normal. On the other hand, there are several viruses that have been identified and carry specific diagnostic criteria in the blood workup. Appropriate antibody studies and elevated liver enzymes can identify all of these.

Treatment is supportive; the patient is put on a low-fat diet and monitored for weight gain/loss. At the same time, the liver studies are monitored to watch for the normal resolution of the infection. Very rarely, a deterioration of the liver enzymes continues, and the patient needs to be watched carefully and monitored for possible liver failure. Antibiotics serve no purpose in viral infections and, therefore, are not used in these infections.

Since the Epstein-Barr virus can cause an inflammation of the liver, it is not a bad idea to check for mononucleosis when a patient has abnormal liver function studies (see "Mononucleosis," p. 344).

Hepatitis

Any inflammation of the liver is called *hepatitis*. The use of the term does not tell us what is causing the inflammation, only that the liver is temporarily damaged.

■ Hepatitis A

This is the virus that used to be referred to as "infectious hepatitis." It is transmitted by foods tainted with infected fecal matter. Patients will have fever and nausea approximately two weeks after exposure. The patient feels terrible, has a poor appetite and fever, and soon will look jaundiced. Tests of the liver will show a high level of bilirubin enzyme, and all she wants to do is rest. After a few weeks, the patient will regain her health, and relatively speaking the duration of the illness is short.

The stool of these patients contains the very virus that caused the illness, so there is the chance of spreading it to other family members—careful hygiene is crucial. The patient's eating utensils need to be isolated, and family members should receive adequate protection against hepatitis A virus with the vaccine, and even gamma globulin, if available, in selected cases.

Prior to 1998, patients traveling to high-risk areas would have received gamma globulin to give them immunity. Today, the hepatitis A vaccine is given instead (see "Immunizations," p. 330).

▪ Hepatitis B

This is the virus that was called the "serum hepatitis" virus for years. It is of great concern because it is transmitted through all body fluids. Clearly, then, it can fall into the category of a sexually transmitted disease. The problem is compounded by the fact that the patient who is infected may not actually know it, because there is a period of a few months in which the patient is infected and contagious but does not appear ill. Some people have chronic hepatitis B, but have no symptoms—if they remain undiagnosed, they can unwittingly infect others.

Since teenagers have a certain lack of discretion and impulse control when it comes to sex, the concern has been that they will be exposed to a hepatitis B patient who is unaware of the infection. (Once a patient has acute hepatitis B, he will demonstrate jaundice, malaise, and even arthritis.)

Patients with hepatitis B are not as common as those with hepatitis A. This is fortunate since the patient with B can be ill for months, and some go on to develop a chronic liver infection. The severity of hepatitis B means that all children, even before they reach twelve, should have hepatitis B vaccine protection. Most children now receive this immunization very early in life (see "Immunizations," p. 330).

▪ Hepatitis C

The patient with hepatitis C is infected in one of two ways: either she had a transfusion, which was contaminated with hepatitis C, or she injected drugs with an infected needle. While donated blood and other blood products have been screened since 1972 (blood) and 1987 (blood products), the street-sharing of needles continues, keeping the hepatitis C transmission level high for illegal drug users.

Treatment for hepatitis C is complicated and involves the need for a biopsy of the liver to ascertain the full extent of the infection. Antibodies against the hepatitis C virus may confirm the exposure but the biopsy must precede any of the expensive, painful, and prolonged injection treatments.

Fitz-Hugh-Curtis Syndrome

Sexually active girls with either gonorrhea or with chlamydia may show symptoms of hepatitis, and this is called Fitz-Hugh-Curtis syndrome. The infection travels through the fallopian tubes to infect the liver, and the patient may present with right upper quadrant abdominal pain and all the symptoms of hepatitis. There will also be a purulent discharge from the cervix. In most cases, there are enough symptoms of a uterine infection that treatment begins before the hepatitis ever occurs.

Liver Toxicity Due to Drugs

Drugs, both legal and illegal, can damage the liver. With any patient who has liver abnormalities, it is imperative to go through all the drugs the teen has taken (or used) one by one. Even those that you would think are innocent may prove to be a problem. Taken in great quantity, even acetaminophen (Tylenol) can cause liver damage.

Alcohol clearly can cause elevated liver enzymes. Some physicians will argue that you need to drink steadily for weeks before you see these liver abnormalities. I have many teens who come in for an annual exam in the summer. They needed school or camp forms and see the visit as routine. Slight liver enzyme elevations are noted, and they sheepishly admit that they had "a few drinks" the night before. Within three or four days, the repeat results come back normal. Obviously the one whose alcohol consumption is in the "alcoholic" range is at great risk for liver damage and elevated liver enzymes.

Philip is a college student *who is active in his fraternity. He parties on weekends, and over the course of three years of hamburgers, beer, and little activity, Philip has added about fifty pounds to his high school weight. During the Christmas vacation he came in because he was not feeling well. Since his complaints were vague, I ordered a set of blood tests. The liver studies were notable for increases in the enzyme levels. Indeed, he had had some* *beers with his buddies just prior to coming home. He allowed me to have a full conversation with his parents and they noted that he would party a bit too much during the holidays, but this was okay since he was doing well in college and "he needed to unwind." I mentioned my concern about alcohol and fatty livers, and they agreed to another set of tests in a week. Once again, the levels were elevated and a consultation with a gastroenterologist was obtained. The consulting physician felt that this was weight- and alcohol-related, and we "should wait" for a month or more with Philip abstaining from alcohol. Philip agreed but, within two weeks, he became concerned about his liver problem and wanted a more definitive answer. He had a closed liver biopsy (a needle is put through the skin and into the liver). The diagnosis was confirmed that he had fatty infiltrates, and the treatment was nothing more than a diet to lose the fifty pounds. Despite the pressure to "drink with the guys," he also reduced his alcohol intake. Since that time, he has lost weight and his enzymes are lowering.*

Parasitic Infections of the Liver

This is a difficult condition to pick up unless the patient has been traveling to areas where parasites are more likely. Because symptoms generally present as garden-variety hepatitis or gallbladder disease, a physician may assume something other than parasites. However, as the illness continues, a doctor may request a liver scan, and parasites may show up as cysts or nodules. Amoebic dysentery will give the patient diarrhea and abdominal pain. An analysis of the stool will often yield the answer as the parasite or the eggs of the parasite are visible. Treatment of parasites requires antibiotics. Many have some toxicity themselves, so the identity of the parasite is important.

Wilson's Disease of the Liver

A rare genetic disease of the liver that must be inherited from both parents is Wilson's disease, a condition where the body cannot metabolize copper correctly. If a teen has hepatitis as well as neurologic abnormalities, which may present as gait disturbances, slurred speech, and a sardonic smile, it is important to consider this condition. Because the symptoms might also lead a physician to consider drug use, it is worth knowing about this illness. Its rarity will be obvious when you realize that any patient with Wilson's disease is immediately presented to the medical staff as a teaching exercise.

Pancreatitis

Although it is rare in teenagers, it is something to consider with anyone who drinks heavily.

The pancreas sits in the upper left side of the torso just behind the stomach. Because of its location the patient with an infected pancreas will complain of severe pain on the upper left side of the abdomen. The inflammation causes nausea and decreased appetite. Gradually the pain increases and the area is very tender. The pain of pancreatitis is such that even the most stoic teen will double over and cry with pain. The physician may order X rays or CAT scans in making a diagnosis.

The pancreas is divided into two parts. The acini produce a protein that is involved in digestion (this is called an exocrine process), while the islets produce a hormone that is critical in the control of sugar metabolism (an endocrine process). It is this damage to the endocrine process that is the basis for diabetes type I, or insulin-dependent diabetes.

Diabetes

The symptoms of diabetes mellitus type I are the classic triad of increased drinking of water, increased urination, and increased hunger. When you analyze the pathology of DM-I, you can understand the three symptoms. Since the type-I patient fails to produce insulin, the blood sugar gradually accumulates in the blood. It is so high a blood level that the kidney begins to leak sugar. Normally sugar is not present in the urine. Since there is an ongoing loss of sugar, there is a concomitant loss of water as the sugar attracts the water. Think of placing sugar on top of strawberries and you see the similarity. Now that the patient has lost sugar and water, he has lost calories and is dehydrated. Hence, he is hungry (loss of sugar and calories), he is thirsty (loss of water in urine), and is also voiding excessively.

The teen with type I diabetes poses all sorts of problems in management. Not only is the need for daily insulin an issue, but the teen has to monitor his own blood several times a day in order to adjust the amount of insulin given. As a diabetic, he has to be careful about diet and is prone to such problems as wound infections that take an overly long time to heal. If the diabetes isn't brought under control, there are the very real dangers of high blood pressure, retinal damage, and kidney disease. However, the newer medications and treatments are doing marvels to prevent these future complications.

Perhaps one of the most complex parts of type I diabetes for the teen is the loss of control that accompanies this disorder. As with any chronic illness, the teen will have to see a physician frequently and have his parents constantly balancing a tightrope as they try to monitor his health enough to be sure he stays healthy but at the same time allow him enough freedom to learn to manage his illness in his own way. In this regard, diabetes is no different from the patient with a seizure disorder or one who has chronic bowel pathology. It is a challenge to keep parent and teen from coming to loggerheads over the parents' very real need to protect versus the teen's very real need to achieve more independence.

Type II diabetes used to be seen in the adult population only. In fact, it was called "adult-onset diabetes" for many years. The idea was that the patient had a pancreas that was still capable of producing insulin but it was overwhelmed with the amount of food, and therefore elevated blood sugar, the individual consumed. It soon became apparent that age was not the critical issue but rather the weight of the person. With that realization we changed the term to type II. We are witnessing a population of teens at high risk for this disorder as their sedentary lives and poor food choices are yielding an obesity epidemic. The patient with type II does not present with the same dramatic triad as does type I. Yet they do have the thirst, the hunger, and the urine sugar but in a more subtle way. Treatment is directed at the weight and at modification of diet. Left untreated the obese person not only has type II looming but also the long-term risk of heart disease (see discussion of obesity on p. 103).

The Umbilicus, or Belly Button

Umbilical Hernia

A hernia simply means a mass pushing through the skin layers. An umbilical hernia can result when there is a larger than acceptable opening between the inside abdomen and the belly button resulting from the way the umbilical cord was tied off at birth. These usually disappear without treatment by age two. If this condition is present in the adolescent, the rule of thumb is that if you can push it back in, and there is an opening about the width of a finger, then this opening may have to be surgically closed.

The Urinary Tract

The Bladder

Infections

Both genders can get bladder infections, but girls are more likely to due to their short urethra (the portion between the bladder and its outlet). Any bacterial infection that starts on the outside of the female urethra has little traveling to do before it gets into the bladder. Moreover the outside of the female urethra is prone to trauma either by incorrect wiping, by irritation of the area with clothing, horseback riding, bubble baths (if you can appreciate soap in your eyes as irritating, then you understand soap in the urethral opening) and, certainly, by intercourse.

Cystitis, a bladder infection, is accompanied by blood in the urine, microscopically or visible to the patient when voiding. The patient, usually female, will be quite uncomfortable. She may have the urge to empty her bladder even when there is little urine in the bladder, and it will likely be painful when she does urinate. An examination and culture of the urine should be taken, and if an infection is found, the patient may be started on a short course of antibiotics. If the infection is limited to the bladder, one type of treatment used involves a single dose of strong antibiotics in combination with a urinary tract anesthetic. Patients are told to acidify their urine with cranberry juice so as to

The Urinalysis

The routine urinalysis yields a remarkable amount of information. Not only do we get information about blood in the urine, but it can also reveal quantities of ketones (breakdown products of fat), glucose, white cells, bacteria, acidity, concentration (useful in deciding about weight and hydration), bilirubin, and protein. Today all of this is available in the doctor's office with a single urine dipstick, which can determine each of these parameters.

When I ask teenagers for a specimen, it is telling if there is hesitation. The loud, quizzical "Why do you want it?" raises my suspicion that they are hiding something. I counter with "Why is that a problem?" or more directly with "Don't worry, this is not for a drug screen," and I explain how I cannot do a drug screen without their permission. I also make a note to deal with this issue later.

Any female who is menstruating or has a vaginal discharge should not have a urinalysis to look for red cells or protein, as the slight contamination from the menses or infection may show up in the urine. This teen will need a "midstream"or "clean" catch in order to avoid as much contamination as possible. (This is done by first letting the first drops of urine fall into the toilet and then catching the middle in the cup, and finally allowing the last drops to fall into the toilet.) Likewise, postcoital urine may show some red cells from irritation.

make it harder for bacteria to grow. Some doctors will treat with antibiotics for a few days to be sure that the patient is totally free of bacteria; others will wait for the results of the culture, usually forty-eight hours. (If the kidney is infected, a longer course of treatment is necessary. See below for an explanation.)

When girls come to me with cystitis, I always ask in what manner they wipe themselves after going to the bathroom. There is a fifty-fifty chance that the response will be "I don't know," or "Back to front." It is critical that all girls and women wipe from "front to back." The urethra is located forward of the vaginal opening and the anus, thus the back-to-front wiper will bring bacteria from theses areas to the urethral opening. Since the urethra is so short in women, it then takes little to enter the bladder. The correct front-to-back method eliminates this likelihood. As they get older and the bacterial content of the vagina alters, the poor wiper is even more prone to cystitis.

Girls compound the problem if they do not drink enough fluids or if they go for long periods without voiding. Urination flushes the urethra, removing any bacteria. The less frequently you urinate, the more time bacteria has to proliferate. If the urine is too concentrated, it can also set the stage for bacterial invasion. Girls' consumption of water has improved now that it is stylish to lug bottled water around, but they still don't necessarily make time to go to the bathroom frequently enough. (Boys simply don't do that to themselves. In addition to the fact that their urethral opening is far from their bladder, teen boys urinate more often than adolescent girls do; perhaps because it is easier, and boys are not as self-conscious about such things.)

In the sexually active girl the possibility of an infection increases dramatically, since the penis can irritate the urethral opening during intercourse, allowing an entryway for bacteria. All teenage girls with urinary tract infections should be asked about the possibility of intercourse as a reason for the infection. As embarrassing as it is, during the time I have to talk privately with the patient, I always ask the sexually active girl if she engaged in anal sex, because the bacteria from this sexual act will easily contaminate the urethra if proper protection is not taken. (The number of girls who admit to me that they do is high enough that it is worth asking.) Some girls will "not go all the way" but only "fool around." They have to understand that any manual stimulation of the area may irritate the urethral opening and infection may occur.

If a girl has frequent cystitis and issues of hygiene and sex have been ruled out, the possibility of an anatomical abnormality should be investigated. A study of the anatomy of the kidney can be done with sonograms and with the injection of a dye into a vein that eventually enters the kidney that outlines its size and structure.

In contrast, boys do not tend to get urinary tract infections, unless they have contracted a sexually transmitted disease such as chlamydia or gonorrhea. This causes painful urination, and the boy will come in complaining that it "burns to pee." He may or may not see a white or yellow discharge from his penis, but the symptoms are enough to treat him (see Chapter 10, "Sexually Transmitted Diseases"). If a boy has even one urinary tract infection and it is not sexually transmitted, it raises questions about abnormal genitourinary anatomy and further investigation is merited.

The Kidneys

Benign Hematuria

This is a benign condition, generally picked up in a urinalysis, where small amounts of red blood cells are found in the urine. In most cases the "benign hematuria" occurs as a result of a minor sports injury. No one should be surprised that after a football, hockey, basketball, soccer, or rugby game there will be some injury to the kidney. Technically we would call that a traumatic hematuria; yet in some teens the slight amount of blood present in the urine will occur after track or tennis or even marching. This condition can be found in all kids, and is more common that appreciated. Some kids, eager to make it on time for their appointment, will run to my office and their urine will demonstrate slight amounts of red cells. For this reason, all teens should have their urine assessed on an annual basis.

By examination under the microscope one can determine, with some accuracy, if the cells are coming from the kidney or from the lower urinary tract. If the kidney is producing the cells, then follow-up tests are required. If the urine is filled with cells from the lower tract, this tends to be less serious and, if one can find a few days in which the teen is not running around, the urine will be free of red cells. One condition that is confused with benign hematuria is called IgA nephropathy, in which, following an upper respiratory infection, the teenager will have red cells in the urine for a few days after the beginning of a cold. As the infection disappears, the red cells go away. Since IgA nephropathy can, in some cases, progress to a more serious condition, the question comes up how to distinguish it from benign hematuria. Frankly, you cannot do it easily. IgA nephropathy is diagnosed after a kidney biopsy and that is not an easy undertaking. So what do we do to monitor this? First you appreciate that if the teen does not have elevated blood pressure and is not spilling protein in the urine, and the amount of red cells is insignificant, it is most likely benign hematuria. If the above symptoms are present, at some point one has to consider the more important IgA nephropathy and a referral to a nephrologist, a kidney expert, to consider a biopsy. Even then, not all of these patients go on to severe renal disease and treatment as IgA nephropathy has a considerably variable course.

One of the main concerns of hematuria is the possibility of a glomerulonephritis, a more serious condition. Damage to the filtration system of the kidney can occur if a post-streptococcal skin infection is not treated in time. In this condition, acute glomerulonephritis, the body's own immune system damages the kidney while killing the strep bacteria. About two weeks after an infection, the patient may demonstrate swelling, elevated blood pressure, and blood in the urine. Fortunately in most cases the disease is self-limited and penicillin and observation are all that are needed. However, occasionally, the patient may go into acute renal failure and need to be treated with steroids.

There are other forms of glomerulonephritis in teenagers that are much more severe and chronic. They manifest with low serum protein due to the ongoing loss of protein in the urine. The patient will show the signs of swelling and hypertension that were seen transiently in the post-strep disorder. Ultimately the diagnosis will rest with a kidney biopsy. Treatment depends on the kind of nephritis, but steroids are commonly used.

Some inherited and congenital kidney disorders may not manifest until adolescence. Alport's syndrome, in which the teenager has blood in the urine and a progressive loss of protein, or cystic diseases of the kidney may not be evident during childhood, for example. Any time there is blood or protein in the urine of a teen and trauma is not an integral part of the history, the kidney should be considered as a possible source of the problem.

Infections

The kidneys are located behind the abdominal cavity and about a hand's width below the shoulder blades. When the kidney is infected (called "pyelonephritis"), it is a more severe illness than an infection of the urinary tract. The patient will generally come in with fever and chills and possibly pain in the lower part of the back, and the physician will find signs of infection in the urine, which will contain a higher level of bacteria than in a urine infection.

The patient with a kidney infection may not complain of pain on urination, since the bladder and urethra are not irritated. Upon examination, the physician will find tenderness in the kidney area, found through pounding the back. Accurate treatment can be started if the results of the culture are known and the exact bacteria is identified; however, the doctor doesn't have this luxury with a kidney infection since the patient may become quite ill during the two days it takes to produce a culture. Treatment needs to start immediately using an antibiotic that will provide broad coverage. Even then the patient has to be monitored for signs of deterioration until an exact diagnosis confirms the choice of antibiotic. Hospitalization is necessary if the patient cannot take oral medication or fluids due to vomiting. However, newer medicines, which are absorbed very well, usually mean patients can stay at home during treatment.

After a forty-eight-hour wait the cultures hopefully will reveal that the correct antibiotic has been chosen, but two weeks observation will be required to be sure that the patient is healed. It is critical that the teenager complete the full course of antibiotics, even if she feels better after a few days. Untreated kidney infection may lead to a loss of the kidney or so severe a sepsis that the patient's life is in danger.

Claire, a freshman in college, *was suffering nausea and had a fever of 102 degrees. A doctor at the student health facility diagnosed it as the flu, and she was told to take ibuprofen to lower her temperature. By the next day she was still feeling miserable, her temperature had risen to 104 degrees, and she felt cold and was shivering. She returned to the center and was told that she needed a throat culture to rule out "strep throat." It proved negative, and she was told that she did not need antibiotics since it was "probably viral." She called home and her parents drove to college to get her.*

Her parents brought her into my office, and she promptly asked to lie down on the examination table because she felt chilled and dizzy. Her throat did not hurt but she reported that "everything else did." After settling her on the exam table, I asked her mother to leave so I could get a further history: Three days prior to her fever, she had intercourse for the first time. She was pleased that she had used a condom and asked me not to tell her mother that she wasn't a virgin. She also noted that passing urine was a little painful but not so terrible. She thought that this was due to postcoital irritation. When I examined her back and pounded over the kidney area, she let out a loud "ouch" and the diagnosis started to become clear. Her urine specimen was filled with white cells, and under the microscope one could see thousands of bacteria floating in the urine. A culture was set up, and she was immediately started on antibiotics. Mom was concerned and upset that this infection had happened away from home, and my explanation that "She got a bladder infection that traveled up to the kidney" was enough information to satisfy her—and Claire, too. I kept in touch with Claire over the phone for the next forty-eight hours, and she improved quickly. Over the next two weeks, she told her mother the truth and later saw a gynecologist for birth control.

Claire's story is classic in that she had the fever, chills, back pain and tenderness, and general aches that accompany an infected kidney. The mistake made by the student health center was in not getting a urine sample. Anyone with high fever and chills needs to have a urine specimen as part of the workup.

Kidney Stones, or "Nephrolithiasis"

Despite the fact that we associate the presence of kidney stones with adults, it is not that unusual to see this in the teenager of both genders. Most teens will have stones that are high in calcium. Hydration, diet, vitamins, and heredity play a strong role in developing the stone. If possible, all stones need to be collected for analysis so that a diet can be modified.

When the problem occurs, the teen may have blood in the urine but not yet have any other symptoms. Then one day, he may unexpectedly complain of pain in the back, or in the abdomen, and then he passes a stone—an exceedingly painful process that one mother described as "more painful than childbirth." I took her word for it.

> **George was a junior** *in high school who, upon an annual physical exam, had some red blood cells in his urine but nothing to suggest that the cells were coming from the kidney. He had no history of trauma, although he was on the soccer team. After a few other tests and a sonogram of the kidney, I made the general diagnosis of "benign hematuria" (see above) since I could find no pathology of his kidney, neither clinically nor on the sonogram. He had no evidence of obstruction and no evidence of a kidney stone. George maintained a normal blood pressure and no health complaints over the next few years, but he continued to have a few red cells in his urine whenever he came in for an annual exam. When he went to college I made a note on his form that he had "benign hematuria." One day I got a call from the emergency room near his college. George had come in with severe abdominal pains. Finally, a sonogram in the emergency room revealed a small stone lodged at the point where the kidney met the ureter.*

George illustrates the point that some patients can have a stone that is too small to be picked up on sonogram for quite a while, and the situation merits watching for possible changes.

Proteinuria

Protein does not belong in urine, and its presence signals reason for concern. This large molecular entity should not be passed through the strainer of the kidney's filtration, and it can signal a major problem that will need to be investigated.

If teenagers get their urine analyzed as part of total care, the presence of protein is quite frequent. It usually signals concern for the parent and the teen because he is unaware of two benign explanations: Sometimes the collection method can be at fault, and a different sampling will correct the situation. The urine collected after the patient has been lying down overnight will fail to show the protein, but a specimen collected in the midst of a busy day will have a greater hydrostatic pressure on the kidney and yield a small amount of protein. This is felt to be benign and labeled "orthostatic proteinuria." No treatment is necessary. Another "benign" reason for having protein in the urine is that ejaculate contains protein. If a boy has ejaculated or a girl has had unprotected sex prior to the urinanalysis, semen may have tainted the sample.

The Female Reproductive System

While men's reproductive anatomy is easy to examine, the female, with her internal "hidden" system appears more complex. The female genitalia appear mysterious, and certainly, society considers the female anatomy to be more private and sensitive than the male. Moreover, the fact that the female body may be called on to sustain a pregnancy makes it all the more important to address diseases and irregularities.

Timing of the First Pelvic Exam

If you are fortunate, your pediatrician has done a visual examination of your daughter's external genitalia throughout her childhood, just as he checks a boy's genitals. Unfortunately, not all doctors do this, and this often leaves teenage girls feeling quite awkward about having their genital area examined.

Any physician who is trained to do pelvic exams can do them, including a pediatrician or adolescent medicine doctor. Yet because it is a delicate exam from the point of view of modesty, many physicians shy away from examining teenage girls. Realistically, many girls, or their mothers on their behalf, prefer that the examining physician be a woman.

If I had to make a choice, I would probably opt for a woman doctor for the first examination for most teenage girls. Having undergone it herself, she is likely to be sensitive to a girl's feelings. However, unfortunately, a woman physician does not guarantee compassion—a first exam on a teenager does require more time to explain the process, and in some offices, the pace is just too frantic to take that time. I have had kids come back and report that "She just poked me with that thing!" While this may be an exaggeration, the perception of the exam being conducted in that manner is almost as bad as having it happen.

What is more important than the gender of the physician is the way the girl is treated and the level of confidential care that she gets. The room should be adequately equipped for the pelvic exam. That means a pelvic exam table with stirrups and proper speculum and lights. I personally dislike the use of paper gowns as they rip easily. If their purpose is to assure some privacy, I prefer cloth gowns. All of my patients get cloth ones that wrap well enough to close the back opening.

While on the subject, the gynecologist who is terrific for mom or Aunt Ruthie may be inappropriate for your daughter. As simplistic as it sounds, some people just don't like teenagers as people or as patients. What's more, your teen may prefer to go to someone other than "Mom's gynecologist," since this is an age when privacy and confidentiality are paramount.

Screening for the right physician can only be done by word of mouth or by referral from a physician who has experience with teens. In my own practice, I have narrowed the search down to a precious few physicians whom I know to be particularly kind and compassionate with teens.

The Pelvic Exam

Before a teen is flat on her back with her feet in the stirrups, she should be given an explanation as to what to expect. I have a plastic transparent model of the female pelvis that I use to demonstrate the anatomy and position of the speculum. Doctors performing first pelvic exams also need to reassure teens that the examination may be uncomfortable but it is not painful. They should show the instruments and point out that they may be cold.

What exactly does the examination yield? Mothers who are reading this will be familiar with the exam and its purpose, but for fathers this may be new information.

A visual inspection begins the examination, and wise doctors explain as they go through the process. The first obvious point will be the presence of pubic hair and its distribution. What is her sexual stage of pubic hair relative to her age? Does she actually have hair? Too much hair may give rise to concerns about excessive male hormones. Next, the doctor looks for signs of infec-

Reasons Why Pelvic Exams Are Needed

At the very least the following girls need a pelvic examination:

■ Any girl with unexplained abdominal pain that could be related to the reproductive system. One could bypass the examination with a pelvic sonogram but good care should include a bimanual pelvic examination *and* a sonogram.

■ Any girl who has a vaginal discharge or pain.

■ A girl who has reached sixteen and has not had menses. Some would argue that you can extend this to eighteen, but in a healthy girl sixteen is well within the norm for a first period.

■ A girl who has unusually prolonged menstrual bleeding.

■ Any sexually active girl needs to be assessed for infection and for birth control. Because some girls will not admit to their parents such a problem or need, they often don't get properly examined. In many states, girls can go to a funded clinic, or even to a private doctor without parental consent.

■ Girls who are about to go to college. This should be done so that issues of birth control can be discussed (without parental intervention) and a Pap smear can be done. Your college-age daughter should have a relationship with someone beyond the campus nurse practitioner or gynecologist. These people are fine for dispensing birth control, or for the occasional *ad hoc* concern about an infection, but it is important for a girl to have a more permanent medical *relationship* that establishes ongoing trust.

■ Any girl who has been sexually abused. Here I draw the line on the gender of the physician. My opinion is that only a woman physician should do this examination. There will be exceptions to this "rule," but in general, this is the best choice.

tion, swelling, or discharges. (A bad odor may signal an infection.) Then the doctor will use her fingers to spread the labia and the clitoris is visually checked for size; again, this is critical, since in some conditions of increased male hormones the clitoris will be large. By simply spreading the labia a bit more the hymen is visible; if not, the patient can bear down a bit and the slight increase in pressure makes it easier to see.

Dispel, dear reader, the notion that virginity is predicated on an intact hymen. (Even in this modern age, I will get an occasional parent who wants to "check" for virginity by asking about the hymen!) An intact hymen is likely, but not necessary, for virginity. Most hymens will have enough of an opening to allow a tampon or an examining finger, and a torn hymen does not imply that the girl had intercourse.

Next, as the teen relaxes, the examiner can gently insert a finger to make it easier for the patient to accept the insertion of the speculum. With one finger in the vagina and the other hand on the abdomen, the doctor can evaluate the presence, location, and size of the ovaries and uterus. In many situations, it is also necessary to do a rectoabdominal examination, in which one finger is inserted in the vagina and the other in the rectum. This allows for further assessment of the internal organs. I can't emphasize enough how important it is to have the girl aware, not only of the examination itself, but of the sensation of wanting to have a bowel movement as the finger is inserted in the anus. (This courtesy should be afforded to all who have a rectal exam. I routinely tell older boys ready for their first prostatic examination that the rectal will make them want to "go to the bathroom.")

The ovaries are about one to two inches long by about one inch wide and roughly three-quarter inches thick. The ovaries eventually end up in the left and right lower quadrants of the abdomen and can, in skilled hands, be palpated with a bimanual pelvic examination.

Finally, a warm-to-the-touch speculum is inserted to observe the cervix and vagina. Most new specula are disposable plastic ones and have a place for a light so that the entire inside of the vagina is illuminated and easy to see. The plastic ones also have the advantage of not being as cold as the metal reusable ones. Once the speculum is gently inserted, it is spread, and the doctor can do an examination, culture, and Pap smear. The smear is performed with a combination of a "Q-tip" type of probe to scrape cells from the surface of the cervix, and a "cytobrush" to scrape cells off the lining of the cervix and place the gathered cells on a microscope slide. A newer technique using a small brush and a special solution (called a wet smear specimen) is making the wooden sticks obsolete. The speculum is then closed and gently withdrawn. From a girl's point of view what counts is that the exam is now over.

As complex as all this sounds, the total time of the examination is about ten minutes. What takes longer is the explanations and assurances that the teenager needs to have. They are worth making.

The mere mention of the pelvic exam to most teenage girls draws facial contortions, even among sexually active tenth graders. By the eleventh grade there seems to be a marked improvement in the acceptance for the need to do a pelvic in certain situations.

The Time for a Gynecologist

Some physicians are comfortable with teenagers and with doing a pelvic examination. For the routine examinations these physicians are optimal since the teenager has already established a relationship and the pelvic is an extension of her care. There is nothing "extra" or "special" that requires a new physician. However, in situations where a surgical procedure, or a pregnancy termination is involved, a gynecologist is often required.

Some of my patients are perfectly comfortable with a male physician. They allow a chest examination, or a breast palpation, and allow me to examine their abdomen, and even their back for scoliosis while they are not wearing a gown. Yet they draw the line when it comes to doing a pelvic examination. I simply refer to one of several gynecologists who treat teenagers with the proper respect and patience. Interestingly, these patients will ask me to go over what is involved with the exam before they agree to see the new doctor. This is a good way to foster a link between myself and the new physician.

The Rate of Female Development

The question on every predolescent's mind is the "when" of the entire process. Sixth- and seventh-grade girls range from flat-chested to being nearly fully developed, and there is no doubt that those on either side of the spectrum are wondering, "Is there something wrong with me that I developed so early (or that I am developing so late)?"

Most girls will begin to show visible signs of puberty by the sixth grade. Though the age of onset seems to be getting younger, the average American girl today can expect her first menses (menstrual period) will take place at twelve years of age plus or minus one year (see Chapter 2 on puberty for more information).

In almost all cases, the rate of development is genetically determined, but a good physician will investigate further whenever he sees signs of what might be either delayed puberty or precocious puberty.

Delayed Puberty

If an eighth grader (age thirteen to fourteen) is not yet showing signs of puberty, most physicians will want to assess what is happening to the ovaries. Why are they not producing the necessary estrogen to develop breasts, curves, and an increase in body fat? The most common "problem" will be that the girl is programmed to follow her mother's and sister's course, and she will develop later. However, one has to at least check for a potential problem. If you are concerned about your daughter's development, talk to your doctor.

If only the menstrual period is delayed, refer to "Primary Amenorrhea," which is later in this section.

Precocious Puberty

The other end of the spectrum is the girl who develops early. Her breasts, her figure, her increase in growth, and her menses take place long before her peers. She is the one who at eight is already showing significant pubertal changes and at ten has her menses. It is important to distinguish precocious puberty from an isolated development of breasts (premature telarche) or of pubic hair (premature adrenarche). With precocious puberty, all normal development has been accelerated; the sequence of pubertal changes is intact but occurs much sooner than the norm. In most cases, there is no pathology involved—everything just happens earlier.

As we realize that girls are developing earlier, we are even beginning to think that girls are "normal" if they develop *before* eight. Arguments about milk and its hormonal products have been invoked as possible causes. The bottom line is that there seems to be a trend to earlier development, and this is still within the range of "normal."

However, the girl who has any central nervous system disorder appears "at risk" for initiating an early puberty. It doesn't matter if the disorder is a history of seizures or evidence of concussions. We are not clear why the process begins in the first place, but it would appear that any brain pathology triggers it earlier. The physician who is doing the evaluation may order scans of the brain to rule out a pathology that is manifesting itself through, and only through, early pubertal onset.

Any girl who develops before the age of eight, although potentially normal, needs an evaluation for pathology of the brain, of the ovaries, or of the adrenal glands. Based on family history and personal development, she may be perfectly normal but it is still worth giving her a full checkup.

Menstruation

Most girls today no longer "fear" their first periods. Sex ed classes and mothers openly address the first period. If the girl has reached the third stage of breast development (see Chapter 2, "Puberty: Your Developing Child, Your Developing Teen") and she has pubic hair on the mons (the visible top part) she is close to being ready. If she also has hair in the armpits, and a slight white or clear vaginal discharge, we have all the signs that she has made enough estrogen. Finally, if she weighs about 88 pounds or more (assuming average height), the brain realizes that she has enough weight to signal adequate nutrition. Within six months of the appearance of these characteristics, one can anticipate a first period, menarche.

Most girls will produce only estrogen for a year or two. When the lining of the uterine wall is produced by estrogen alone, it is very fragile, and this is why young girls have irregular bleeding at the start. For the wall to be prepared for a pregnancy, progesterone needs to be made by the ovary, and it is this hormone that holds the fragile lining in place for an egg to implant.

Menstrual Cycle

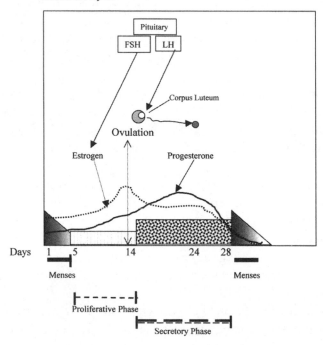

The Dos and Don'ts of Menstrual Periods

Dos:

1. When your daughter is beginning to develop, show her both sanitary napkins and the tampons. Many girls cannot appreciate the idea of the blood coming out almost uncontrollably. Assure her that the sanitary napkins will handle almost all situations, and that they are comfortable and most important, the pads *do not* show when worn.
2. Assure her that tampons are quite safe and with a little practice she will be able to insert it. Though it takes practice to become accustomed to the proper angle for insertion, the illustrated instructions within the packaging are generally helpful. Tell her that you can't think of a single woman who wanted to use a tampon who wasn't able to master it. All eventually get the knack of it.
3. Let her know that she will be able to sleep wearing a tampon and even go swimming with it. She can climb, run, sweat, and do somersaults as well. The current tampons no longer give rise to concerns about Toxic Shock Syndrome.
4. Let her know she can come to you if any problems or concerns arise.

Don'ts:

1. Don't tell her that periods will be painful. Since she will not be ovulating before the first period, there is every expectation that no premenstrual pain will accompany the cycle.
2. Don't tell her that she cannot wear a tampon because they are "too big" or too hard to use. They come in junior sizes and therefore can be inserted in younger girls. Unless culturally you, as a parent, have a major objection, tampons are safe.
3. Don't make it secretive, but don't advertise it either. I have had mothers who "didn't want to tell Daddy," while others called grandmother and nearly took out an ad in the *New York Times*.

Both estrogen and progesterone are under the direct control of the pituitary gland, which send two major messages through hormones, follicle stimulating hormone and luteinizing hormone. The first (FSH) is responsible for the release of an egg from the ovary, and the second (LH) will maintain the production of progesterone. As early as eight years old, a girl's ovaries can respond to each of these hormones and begin the process of puberty. It will take a few years for the ovary to mature sufficiently to respond with some rhythmic cycle so that the menses occurs approximately every twenty-eight days.

Anatomy, sexual hormones, stress, and even who lives in the household are all important in determining a teenager's menstrual cycle. When one stops to think about the intricacy of the process, it is not surprising that a girl will miss a period or two occasionally. If a girl changes environments, such as going to camp in the summer, the delicacy of the ovulatory cycle may be disturbed and a menses may be missed.

Another interesting piece of information is that girls who live together in groups will have a "leader" who will alter the other girls' cycles via the strength of a hormone called a pheromone. One female in a dorm or a bunk or in a predominantly female household will send a hormonal message to the others, and they unconsciously respond. They are literally smelling their way to having cycles at the same time!

Premenstrual Syndrome (PMS)

Few people today question the fact that mood alterations and various physical symptoms occur in the days prior to a girl's period. Long the butt of jokes, this is as real as a kick in the groin. (The analogy is given for any father who happens to be reading at the present time. Your daughter's mood *has* changed just before her menses starts, and it is due to hormones, not to some psychological "female" trait.)

Each girl will have her own version and time frame, though some girls' symptoms may prove only a small nuisance to them. Others will have symptoms for one to two weeks before their period, while some realize that the onset of their symptoms means they are about to start bleeding. Almost all report that the symptoms go away once their menses start.

Symptoms range from depression, anxiety, and mood swings to a host of physical symptoms ranging from breast tenderness and fluid retention to diarrhea. Headaches, tiredness, nausea, increased appetite, weight gain, and feeling "bloated" are all part of the profile. (No male will ever understand or use this term, "bloat," but trust me as a thirty-year practitioner, it's real. For Dads,

Relieving the Symptoms of PMS

Exercise. Many girls find that exercise is quite helpful. Is this a way of releasing endorphins in the brain and lessening symptoms? Or, is it a relaxation of muscles that need to loosen up? We don't know, but it works. Running, swimming, or just a good workout at the gym are great choices. One of my patients likes to box, so that she can exercise and get out aggression at the same time.

Prescription medication. Because of the swelling that most experience, attempts at fluid loss through diuretics is a frequent response. Some women use spironolactone, which has the effect of blocking the kidney production of a fluid-retaining hormone. The doses for both diuretics and spironolactone tend to be on the low side but the physician who prescribes them will monitor any side effects, such as a lowering of potassium levels. In most cases, short-term use will pose no problems.

For teens who have severe depression with PMS the recent use of the SSRI (selective serotonin reuptake inhibitor) antidepressant Prozac has proven successful. This has shown significant promise since it raises the serotonin levels in the brain and helps to stabilize moods. Fluoxetine, the generic name for Prozac, is marketed as Sarafem for the specific use in "premenstrual dysphoric disorder" or PMDD. This relatively new term is used to distinguish the severity of the depression and irritability that can accompany the weeks preceding menses from normal mood fluctuations.

To diagnose PMDD, the teen should have symptoms severe enough to interfere with work, school, or social functioning. The initial data suggested that fluoxetine should be given for six cycles to stop the symptoms. Subsequent studies are suggesting that taking the medication for the two weeks preceding menses is effective. As new studies with different antidepressants become available, the treatment for PMDD may be altered. Your physician will decide the best course for your teen.

Diet. Avoidance of salt, despite the craving, is recommended as salt tends to cause fluid retention in the body. Complex carbohydrates (starches) are preferred to simple sugar (which cause a rapid rise and fall in bood sugar that may affect mood and energy level, and it is recommended that the latter be decreased prior to menses. Caffeine seems to aggravate breast tenderness and may exacerbate irritability so coffee, teas, and caffeinated sodas should be minimized at this time. This hurts—

chocolate also can worsen PMS because of its caffeine and simple sugar content, and cigarettes and alcohol can also make PMS worse.

In most cases, the use of a birth control pill will alter many of the symptoms. Since the pill provides a steady dose of hormones, the variations of mood and symptoms may decrease.

Vitamins and herbal medicines. It has been observed that the following vitamins and minerals are useful in alleviating PMS symptoms (your doctor can recommend dosages): Vitamin B$_6$ is good for moodiness and for breast pain. While effective, it must be used carefully as it can cause toxicity to nerves in high doses. Some women take the vitamins on a regular basis while others can take it for the two weeks preceding menses. Your doctor will recommend dosages and how to take the medication. Vitamin E has also been used to reduce breast pain. Magnesium at 300 to 500 mg per day has been used to lower breast pain. Calcium is also effective. Chamomile tea is often cited as beneficial for its mild sedative quality.

think of how you feel after beer, pretzels, sausages, and pie—it's close enough!) Some will complain of not being able to think as clearly. A craving for sugar and salt is common and I have heard more than one female tell me that they "need" chocolate! (The tryptophan in chocolate, which has a calming effect, may offer a possible explanation for the craving.)

Though PMS is a very real condition, some girls are prone to use it as an excuse for everything. For example, rather than acknowledging that she's cranky because of eating poorly and staying up until all hours, a teen may play the PMS card. Males, too, are willing to dismiss as PMS a girl's display of anger—no matter how valid. It is true that women can be more irritable and tense just before their cycle, but that should not be the first invocation when there is disagreement. If she doesn't have PMS, the argument is trivialized; if she does, she won't even want to listen to you.

The twentieth century has now seen women in power in industry, in medicine, in politics, and in every conceivable walk of life. The notion that a woman cannot govern, lead, or fly fighter planes because of PMS should be laid to rest. We still have some who would argue the point but I suspect they will always be there. Also remember that particularly bad PMS can be treated if need be.

Menstrual Irregularities

■ Dysfunctional Uterine Bleeding

Most of the time, girls who bleed irregularly and frequently have dysfunctional uterine bleeding (DUB), which may be inconvenient, but is actually quite common since it takes time for the menstrual cycle to assume the normal adult flow and regularity. Because rhythmic cycles require ovulation to generate the necessary progesterone, and these early cycles produce only estrogen, young girls frequently have breakthrough bleeding (bleeding between periods). As a result of this imbalance, these young girls may shed uterine lining as often as daily.

Treatment depends on the severity of the bleeding. Iron is often given to correct for the blood loss, but the main part of the therapy is to replace estrogen and progesterone in order to stop the shedding. The mild to moderate flow can be corrected with a birth control pill that delivers a constant amount of estrogen and progesterone on a daily basis. (See Chapter 9 for more information on the Pill.)

In severe bleeding the hemoglobin may be so low that the teenager will feel weak and have low blood pressure. Since this is no different than someone who is bleeding profusely from an injury, the patient may be admitted to the hospital until the bleeding is brought under control. One of my patients was so weak that she nearly collapsed in my office. She bled so much that her hemoglobin was close to 7; the normal level is 13 to 15. In order to stop this amount of flow, the birth control pill may be given as often as every four hours. In fact, with some girls one has to resort to intravenous estrogen replacement with Premarin, followed by a high dose of an oral contraceptive for one cycle. After the cycle ends, she is placed on a lower dose of birth control pill for at least three to six months.

In many ways, this is a diagnosis of exclusion. Yes, the young girl is the right age, and it all fits that she is having anovulatory bleeding. However, there are other possibilities to entertain. The only way to diagnose is to rule out other causes.

■ Excessive Bleeding

Teenagers frequently suffer from too heavy or too frequent menstrual bleeding. The periods come too soon and, in fact, may be a daily or weekly issue. Alternatively, the flow itself is "too heavy."

With dysfunctional uterine bleeding (see above), there is no pathology other than a lack of progesterone from a anovulatory cycle. With "excessive bleeding" the cause may be a tumor, a laceration, an infection, etc. Fortunately, DUB is the more common cause.

A thorough and confidential history is paramount. The doctor will inquire about the amount of flow, medications taken, any weakness experienced, and how many pads or tampons are being used daily. Parents are generally asked to leave the room during part of the discussion, as the doctor may explore the possibility of a pregnancy, miscarriage, or abortion.

It is also important for a doctor to determine what a patient means by "excessive." She may say that she got her period "twice this month." She may be referring to a calendar month of thirty days, when she has a twenty-four-day interval for this cycle. In her mind, it *is* twice a month. She may say that she is using "a lot of pads," when she is actually using a reasonable five or six per day. (A pad count is unreliable as some girls change more often because they feel they "need to.") To qualify as "excessive," a doctor is looking for a report of thirteen or more soaked pads per day.

■ Clotting Disorders

If a girl is bleeding from her vagina, we automatically assume that this is menstrual blood and it "belongs" there, but a subtle disorder of the coagulation system may be interfering with the normal clotting process of the menstrual flow. There are standards for the time that blood should clot. An activated partial thromboplastin time is a blood test that simply gives the time that blood takes to clot. In the event of a prolonged clotting time, the problem with the excessive bleeding is one of a coagulation defect. One of the most common is the inherited von Willebrand's disease in which a protein is missing that allows the blood to clot. Often it is so subtle that it is not picked up in childhood and the clotting time test is not performed. In retrospect, some girls will remember that they bruise easily, that they get nosebleeds regularly, or that their gums bleed easily. They should be checked for von Willebrand, but often there will be no prior history of bleeding. Treatment depends on the severity of bleeding. In some girls, where the vaginal bleeding is not severe, one can treat with hormones to help stop the bleeding. In others, special clotting medications may be needed intravenously if the flow is excessive. In some girls the disorder is so subtle that it will not be picked up in her teens or twenties. She will simply have longer flows.

■ Foreign Body

Probably the most common foreign body in the vagina is the forgotten tampon. The ease of fit and use makes some girls simply forget they are wearing them. After a few days, the girl will note a bloody vaginal discharge. The odor is quite strong in most cases and she will have trouble removing the soaked tampon. To add to the problem, she is embarrassed at her plight and may prolong the call to the physician even further. The offending foreign body, the tampon, has to be removed by the doctor, and the girl is usually placed on some intravaginal antibiotics.

▪ Infection

More on infections is covered in Chapter 10, "Sexually Transmitted Diseases," but it is worth mentioning that the menstrual flow that is combined with a bad odor may actually be the sign of an infection.

▪ Miscarriage, or "Missed Abortion"

A "missed abortion" (in which the woman has a spontaneous abortion and doesn't realize it) can present with irregular or excessive vaginal bleeding. It may be difficult to diagnose because of the teen's reluctance to admit that she might have been pregnant. If in doubt, many physicians order a pregnancy test under the guise that it is a "routine" procedure with any girl who is bleeding profusely. If she is in the process of miscarriage, the hormones will still be elevated. This often saves face for the girl and the parent when the test shows up negative. It's worth the "I told you so" that inevitably follows. Then other reasons can be looked for.

▪ Oral Contraceptives

Since the new birth control pills have low levels of estrogen either for the entire duration of the cycle (tricyclic pills) or, in the case of the triphasic pills, for the first week (the triphasic pill will increase estrogen in the second week), it is possible to bleed during that time. The pills also have incremental amounts of progesterone with the lowest dose in the first week. Many physicians will accept the low estrogen pill's consequences of some breakthrough bleeding during the first month in return for fewer estrogen side effects. As long as the girl knows ahead of time, she, too, is reasonably comfortable with the trade-off. Naturally, if the bleeding is excessive, the pill has to be changed for one that has a higher estrogen concentration or a steady amount of progesterone.

▪ Thyroid Disorder

Both high and low levels of thyroid hormone can precipitate excessive bleeding and both are easily treated with medication (see p. 371 for a further discussion of the thyroid).

▪ Trauma

Lacerations of the vagina or external genitalia will obviously bleed. Questions about sexual abuse are obviously delicate but should be part of this evaluation. Your teenager has the right to have a private discussion with the physician, as she may not be comfortable sharing this type of information with you. All good doctors will share what you need to know once they have the information; they are legally obligated to report cases of abuse in the case of minors.

■ Vaginal Tumors

Tumors (they need not be malignant) inside the vagina or the uterus can break down and cause bleeding. A pelvic examination may show the mass, or a sonogram may be needed to detect intrauterine tumors. If a mass is identified, biopsies are needed to identify their origin and to determine if they are benign. Fortunately malignant genital-tract tumors are uncommon in teenagers.

Polyps of the cervix or vagina are rare and fortunately they tend to be benign. However, most are biopsied or removed fully. Sometimes the mere size of the polyp warrants removal as it can cause obstruction of blood flow. If the physician is positive that the polyp is benign, and it is small, it can be left in place.

Pain during Menstruation
(Dysmenorrhea)

Pain associated with menstruation used to be one of the leading causes for girls to miss school. However, newer pain medications have made it possible for girls to manage their menstrual cramps more easily.

While some are likely to say that menstrual pain is psychological, this accusation is insulting and demeaning. While teens may, indeed, use the discomfort to their advantage, both parents and doctors should take the complaints seriously so that a correct diagnosis can be made.

The pain of dysmenorreah is generated by contractions of the uterine muscles due to the production of prostaglandins. (These are a relatively newly discovered series of proteins that are critical in many diseases such as arthritis.) Prostaglandins are released because a woman is ovulating, so younger teens rarely have uterine cramping associated with their periods. However, a mild dose of ibuprofen may go a long way in helping alleviate any perceived discomfort. Since menstrual pain comes with ovulation, teens who are on the Pill, which suppresses ovulation, find that their pain disappears for as long as they are on it.

In treating dysmenorrhea, ibuprofen or naproxen (Aleve), both nonsteroidal antiinflammatory agents, or NSAIDs, are usually recommended. If your doctor suggests the over-the-counter-pill versions of either, ask him what dose your daughter should take. Depending on the severity of the pain and your daughter's health, he may recommend taking a higher dose than the package states.

If nonprescription medicines don't work, there are stronger prescription medicines, such as Anaprox DS (naproxen). Because of ease of use, the double strength Anaprox is one of the more popular prescriptions for dysmenorrhea. Some physicians will use Naprosyn, which is in the same family.

A new family of NSAIDs is the fenamates. Ponstel (mefenamic acid) was one of the first drugs in this group available for those who did not do well on the naproxen-like drugs. A newer version is Cataflam (diclofenac), given in the "immediate release" form for fast treatment of pain. Care must be taken with all of the NSAID pills. They cannot be used if there is any possibility of pregnancy, and they cannot be taken for more than a couple of days. Too much use can induce ulcerations of the gastrointestinal tract.

■ Mittelschmerz

This word, taken from the German, literally means "middle pain." For a girl this means as she ovulates midcycle, she may experience lower abdominal pains. Rupture of the follicle during ovulation generates the pain as the egg is released. The small amounts of blood and fluid from the follicle trickle down into the peritoneal space and the patient may experience an irritation of the area for several hours. In some girls the pain may persist for a day or two but that is unusual.

NSAID medications, both over-the-counter and prescription, and a heating pad are used to treat the pain. In some girls, the pain can be as debilitating as premenstrual pain. In those cases, a few months on the birth control pill to suppress ovulation not only will give her a vacation from pain, but when the Pill is stopped she may not have mittelschmerz again.

One has to be cautious when making this diagnosis. Since there are other reasons for pain in the lower abdomen, one has to be sure that urinary tract infections, ovarian cysts, twisted ovaries, tumors, sexually transmitted diseases, and even endometriosis have been eliminated as causes.

■ Primary Amenorrhea

Amenorrhea is the absence of menstrual periods; primary amenorrhea means that there hasn't been a first period. There are many potential issues to be investigated with primary amenorrhea, from poor nutrition to hormonal abnormalities.

Although a workup of the endocrine system is in order, the most obvious place to start is with the girl's diet. A doctor will measure hormone levels, but there are other, simpler questions that need to be answered. Is she eating enough protein? Is she losing weight, or maintaining it when she should be gaining? If the answers to these questions are positive, puberty will be halted because the hypothalamus will signal the pituitary that the body is not ready for puberty. (This is nature's way of preventing pregnancy in the malnourished.) Girls who participate in sports in which body fat is reduced are likely to have this problem. A skater, a dancer, a gymnast, a runner will usually maintain a low percentage of body fat, and this can cause a delay in maturation. Generally 10 percent of body fat is considered the lowest acceptable limit for females.

In most practices that deal with teenage girls, one tends to see the gymnastic girl and the dancer often. Girls who have watched the "little girls" who do competitive gymnastics feel that's how they should look. Dancers, especially ballerinas, strive for the lean and long look, since appearance is as important as movement to their art, but gymnasts and runners also work to maintain slim bodies, and not always because this makes them better athletes. When not-so-lean girls participate in these activities, physicians frequently see unnecessary starvation.

A corollary of nutritional abnormalities is a condition in which the patient does not absorb food properly. The most common cause would be an inflammatory bowel disease, such as Crohn's disease (see p. 418), in which food is consumed but not absorbed because of inflammations in the bowel. Usually the girl will have diarrhea and abdominal pain as part of the malabsorption. Effectively the same scenario takes place as with poor nutrition, with the brain reading a situation in which the pituitary should not allow ovulation.

Another cause of amenorrhea is an imperforate (unbroken) hymen. The virginal hymen has enough of an opening to allow menstrual blood to escape; in the case of an imperforate hyphen, the opening is nonexistent. This problem should have been diagnosed in childhood, yet it may have escaped detection because pediatricians don't always look for it. As a teenager, then, the patient will have normal development but no menses. She will complain of intermittent monthly pain but no bleeding, and the unsuspecting parent may presume that the girl is having "menstrual cramps" and dismiss the issue. The girl is actually menstruating, but the blood has no means of escape and is trapped behind the imperforate hymen. The diagnosis is made by the presence of a painful bulging hymen ready to explode its trapped contents.

Since there is no outlet for the blood, the solution is to make an incision in the hymen (usually under anesthesia) and allow the trapped contents to be expelled. Once the incision opens the hymen, further menstrual blood can escape through the same opening.

If a girl is not developing, there may be ovarian abnormalities, and a chromosomal complication should be considered. The girl's natural chromosomes should include two X "sex" chromosomes. If there is an abnormality in one of these, or if one is missing, then the girl will not develop normally. She may be shorter than five feet and have distinguishing features such as a large webbed neck and a broad chest. The diagnosis of Turner's syndrome is one in which one of the X chromosomes is missing. The development of breasts and ovaries depends on the degree of X chromosome abnormality, and then we see variants of Turner's.

It is important to remember that the girl may develop pubic hair since this is under the adrenal gland's control. With even a slight amount of estrogen, there may be some breast buds in the girl. The question is has she progressed through the normal phases of puberty?

A rare condition is the girl who is making destructive antibodies against the ovaries. These girls often have several other autoimmune disorders, and it will be complications of their thyroid or adrenal glands that bring the problem of the ovary to light.

In terms of abnormal ovaries, nothing could be more "abnormal" than to have gonads (sex organs) that are actually testicles: this is known as testicular feminization. We need to recall that the process of male/female development requires the presence or absence of testosterone. However, in order to develop as a male, the embryo has to *respond* to the testosterone. If the testicle is present, and the testosterone is made, but the end organ fails to do what it should, then we have the equivalent of not having testosterone at all. In other words, if there is androgen insensitivity or, testicular feminization syndrome, there is a failure to develop as a male. These patients will have male chromosomes with the genetically male pattern of normal XY, and they will fail to develop a vagina. However, externally, they look like females, and may even go through pubic hair development, although many do not. Their ability to respond to the stimulus of the adrenal hormones is impaired, and pubic hair and axillary hair may be missing. If the condition is diagnosed at infancy, most of the children will have their gonads (in this case "testicles"; the female gonads are the ovaries) removed and breast tissue will not develop later. If the diagnosis is missed until puberty, breast tissue (they may even have large normal breasts) may develop from the small amount of estrogen made from the testes. The clue to this condition may be the absent pubic hair and the lack of menses.

I first saw Joan *when she was seventeen. She was tall and quite attractive and lived a normal teen life in a suburban setting. She had had her "gonads" (she used this word) removed "when she was little" and was being* *followed medically by the endocrine clinic at one of the major hospitals. She never once referred to her "testes" and told me that she was on estrogen pills to make up for the removed gonad. It was soon clear to me that she was unaware of the diagnosis. I excused myself from the room and talked to her parents, who cautioned me not to bring up the truth to Joan for they saw no reason to tell her what was happening. They also told me that they were very religious and would tell her before she got married, as that would have an impact on her "wedding night." I went back to continue my discussion and examination. Joan then told me in strictest confidence that she had a problem. Despite her upbringing, she had attempted intercourse and had been unable to perform. She blushed as she told me that her boyfriend had been unable to penetrate, and she wondered if her hymen was particularly tough. I contacted the endocrine expert who had been following Joan since she was a little girl and explained the problem. There were plans to have Joan's short vagina repaired and enlarged to enable intercourse. However, part of the surgical procedure required an artificial phallus to be left in place so that the walls of the new vagina would not collapse. Since her parents could not imagine premarital intercourse, they wanted the surgery delayed until Joan was "ready," i.e., engaged. I told the endocrinologist that "ready" had passed. This then precipitated a series of discussions with the family about Joan, her femininity, and her anatomy, which culminated in an open discussion about Joan's present and future sexual concerns. Both patient and parents required a great deal of counseling to come to terms with the situation. Thankfully, this condition is one that is not seen that often.*

Ovarian failure to respond to FSH (follicle stimulating hormone) and LH (leutenizing hormone) can be seen in other conditions. If the chromosomes are normal but there is still no pubertal development, and the girl is making FSH and LH, then a rare condition of premature ovarian failure is possible. Girls who underwent chemotherapy or radiation for a malignancy may fall into this category. The medications or the radiation damaged the ovaries and now the levels of FSH and LH are very high, as the pituitary attempts to get the unresponsive ovary to produce estrogen. Replacement hormone therapy is needed since the girl is not making her own estrogen.

If the girl is not developing, the thyroid gland needs to be evaluated with blood tests (see p. 371).

There is a small amount of circulating male hormone made by a normal female. It comes partially from the adrenal gland and partially from the ovary. The amount is negligible in terms of body hair and interference with the role of estrogen. However, in situations where there is excessive production of male hormones, the normal pubertal process is disrupted; this is called virilization. Adrenal tumors, adrenal enzyme abnormalities, ovarian tumors that may produce male hormones—all can interfere with the pubertal process. Treatment depends on what is happening in the adrenal gland. If a tumor is present it needs to be removed; if there is an overproduction of hormones because of too much stimulation of the adrenal gland or ovary from pituitary hormones, these must be blocked (see "Polycystic Ovaries," p. 460, and "Adult Onset Congenital Adrenal Hyperplasia," p. 461).

▪ Secondary Amenorrhea

In secondary amenorrhea, periods start but then stop. In theory this teen had enough normal hormones, a stable thyroid, and adequate nutrition to produce a menstrual flow. Now something has gone wrong elsewhere. Following are some of the things a doctor will look for.

While most women are aware that dancers, gymnasts, and skaters frequently suffer menstrual irregularities, female athletes of all types place their bodies under similar stresses (heavy exercise, weight issues, and the demands of high performance), and any serious athlete may have problems. The research on the exact reason why athletes have menstrual problems has yielded mixed results. It appears that the nutrition and protein intake of the athlete is most critical in determining if they maintain normal hormones. The amount of exercise is important but that, too, may simply be due to its effect of lowering of the weight as more calories are burnt. Or the hypothalamus may simply read "stress" as inappropriate for a normal cycle, and the result is that FSH and LH are suppressed.

Patients with thyroid abnormalities can miss their cycles. Sometimes it will be the first symptom to note, but usually there are many other features of each (see the section on thyroid, p. 371).

Another cause of secondary amenorrhea is elevated male hormones. Male hormones are responsible for facial hair, body hair, acne, oily skin, and male pattern baldness. Any girl who has facial hair or whose acne persists should have an evaluation for excessive amounts of male hormones (see above discussion of virilization). Investigation of polycystic ovaries (below) or male hormone-producing tumors of the ovaries, or a fairly common disorder of the adrenal gland, adult onset congenital adrenal hyperplasia, needs to be investigated.

In exactly the same way that poor nutrition can interfere with the development of puberty, so, too, can it halt the progression of the normal monthly cycles. Any girl who misses her period and is not pregnant should be monitored for inadequate protein intake and low body fat. She could be eating poorly without actually having an eating disorder, or could be losing protein because of a malabsorption problem.

The girl with anorexia nervosa or bulimia is likely to lose her menses as she loses weight and falls below a certain percentage of body weight for her height. This is covered in Chapter 5, "Teens, Nutrition, and Eating Disorders."

Lest we forget, the main reason for not having a menstrual cycle in a fully developed female is still pregnancy.

■ Progesterone Withdrawal Challenge

A simple test that doctors use with a girl who has stopped menstruating is the progesterone withdrawal challenge. In order to understand this "test," one needs to remember that estrogen primes the uterus for pregnancy with a thick, dense lining, and progesterone converts it into a thicker "mushy" layer so that the egg can implant. If, after this conversion, progesterone is withdrawn, then the lining disintegrates and the girl has a menses.

For the progesterone challenge, either natural or synthetic progesterone tablets are given to the girl over seven days. (Some physicians would give a lower dosage pill for a two-week interval in order to more approximate the "normal" progesterone secretion.) If her period starts within a week after finishing the progesterone, then several questions are answered: the patient has a normal vaginal outlet, her uterus is getting estrogen (otherwise no period could have been stimulated), and she is not pregnant. If a teen will not agree to a pregnancy test or a pelvic exam, this is an alternative. However, if a pregnancy is highly suspect, a natural progestin that will not interfere with a developing fetus will be given by your doctor in the event she is pregnant.

If no period occurs, the physician may suspect pregnancy. If that is unlikely, she will begin to consider ovarian failure, a chromosome abnormality, or poor nutrition. She may also explore whether or not there is an anatomical abnormality preventing menses. For example, a girl with an imperforate hymen will bleed, but we would not see the flow. If there were previous flows, then this is not an issue.

This test has its limitations and is generally used in conjunction with studies of the FSH, LH, prolactin, thyroid, and chromosome tests in assessing amenorrhea.

Disorders of the Reproductive System

Pelvic Pain

The girl who experiences lower abdominal discomfort may have pain due to urologic causes, gastrointestinal causes, or even skeletal problems. The key is always taking a thorough history and allowing her enough time to collect her thoughts and be comfortable with the physician. She may have information for the doctor but, if a parent is in the room, it may not be given. I have no doubt that a teen will let you know when you should be in the room, but it is harder to ask you to leave, for it implies a secret. Preempt the problem and offer her the opportunity to discuss some of the history alone with the doctor. "Honey, I'll step out so you can discuss some of the symptoms with Dr. Jones. I'll be in the waiting room if you need me for anything. Okay?"

■ Pelvic Inflammatory Disease

Since an inflammation of the uterus can cause mild to severe pain, it is worth noting here. For further discussion, see Chapter 10, "Sexually Transmitted Diseases."

Vaginal Irritations

Many of the infections, bumps, and pains of the vagina are due to infections and often are of a sexual nature. The specific diseases are covered in Chapter 10, "Sexually Transmitted Diseases." However some vaginal problems are not related to sexual diseases.

■ Discharge

A discharge is normal with some girls. This is due to the estrogen-primed vaginal lining and the presence of some shed cells. The problem is that the girl may not appreciate the fact that this is normal and become worried that something is wrong. I will never forget a lecture that I was to give to a group of seventh graders at an all-girls school. Another lecturer had preceded me the week before and had spent all of her time on STDs and vaginal discharges. Even before I could start my own talk on acne, several girls raised their hands because they were concerned that a "lot of girls had vaginal infections." It took a while for me to realize that normal discharge had not been discussed, and the class had been left believing that any discharge meant infection.

The normal discharge is thin, white, and does not have an odor. With genuine infections one of the above features changes. The color, the consistency, or the odor will trigger the need for an evaluation of infection. When in doubt, an examination under a microscope usually yields the answer. With normal discharge, the girl is aware of its presence because there may be some light amount on her underwear, or because of an itch or mild discomfort. For some, this discharge will precede each period, and it is important that they understand that nothing is wrong with them.

■ Yeast and Other Fungal Infections

Any time girls disturb the normal acidity and bacteria of the vagina, it sets the stage for a fungal infection. The girl who is on antibiotics for a long time (for acne, ear infections, sinus infections) simultaneously will destroy not only the bacteria that is causing the problem but also the "good" bacteria in the vagina. The small amount of normal yeast in the vagina will take advantage of this shift in the balance of organisms and pH and proliferate. A white cheesy, incredibly itchy discharge is the result. A small amount placed under the microscope will demonstrate the classic branching and budding of a yeast or another fungus. Along with the discharge, the yeast (*candida albicans*) or fungus will infect the girl's labia, and they become swollen and painful. I have had girls come in crying over the pain from infected and swollen labia.

Treatment today has become incredibly easy. A course of an antifungal cream or tablet inserted nightly in the vagina will cure it. Girls who are younger tend to complain about the applicator and the creams (or gels) as they find it difficult to maneuver the applicator into the vagina; the creams also drip, while the pills don't. A simpler solution is an oral pill, Diflucan (fluconazole), which has been found effective in treating the milder to moderate fungal infections. The doctor can best determine what your daughter should take. What a difference since grandmother's day, when women had to be treated with gentian violet, a violet-colored antifungal solution, which caused the whole area to become purple!

The FDA has made some of the antifungal creams available over the counter. Yet without seeing a doctor, one cannot tell if the discharge is really fungal.

Along with the medication, girls are advised to wear loose-fitting pants and cotton underwear. Although this can help, the real treatment is the medication.

While the physician is treating the yeast infection, assuming that the girl's antibiotics precipitated it, he will also check the urine to make sure that the patient does not have an early case of diabetes mellitus. In this condition, the excess sugar in the urine makes the fungus grow more readily.

■ Cysts of the Labia

The Bartholin glands are involved with lubrication. In most cases of infection, one has to consider sexual contact but it is possible to infect this gland with a nonsexually transmitted organism.

Some women will have excessive thick mucous and the ducts of the gland can get obstructed and infected. Normally the Bartholin glands are not easily visible but when they are infected, the back portion of the labia is swollen and there is localized tenderness. Treatment consists of antibiotics and drainage of the infected cysts.

Disorders of the Ovaries

With the advent of sonograms we have been able to identify ovarian pathology without resorting to the surgical intervention of thirty years ago. Following are some of the conditions that can occur.

■ Follicular Cysts

One of the first realizations that occurred with the advent of the sonogram was that women were actually walking around with cysts that were not causing a problem. These "follicular cysts" are commonly noted on sonograms and should be considered a variation of the norm. They can grow to two to three inches in size, are filled with a clear fluid, and shrink as the cycle progresses. All that is required is to monitor for symptoms and, in most cases, they will disappear over the course of a few months. Sometimes the size of the cyst will pose a problem and the gynecologist will insert a needle and remove the fluid; this is done through a laparoscope (a flexible tube inserted into the abdomen to directly visualize internally), and the incisions are minimal. A problem arises when a sonogram is ordered because of abdominal pain or some other symptom, and it reveals a cyst. Once the cyst is discovered, there is a dilemma: Is the cyst causing the pain, or is it "just there"?

Generally the best course of action is to monitor the situation. Cysts occur frequently, and all that is recommended is monitoring with followup pelvic exams or sonograms to watch the evolution of the cyst.

Occasionally the cyst will rupture spontaneously and the patient will experience a sudden, sharp pain in the lower abdomen. Nausea and vomiting may accompany the rupture, and one has to distinguish this from the acute abdominal pain of appendicitis. Sometimes the only way to tell the ruptured cyst from appendicitis is with an MRI scan of the abdomen. Since the cyst contains sterile fluid, there is no need to treat this rupture with antibiotics. The pain can be quite severe, but it usually will subside on its own with little intervention.

◼ Polycystic Ovaries

With excessive male hormones, a girl may experience irregularity, or even cessation, of her periods. Usually there is weight gain and acne, and the girl may note an increase in facial or body hair. All of the features of this syndrome may not be present at the same time, and the severity will vary with each girl because of a varying range of male hormones being produced. Secondary amenorrhea generally triggers the workup necessary to diagnose polycystic ovary (PCO) syndrome.

I have found that parents and teens are confused by these terms. There had been a debate between the endocrinology and gynecology worlds as to the criteria for PCO. The endocrinologists feel that the syndrome is defined by the elevation of the leutenizing hormone from the pituitary and by the increase in the amount of male hormone (androgen). The gynecologists counter that the syndrome requires the presence of multiple cysts if we are to call it "polycystic" (many cysts) in the first place. Today the two worlds have agreed on two different terms for syndromes that share the symptoms of high levels of LH and androgen: Girls who have cysts have PCO, while girls who do not manifest the multiple cysts have androgenizing ovary syndrome.

Regardless of the term, the treatment is aimed at lowering ovarian stimulation by LH. The simplest way of suppressing LH is to give the girl the birth control pill. This often will improve the acne, the menses irregularity, and the hair loss.

One has to decide when to initiate the birth control pill in this treatment. If there are no symptoms but only an elevation of LH, many physicians would opt to monitor and wait. Once there is an increase in testosterone, all the problems with acne, body hair, and weight gain become an issue, and the Pill is called for. As to the length of treatment, one first has to appreciate that the newer pills are very low in both estrogen and progesterone. Their low hormones allow for long-term use without worrying about the side effects that once plagued women who took the Pill years ago. The teenage girl is faced with an alternative between the effects of unusual amounts of testosterone or an artificially given amount of estrogen and progesterone. Given the effects of PCO, it is not much of a choice. I know of few girls who can put up with the effects of this disorder and not want to take any pill that would give relief.

When the girl reaches the age that she wants to conceive, she will have higher risk of infertility, but most women with PCO can conceive.

Unfortunately, once there is an increase in body hair it is difficult to remove. Facial hair does improve, but hair on the chest, thighs, abdomen, and buttocks is more problematic. I have sent several girls to have hair removed by the new laser treatment and the results have been mixed. For now, electrolysis and waxing are still necessary.

■ Adult Onset Congenital Adrenal Hyperplasia (ACAH)

Despite its name, this condition is seen in teens and is one of the most common genetic disorders. The girl who has adult onset congenital adrenal hyperplasia (ACAH) has an overproduction of male hormones because of a minor defect in an enzyme of the adrenal gland. With this small defect a girl makes too much of the male hormone, and her symptoms are very similar to the PCO patient (see above).

Teenagers will complain of acne, of increased body hair, of weight gain, and loss of head hair. The diagnosis relies upon an assessment of adrenal hormones done by a blood test. However, in some patients it may be necessary to do a stimulation of the adrenal gland to see if it is normal. Baseline adrenal blood values are obtained, and then the patient is given a hormone that stimulates the adrenal gland. Blood tests are done over time to see the effects of this stimulation. Treatment may consist of a small amount of cortisol to suppress the stimulation of the adrenal. Newer "antiandrogens" are being used to curb the production of the male hormones.

Often, as part of the disorder, the girl may show a "male pattern baldness," in which hair is lost in the back portion of the head. Although one associates increased body hair with ACAH, we have to remember the girl with less hair on her head is also a likely candidate. The presence of acne unrelated to the menstrual cycle beyond the late teenage years in the girl should also raise suspicion.

Some ethnic populations are particular prone to carry the gene for ACAH. One such group is Ashkenazi Jewish woman; it is estimated that more than 10 percent will manifest ACAH.

It is worth noting that a workup for hirsutism (excessive body hair) in a girl can be quite expensive. Not only are the relatively expensive thyroid tests ordered, but the patient will need tests for FSH, LH, prolactin, testosterone (total and free), sex binding globulin, DHEA-S, androstenedione, and the other adrenal hormones. I have had several patients and parents who were flabbergasted at the laboratory bill for this evaluation. It is an evaluation that should be undertaken, but I always warn the parents about the cost. You can discuss this with your physician who may be able to help you with your insurance company.

■ Other Ovarian Masses

Not all ovarian cysts are filled with clear fluid and go away with time. Some actually will hemorrhage and blood will fill the cyst. In time, the fresh blood deteriorates into a dark coagulated material, and the "chocolate cyst" is formed. These are associated with abdominal pain and even with irregularity of menstrual flow, as some will produce progesterone and disrupt the normal cycle. If the cyst ruptures, all its contents will be discharged into the peritoneal space. The patient's symptoms are those of a ruptured appendix, since the peritoneal lining is irritated. The toxicity to the patient is directly related to the content that spilled.

Treatment usually consists of the birth control pill to suppress the pituitary hormones and remove the cyst's stimulation. In this case, one can be on the Pill for a few months to allow suppression of cysts for a while. If more occur, then the girl may be on the Pill for a few years to prevent cyst formation. In situations where the cyst is very large, then it must be removed. If possible, the ideal route would be through the laparoscope (a flexible tube inserted into the abdomen to directly visualize internally), since this minimizes scar tissue and healing. However, if there is any question that the cyst removal will be complicated and the ovary is in danger of being lost, then a small incision is made in the lower quadrant to expose the ovary. In so doing, the surgeon can do a more careful dissection and, hopefully, salvage the ovary.

One other potential problem with a large cyst is the possibility of the ovary rotating due to the imbalance of the cyst, or the cyst itself may twist. If the former occurs, the patient will be in excruciating pain and without surgical intervention may lose the ovary.

■ Solid Tumors of the Ovary

Some tumors will present with pain or with fullness, but often they are just there waiting to be detected, perhaps by a sonogram ordered for other reasons. Others will be so large that they obstruct the flow of stool and cause constipation. Some have unusual tissue collected internally while others will produce estrogens or androgens.

The most common teenage ovarian tumor is the dermoid cyst, or benign cystic teratoma. This type of tumor arises from germ cells in the ovary and may be located on both sides. If one is discovered, it is important that the other ovary be examined. Since the tumor arises from embryological germ cells, it can contain any of the body tissues. Teeth, skin, nails, muscle tissue may all be found in the tumor. One has to be careful in presenting this to the teenager; she may respond with disbelief and disgust at the idea of "teeth in my ovaries."

The teratoma is a benign tumor but one still wants to remove it since it will inevitably grow and destroy the ovary. It can also undergo malignant transformation, although this is rare. Other benign tumors include fibromas but they are exceedingly rare.

> **Janice was being monitored** *for extreme obesity, and once she reached 300 pounds she was offered the option of abdominal stapling. At twenty-three she had already tried every diet possible, and she agreed to the stapling. As the weight was lost, she felt better daily. However, one day she experienced abdominal pain in her left lower quadrant and felt nauseated. Since she had had surgery, it was deemed important to get an X ray of her abdomen to see if there were any loops of bowel that were not moving. On the X ray a set of miscellaneous teeth were visible in the right lower quadrant. A scan of the pelvis revealed that Janice had a teratoma with teeth as one of its components. With her obesity it had been difficult to detect any pelvic masses and X rays of that area had never been done for any reason. She underwent an abdominal exploration to remove the teratoma and salvage the ovary.*

Malignant tumors can exist in teenagers. The dysgerminoma is the most common of the malignant tumors and, it too, can occur bilaterally. There are several other malignant tumors that can present but they are rare. The key is to believe the teenager who complains of lower abdominal pain and consider an ovarian ailment as an explanation.

No doubt you have been left with a sense of awe and concern after reading about the possibilities of the gynecologic system. Yet, your daughter and the vast majority of girls go through their teen years and their mature years with no problems. They have annual visits for a pelvic examination and no masses, no abnormal discharges, and no abnormal Pap smears. They leave the gynecologist's office reassured that they are healthy and simply note when the next appointment is due. The vast majority of girls have no disorders and eventually have no problem bearing children later.

We monitor all aspects of the teenager's physical growth and development. Parents should appreciate that the gynecological care of the teenager is part of good medical management and should not be postponed until "she needs it." Sexual activity is not the only aspect of gynecology, and parents need to understand this or their daughters will not get the best care possible.

The Male Reproductive System

The Prostatic Gland

The prostate sits directly behind the bladder, and every male over fifty is well acquainted with the pressure this exerts nightly as he ventures to the bathroom several times during sleep. Mothers can relate to this if they recall what it was like during pregnancy to feel pressure on the bladder and the need to void frequently.

Most boys have the luxury of small, firm, normal prostates. They can go for hours and not think of voiding. They take their prostates for granted, as they should. Unless they get a sexually transmitted disease and they complain of irritation on voiding, they couldn't care less where the prostate is located. They quickly decide that it is important when the physician needs to do a rectal to decide about infection and tenderness.

"Oh no, Doc, not that! Are you serious? Just give me a shot, I mean it. You can't possibly be thinking of putting, what . . . a finger! Wow! Do you do this a lot, I mean to other kids?" The reason for the examination is to ascertain prostatic swelling, tenderness, and texture. At the same time, one massages the gland in the hopes of producing some bacterial discharge from the penis during the next void. This voided specimen would potentially contain material "squeezed" out of the prostate during the massage, and it may yield a clue as to the organism that is causing the infection.

Teenagers can, and do, develop infections of the prostate; in most cases, it will be sexually transmitted. The teen may complain of urinary symptoms and possibly fever associated with chills. In a way, it mimics an infection of the kidney. The history of sexual exposure is important. If the cultures are negative, the doctor may treat with an antibiotic and the patient will be advised to abstain from sex for two weeks to rest the area.

Another possible finding in prostatitis may be the presence of blood in an ejaculate. Sometimes this happens because of trauma, but the possibility of an infected prostate should also be considered.

The Penis

In some boys the opening of the urethra (meatus) is located toward or on the underside of the penis; this is called hypospadias, and it is almost always caught by the pediatrician. If the opening (meatus) is slightly off center, it matters little except for aiming at the toilet. However, if the opening is significantly below the center and on the underside of the penis, problems with ejaculation and urination may arise. Again, these rarely escape the pediatrician.

The penis also contains small oil glands that can get irritated and swollen, and this is very alarming to teens who have heard over and over about some of the symptoms of sexually transmitted diseases. Even those who are not having intercourse will call me about an irritated area they found after they masturbated or after some "fooling around with a girl." In the back of their heads, they are worrying about herpes or even syphilis. That's fine; they should be concerned as these are possible.

Sometimes patients will show me very small pearly nodes along the edge of the glans (the tip, or head, or the penis). These are commonly mistaken for an infection. They have been there all along, but now that puberty has made the penis larger, and there is more concern about this area, they have been found (also see "Balanitis" below). The teen's great sigh of relief attests to the level of anxiety. (See Chapter 10, "Sexually Transmitted Diseases," for more information on lesions.)

If a teen says that it burns when he urinates, it may be an irritated meatus from something as simple as rough underwear (a problem that can occur in a young teen who is having unwilled erections that come in contact with the underwear). However, a sexually transmitted disease may also need to be considered. A discharge may or may not be present, but antibiotic treatment usually is undertaken in cases where there is doubt. The implications of this are also covered in Chapter 10.

Any time that one has to probe the meatus for cultures, the patient will wince with discomfort as the culture probe, albeit a minute one, enters the opening. The opening is exquisitely sensitive to trauma.

Boys rarely shave their pubic area or go to a salon to get a wax. However, occasionally I do have a teen who has decided to remove his hair. Certainly in swimmers this has been done often. If they do shave down, then folliculitis is of concern (see p. 129). The plucked hair follicle, whether on the eyebrow or on the groin, can get invaded by bacteria and has to be treated with antibiotics. (Girls are the more likely candidates for this. See also Chapter 6, "The Teen Obsession: Skin.")

Infections of the groin in males are often fungal. This is covered in Chapter 6. For now remember that "jock itch" is not limited to the athlete.

Balanitis

The glans of the penis is subject to infection. It can be the direct result of contact with bacteria or fungus, and the teenager may complain of burning or itchiness in the area. Teens who have been circumcised have an advantage in hygiene (they don't have to move the foreskin to clean the penis) and a disadvantage from an infection point of view in that the circumcised glans is easily exposed to infecting organisms, sexually transmitted or not. (The only medical reason for a circumcision is to make it easier to clean the area.)

The uncircumcised male has to retract the foreskin while he bathes or showers so that it does not adhere to the penis. Since the tip of the penis is not readily available for inspection, it is important to check for bacterial infections that may be hidden inside the foreskin. If the foreskin cannot be retracted, the glans cannot fully be exposed, and infection becomes easier. A vicious cycle develops.

All sorts of rumors have persisted about females having a high risk of cervical cancer through contact with the uncircumcised male. It turns out that the risk is related to hygiene and the ability of the male to appreciate that.

Louis is a thirteen-year-old *who had a normal examination. He was uncircumcised, and when I asked him to demonstrate the foreskin retraction to me, he was unable to do so. I explained that this was a problem with good hygiene, and I needed him to gently pull the foreskin back when he showered. A month later he came back and we had not accomplished anything. His foreskin was still tightly adhering to the glans. I discussed a referral to the parents and they saw a pediatric urologist. One quick strong pull by the* *urologist on Louis's foreskin and the adhesions were gone. (Sometimes you need surgical skills to be effective.) I knew then that Louis would maintain daily retraction.*

If Louis's situation could not be corrected and infection were a recurring problem, circumcision would be a possibility, but I have not had too many teens opt for circumcision. Generally speaking the idea of knives to that area repels most teen males, and even most adults.

The Scrotum

Scrotal Masses

■ Hydrocele

A hydrocele is a fluid-filled area in the scrotum that surrounds the testicle's covering. Most of these will be seen in the pediatrician's office, but an occasional one will present in the teenager. Usually there is no explanation for the hydrocele, although trauma can cause the fluid to accumulate. Following a correction for a varicocele (a varicose vein of the testicles—see below), one may find a hydrocele, if the surgeon ties off some of the normal drainage. A hydrocele may enlarge the size of the scrotum. I have a few boys whose scrotum swelled to the sizes of large oranges and were both uncomfortable physically and emotionally. Despite the bragging about penis size associated with adolescents, no one wants to have a huge scrotum! Treatment requires surgical correction to tie off the leaking lymphatics that are causing the swelling.

Andrew was seen in my office *as a new patient at the age of fourteen. He came in because he was not doing as well in school as one hoped. In the course of the examination, I found a large hydrocele and the remnant of a scar that signaled previous surgery for either a hernia or varicocele. I had not been told of the surgery because "It had gone so well, I forgot." Andrew was clearly uncomfortable that I was examining his testicle but ventured a shy, quiet, "Is that swelling okay?" I explained that this appeared to be a hydrocele and what it meant. He told me that it wasn't painful, but asked, "Can you fix it?" I told him that I couldn't but that I would make sure we found a surgeon who would. Even the thought of surgery to correct it didn't faze him a bit. After the consultation with the urologist, Andrew broke* *down and started to cry to his parents that he wanted the operation done as soon as possible. He had been hiding his concern because he didn't know how to discuss it.*

■ Neoplasm

A neoplasm is a tumor. In most cases, the concern regarding a mass is whether it is malignant. Statistically we should not find cancer in the testicle of the teenager since this is more prevalent in men in their twenties and thirties. Yet, it is worth the effort to make sure that any mass is benign and, if it is not, that we detect it as early as possible.

Boys who had undescended testicles have a slightly higher chance of malignant tumors on the affected testicle. The odds are not great enough to merit worry. However, the physician should examine the area a bit more carefully during the annual visit. When indicated, a sonogram is performed. As a rule, the key distinguishing feature is that the malignant mass is solid, not filled with fluid. Cystic lesions of the scrotum tend to mean good news for the patient.

Patients with a malignant neoplasm, or cancer, will only complain of a dull ache or none at all. They may even present with back pain as the tumor has spread to the lymph nodes in the back. Again, it is worth noting that cancer of the testicle is not a common concern in the teenager. It is the exception and not the rule.

■ Spermatocele

Another mass that is likely to be discovered during a routine exam is the spermatocele. This hard mass is benign and arises from the vas deferens (the cord that carries the sperm from the testicle to the ejaculate). Because it is found casually and tends to be quite hard, it usually elicits concern from the patient. One sure sign that it is benign is the fact that it is cystic, or fluid filled, and is separate from the testicle. A sonogram of the scrotum is usually done to distinguish the features of the spermatocele.

The Testicles

Teenage boys generally express concerns to me about the size of their penis; rarely do they mention their testicles. Yet, these are monumentally important if they are to produce testosterone and sperm. I have a chart in the office with details of the male anatomy to show where the prostate is located, what the epididymis (a tube on the posterior of each testicle) is and how it wraps around

Testicle

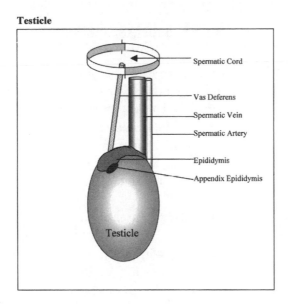

the testicle. It is quite a different story to discuss your own anatomy as opposed to theoretical anatomy in sex ed class.

One thing I point out to them is that the testicles do not lie in the same horizontal plane. If they did, they would bang against each other, and no male would be able to walk. Ingeniously, the male is designed to have one testicle slightly lower than the other; it doesn't matter which.

As the teen goes through puberty, the testicles grow until they mature to about one-and-a-half to two-and-a-half inches each. After many years of doing male examinations, a doctor should have a sense of the norm with a manual exam. I cannot emphasize how important this examination is and how often it does not get done.

The most common mass that is found on examination is actually a normal finding. The top of the testicle has a small nodule that is shaped like a baseball cap; it is the head of the epididymis. In our analogy, the peak of the hat would be the appendix of the epididymal head. This is important in assessing testicular pain, as we will discuss.

The testicle hangs suspended by veins and nerves, and by a thin tube that delivers sperm, the vas deferens.

Monthly Self-Examination

Recently a well-known comic actor was diagnosed with testicular cancer. This drove many boys into my office after they discovered their normal epididymis on self-examination. Frankly I was pleased with the opportunity to demonstrate the male anatomy again to these boys and to assure them that what they were examining was normal. As part of adolescent male care, we should be teaching all boys to self-examine. Not only is it teaching responsibility for their health, but it also may pick up some pathology.

The monthly testicular exam begins while standing, in order to make the testicles fall into the scrotum, and the patient should gently grasp the testicle to determine tenderness. With one hand he can run two or three fingers and the thumb along the edges of the testicle; it should feel smooth. There is a very small ridge at the bottom and back (the epididymis) and another small bump on the top of the testicle (the head of the epididymis). Neither should be tender to the touch, and they should show no growth in followup exams. At the top of the testicle there is a cord holding the testicle in a pendulum position. This spermatic cord contains the blood vessels, both arteries and veins, as well as the nerves to the area. It should feel like a thin rope. Masses in this area can include the common varicocele or the spermatocele. Tenderness should not be present. Since these are serial exams, they should be done monthly if possible to judge for size difference.

I am impressed with the recent degree of conscientiousness that teens are having about this exam. Once told that cancer is a possibility and that celebrities are discussing the monthly exam, they participate.

Scrotal Hernia

A hernia is a protrusion of one piece of anatomy into another, and they occur more frequently than most people think. There are two types of scrotal hernias: the direct hernia presses directly onto the inguinal canal's side; these generally don't create a problem. The indirect hernia slides down the inguinal canal opening left when the testicle migrated into the scrotum. This canal should have closed after the testicle arrived safely; in some cases it stays open and a piece of gut can find its way into the top opening and down into the same canal where the testicle migrated. That in and of itself is not a big deal. But a dangerous situation occurs if the piece of gut gets stuck and compromises the blood supply. In most cases, one can push the hernia back with a finger as the patient is lying down. This *reduction* of the hernia gives one time to set up a surgical date, since this situation will not heal by itself.

Sometimes the hernia cannot be pushed back, and the patient will be in a lot of pain from this strangulated hernia. This calls for immediate surgery.

The operation for a hernia is now so simplified that the patient is out of the operating room, into the recovery room, and home on the same day. The scar is quite small, and after a few days many patients feel quite well. Discomfort is minimal and dissolvable stitches may be used, eliminating the need for a return visit to remove them.

> **Andre had his college physical** *in June and left in August to meet his new professors before the upperclassmen arrived. He had spent the summer working on a construction crew and after being in class for a day he noted a pain in his left scrotal sac. He ignored it, but when it came back he called me to ask what he should do. "Go to student health and let them see what is going on," I suggested. "Nah, I told my Dad that I wanted to come down to see you. It's only an hour away and I don't want these guys examining me down there!"*
>
> *I saw Andre the next day and his left scrotal sac was markedly swollen. He said that the examination was causing him some discomfort and he felt a bit woozy. Clearly there was a large cystic structure on top of the testicle. I had him lie down and told him to bring his legs up with his knees bent. As he did so, he said he felt better and I pointed out that his hernia had just been reduced by this maneuver. We set up a surgical appointment for the next day, so he could quickly return to school.*

Testicular Pain

Discussions about testicular and epididymal pains from infection are covered in Chapter 10, "Sexually Transmitted Diseases."

Torsion

Torsion of the testicle is most likely to occur in the teenager, and this condition will be accompanied by sudden, extreme pain. There are minor abnormalities that predispose the testicle to twist; primarily that it lacks a normal anchor in the back. As the testicle grows in size and is more pendular it can twist suddenly and inexplicably. The teenager will double over in pain and point to the testicle involved, or to the general area of the groin.

The "corkscrew" action of torsion can actually "strangle" and kill off the testicle because of a lack of blood flow to the area. If a patient or his parents call in with symptoms that make me think of testicular torsion, I send them directly to an emergency room, because immediate surgery will be necessary. With testicular torsion you have four to six hours to save the testicle from permanent death.

Once at the hospital, experienced hands will be able to tell that the testicle is lying in the wrong direction, though the pain and tenderness may not allow for a full examination. X rays and bloodflow studies may be necessary in doubtful cases; when in doubt, however, it is best to explore the scrotum.

In some cases, the patient may have had a "partial" torsion. The theory holds that the testicle started to twist but partially unwound spontaneously. The teen may not even reveal that this happened out of fear. I have had several boys who first "confessed" the pain to me at a checkup because they could no longer keep to themselves their fears of what might be wrong with them. I ask permission to discuss this occurrence with parents who are always in disbelief that their son kept this a secret.

If a partial torsion happens a second time, some surgeons argue that this is a catastrophe waiting to happen and suggest "tacking" down the testicle before it actually twists for good. Other surgeons don't buy that argument and simply take a "wait-and-see" attitude. However, if it occurs once, you may want to rethink your son's travel plans. There are few urologists in the mountaintops of Peru, and the first occurrence may only be a warning.

The small appendix of the epididymis can also twist and this can be difficult to differentiate from a general torsion. Generally, this pain is localized to the upper pole of the testicle, and the testicle is lying in the normal north-south direction. Surgery is not indicated, and the parents and frightened teen can be sent home. Treatment consists of analgesics.

Varicoceles

The testicle must be cooler than the rest of the body for it to maintain proper function, and its placement outside the body is perfect for this. Occasionally, a collection of veins (like varicose veins of the leg) may be found in the spermatic cord. These veins, known as varicoceles, can result in increasing the temperature of the scrotal sac. With increased temperature comes the risk of damage to the testicle, so if varicoceles are found, they usually are removed surgically once deemed of sufficient size to affect the temperature of the testicle. The surgery is not a major procedure.

Most varicoceles drain when the teen is lying down, so if a physician has always examined the teen when the youngster is lying on the examination table, the varicoceles will be missed. The patient must be standing in order to feel it, and it will be easier to feel if the patient holds his breath and bears down. This increases the pressure in the abdomen and makes it harder for the varicoceles to drain. Rarely will it be large enough in the young teen to have permanently compromised testicular growth. In most cases, the removal of the varicoceles will return the testicle to full size.

Undescended Testicle

In a few teens, an undescended testicle is not discovered until adolescence. Since the warmth of the abdominal cavity poses damage to the testicle, it is important that the testicle be brought into the scrotal sac as soon as possible. The longer it stays internal, the more the risk of damaging the production of sperm and testosterone later in life. Indeed, it is one of the principal reasons for low testosterone in the adolescent and in the adult.

In some teens the testicle will appear to be undescended but it actually is hiding in the inguinal canal, a primitive reflex that comes into play in any situation in which there is potential danger to the testicles. This is handy if you happen to be a bull moose about to battle and want to preserve one part of the anatomy from danger; you simply retract it out of harm's way. Sometimes the examining hand of the physician is sufficient to drive the testicle north. Moreover most examination rooms tend to be cold and that, too, will make the testicle rise into the canal. The remedy involves examining the teen in as warm a room as you can get, while he is standing, or better yet, squatting. This will assure a more accurate assessment of the testicle.

The Hips, Legs, and Feet

Hip Problems in Adolescents

Most hip problems in the adolescent population are attributable to trauma, in particular to sports' injuries, and these usually involve muscle strains. However, if the teenager complains about pain in the hip, two other concerns arise:

If the teenager is overweight, the head of the femur can slip from the rest of the bone at the growth plate because of the weight load that it has to bear. This is called a slipped capital femoral epiphysis. The teen will limp and complain of pain at the hip. The diagnosis is made by X ray. This injury is more common in the overweight and young teenager since you need an open growth plate and inordinate force (in this case, weight) to fracture the plate. Because the patient is likely to slip the bone again and cause further disruption to the blood supply, immobilization and potentially pinning the bone with screws is part of the treatment.

If the weight is normal, the teen may suffer from Legg-Calvé-Perthes (LCP) disease, where the patient's hipbone is compromised by a diminished blood supply. If the bone becomes brittle enough, the hipbone can break. In children with hip pain, a frequent diagnosis is an inflammation of the hip joint called toxic synovitis, and it is felt that LCP is the end product of the inflammation or comes from local trauma to the area. The teenager may complain of pain and difficulty walking or thigh pain. Treatment requires limiting weight-bearing; yet it will interfere with the whole of the pubertal years as the teens will have a limp and many limitations on activities.

The Legs

Thigh Muscle Pains

The femur is the sole bone in the thigh and one of the strongest bones in the body. Its head (sitting in the hip socket) is incredibly strong, as would be expected since it carries our whole weight. It is unusual for a teenager to complain about thigh pains related to the bone unless there has been trauma.

The quadriceps muscle is the main one in the front of the thigh, and it anchors the front of the leg to the knee. Pain from damage to the quadriceps may be felt in the knee, not in the muscle itself. Treatment consists, as with any muscle injury, of rest and antiinflammatory medications. Cold compresses are usually applied immediately to prevent swelling of the muscle and to stop any bleeding. By the next day, heat to the area will help the muscle loosen up and begin healing.

Tumor of the Femur

The most common malignant tumors of childhood and adolescent are osteogenic sarcoma and Ewing's sarcoma. Although they are "common" tumors, this does not mean that they occur frequently; it means that most bone tumors are of this type. Annually there are about 700 reported bone tumors in this age group; 400 were osteogenic sarcoma, and about 250 were Ewing's sarcoma. Generally speaking, the osteogenic sarcomas occur in girls twelve to thirteen and boys fourteen to fifteen. This corresponds to the growing period for each. By contrast, Ewing's tumors occur in the very young teen, even as early as ten or eleven.

Both tumors can present with a lingering pain in the thigh and a mass that is not easy to palpate on physical examination. In most cases, an X ray is necessary for diagnosis. Since the tumors respond to radiation (Ewing's more so) and chemotherapy, they need to be assessed as soon as possible. In a teenager who is limping or complaining because of unresolved pain in the thigh, X rays are warranted. Also any teenager who has an "easy" fracture (relatively little trauma involved) is suspect for a bone that is weakened by a tumor.

The Knees

Teenagers are not proportionally balanced during pubertal growth, and since their legs will grow before their trunks, they will be "off center" for a while (for a full discussion, see Chapter 2 on puberty). This imbalance places a great deal of stress on the knee. Kids who never set foot in a gym, or on the athletic field, will often come in with mysterious knee pains.

The knee is kept in place with ligaments, cartilage discs, and muscles. It is a marvel of limited motion and it has to sustain the entire weight of the individual, to say nothing of someone who decides to jump up and down while dribbling a ball, or go down a snow slope on thin pieces of plastic! Since the hipbone is connected to the thighbone and that, in turn, is connected to the knee bone (if you remember the song), it stands to reason that any teenager with a pain in the knee has to have the joints above and below assessed as well. In other words, the pain may be in the knee but the problem may be in the hip or the ankle. Most injuries will be sports-related and are dealt with in Chapter 7.

The Kneecap

Our coach potato teen may also be the unfortunate progeny of genes that misaligned his knee. He needs to do little to feel the discomfort of a poorly centered kneecap (patella), which should sit in the center of the joint with rubber bands (ligaments) connecting it to the appropriate muscles and bones. During adolescent years, the teen with a misaligned knee may complain of a sore feeling when he bends his knee or say that it feels like the knee is "catching on something" when he walks. It may even buckle at times. Going up stairs may hurt, though the pain occurs *after* climbing the stairs, not during. Often the teen will complain that the sides of the knee will hurt, and this is consistent with a strain of the lateral, or outside, ligament. This is usually due to a slightly misaligned kneecap, or the result of sports-related stress. Treatment will often involve rest and muscle exercises to strengthen the major muscles of the thigh that stabilize the knee. It is hard to have teenagers stop their favorite sport temporarily in an effort to rest the knee, though this would be ideal.

Sometimes the knee is aligned properly but there is still a problem with the underside of the knee, which results from misuse or overuse. This latter condition carries the diagnosis of chondromalacia patella, or "bad cartilage under the kneecap." Again, most patients will improve with some physical therapy to strengthen the appropriate muscles.

The kneecap is supposed to move from side to side. However, in some teens the movement is so marked that it goes to one side and stays there. The kneecap has actually dislocated from the center point and is stuck. During the course of a normal examination, a doctor will move the kneecap from side to side. The teen with normal knees will watch this being done and will not feel any discomfort. Yet, the teen whose knee can dislocate watches closely and waits for pain. This teen is aware that his kneecap can dislocate and is apprehensive about your moving it and may complain as you do the examination. Indeed, some have actually reached out to stop the examination.

The kneecap does not tend to pop out spontaneously; some trauma is usually needed, and it can generally be repositioned relatively easily by applying moderate pressure. I once watched a girls' basketball game and saw a slight hit of a girl's knee end up in a dislocation. She fell to the floor in pain and acknowledged that this had happened before. In her case there was enough pain (because of it happening before) that a muscle tranquilizer was needed before her kneecap could be tapped into place.

Treatment for most types of knee pain, including incomplete dislocations (subluxations), involves muscle strengthening through physical therapy. Rest and antiinflammatory medications help relieve some of the pain. In some cases, a misalignment of the kneecap is so severe that the patella has to be tacked down in an operation lest it continue to dislocate.

Nonossifying Fibroma, or Bone "Hole"

These benign lesions are found on X rays only. The teen, usually a male, may have had an injury and because of pain to the area, an X ray is ordered. The presence of the hole immediately poses a problem about potentially having a fracture at the site. The argument is simple: If the bone is weakened by a "hole," isn't the bone itself subject to a possible fracture with less injury? Many orthopedists will warn against playing a contact sport such as football, but otherwise the advice is to "watch" and X ray the lesion at six-month intervals.

Harry was seen by an orthopedist *because of knee pain. He was very involved with athletics and his knee required evaluation. The orthopedist felt that Harry's lesion was incidental and did not require any surgery. He wrote that the lesion would eventually heal on its own and* *that the best course of treatment was to observe the lesion until it healed. It did just that.*

In Harry's case the prediction ultimately came true and nothing was ever done. In some cases the hole size is of such magnitude that some orthopedic surgeons suggest grafting bone tissue into the hole to heal and strengthen the bone. In Harry's case, it was a close call but it was decided that he had already begun to close the fibroma.

Osteochondritis Dissecans

Since knee pains are so common with teenagers, it takes quite a bit of complaining before X rays are done to search for unusual or dangerous conditions. A rare finding that causes needless alarm is osteochondritis dissecans. The X rays will show a thin "fracture" in the lower portion of the femur at the point where it becomes the top part of the knee. As bad as that sounds, nothing really happens to the bone, and it is believed that the disorder will not cause any problems. It takes a bit of convincing, both to parents and to patient, that nothing pathologic is happening. Most patients will have no symptoms and the finding is by accident. Occasionally, knee pain will force the issue, and X rays are ordered. Once the osteochondritis is found, most orthopedists will not limit activity unless the patient is complaining of severe knee pain. Even with pain, it is not felt that the condition causes the pain. Whereas girls are more likely to dislocate their kneecaps, boys are more likely to have osteochondritis dissecans. In general, the prognosis for the teenager is quite good since there seldom is a full separation of the bone. Only in rare cases will there be a full separation requiring more aggressive treatment.

Osteoid Osteoma

This is also found incidentally after an injury that required an X ray. While osteochondritis is due to a lessening of bone growth, there is an overabundance of growth in this type of lesion. An X ray will reveal an increase in the density of the bone and in the center there is a small translucent spot. As opposed to the nonossifying fibroma, this lesion is more likely to be found in girls, who will have pain at the site. Again, an X ray is needed and the typical hole surrounded by increased bone density is seen. Most of these masses are seen in the femur and tibial bone, although they can be found anywhere.

Since there is accompanying pain, it becomes important to differentiate this lesion from a malignancy. Pain is the main reason to do an excision of the lesion and, in a way, the treatment becomes the biopsy that confirms the diagnosis. Treatment requires removal of the translucent area and the surrounding overgrowth; the doctor may do that during the biopsy.

The Lower Leg

Shin Splints

The muscle that runs down the tibia (the front bone in the leg, below the knee) is the one that is implicated in "shin splints." It takes little to aggravate this muscle—all you need to do is run or walk with an improper gait and the muscle will hurt. People who have slightly longer legs, people who wear incorrect shoes (with worn-down sides), or people with turned-in ankles or feet will strain this muscle. Often corrective measures with orthotics can straighten the foot, or lengthen the leg slightly, which then alleviates the pressure on the muscles in the leg.

Osgood-Schlatter Disease

This common condition of the top portion of the tibial bone, just below the knee, is a frequent finding in the athlete. It is discussed in Chapter 7, "Teens and Sports: Sports-Related Injuries."

The Feet

When it comes to the foot, the two most common teen complaints are stress fractures and flat feet. The former is usually the result of too much strain on the metatarsal bones, the long bones of the foot. In most cases, the teenager will be a runner or involved in sports. I have had a few teens who simply walked for a long time and got stress fractures. Rest and arch supports are the treatment.

Flat feet are very common, and not all need to be treated. In most cases that I have diagnosed, a teenager with flat feet has parents with the same. Most teens with severe flat feet have already been prescribed orthotic appliances to help support the arch. If they haven't and there is no discomfort, I simply tell them that the foot is flat, and that nothing needs to be done for now. However, if there is pain in the ankle, or even in the knee, it may be necessary to get proper-fitting supports for the feet. Remember that the foot is still growing in the early part of puberty. A set of supports molded for a specific arch can cost hundreds of dollars. I usually tell them to try the ones that are sold generically in the drugstore first. If they work, but not quite enough, *and* if the family can afford them, I send them to the podiatrist for molds specific to their foot. As the foot changes with puberty, you need to spend more money on new molds.

Heel Pain

Heel pain is usually the result of trauma. Jumping and landing fully on the heel will cause severe pain. Sometimes a stress fracture of the metatarsal bones (the long bones of the foot) may be reflected by a painful heel.

The Toes

The first toe can cause great pain if it is turning inward and points to the fifth, or little toe. Although this is a condition that one sees more often in the adult population, it may begin in the adolescent years. Occasionally, the older teenager has so advanced a condition that the only correction is a surgical one. It is not a minor procedure and should only be undertaken in severe cases.

Fractured Toe

If a toe is suspect for fracture, simply tape it to the next one. This will help to stabilize the potential fracture until an X ray can be obtained. There really is no rush unless there is tremendous pain. Generally, a doctor will do very little for a fractured toe unless the fracture involves the metatarsal bones. (These are the long bones just behind the toes.) If these are fractured, the orthopedist will place the foot in a walking cast.

Proper Toenail Cutting

One point that cannot be overemphasized is that the proper cutting of the toenail has to be taught. A correct cut of the nail is concavity out, that is, one cuts deeper in the center and leaves the two edges intact. Too many teens have mistaken a large fingernail clipper as a toenail clipper. The correct one for toes looks like this:

The nail clipper for the hand nails looks like this:

Toenails should be cut straight across to prevent the edges from growing into the skin.

Subungual Hematoma

The other main trauma to the toe is the subungual hematoma, or a blood clot under the nail. For those who have never had one of these, please believe your teenager when he tells you it is unbearable—whether on the toe or on the fingernail. What happens is that the blood oozes under the nail from the injury and it has nowhere to escape. Since the pressure from this trapped blood is what causes the pain, the treatment involves releasing the blood. Between their own squeamishness and their teen's jumpiness, parents will have a hard time treating their teen at home. Your doctor, working under sterile conditions, will slowly but firmly puncture a small hole in the nail with a small drill or other sharp object. Boring through the nail, the blood can leave through this opening, and the symptoms improve dramatically. Some even have a small drill that allows the nail to be punctured more easily.

Toenail Infections

Statistically the most common complaint I see in toes is an infection of the toenail, a paronychia. This infection is due to trauma to the nail, usually at the side where the nail meets the skin. Although boys are the ones who usually call, as they mangle their toes in sports, girls are not immune to the infection. However, girls (in general) take better care of their toes. At least it is safe to say that boys will rarely get pedicures! Instead, boys will absentmindedly pick at their toenails while watching television. I know, dear reader, this sounds disgusting, but that's the reality of how most paronychial infections are born. The nailbed at the side tends to hurt, and the surrounding tissue is raised, red, and tender. If you press gently some pus can be seen oozing from the edge, and the torn nail is visible immediately.

Treatment depends on severity. One starts with soaking the toe with warm water to loosen the edge and promote drainage. Antibiotics are often necessary to stop the infection and, in severe cases, the nail may have to be removed to allow drainage.

We have reached the bottom of the teenager . . . but only in anatomy.

Web Sites for Parents and Teens

General Adolescent Information

www.aap.org.   American Academy of Pediatrics web site. Information from the Academy on all phases of child and adolescent care.

www.adolescenthealth.org.   Society of Adolescent Medicine home page. Information on doctors who practice Adolescent Medicine.

www.cdc.gov.   General topics from the Centers for Disease Control and Prevention (CDC). Includes immunizations, infections, travel information, and injuries related to sports.

www.school_file.com.   General information on teenagers.

www.teenhealthfx.com.   A question-and-answer site for teens on all aspects of their lives.

Immunizations

www.aap.org/family/parents/immunize.htm.   American Academy of Pediatrics schedule of immunizations.

www.acpm.org/adult.htm.   The American College of Preventive Medicine policy statement on vaccines.

www.cdc.gov/nip/default.html. The CDC home page. It links to information on immunizations for children, adolescents, and adults. Also has information on travel.

www.cfsan.fda.gov/~mow/intro.html. Site that discusses different bacteria, viruses, and toxins. Can be useful to look up for travel and for infections.

www.fda.gov/cber/vaers/vaers.htm. The home page for the FDA's Vaccine Adverse Event Report System (VAERS).

www.WHO.int/vaccines/index.shtm. World Health Organization home page.

Sleep

www.asda.org. American Academy of Sleep Medicine home page. Information about sleep and disorders of sleep.

www.sleepfoundation.org. Overall view of sleep and disorders.

www.sleepnet.com. Useful site for links on sleep issues.

Birth Control and Sexual Information

http://ec.princeton.edu. Information on emergency contraception, or the "morning after" pill. Run by Princeton University. Home page has a search engine that will find resources based on area code for the "emergency pill."

www.agi-usa.org. The Allan Guttmacher Institute home page. Information and statistics on sexual practices in the United States. Statistics on STDs, birth control, pregnancy in teens.

www.plannedparenthood.org/bc. Information on birth control methods. Also links to issues of sexually transmitted diseases and sexual issues in general that are of interest to teens.

www.safersex.org/barriers/femalecondomclip.html#6. A series of press release articles on the "female condom."

www.stopaids.org. AIDS prevention in homosexuals.

www.teenwire.com. Run by Planned Parenthood. General topics for teens on birth control and STDs.

www.wdxcyber.com. An article on which drugs interfere with birth control pills.

Nutrition

www.caloriecontrol.org/bmi.htm.   Calculates BMI and provides a chart for normal BMI-based height.

www.cdc.gov/nccdphp/dnpa/bmi/bmi-for-age.htm.   Discussion of BMI for age.

www.cspinet.org.   Nutritional contents of fast foods.

www.diabetes.com/dd/nutrition2.htm.   Discusses the Glycemic Index.

www.nal.usda.gov.   National Agricultural Library. Filled with information about nutrition and foods.

www.nal.usda.gov:80001/py/pmap.htm.   Food Pyramid.

www.nal.usda.gov/fnic.   Food and Nutrition Center at the National Agricultural Library.

www.nutrition.gov.   USDA (United States Department of Agriculture) page on nutrition.

www.thusness.com/bmi.t.html.   Calculates BMI in inches and pounds.

www.usda.gov.   Home page for USDA on dietary guidelines.

Drugs and Alcohol

www.alcoholism.about.com.   Information about alcohol abuse and alcoholism. Links to other sites for information about other drugs.

www.cdc.gov/tobacco.html.   Information on tobacco.

www.doitnow.org.   Talks about each drug in a language suited for the teen. Lists a series of pamphlets on each drug that can be viewed on screen or purchased. A "game" illustrates how sex sells alcohol.

www.doj.gov/dea.   Drug Enforcement Agency of the Department of Justice home page. Click "Drugs of Concern" and you are linked to a page that has all of the drugs of abuse. Excellent source of information on each drug.

www.drugfreeamerica.com.   Drugs and alcohol information.

www.drugtext.org/sub/alchohol.html.   Information on alcohol.

www.home-drugtest.com.   Information on drug test kits for home testing.

www.marijuana.com.   Marijuana page. Tends to be "pro use" but does have information on laws. It is useful for parents to see what the counterarguments are.

www.nida.nih.gov.   Home page from the National Institute on Drugs and Alcohol, which is a part of the National Institute of Health.

www.shroomery.org.   Information on "how to" use mushrooms. Does have a good section on pharmacology of the mushrooms.

www.xs4fall.nl.htm.   Drug information.

Sports and Injuries

www.cdc.gov/safeusa/sports/child.html.   CDC page on sports and sports-related injuries in adolescents.

www.orthoino.org.   Orthopedic information about sports and injuries.

Dermatology

www.aad.org/kids.html.   American Academy of Dermatology home web site page.

Index

AA (Alcoholics Anonymous), 268–69, 271
abdominal muscles, stretching exercises for, 151–52
abdominal pain, 164, 217, 230, 307, 415–20, 424, 438, 462
   appendicitis and, 415–16
   gastrointestinal bleeding and, 419–20
   pancreatitis and, 426
   reproductive disorders and, 457
   see also bowel problems and disease
abortion, 189, 214–17, 448
   complications of, 217
   mifepristone (RU 486) and, 215–16
   "missed" (miscarriage), 448, 449
   procedures for, 217
   religion and, 214, 215–16
abstinence, 188, 195, 196
ACAH (adult onset congenital adrenal hyperplasia), 461–62
Accutane, 124–25
acetaldehyde, 256
acetaminophen, 348, 349, 362, 363, 424
ACL (anterior cruciate ligament), 170
acne, 27, 36, 119–26, 369
   causes of, 119–20
   oral medications for, 123–26
   ovarian disorders and, 460, 461
   surgery for, 126
   topical care for, 121–23
   treatment of, 120–26
   vitamin A and, 97
acquired immune deficiency syndrome, *see* AIDS; HIV
acromion-clavicular (AC) joint, 166

acupuncture, 280
Acyclovir, 136, 223
ADD (Attention Deficit Disorder), 79, 308, 309
Adderall, 309
adenoids, 351
adolescence:
   defined, 31
   emotional life in, *see* emotional life
   nature of, 56–58
adolescent gynecomastia, 41
adoption, 63
adrenal gland, 453, 454–55, 461
adrenal hyperplasia, adult, 461–62
adrenaline, 148
aggression:
   steroids and, 147
   testosterone and, 42, 43
Agriculture Department, U.S., 84
AIDS (acquired immune deficiency syndrome), 193, 226–28, 299
   see also HIV
alcohol, alcohol use, 17, 102, 232, 241–72, 277, 319, 346, 485–86
   college drinking, 269–72
   content in beverages, 257
   discovering teen use of, 248–49
   drunk driving and, 69, 254, 258, 264
   effects of, 255–56, 424–25
   equivalent volumes of, 257
   factors in absorption of, 258–59
   heartburn and, 410
   learning about, 243
   marijuana compared with, 259, 287

alcohol, alcohol use (*continued*)
  measuring consumption of, 257–60
  parental response to, 262–65
  as part of teen scene, 243, 254–55, 257, 269, 271
  providing help for, 268–69
  responsible use of, 260–63
  as rite of passage, 262, 270–71, 273
  STDs and, 221, 226, 227
  talking about, 244–47
  weekend sleep and, 76
  weight loss and, 104
alcoholics:
  parents as, 246, 262–63, 267
  teens as, 267–69, 271–72
Alcoholics Anonymous (AA), 268–69, 271
Aldara, 225
allergies:
  to benzoyl peroxide, 121
  coughs due to, 391–92
  eyes and, 353
  fatigue and, 340
  food, 116–17, 127
  nose and, 355–57
  prophylactic treatments of, 356
  side effects of, 357
  skin, 126–31
allowances, 58
Alport's syndrome, 432
amenorrhea, 109, 171, 451–56
  primary, 49, 438, 441, 451–55
  secondary, 455–56, 460
American Academy of Neurology, 159
American Academy of Obstetrics and Gynecology, 221–22
American Academy of Orthopedic Surgeons, 151
American Academy of Pediatrics, 151, 331, 333
American Cancer Society, 280
American Lung Association, 280
amino acids, 106
amnesia, 159
"amotivational" syndrome, 298
amphetamines, 100, 103, 308–10, 397
ampicillin, 124, 209
amyl nitrate (poppers), 317
anal sex, 430
androgens, *see* testosterone
androstenedione, 148, 461
anemia:
  fatigue caused by, 340–41
  iron deficiency, 99–100, 147, 340–41
  pernicious, 98
anesthesia, 162, 211
angel dust (phencyclidine; PCP), 306–7
Animal House (movie), 271

ankles, injuries to, 172
anorexia nervosa, 64, 95, 100, 106–13, 373, 456
  damage from, 109–10
  diagnosis of, 109
  signs of, 110–11
antacids, 410, 411, 412
anterior cruciate ligament (ACL), 170
antianxiety medications, 340
antibiotics, 344, 345–46, 354, 357, 366, 407, 413, 414, 419
  birth control pills and, 209
  for bronchitis and pneumonia, 389, 390
  for ear problems, 360, 361
  for skin treatment, 122–24, 129, 130
  for STDs, 228, 229, 231–34
  for urinary tract infections, 428, 429
  vaginal infections and, 124, 229, 232, 458
antibodies, 74, 372, 411, 420, 424, 453
anticonvulsant medications, 209
antidepressants, 79, 114, 310, 340, 397, 445
antihistamines, 127, 340, 344, 356
antiinflammatory drugs, 171, 385, 386, 475
antioxidants, 97
antiviral drugs, skin problems and, 136, 137
anus, tear or fissure in, 417
anxiety, 58, 67, 81, 157, 305, 311, 319, 328, 444
  "Dumbo" ears and, 361
  heart rate in, 402–4
  thyroid and, 374, 375
apocrine glands, 36
appendicitis, 415–16, 460
appointments, medical, 27
  honoring of, 58
armpit hair, 36, 50, 442
arteriosclerosis, 93, 97
artery blockage, 206–7
arthritis, 131, 216, 343, 344, 423, 450
ascorbic acid (vitamin C), 97–98, 99
Ashkenazi Jewish women, 461
Asian Americans, lactose intolerance of, 117
aspirin, 121, 362, 413
asthma, 128, 145, 388–89
  exercise-induced, 388–89
  sports and, 155
athletes:
  drug use by, 241
  early developers as, 154
  female, 154–55, 169–72, 452, 455
  menstrual problems of, 452, 455
  skin problems of, 120, 132, 133–34
  see also sports
athlete's foot, 131, 132, 133
Attention Deficit Disorder (ADD), 79, 308, 309

automobiles:
  accidents in, 69, 254, 307, 362, 368
  drunk driving and, 69, 254, 258, 264
  family rules for, 249
  sobriety and, 261–62
axilla, 36, 50, 442
azelaic acid, 122

babies, 132, 333
  growth of, 34
  health care of, 26–27
back, 381–83
  pain in, 164–65, 327–28, 380–83, 468
backpacks, 382
bacteria:
  appendicitis and, 415–16
  HIB and, 331
  meningitis and, 335–36
  STDs and, 220, 228–32; *see also* chlamydia;
    gonnorhea
  ulcers and, 411
  urinary tract infections and, 428–30
bad breath, 290
  smoking and, 276, 279–80
balanitis, 466–67
barbiturates, 322–23, 343
barrier methods of birth control, 195, 197–203
  diaphragm and cervical cap, 202–3
  spermicides, 201–2
  see also condoms
Bartholin glands, 459
  infection of, 229, 459
Basal Metabolic Rate (BMR), 87
baseball, 148, 150, 155, 161, 165, 166
basketball, 149, 155, 158, 161, 164, 165,
    169–70, 477
bathing and washing, 36, 120, 466
beards, 42–43, 455, 460, 461
bedding, 235
bed-wetting (enuresis), 81
beer, 270
  alcohol content of, 257
  calories in, 260
  as rite of passage, 262
Bell's palsy, 344
belly button (umbilicus), 427
Benadryl, 79, 210, 356
benign virginal mammary hyperplasia, 398–99
benzodiazepines, 79, 319, 403, 404–5
benzoyl peroxide, 121, 123
biking, 105
bilirubin, 420–21, 423
biological clock, 76
biological model of homosexuality, 190, 191

bipolar disorder, 251
birth control, 18, 27, 188, 195–219, 438, 484
  abstinence as, 188, 195, 196
  barrier methods of, *see* barrier methods of birth
    control; condoms
  hormonal methods of, *see* birth control pills;
    hormonal methods of birth control
  IUDs, 195, 197
  new methods of, 212–13
  rhythm method as, 195, 197
  withdrawal as, 195, 197
birth control patch, 212–13
birth control pills, 204–9, 218, 221, 395, 397, 462
  Accutane use and, 124
  acne caused by, 120
  cost of, 206
  decline in use of, 180
  estrogen in, 204, 206, 208, 209, 395, 447, 449
  menstrual irregularities and, 449
  progesterone in, 204, 208, 209, 447, 449
  risk factors and, 206–7
  side effects of, 208
  as skin treatment, 125–26
  smoking and, 206–7, 275
  types and uses of, 205, 208–9
  warnings about medicine combinations with, 209
  workings of, 204, 205
birth defects, 124, 216, 332
black eye, 354
blackheads, 120, 126
bladder infections, 428–30
blood, bleeding:
  alcohol levels in, 258, 259
  anemia and, 341
  in ejaculate, 465
  gastrointestinal, 416, 417, 419–20
  hemorrhoids and, 417–18
  in mouth, 362
  nose, 358
  recycling of, 420–21
  in urine, 429, 431, 432, 434
  see also vaginal bleeding
blood clots, 206, 275
  menstrual disorders and, 448
blood pressure, 400–401
  high (hypertension), 103, 207, 208, 401–2, 426
  low, 342, 447
  sports and, 145, 148, 156
  substance abuse and, 276, 288, 306, 307, 309,
    311, 317
  systolic vs. diastolic, 401
blood sugar, low (hypoglycemia), 115–16
blood tests, 416, 421–22
  for drugs, 293

blood transfusions:
  hepatitis B and, 333, 423
  HIV and, 226
BMR (Basal Metabolic Rate), 87
Body Mass Index (BMI), 91–93
body size, distorted view of, 83, 102, 109
body types, sports participation and, 149–50
bone age, assessment of, 110
bone density, loss of, 110, 113, 171, 211
bone "hole" (nonossifying fibroma), 477–78
bowel problems and disease, 415–19
  constipation and, 109, 416–17, 462
  hemorrhoids, 417–18, 420
  inflammatory bowel disease, 418–19
boxing, 162
boys:
  average height-weight and caloric tables for, 87
  body fat of, 90–91
  breasts of, 40–41, 147, 392–94
  double standard and, 184, 186, 187, 219
  eating disorders of, 108, 112–13
  facial hair of, 42–43
  food supplements for, 100
  genital development of, 38–42
  growth of, 34–35, 36–37, 75
  hygiene and, 36
  iron deficiency in, 340–41
  muscular development of, 56, 100
  need for body fat in, 90–91
  oral sex and, 178–79, 180, 186–87
  pecs of, 386
  reproductive system of, see reproductive system, male
  at risk for STDs, 221
  scoliosis in, 378, 380
  skin problems of, 120, 129–30, 132–33
  sleepwalking of, 81
  Tanner stages of sexual changes in, 39–42
  urinary tract infections in, 430
braces, 383
  for scoliosis, 378–79, 380
  for teeth, 362–63
bradycardia (slow heart rate), 405–6
brain, 110, 143, 207, 317
  alcohol and, 255, 256, 257
  concussion and, 160
  contusions of, 161
  eating and, 104
  fainting and, 156
  gender and, 190
  hallucinogens and, 304–5, 307
  marijuana and, 286–89
  meningitis and, 335–36
  neurotransmitters in, 144
  receptors of, 288, 289
  in REM vs. NREM sleep, 74, 76
  smoking and, 275, 276
brain tumors, 347, 352
Brand-Miller, Jennie, 116
bras, 47, 56, 127, 397
breast cancer, 207
breast implants, 398
breasts, 386, 392–99
  birth control pills and, 208
  development of, 32, 39, 40–41, 45–48, 442, 453
  hair on, 395
  injuries to, 164
  lumps in, 395–97
  of males, 40–41, 147, 392–94
  nipples of, 45, 47, 394, 396–97
  pain in, 397
  as "silent word," 32, 33
  size of, 397–99, 453
  skin problems of, 127, 133
  tenderness of, 208, 211, 444, 445
  trauma in, 397
breath analysis, 258, 265
Brighton Beach Memoirs (Simon), 30
bronchitis, 389
bulimia, 106–8, 113–14, 363, 371, 420, 456
butyl nitrate, 317
B vitamins, 98, 341, 446

caffeine, 147, 148, 309, 397, 405, 410, 412, 413
  premenstrual syndrome and, 445, 446
  sleep disorders and, 78–79
calcium, 97, 99, 117, 376, 434, 446
calories, 100, 110
  activity factor and, 87–88
  in alcohol, 259–60
  average height-weight and, 87
  and fear of obesity, 106–7
  meaning of, 86–88
  weight loss and, 104, 105
camps, "overweight," 103
Campylobacter, 413
cancer, 97, 299, 468
  smoking and, 276, 277, 290
  see also specific sites
candida, 220, 233–34
canker sores, 364
carbohydrates, 88, 106, 259–60
  Glycemic Index and, 115–16
carbo loading, 146–47
carbon dioxide, 156–57
cardiac surgery, 145
cardiovascular system, smoking and, 273, 275, 276
carotenemia, 97

Carroll, Lewis, 348
catecholamines, 276
CAT scans, 159, 397, 417, 426
"cauliflower" ear, 162
Centers for Disease Control and Prevention
    (CDC), 201, 230, 336, 338, 342
cephalosporins, 124
cervical cancer, 207, 466
cervical cap, 202–3
cervical injury (neck injury), 163, 368
cervix:
    dilation of, 217
    discharge from, 424
    Pap smears and, 222, 224
CFS (Chronic Fatigue Syndrome), 341–43
chalazion, 354
cheerleading, 149
chemotherapy, 288, 299, 370, 454
chest, 386–99
    coughs and, 389–92
    misshapen wall of, 387
    pain in, 163–64, 400
    pecs in, 386
    rib trauma and, 386–87
    see also breasts; lungs
chewing tobacco (dip), 277
chicken pot pie meal, calories in, 89–90
chickenpox (varicella), 136, 137, 222, 225,
    334–35
children, 225, 347, 350, 365
    blood pressure of, 400–401
    growth of, 34
    immunizations for, 331, 332
    "pre-teens" as, 183
Chinese food, MSG in, 127
chips, calories in, 90
chlamydia, 201, 220, 228–31, 424, 430
    symptoms of, 229
cholera, 337
cholesterol, 93–96, 106
    Accutane and, 124
    HDL (high-density lipoproteins), 93, 94
    LDL (low-density lipoproteins), 93, 94, 97
    testing levels of, 28
chondromalacia patella (patellofemoral syndrome),
    169, 170, 476–77
chromosomes, 28, 394, 453, 454, 456
Chronic Fatigue Syndrome (CFS), 341–43
cigarettes, *see* smoking
cigars, 274, 276–77
circumcision, 221, 466, 467
clindamycin, 123, 232
clitoris, 438
clonazepam (Klonopin), 319

clothes, 107, 155, 156, 183, 235
    sexy, 182, 183
cobalamin (vitamin B_{12}), 98, 341
cocaine, 277, 278, 312–14, 317, 357, 402
Cocaine Anonymous, 314
codeine, 319, 320, 391
colds, 351, 355, 357
cold sores (fever blisters), 135–36, 222, 223,
    364–65
collagen, injections of, 126
college students:
    alcohol use by, 269–72
    immunizations for, 335, 336–37
    smoking of, 274
"coming out," 190–94
commitments, honoring of, 58
competition:
    parental, 42
    in sports, 143, 147
computers, 349
concerts, drug use at, 295, 297
concussion, 158–61, 264, 351
condoms, 128, 180, 182, 198–201, 205, 218
    female, 203
    proper use of, 199–201
    spermicides and, 201
    STDs and, 201, 220, 224, 227, 229, 237
confidentiality, 17, 250, 285
    importance of, 25–29
conjunctivitis, 353–54
constipation, 109, 416–17, 462
Consumer Product Safety Commission, U.S., 161
contact lenses, 161, 353
contusions, 161
copper, 425
cornea, scratched, 354
corticosteroids, 356–57
cosmetics:
    allergic reactions to, 127–28
    hypoallergenic, 128
costochondritis (Tietze's disease), 163, 386
coughs, 386, 389–92
coxsackie virus, 364
crabs (pubic lice; pediculosis pubis), 220, 234–35
crack, 313
cramps, abortion and, 217
creatine (creatine kinase), 148
Crohn's disease, 418–19, 452
cromolyn medications, 356
crossover exercise, 152
crown to pubis: pubis to heel ratio, 34
culture:
    emotional life and, 63
    food rules and, 109

cystitis, 428–30
cysts (pustules), 120, 359
  breast, 395–96
  follicular, 459–60
  of labia, 459
  ovarian, 417, 451, 459–62
cytomegalovirus, 345

dancing, 149, 452, 455
  eating disorders and, 107, 108
D & C (dilation and curettage), 215, 216, 217
D & E (dilation and evacuation), 217
dandruff (seborrheic dermatitis), 131
date rape, 253, 318, 319
DEA (Drug Enforcement Agency), 303, 304
death:
  from anorexia nervosa, 110
  parental, 63
  see also suicide
dehydration, 252, 256, 371, 413
delta-9–tetrahydrocannabinol, *see* THC
dental care, 363–64
dental dams, 227
Depo-Provera, 211
depression, 18, 66–69, 208, 328
  abortion and, 216, 217
  Accutane and, 124–25
  alcohol and, 255, 266, 319
  fatigue and, 339–40
  premenstrual syndrome and, 444, 445
  substance abuse and, 310, 312, 318–19
  suicide and, 67–69, 124–25
dermabrasion, 126
dermal layer, 118, 119, 129
dermatitis, 126–31
detergents, 127
dextromethorphan, 391
DHEA-S, 148, 461
diabetes, 207, 426–27, 459
diaphragms, 202–3
diarrhea, 103, 109, 114, 117, 256, 276, 309, 313, 416, 418, 425, 452
  food poisoning as cause of, 412–13
Dietary Guidelines for Americans, 84
dietary reference intakes (DRIs), 101
  adequate intakes (AIs), 101
diets, dieting, 28, 434
  abdominal pain and, 415–17
  amenorrhea and, 451–52, 455–56
  food poisoning and, 412–15
  heartburn and, 409–10
  low-fat, 96, 342
  premenstrual syndrome and, 445–46
  puberty and, 49

  special, 84, 114–17
  weight loss, 102–5
difference, desire for, 59–60
digestive system, 256, 409–14
dilation and curettage (D & C), 215, 216, 217
dilation and evacuation (D & E), 217
"ding" injury, 159, 160
dip (chewing tobacco), 277
diphtheria, 331
directions for treatment, following of, 123
disabled teenagers, 64
diuretics, 111, 113, 114, 148, 445
divorce, 64, 296
  rebellious teens and, 59–60
DNA test, for HIV, 228
doctor-patient relationship:
  confidentiality and privacy in, 25–26, 27, 250, 285
  finding the right match and, 26–27
doctors:
  eating disorders and, 108
  making appointments with, 27
  selection of, 26
  sports medicine, 172
  substance abuse and, 241–42, 250–51, 268, 281, 285–86, 293–94
  see also specific specialists
doctor's office, as teen-friendly environment, 24
dopamine, 104, 144, 275, 304–5, 308
Dorland's Medical Dictionary, 33n
double standard, sex and, 184, 186, 187, 219
douching, 202
doxycycline, 229
DPT (diphtheria, pertussis, and tetanus) immunization, 331
dreams, "wet," 41–42, 43
DRIs (dietary reference intakes), 101
  AIs (adequate intakes), 101
driving, *see* automobiles
Dr. Jekyll and Mr. Hyde (Stevenson), 312
Drug Abuse Warning Network, 303
Drug Enforcement Agency (DEA), 303, 304
Drug-Induced Rape Prevention and Punishment Act (1996), 318
drug rehabilitation programs, 242–43, 251, 252, 297, 321–22
drugs, drug use, 17–18, 241–324, 485–86
  amyl nitrate (poppers), 317
  barbiturates and Quaaludes, 322–23
  cocaine, 277, 278, 312–14, 317, 357, 402
  confidentiality and, 25–26, 27, 250
  discovery of, 248–49
  family plan for dealing with, 297
  fatigue and, 343

GHB, 318
  hierarchy of, 254
  HIV and, 226
  inhalants, 253, 315–16
  ketamine ("vitamin K"), 18, 317–18
  Klonopin, 319
  learning about, 243
  liver toxicity due to, 424–25
  needle-sharing and, 226, 333, 423
  opiates, 319–22
  parental use of, 246–47
  rapid heart beat and, 402–3
  rashes and, 127
  sleeping patterns and, 73, 78–79, 81
  STDs and, 221, 226
  suicide gestures and, 68
  talking about, 244–47
  tattoos and piercings and, 141, 244
  weight loss and, 103
  see also alcohol, alcohol use; hallucinogens;
      marijuana; medications; smoking
drug tests, 17, 25–26, 242, 250–51, 285, 305, 314
  drugs screened in, 294
  for marijuana, 293–97
drunk driving, 69, 254, 258, 264
"Dumbo" ears, 361
duodenal ulcers, 411, 420
duodenitis, 411–12
dysentery, 425
dysfunctional uterine bleeding (DUB), 447
dysmenorrhea (pain during menstruation), 52,
      450–51

eardrum, ruptured, 360–61
earrings, 361
ears, 358–62
  cleaning of, 359–60
  cosmetics and piercings for, 361–62
  infection of, 141, 331, 358–61
  injuries to, 162
  pain in, 35, 349
  swimmer's, 361
eating disorders, 16, 49, 106–15
  bulimia, 106–8, 113–14, 363, 371, 420, 456
  as psychological illnesses, 107, 108, 111
  sports and, 107, 149
  vegetarians and, 114–15
  vitamins and, 96, 98
  weight loss and, 16, 27
  see also anorexia nervosa
eccrine glands, 36
echocardiograms, 407
Ecstasy (MDMA; methylenedioxymethampheta-
      mine), 310–12

eczema, 128–29
  keratosis pilaris, 129
  nummular, 129
EIA (exercise-induced asthma), 388–89
ejaculation, ejaculate, 435
  blood in, 465
  first, 43
  "wet dreams" and, 41–42, 43
electrical cautery, 134–35, 224
electrocardiogram, 145, 403
electroencephalograph (EEG), 74
electrolytes, 113
Elmite Cream, 236
embarrassment:
  about erections, 41, 43–44
  about menstruation, 53
emergency rooms, 252, 266, 305, 306, 358
emotional life, 18, 55–82
  abortion in, 217
  adoption in, 63
  culture and, 63
  death in, 63
  disease in, 63–64
  divorce in, 59–60, 64
  external pressures on, 62–65
  fatigue caused by, 338, 339–40
  feelings of isolation in, 59
  friends and, 60–61
  insecurities in, 58–59
  internal pressures on, 58–62
  nature of adolescence and, 56–58
  normal, 65–66
  parental role and, 60
  puberty abnormalities and physical disabilities
      in, 64
  rational thinking and, 61–62
  rebellion in, 59–60
  religion and, 64–65
  and three spheres of life, 65–67
enablers, 268
Encare, 201–2
encephalitis, Japanese, 338
endocrine system, marijuana and, 289
endometriosis, 451
endometrium, 50, 51, 442, 447
endorphins, 320, 445
enuresis (bed-wetting), 81
enyzmes, liver, 420–24
ephedra, 100, 148
epidermis, 118, 129, 134, 136
epididymis, 468–72
epinephrine, 148
Epstein-Barr virus, 341, 345, 422
equipment, sports, 150–51, 160–63

erections:
    embarrassing, 41, 43–44
    spontaneous, 41–42
    see also ejaculation, ejaculate
ergot, 302
erythromycin, 122, 123, 229, 390
esophageal area, 409–10
estradiol, 204
estrogen, 90, 110, 171, 373
    in birth control pills, 204, 206, 208, 209, 395,
        447, 449
    breast size and, 398–99, 453
    cysts and, 395–96, 460
    in menstrual cycle, 204, 442, 444, 447
Eurax, 236
Evra, 212
Ewing's sarcoma, 475
exercise, 342
    caloric requirement and, 87–88
    eating disorders and, 107, 111, 112
    general, 151
    neurotransmitters and, 144
    premenstrual syndrome and, 445
    prone, 152
    standing, 152
    stretching, 151–52
    weight issues and, 102, 103, 105, 149–50
exercise-induced asthma (EIA), 388–89
eyebrows, piercing of, 140–41
eye exams, 349, 352–53
eye guards, 161
eye-hand coordination, 143
eyes, 352–55, 374
    allergies and, 353
    injuries to, 161, 354–55
    reshaping of, 35
    strain on, 349, 353

face:
    hair on, 42–43, 455, 460, 461
    washing of, 120
fainting, 156–57
fallopian tubes, 424
family, 65
    culture of, 63
    illness in, 63–64
    plan for dealing with drug use by, 297
    rules of, 249
    scheduling meals for, 84
    teen depression and, 67
family therapy, 111, 297
fast food, 83, 84, 86, 89–90, 117
fat, blood, 256
fat, body, 109, 259, 452

breast development and, 45
    complaining about, 107
    need for, 90–93
    percentage of, 91
fat, dietary, 88, 106, 147, 259
    anorexia nervosa and, 110, 111
    saturated, 93, 95
    unsaturated, 93
fathers:
    competitive, 42
    in sex discussions with sons, 186–87
    in theories of homosexuality, 191
fatigue, 338–46, 444
    emotional causes of, 338, 339–40
    organic illness as cause of, 338, 340–46
    physical activity as cause of, 338, 339
    skin problems and, 135
fat-soluble vitamins, 96–97, 103
fatty acids, 256
FDA, *see* Food and Drug Administration
feet, 479–82
    flat, 480
    growth of, 36
    toes and, 480–82
females, *see* girls
femininity, 57
femur, tumor of, 475
fever, 332, 333, 335, 336, 344, 345
    hepatitis and, 422–23
    kidney infection and, 432, 433
fever blisters (cold sores), 135–36, 222, 223,
        364–65
fibroadenomas, 396
fibrocystic disease, 395–96
Fitz-Hugh-Curtis syndrome, 229, 424
5–hydroxytryptamine, 348
Flagyl, 232
fluid retention, 208, 444, 445
flunitrazepam, 319
fluoxetine, 445
flu shots, 336
folic acid, 98, 341, 419
follicle stimulating hormone (FSH), 211, 461
    birth control pills and, 204
    in menstruation, 204, 444, 454, 455, 456
follicular cysts, 459–60
folliculitis, 129–30, 466
food:
    allergic reactions to, 116–17, 127
    "bad," 106
    energy activity and, 87–88
    fast, 83, 84, 86, 89–90, 117
    "low fat," 104
    migraines and, 348

religious and cultural prohibitions of, 109
sources of, 88–90
vitamins and minerals in, 96–100
Food and Drug Administration (FDA), 84, 103,
207, 215, 225, 458
birth control methods newly released by, 212–13
condoms and, 198
Food Guide Pyramid, 84–85
food poisoning, 412–15
football, 147, 150, 155, 160–61, 164, 165,
169–70, 383
forward lunge, 152
fractures:
finger, 166
stress, 171–72
wrist, 167
fraternities, alcohol and, 270–71
freckles, 137
friends, 60–61, 66
best, 60
FSH, *see* follicle stimulating hormone
fungal infections:
skin, 131–34
STDs, 220, 233–34
vaginal, 124, 458

gallbladder disease, 207, 425
gamma globulin, 423
gamma-hydroxybutyrate (GHB), 318
ganja, 286
gastritis, 412
gastroenterologists, 411, 418
gastroesophageal valve, 409
gastrointestinal bleeding, 416, 417, 419–20
gastrointestinal tract, 276, 341, 451
gateway theory, 277–78
gender:
alcohol use and, 259
STDs and, 221, 224, 229, 230, 232, 233, 234
genetics:
lactose intolerance and, 116–17
obesity and, 102
genital warts, 135, 220, 221, 223–25
German measles (rubella), 332
GHB (gamma-hydroxybutyrate), 318
GH (growth hormone), 74
Gilbert's syndrome, 421–22
girls:
as athletes, 154–55, 169–72
average height-weight and caloric tables for, 87
body fat of, 90, 91
developmental rate of, 440–42
eating disorders of, 107–14
growth pattern of, 44

hygiene and, 36
iron deficiency in, 340
physical exams of, 25
pubertal growth in, 34–35, 39, 44–48, 75
pubic hair of, 44–45
reproductive system of, *see* reproductive system,
female
at risk for STDs, 221
scoliosis in, 377–80
skin problems of, 120, 124, 125–26, 129–30, 133
smoking of, 274, 275
stress fractures of, 171–72
Tanner stages of sexual changes in, 45–48
testosterone use by, 147
urinary tract infections of, 428–30
glandular changes, 36
glasses, 35, 147, 161, 353
glaucoma, 299
glomerulonephritis, 431–32
glucose, glucose levels, 115–16, 146, 413–14, 426
Glucose Revolution, The (Brand-Miller and Wolver),
116
glucuronyl transferase, 420, 421
glue sniffing, 316
Glycemic Index (GI), 115–16
gonorrhea, 201, 220, 230–32, 424, 430
symptoms of, 230–31
grades, decline in, 242, 263, 265
Graves' disease, 374
growing pains, as catch-all explanation, 328
growth:
critical proportions and, 34
female pattern of, 34–35, 44
male pattern of, 34–35, 36–37
nutrition and, 83, 106
pace of, 27
before puberty, 34
of skull, 34–35
sleep requirements and, 74–75
growth hormone (GH), 74
guaifenesin, 390
guilt, anorexia nervosa and, 108–9
gymnastics, 108, 149, 161, 383, 452, 455
gynecologic exams, 218, 221–22, 229, 436–40, 450
description of, 437–39
first, 436–37
need for, 438
time for, 440

hair:
armpit, 36, 50, 442
body, 460, 461
breast, 395
facial, 42–43, 455, 460, 461

hair (*continued*)
    pubic, 39–42, 44–48, 437, 442, 453, 466
    thin and brittle, 111
Hallucinogen Persisting Perceptual Disorder
    (HPPD), 305
hallucinogens, 253, 300–307
    LSD, 253, 301–7
    mescaline, 305–6
    mushrooms, 307
    PCP, 306–7
hamburger meal, calories in, 89
hands:
    growth of, 36
    injuries to, 166
Harvard College Alcohol group, 274
Hashimoto's thyroiditis, 372
hashish, 286
Havrix vaccine, 334
HCG, measurement of, 213
HDL (high-density lipoproteins), 93, 94
head, 347–67
    injuries to, 158–61
    see also ears; eyes; headaches; mouth; nose; throat
headaches, 35, 159, 317, 327, 335, 347–53, 444
    birth control pills and, 207, 208
    fatigue and, 341–44
    migraines, 117, 347, 348
    muscle contraction (tension), 347, 349–50
    sinus, 350–51
    systemic diseases and, 351
    trauma as cause of, 351
    tumors and, 347, 352
health care, teen, 23–29
    changing thoughts on, 23–24
    communication problems in, 327–28
    confidentiality and privacy issues in, 24–29
    finding the right patient-doctor match in, 26–27
    friendly environment for, 24
    ideal medical visit in, 29
    selection of new doctor in, 26
    shifting responsibility in, 27–29
    STDs and, 221
    see also specific topics
health clubs, 105
hearing impaired, 64
heart, heart rate, 400–408
    alcohol and, 255–56
    blood pressure and, 400–402
    drugs and, 276, 288
    extra beats of, 406
    marijuana and, 288
    murmurs, 145, 407–8
    rapid (tachycardia), 145, 306, 307, 309, 311,
        402–5

    slow, 405–6
    sports and, 145, 148
heartburn, 98, 163, 409–10
heart disease, 93, 97, 145, 275
heat-related illnesses, 155–56, 163
heatstroke, 156
heel pain, 480
Helicobacter pylori, 411
helmets, 160–61, 162
hematuria, benign, 431–32
heme iron, 99
hemoglobin, 98, 147, 447
Hemophilus influenza, 331
hemorrhoids, 417–18, 420
hepatitis, 207, 332–34, 346, 421–25
hepatitis A, 332, 333–34, 422–23
hepatitis B, 223, 306, 332–33, 423
hepatitis C, 139, 332, 423–24
herbal medicine, PMS symptoms and, 446
hernia:
    scrotal, 470–71
    umbilical, 427
herniated disc, 381, 383
heroin, 278, 320–21
herpes simplex virus (HSV), 220, 222–23
    condoms and, 201, 223
    mouth and, 364–65
    1 (HSV-1), 135–36, 222
    2 (HSV-2), 222–23
herpes zoster, *see* chickenpox
HIB immunization, 331
high-density lipoproteins (HDL), 93, 94
hips, injuries to, 167, 474–75
Hirschsprung's disease, 417
hirsutism, 120
hives, 126–27
HIV (human immunodeficiency virus), 139, 179,
    181, 220, 226–28
    condoms and, 198, 201, 220, 227
    homosexuality and, 193
    practices that increase risk of, 226, 306
    testing for, 29, 201, 220, 227–28
hockey, 161, 164
Hodgkin's disease, 370
Hofmann, Albert, 302–3, 304
homework, sleep and, 75, 76, 77
homosexuality, homosexuals, 189–94, 317
    biological model of, 190, 191
    "coming out" of, 190–94
    hepatitis B and, 333
    psychosocial model of, 191–92
"hook up", use of term, 179–82, 187, 231
hordeolums (sties), 354
hormonal methods of birth control, 204–12

Depo-Provera, 211
"morning after" pill, 210–11
Norplant, 211–12
see also birth control pills
hormones:
  abnormality in production of, 48
  endocrine system and, 289
  homosexuality and, 190
  male breast development and, 40–41
  ovarian disorders and, 460–61
  skin and, 118, 120
  see also specific hormones
hospitalization, 111, 432, 447
HPPD (Hallucinogen Persisting Perceptual
    Disorder), 305
HSV, *see* herpes simplex virus
human immunodeficiency virus, *see* HIV
human papilloma virus (HPV), 223–25
humidifiers, 356
hunger, 309, 426
  marijuana and, 291, 299
hydrocele, 467–68
hygiene, 36, 120, 235
  cystitis and, 429
  penis and, 466–67
  urinary tract and, 429
hymen, 438–39
  imperforate (unbroken), 452, 456
hypertension (high blood pressure), 103, 207,
    208, 426
  labile (unstable), 401–2
hyperthyroidism, 371, 374
hypertonic solutions, 217
hyperventilation, 156–57
hyphema, 354
hypnosis, 280
hypnotics, 79
hypoglycemia, 115–16
hypothalamus, 373, 452, 455
  marijuana and, 288, 289
hypothyroidism, 371–74

ibuprofen, 171, 348, 363, 413, 420, 450
ice (methamphetamine), 308–9
identity, 56–57
  adoption and, 63
  culture and, 63
  friends and, 60–61
  sexual, 57
IgA nephropathy, 431
Imitrex, 348
immune system, 74, 96
  immunization and, 330
  macrophages in, 139

immunizations, 330–38, 483–84
  DPT, 331
  flu, 336
  hepatitis A, 333–34, 423
  hepatitis B, 223, 332–33, 423
  HIB, 331
  HPV, 225
  meningococcal, 335–36
  MMR, 332
  passive vs. active, 330–31
  polio, 331
  summary of, 337
  for travel, 331, 334, 337–38
  tuberculosis, 336–37
  varicella (chicken pox), 334–35
impetigo, 130
independence, 57–58, 63
infections:
  ear, 141, 331, 358–61
  eye, 353–54
  fungal skin, 131–34
  of glans of penis, 466–67
  measles, mumps, and rubella, 332
  nose, 357
  prostate, 464–65
  sinus, 350–51, 357
  toenail, 482
  urinary tract, 428–30, 432–33, 451
  uterine, 424
  vaginal, *see* vaginal infections
  viral skin, 134–37
infertility, 332, 461
inflammatory bowel disease, 418–19
inhalants, 253, 315–16
inhalers, 280, 283–84
insecurities, 58–59
insomnia, 78–79, 148, 309, 319
insulin, 146, 426, 427
insulin-dependent diabetes, 426, 427
insurance, drug rehabilitation and, 251
Internet, 30, 483–86
  BMI published on, 92
  nutrition sites on, 84, 100, 485
  pharmacological information available on, 18
  pornography on, 30, 178–79
  regulating time spent on, 77–78
intrauterine devices (IUDs), 195, 197
ipecac, 113
IPV (Inactivated Polio Vaccine), 331
iron, 97, 99–100, 147, 340–41, 419, 447
isolation:
  anorexia nervosa and, 110
  feelings of, 59
isotretinoin, 124

itchiness, STDs and, 230, 233–36
IUDs (intrauterine devices), 195, 197

Japanese encephalitis, 338
jaundice, 353, 420–23
jaws, 371
    headaches and, 35, 349–50
    reshaping of, 35
    trauma to, 362
jewelry, allergic reactions to, 128
"jock itch," 132–33, 167, 466
jogging, 105
joints, pain in, 131, 342, 343, 344

"keeping up with the neighbors," 183
keloids, 141, 361–62
keratosis pilaris, 129
ketamine ("vitamin K"), 18, 317–18
kidneys, 95, 351, 426, 431–35, 445
    alcohol and, 256
    back pain and, 164–65
    benign hematuria, 431–32
    infections of, 429, 432–33
    proteinuria and, 434–35
kidney stones (nephrolithiasis), 434
Klinefelter's syndrome, 394
Klonopin (clonazepam), 319
kneecap, 476–77
knees, 476–79
    injuries to, 168–70, 476–79
knees-to-chest exercise, 152
Kwell, 235
kyphosis, 378, 380–81

labia, 229
    cysts of, 459
labia majora, 45
lacrimal gland, 354
lacrosse, 161
lactase, 117, 414
lactic acid, 256
lactose intolerance, 116–17, 413–14
lasers, Q-switched YAG, 140
laser surgery, 224, 353
latex, allergic reaction to, 128, 199
laxatives, 111, 113, 114
LDL (low-density lipoproteins), 93, 94, 97
lean body mass, 91
learning disabilities, 27
Legg-Calvé-Perthes (LCP) disease, 474–75
legs, 475–79
    knee injuries and, 168–70, 476–79
    lower, 479
    stretching exercises for, 151–52

leukemia, 370
LH, *see* luteinizing hormone
lice, pubic (crabs; pediculosis pubis), 220, 234–35
lifestyle issues, 71–173
    see also nutrition; skin; sleep; sports
light therapy, 131
limits, parental setting of, 59–60, 184, 249
limps, 327
Lindane, 236
liquid nitrogen, 134–35, 224
liquor, 271
    alcohol content of, 257
    calories in, 260
listening, 183, 244, 245
liver, 95, 147, 207, 332, 346, 420–27
    alcohol and, 256, 424–25
    diabetes and, 426–27
    drug toxicity and, 424–25
    malfunctioning of, 420–22
    parasitic infections of, 425
    Wilson's disease of, 425
    see also hepatitis
liver cancer, 333
Lo/Ovral, 210
loss, *see* death; suicide
low-density lipoproteins (LDL), 93, 94, 97
LSD (lysergic acid diethylamide), 253, 301–7
    bad trips and, 303–4, 305
    physical effects of, 304–5
Lunelle, 212
lung cancer, 290
lungs, 103, 273, 387–90
    bronchitis vs. pneumonia in, 389–90
    marijuana and, 289
    smoking and, 276, 290
    see also asthma
luteinizing hormone (LH), 211, 460, 461
    birth control pills and, 204, 460
    in menstruation, 204, 444, 454, 455, 456
lying quad stretch, 152
Lyme disease, 233, 342, 343–44
lymph glands, 369–70
    swelling of, 136, 369–70
lymphocytes, 74, 369, 370
lymphoma, 370, 421
    coughs due to, 392

macrophages, 139
magnesium, 446
malabsorption syndrome, 96, 97, 106, 113
males, *see* boys
malnutrition, 49
mammograms, 395
mandible, 35

Mantoux test, 336–37
marijuana, 17, 242, 253, 285–99, 317, 388,
        392, 397
    alcohol compared with, 259, 287
    chemistry of, 287–89
    definitions and, 286–87
    drug testing and, 293–97
    effects of, 286–91
    gateway theory and, 277–78
    as illegal, 298–99
    mind-altering aspects of, 290–93
    paraphernalia for smoking of, 289–90
    parental use of, 246
    passive smoking and, 295
    rapid heart beat and, 402–3
    reaction time slowed by, 291
    sports and, 148–49
    statistics on, 286
    therapeutic use of, 288, 299
    see also THC
marketing, of smoking, 274
Marley, Bob, 286
masculinity, 43, 57
maxilla, 35
MDMA (methylenedioxymethamphetamine;
        Ecstasy), 310–12
measles, 352
medications:
    for acne, 123–26
    for allergies, 356–57
    for asthma, 155
    for depression and anxiety, 67
    fatigue caused by, 344
    for headaches, 348, 349
    for HIV, 228
    for insomnia, 79
    for menstrual pain, 450–51
    for premenstrual syndrome, 445
    see also specific medications
melanoma, 137
melotonin, 79
memory, 310, 344
    long-term, 291
    marijuana and, 290, 291
    short-term, 291, 311, 342
menarche, effect of nutrition on, 52
meningitis, 331, 335–36
meningococcal vaccine, 335–36
menstrual irregularities, 27, 373, 374, 447–50
    clotting disorders, 448
    dysfunctional uterine bleeding, 447
    excessive bleeding, 447–48
    foreign bodies and, 448–49
    infection and, 449; *see also* vaginal infections

miscarriage, 449
mittelschmerz, 451
    oral contraceptives and, 449
    pain, 450–51
    primary amenorrhea, 49, 438, 441, 451–55
    progesterone withdrawal challenge, 456
    secondary amenorrhea, 455–56, 460
    thyroid disorder and, 449
    trauma and, 449–50
    vaginal tumors and, 450
menstruation, 44, 48–54, 395, 397, 419, 442–56
    delayed, 49
    dos and don'ts of, 443
    early, 49, 440, 441
    eating disorders and, 107, 109, 110, 111
    first, 35, 43, 45–50, 52–53, 442
    iron and, 99–100
    pain and, 52
    premenstrual syndrome and, 444–46
    as "silent" word, 52
    skin problems and, 120, 135
    sports and, 147, 171
    talking about, 52–54
mental health experts, 108
Meridia (sibutramine), 103
mescaline, 305–6
mestranol, 204
metabolism, 103, 256, 351, 426
    accelerated, 105, 106
    caloric requirements and, 86–87
methadone, 320
methamphetamine (ice), 308–9
methimazole, 374
methylphenidate (Ritalin), 308, 309
metronidazole, 232
Mexican food, calories in, 90
MFS (Monitoring the Future Study), 309
mifepristone (RU 486), 210, 215–16
migraines, 117, 347, 348
milk:
    lactose intolerance and, 116–17, 413–14
    vitamins in, 97
    warm, 79
minerals, 95–96, 99–100
minocycline, 123, 124
Mirena, 213
miscarriage ("missed abortion"), 448, 449
mitral valve prolapse (MVP), 407
mittelschmerz, 451
MMR vaccine, 332
molds, as allergens, 355, 356
moles and spots, 137
molluscum contagiosum, 220, 225
Monitoring the Future Study (MFS), 309

mononucleosis, 164, 341, 344–46, 366, 422
mons veneris:
    of females, 45, 46, 48, 442
    of males, 41, 42
mood swings, 18, 67
"morning after" pill, 210–11
morphine, 319, 320, 391
Mortality and Morbidity, 201
mothers:
    sexual secrets and, 188–89, 214–15
    in theories of homosexuality, 191
motorcycle accidents, 309–10
mouth, 362–65
    braces and, 362–63
    coxsackie virus and, 364
    dental care for, 363–64
    herpes simplex and, 364–65
    injuries to, 162–63
    lesions of, 364
    tongue problems and, 365
mouth guards, 162–63
MRI (magnetic resonance imaging), 157–60,
        327–28, 352, 368, 370, 383, 393, 397, 460
MSG, allergy to, 127
multiple partners, 220, 221, 227, 230
mumps, 332
muscle contraction (tension) headaches, 347, 349–50
muscles, 421
    development of, 56, 100, 143, 149–50
    pain in, 342, 344, 475
    protein and, 88
    warm-ups for, 151–52
mushrooms (psilocybin), 307
MVP (mitral valve prolapse), 407

nail infections, 133
naproxen, 450, 451
nasal septum, deviation of, 358
nasal spray hormone, 81
nasal sprays, 280, 283–84
National Household Survey on Drug Abuse
        (NHSDA), 309
nausea, 159, 210, 333, 351, 359, 459
    in food poisoning, 412–13
    in substance abuse, 256, 276, 288, 307, 313,
        316, 317–18
neck, neck area, 368–76
    glands in, 369–74
    pain in, 349, 368–69
    sports injuries and, 163, 368
needle-sharing, 226, 333, 423
Neisseria meningitis, 335–36
neoplasm, 468
nephrolithiasis (kidney stones), 434

nerves, pinched, 368
nervous system:
    central, 276, 286, 317, 322, 441
    peripheral, 276
    smoking and, 276
neurotransmitters, 144, 304–5
niacin (vitamin B$_3$), 98
nicotine, 275–77, 290
    effects of, 275
nicotine gum, 280, 282
nicotine patch, 280, 283–84
Nicotrol Inhaler, 283
nightguards, 350
night terrors, 81
nipples, 45, 47
    discharge from, 396–97
    extra, 394
non-heme iron, 99
nonossifying fibroma (bone "hole"), 477–78
nonoxynol-9, 201
non-Rapid Eye Movement (NREM) sleep,
        73–74, 76
non-steroidal antiinflammatory agents (NSAIDs),
        450–51
Norplant, 211–12
nose, 355–58
    allergies and, 355–57
    broken, 358
    infections of, 357
    injuries to, 162, 358
    polyps in, 350, 357
nosebleeds, 358
NREM (non-Rapid Eye Movement) sleep, 73–74, 76
NSAIDs (non-steroidal antiinflammatory agents),
        450–51
nummular eczema, 129
nurses, 24, 25, 27
nutrition, 83–117, 485
    and age of menarche, 52
    calories in, 86–88
    cholesterol and, 93–96
    fat needed in, 90–93
    good, 83, 84–85, 100–102
    measurements and, 86
    sports and, 146–49
    vitamins and minerals in, 95–100
    weight issues and, 102–6
    see also diets, dieting
nutritionists, 108
Nuvaring, 213

obesity, 83, 149
    birth control pills and, 206–7
    BMI and, 92–93

diabetes and, 427
fear of, 106–7
genetics and, 102
morbid, 93
sleep apnea and, 81
obstetricians, 213
odor, glandular changes and, 36
ophthalmologists, 349, 353, 354
opiates, 319–22, 397
opium, 319, 320
oral sex, 178–80, 182, 227
myths about, 179
STDs and, 222, 230
talking about, 186–87
orchidometer, 41
orlistat (Xenical), 103
orthodontists, 350, 363
Osgood-Schlatter disease, 168–69, 479
osteochondritis dissecans, 168–69, 478
osteogenic sarcoma, 475
osteoid osteoma, 478–79
osteoporosis, 90, 110
otorhinolaryngologists, 371
ovarian cancer, 207
ovaries, 110, 439, 451
disorders of, 453–54, 459–63
hormones from, 74, 204, 442
in menstrual cycle, 204, 442, 453–54
mumps and, 332
other masses of, 462
polycystic, 455, 460–61
tumors of, 455, 462–63
overweight, 102–3, 107, 113
BMI and, 91–93
distorted view of, 83
Ovral, 210
ovulation, 50–52, 90, 443, 447, 450, 452

pain:
abdominal, *see* abdominal pain
back, 164–65, 327–28, 380–83, 468
breast, 397
chest, 163–64, 400
Chronic Fatigue Syndrome and, 341, 342
ear, 35, 349
"growing," 328
knee, 168–70, 476–79
during menstruation (dysmenorrhea), 52,
450–51
mouth, 362
muscle, 342, 344, 475
neck, 349, 368–69
opiates and, 319–20
shoulder, 165–66

testicular, 229–30, 471, 472
"palatal speech," 351
pancreas, acini vs. islets of, 426
pancreatitis, 426
panic attacks, 403–5
Pap smears, 222, 224, 438, 439
parasites:
in liver, 425
STDs and, 220, 234–36
in stomach, 414
parathyroid gland, 376
parents:
alcoholism of, 246, 262–63, 267
confidentiality and issues and, 25–26, 28–29
death of, 63
divorced, 59–60, 64, 296
drug testing and, 294–97
drug use of, 246–47
illness of, 63–64
legal rights of, 28, 285
limits set by, 59–60, 184, 249
nonathletic, 143–44
privacy issues and, 24–25, 246–47
proper role of, 60
puberty discussed by, 31–32, 43–44, 52–54
quitting smoking and, 278–81
as role models, 181–82, 183, 261–63
sexual information shared by, 188–89,
214–15
teen memories of, 55
weight complaints of, 107
paroxysmal atrial tachycardia (PAT), 405
parties, alcohol at, 243, 254–55, 269, 271
patellofemoral syndrome (chondromalacia patella),
169, 170, 476–77
PCO (polycystic ovary) syndrome, 460–61
PCP (angel dust; phencyclidine), 306–7
pecs (pectoralis major), 386
pediatricians, 23, 25, 26–27, 67, 452
pediculosis pubis (crabs; pubic lice), 220,
234–35
peeling agents, 121–22
peer groups:
"bad," 61
experimenting with, 60–61
leaders of, 56
"right crowd" as, 182
sexual behavior accepted by, 184
smoking and, 276
substance abuse and, 247–48, 249
pelvic exams, *see* gynecologic exams
pelvic inflammatory disease, 197, 229, 457
pelvic pain, 457
penile warts, 221, 224

penis, 234, 465–67
  development of, 40–42
  discharge from, 229, 230, 233, 430, 465
  glans of, 465, 466–67
  as "silent" word, 32, 33
  see also ejaculation, ejaculate; erections
peritonitis, 416
pertussis, 331
phencyclidine (angel dust; PCP), 306–7
pheromones, 444
physical activity, fatigue caused by, 338, 339
  see also exercise; sports
physical appearance, control over, 107
physical disabilities, 64
physical exams:
  birth control pills and, 218
  eyes in, 352–53
  sports and, 144–45
  see also gynecologic exams
piercings, 118, 138–42, 183
  of ears, 361–62
  HIV and, 226
pinched nerves, 368
pituitary gland, 204, 374, 393, 444, 452,
  455, 460
pityriasis rosea, 130–31
pizza, 89, 414
plantar warts, 135, 137
plastic surgery, 35, 161, 361, 393, 394
PMDD (premenstrual dysphoric disorder), 445
PMS (premenstrual syndrome), 444–46
pneumonia, 389–90
poison ivy, 128
polio, 331
polycystic ovary (PCO) syndrome, 460–61
polyps, 420, 450
  in nose, 350, 357
poppers (amyl nitrate), 317
pornography, on Internet, 178–79
postnasal drip, 350–51, 352, 357, 365–66, 369
potassium, 113, 114, 445
"power lifting," 153
prednisone, 346
pregnancy, 179, 180, 213–17, 448, 456
  abortion and, 189, 214–17
  Accutane and, 124
  incidence of, 221
  rubella during, 332
  tests for, 28, 124, 213, 397, 449
premenstrual dysphoric disorder (PMDD), 445
premenstrual syndrome (PMS), 444–46
Preparation-H, 418
"pre-teen" marketing concept, 183
privacy:

  increasing need for, 24–25, 127
  of parents, 246–47
  sex and, 182, 184, 185
progesterone, 50, 52, 373, 395, 460
  in birth control pills, 204, 208, 209, 447, 449
  in menstrual cycle, 204, 442, 444, 447
  Norplant and, 211–12
progesterone withdrawal challenge, 456
prolactin, 74, 392–94, 396–97, 456, 461
promiscuity, 180, 181, 235, 333
prone exercises, 152
propranolol, 374
propylthiouracil, 374
prostaglandins, 217, 450
prostate, 417, 464–65
prostitutes, 227
protein, 88, 147, 455–56
  in urine (proteinuria), 432, 434–35
Prozac, 80, 445
pseudofolliculitis barbae, 130
psoriasis, 131
psychopharmacologists, 67
psychosis, 303, 308, 309
psychosocial model of homosexuality, 191–92
puberty, 21–69, 440–41
  abnormalities of, 64
  defined, 31
  delayed, 440, 441
  female growth pattern in, 34–35, 39, 44–48
  genital development in, 38–42
  glandular changes in, 36
  growth before, 34
  male facial hair in, 42–43
  male growth pattern in, 34–35, 36–37
  as more than body changes, 32–33
  precocious, 49, 440, 441
  same-gender talks in, 43–44
  "silent" words and, 32, 33, 40
  skin changes in, 36
  talking about, 31–32, 43–44, 52–54
  see also emotional life; health care, teen
pubic hair:
  of females, 44–48, 437, 442, 453
  of males, 39–42, 466
  shaving of, 466
purging, bulimia and, 113–14
pustules, see cysts
pyridoxine (vitamin B$_6$), 98, 446

Q-switched YAG lasers, 140
Quaaludes, 322, 342

rabies, 338
race, STDs and, 221

racquetball, 161
rape, 210, 226
    date, 253, 318, 319
Rapid Eye Movement (REM) sleep, 73–74, 76
rational thinking, 61–62
rebellion, 59–60, 63
recommended daily allowances (RDA), 86, 96–98,
        100, 101
rectal exams, 417
Reefer Madness (movie), 286
REE (Resting Energy Expenditure), 87, 106
relationships, sexually active, 180, 182, 184, 187
religion, 64–65
    abortion and, 214, 215–16
    food rules in, 109
    values in, 188
REM (Rapid Eye Movement) sleep, 73–74, 76
reproductive system, female, 436–63
    development rate of, 440–42
    disorders of, 457–63
    pelvic exam and, 436–40
    see also menstrual irregularities;
        menstruation
reproductive system, male, 464–73
    see also penis; testicles
responsibility, 58
    birth control pills and, 206, 217
    drinking and, 260–63, 269
    for teen health care, 27–29
Resting Energy Expenditure (REE), 87, 106
Retin-A and derivatives, 122, 129, 135
retinoic acid, 124
Reuben sandwich, calories in, 90
rhythm method, 195–97
riboflavin (vitamin B$_2$), 98
ribs:
    broken, 163–64
    trauma to, 386–87
RICE method (rest, ice, compress and elevate),
        157, 170, 172
RID, 235
ringworm, 131, 133
risk-taking behaviors, 68
    sex and, 68, 221, 226, 229–30, 231, 333, 435
Ritalin (methylphenidate), 308, 309
roofies (rohypnol), 318–19
rubella (German measles), 332
RU 486 (mifepristone), 210, 215–16

SAD (Seasonal Affective Disorder), 80
salabrasion, 140
salicylic acid, 121, 135
salivary glands, 371
Salmonella, 413

salt, 413, 445
sanitary napkins, 53, 443, 448
saturated fats, 93, 95
scabies, 220, 235–36
Scheuermann's disease, 381
school performance, dramatic shift in, 69
schools, opening time of, 75
scoliosis, 164, 377–80
scrotal hernia, 470–71
scrotum, 40, 41, 467–68
Seasonal Affective Disorder (SAD), 80
seat side straddle, 151–52
seat straddle lotus, 151
seat stretch, 152
seborrheic dermatitis (dandruff), 131
sebum, 119–20
sedentary habits, 83
selective serotonin reuptake inhibitors (SSRI), 80,
        445
self-destructive acts, 69
self-mutilation, 69
sense, 286
sepsis, 416
serotonin, 144, 275, 304–5, 311, 312
serving sizes, 85
sex binding globulin, 461
sex education, 30
sexual abuse, 438, 449–50
sexual intercourse, 179–82, 184, 188, 454
    danger of, 179
    prevalence of, 221
    unprotected, 68, 221, 226, 229–30, 231, 435
    urinary tract infections and, 428, 430
sexuality, sex, 18, 175–237
    alcohol and, 256
    confidentiality and, 27
    culture and, 63
    Ecstasy and, 311
    "hooking up" and, 179–82, 187, 231
    Internet and, 30, 178–79
    language of, 179–80
    normal, 181–84
    oral, 178–80, 182, 227
    parental discussion of, 31–32
    physical development and, 56
    physical vs. emotional readiness for, 188
    places for engaging in, 180–81
    talking about, 183–87
    values and, 182, 183, 187–89
    see also birth control; homosexuality,
        homosexuals; reproductive system,
        female; reproductive system, male
sexually transmitted diseases (STDs), 18, 68, 134,
        179, 188, 220–37, 423, 430, 451

sexually transmitted diseases (STDs) (*continued*)
 bacterial, 220, 228–32; *see also* chlamydia;
  gonorrhea
 and barrier methods of birth control, 198, 201,
  220, 224, 227, 229, 237
 fungal, 220, 233–34
 parasites and, 220, 234–36
 prevalence of, 221–22
 risk-taking behavior and, 220, 221, 226
 spread of, 221
 syphilis, 131, 201, 220, 227, 232–33
 teen awareness of, 236–37
 testing for, 28
 viral, 220, 222–28; *see also* genital warts; herpes
  simplex virus; HIV
Sexual Staging System, *see* Tanner System
shaving, 42–43
 folliculitis and, 129, 466
shingles, 136–37, 222, 335
 see also chickenpox
shin splints, 171, 479
shoes, sports, 151, 171
shoulders:
 dislocated, 385
 pain in, 165–66
 trauma to, 384–85
showers, 36
siblings:
 illness of, 63–64
 older, 59
sibutramine (Meridia), 103
side lunge exercise, 152
"silent" words, 32, 33, 40, 52, 184–85
Simon, Neil, 30
sinus headaches, 350–51
sinusitis, 357
skateboarding, 160, 167
skating, 149, 160, 167, 455
 eating disorders and, 107, 108
skin, 118–42, 486
 alcohol and, 256
 allergic reactions and dermatitis of, 126–31
 changes in, 36
 facial growth and, 35
 fungal infections of, 132–34
 layers of, 118
 moles and spots on, 137
 sunscreens for, 118, 122, 137–38
 tattoos and piercings of, 118, 138–42
 viral infections of, 134–37
 vitamin A and, 96, 97, 122
 see also acne
skin cancer, 118, 137
skull, growth of, 34–35

sleep, 73–82, 342, 374, 484
 deprivation, 73, 75–76, 339
 disorders of, 78–82
 physiology of, 73–74
 requirements for, 74–75, 339
 time management and, 77–78
 "wryneck" and, 369
sleep apnea, 81–82
sleepwalking (somnambulism), 80–81
slouching, 382
"sluts," 180, 184, 187, 188
smoking, 253, 273–84, 357, 388, 392
 addictive qualities of, 273, 275, 279
 birth control pills and, 206–7, 275
 coughs due to, 392
 effects of, 275–76
 gateway theory and, 277–78
 heartburn and, 410
 incidence of, 273–74
 marijuana compared with, 290
 marketing of, 274
 new habits and, 280, 284
 quitting of, 273, 278–84
 reasons for, 274–75
 STDs and, 221
snacks, weight loss and, 104, 105
soccer, 147, 155, 161, 169–70
Society for Adolescent Medicine, 26
socioeconomic groups, STDs and, 221
soda, 104, 412
 caffeine in, 78–79, 410, 445
sodium, 113, 413
somnambulism (sleepwalking), 80–81
sonograms, 395, 407, 417, 421, 430, 438, 450,
  459, 468
sore throats, 230, 280, 327–28, 342, 344–46,
  366–67, 369
sororities, alcohol and, 270–71
spermatocele, 468, 470
spermicides, 201–2
spinal cord, 288
spine, 377–81
 injuries to, 163
 kyphosis and, 378, 380–81
 scoliosis and, 164, 377–80
spironolactone, 445
spleen, swollen, 164, 346
spondylolisthesis, 381–83
spondylolysis, 381–83
sports, 143–73, 327, 362, 486
 body types and participation in, 149–50
 competition in, 143, 147
 eating disorders and, 107, 149
 equipment for, 150–51, 160–63

general health problems and, 155–58
injuries and treatment in, 158–72, 368
nutrition and, 146–49
physical exams and, 144–45
supplements in, 100, 147–49
types of, 146; *see also specific sports*
warm-ups for, 151–52
weight lifting, 150, 152–54, 156, 421
weight loss and, 149
see also athletes; exercise
sports drinks, 156
spots and moles, 137
sprains and strains, 157–58
SSRI (selective serotonin reuptake inhibitor), 80, 445
standing exercises, 152
standing quad stretch, 152
staphylococcus, 129
STDs, *see* sexually transmitted diseases
stepparents, 64, 296
steroids, 356–57, 388, 418, 432
anabolic, 147–48
for Crohn's disease, 419
for poison ivy, 128
skin problems and, 120, 128, 131
Stevenson, Robert Louis, 312
sties (hordeolums), 354
stimulants, 308–14
amphetamines, 100, 103, 308–10, 397
cocaine, 277, 278, 311–14, 317, 357, 402
Ecstasy (MDMA), 310–12
stomach, 409–14
alcohol use and, 256, 259
duodenal ulcers and, 411, 420
duodenitis and, 411–12
food poisoning and, 412–13
lactose intolerance and, 413–14
parasites in, 414
strawberries, 127
strength training, 153–54
streptococcal infection, 131, 366
stress, 411, 444, 455
divorce and, 64
external pressures, 62–65
fatigue and, 339
insomnia and, 79
internal pressures, 58–62
skin problems and, 120, 129, 135
stress fracture, 171–72, 383
stretching exercises, 151–52
subcutaneous layer, 118
substance abuse, 239–324
additional advice on, 250–51
discovery of, 248–49

identifying emergencies in, 252
improving your knowledge about, 252–53
information pipeline and, 247–48
talking about, 244–47
see also alcohol, alcohol use; drugs, drug use; hallucinogens; marijuana; stimulants
subungual hematoma, 481–82
sugar, low blood level of (hypoglycemia), 115–16
suicide, 62, 65, 67–69
Accutane and, 124–25
precursors of, 69
suicide gestures, 68–69
suicide ideation, 68–69
sulfur, 121, 236
sumatriptan, 348
sunburn, 125
sun protection factor (SPF), 138
sunscreens, importance of, 118, 122, 137–38
supplements, nutritional, 96, 99
in sports, 100, 147–49
surgery:
for appendicitis, 46
breast, 398, 399
cardiac, 145, 405–6
for dislocated shoulder, 385
heart murmurs and, 407–8
for hernia, 471
laser, 224, 353
Norplant and, 211
plastic, 35, 161, 361, 393, 394
for skin, 126, 137
for sports injuries, 157, 158, 161
sweating, 36, 374
skin problems and, 118, 132
swelling:
of eye, 354–55
of nose, 358
swimmer's ear, 361
swimming, 149, 361
swollen glands, 136, 369–71
syphilis, 201, 220, 227, 232–33
secondary, 131

tachycardia (rapid heart beat), 145, 306, 307, 309,
311, 402–5
talks, talking:
about menstruation, 52–54
about puberty, 31–32, 43–44, 52–54
same-gender, 43–44, 52, 184–87
about sex and sexuality, 183–87
about substance abuse, 244–47
about values, 183, 187–88
tampons, 53–54, 443, 448–49
Tanner, J. M., 38–39

Tanner System (Sexual Staging System), 38–42
    of female sexual changes, 45–48
    of male sexual changes, 39–42
tattoos, 118, 138–41
    removal of, 140
teeth:
    braces for, 362–63
    broken, 163, 362
    grinding of, 347
    wisdom, 363–64
telephones, regulating time spent on, 77–78
television, sex on, 78, 185
temporomandibular joint syndrome (TMJ), 35,
        349–50
tendonitis, 166, 171
tennis, 149, 155, 165
tennis elbow, 166
tension (muscle contraction) headaches, 347,
        349–50
testicles, 74, 392–93, 453–54, 468–73
    development of, 38–42
    monthly self-examination of, 470
    mumps and, 332
    pain in, 229–30, 471, 472
    scrotal hernia and, 470–71
    size of, 38–42
    sports supplements and, 147, 148
    torsion of, 472
    trauma to, 167
    undescended, 468, 473
    varicoceles of, 470, 472–73
testicular cancer, 470
testicular feminization, 453–54
testosterone, 43, 190, 289, 453, 460, 461
    aggression and, 42, 43
    breast enlargement and, 392–93
    genital development and, 41–42
    skin and, 120
tetanus, 331
tetracycline, 122, 123, 209, 390, 412
THC (delta-9–tetrahydrocannabinol), 242,
        286–95, 299
    absorption of, 291–93
    long-term use of, 298
therapy, 67, 251, 297, 306, 310
    for anorexia nervosa, 111
thiamin (vitamin B$_1$), 98
thigh muscle pains, 475
three spheres of life, 65–67
throat, 365–67
    sore, 230, 280, 327–28, 342, 344–46, 366–67,
        369
    strep, 366
    tonsillitis and, 366–67

thrush, 365
thyroid, thyroid level, 148, 342, 346, 371–75
    amenorrhea and, 454, 455
    high, 401, 449
    low, 95, 103, 113, 449
    menstrual irregularities and, 449
thyroid cancer, 375
thyroiditis, 372
ticks, deer, 343
Tietze's disease (costochondritis), 163, 386
time management, sleep in, 77–78
"tinea", use of term, 132
tinea versicolor, 133–34
tinnitus, 162
TMJ (temporomandibular joint syndrome), 35,
        349–50
tobacco:
    chewing, 277
    see also smoking
toddlers, 34, 74
toenails:
    infections of, 482
    proper cutting of, 481
toes, 480–82
    fractured, 480
tolerance, drug use and, 298
tongue, 365
    piercing of, 141
tonsillectomy, 366–67
tonsillitis, 366–67
tonsils, 351, 365, 366–67
torsion, 472
torticollis ("wryneck"), 369
Toxic Shock Syndrome (TSS), 53–54
track, 108, 149
tranquilizers, 306, 310
transsexuals, 190
transvestites, 190
travel:
    ear infections in, 360
    immunizations for, 331, 334, 337–38
    parasites in, 414
triglycerides:
    Accutane and, 124
    testing levels of, 28, 93–94
tryptophan, 79
TSS (Toxic Shock Syndrome), 53–54
tuberculosis, 336–37
tumors, 455
    brain, 347, 352
    femur, 475
    neoplasm, 468
    ovarian, 455, 462–63
    vaginal, 450

Turner's syndrome, 453
Twain, Mark, 280
twin studies, homosexuality and, 190
Tylenol, 320
typhoid, 338

ulcerative colitis, 418
ulcers, duodenal, 411, 420
umbilicus (belly button), 427
underweight, 105–6, 109
unsaturated fats, 93
urethra, 428–30
urinalysis, 429, 431, 435
urinary tract, 428–35
    bladder infections and, 428–30
    chlamydia and, 229
    see also kidneys
urine, urination:
    blood in, 429, 431, 432, 434
    burning sensation in, 465
    protein in, 432, 434–35
    smoking and, 276
urine tests, for drug use, 17, 25–26, 293–97
uterine cancer, 207
uterus, 439
    chlamydia and, 229
    contractions of, 52, 217, 450
    infection of, 424
    lining of, 50, 51, 442, 447

vaccination, *see* immunizations
vagina, 439
    tumors of, 450
vaginal bleeding:
    abortion and, 217
    breakthrough, 211, 447, 449
    irregular, 207
    see also menstrual irregularities; menstruation
vaginal discharge:
    abnormal, 229, 230, 232, 233, 234, 438
    normal, 49–50, 457–58
    urinalysis and, 429
vaginal infections, 437–38, 439, 458–59
    after abortions, 217
    antibiotics and, 124, 229, 232, 458
    chlamydia, 201, 220, 228–31, 424, 430
    vaginosis, 232
    yeast, 458–59
vaginal ring, 213
vaginosis, 232
Valium, 319, 343, 411
Valtrex, 136
values, 182
    talking about, 183, 187–88

teaching or reaffirming, 187–89
Vaqta vaccine, 334
varicella, *see* chickenpox
varicoceles, 470, 472–73
Varivax vaccine, 335
vas deferens, 468, 469
vasovagal response, 156
vegetables:
    green leafy, 97, 98, 99
    yellow, 96–97
vegetarians, 100, 114–15, 341
virginity, 179, 182, 188, 438–39
virilization, 455
viruses:
    coxsackie, 364
    herpes zoster, 136–37, 222, 334
    skin infections and, 134–37
    STDs and, 220, 222–28; *see also* genital warts;
        herpes simplex virus; HIV
    see also hepatitis
vision, 256
    blurred, 353
    double, 159, 354
vitamin A, 96–97
    skin and, 96, 97, 122
vitamin B_1 (thiamin), 98
vitamin B_2 (riboflavin), 98
vitamin B_3 (niacin), 98
vitamin B_6 (pyridoxine), 98, 446
vitamin B_{12} (cobalamin), 98, 341
vitamin C (ascorbic acid), 97–98, 99
vitamin D, 97
vitamin E, 97, 446
"vitamin K" (ketamine), 38, 317–18
vitamins, 95–98, 419, 434
    defined, 96
    fat-soluble, 96–97, 103
    PMS symptoms and, 446
    water-soluble, 96, 97–98
vomiting, 210, 232, 333, 351, 459
    bleeding and, 420
    bulimia and, 107, 113–14, 371
    food poisoning and, 412–13
    sports injuries and, 159, 161
    substance abuse and, 276, 306, 318, 320
von Willebrand's disease, 448

walking, 105
warm-ups, for sports, 151–52
warts:
    common, 134–35
    genital, 135, 220, 221, 223–25
    molluscum contagiosum and, 225
    plantar, 135, 137

warts (*continued*)
  as skin infections, 134–35
washing and bathing, 36, 120, 466
water consumption, 99, 104, 147, 156, 416, 417, 430
water-soluble vitamins, 96, 97–98
wax, ear, 359–60
waxing, folliculitis and, 129–30
weekends, sleep deprivation on, 75–76
weight:
  criticizing others for, 107
  normal, 107, 109, 111, 113
  nutrition and, 102–6
  see also obesity; overweight; underweight
weight gain, 111
  alcohol and, 259–60
  birth control pills and, 180, 208
  fear of, 108, 109, 112
  hypothyroidism and, 372, 373
  of males, 93
  before menses, 49, 50, 93, 444
  ovarian disorders and, 460, 461
  sports and, 149–50
weight lifting, 150, 152–54, 156, 421
weight loss, 313
  blood fat levels and, 28
  "easy," 104–5
  eating disorders and, 16, 27
  hyperthyroidism and, 374
  sports and, 149
  supplements and, 100

zinc and, 100
weight maintenance, 105
weight training, 153–54
Western blot test, 228
"wet dreams," 41–42, 43
whiteheads, 120, 122
wilderness programs, 242–43
Wilson's disease, 425
wisdom teeth, 363–64
withdrawal, as birth control, 195, 197
Wolver, Thomas M. S., 116
work, 66
wrestling, 149, 150, 162, 225
wrist injuries, 167
"wryneck" (torticollis), 369

Xanax, 403, 404–5
X chromosome, 394, 453
Xenical (orlistat), 103
X rays, 337, 358, 362, 368, 378–81, 383, 395, 416, 417, 419, 426, 472, 474
  chest, 370, 388, 389, 390, 392
  for leg problems, 475, 477, 478
  scoliosis and, 378–80
  sports injuries and, 159, 162, 163, 165, 166, 168, 169, 171, 172

yeast infection, 458–59
yellow fever, 338

zinc, 99, 100

About the Author

Ralph I. López, M.D., has practiced adolescent medicine for over thirty years. He received his medical degree from New York University Medical College, did his residency at Bellevue Hospital, and completed a fellowship in adolescent medicine at Boston Children's Hospital. Dr. López initiated the first adolescent medical unit in the navy in 1971 at the Portsmouth Naval Hospital in Virginia. Following the navy, he was the director of adolescent medicine at Cornell Medical College–New York Hospital. He also set up the first full-time adolescent medical practice in New York City in 1983 and currently is a Clinical Associate Professor of Pediatrics at the Weill Medical College of Cornell University and a member of the senior medical staff at Lenox Hill Hospital. *New York* magazine chose Dr. López as one of the ten best New York City children's doctors, and he has been on the Best Doctor's List in that magazine for the past several years. He has served on numerous boards and advisory committees focused on children, including a term as chairman of the board of Camp Rising Sun, which brings together teens of diverse ethnicity and backgrounds. He has also served on the advisory boards of the Girls Scouts of America in New York and on Parents in Action, a New York City parents group. Dr. López is married and the proud father of a daughter, Abigail.